JOURNAL FOR THE STUDY OF THE NEW TESTAMENT SUPPLEMENT SERIES
128

Executive Editor
Stanley E. Porter

Editorial Board
Richard Bauckham, David Catchpole, R. Alan Culpepper,
Margaret Davies, James D.G. Dunn, Craig A. Evans, Stephen Fowl,
Robert Fowler, Robert Jewett, Elizabeth Struthers Malbon

Sheffield Academic Press

The Motif of Wonder in the Gospel of Mark

Timothy Dwyer

Journal for the Study of the New Testament
Supplement Series 128

BS
2585.2
.D89
1996

Copyright © 1996 Sheffield Academic Press

Published by Sheffield Academic Press Ltd
Mansion House
19 Kingfield Road
Sheffield S11 9AS
England

Printed on acid-free paper in Great Britain
by Bookcraft Ltd
Midsomer Norton, Bath

British Library Cataloguing in Publication Data

A catalogue record for this book is available
from the British Library

ISBN 1-85075-603-1

CONTENTS

Acknowledgments 7
Abbreviations 8

Chapter 1
INTRODUCTION 11

Chapter 2
WONDER IN THE GRECO-ROMAN WORLD 26

Chapter 3
WONDER IN EARLY JEWISH LITERATURE 48

Chapter 4
WONDER IN EARLY CHRISTIAN LITERATURE 68

Chapter 5
MARK I 92

Chapter 6
MARK II 145

Chapter 7
CONCLUSION 196

Bibliography 203
Index of References 224
Index of Authors 238

ACKNOWLEDGMENTS

I would like to offer a word of thanks to those who aided in the production of this work. Ruth Edwards and I. Howard Marshall were helpful guides in the original project at the University of Aberdeen. Logistical support was provided by Larry and Mary Rosine of La Crescenta, CA, and Ed and Anne Dwyer of Ceres, CA. Special help at later stages was provided by Franklin Shirbroun in California, and Fred Burnett in Indiana. I would also like to thank Stan Porter, and the Sheffield Academic Press staff for their help and suggestions. Most of all, I would like to thank my wonderful wife, Paula, for support in so many ways over the years.

Shortly after this project was begun, I was saddened by the loss of my father. By the time it comes to publication, I have been cheered by the birth of my sons Peter and Philip. 'A generation goes and a generation comes' (Eccl. 1.4). I dedicate this to the generation which is now gone, with sadness and blessed memory:

    Katherine 'Pat' Dwyer 1919–1981
    Charles Patrick Dwyer 1915–1987
    Daniel Dwyer 1905–1988

                 Timothy Dwyer
                 Daleville, IN
                 February, 1996

ABBREVIATIONS

AASOR	Annual of the American Schools of Oriental Research
AB	Anchor Bible
AnBib	Analecta biblica
AUSS	*Andrews University Seminary Studies*
BAGD	W. Bauer, W.F. Arndt, F.W. Gingrich and F.W. Danker, *Greek–English Lexicon of the New Testament*
BETL	Bibliotheca ephemeridum theologicarum lovaniensium
Bib	*Biblica*
BNTC	Black's New Testament Commentaries
BZ	*Biblische Zeitschrift*
CBQ	*Catholic Biblical Quarterly*
CBQMS	*Catholic Biblical Quarterly*, Monograph Series
CGTC	Cambridge Greek Testament Commentary
CNT	Commentaire du Nouveau Testament
CRINT	Compendia rerum iudaicarum ad Novum Testamentum
EcumRev	*Ecumenical Review*
EKKNT	Evangelisch-Katholischer Kommentar zum Neuen Testament
ETL	*Ephemerides theologicae lovanienses*
EvT	*Evangelische Theologie*
ExpTim	*Expository Times*
FB	Forschung zur Bibel
FRLANT	Forschungen zur Religion und Literatur des Alten und Neuen Testaments
HNT	Handbuch zum Neuen Testament
HTKNT	Herders theologischer Kommentar zum Neuen Testament
HTR	*Harvard Theological Review*
HUCA	*Hebrew Union College Annual*
ICC	International Critical Commentary
Int	*Interpretation*
JBL	*Journal of Biblical Literature*
JR	*Journal of Religion*
JSNT	*Journal for the Study of the New Testament*
JSNTSup	*Journal for the Study of the New Testament*, Supplement Series
JSS	*Journal of Semitic Studies*
JTS	*Journal of Theological Studies*

JThSAF	*Journal of Theology South Africa*
MeyerK	H.A.W. Meyer (ed.), Kritisch-exegetischer Kommentar über das Neue Testament
NedTTs	*Nederlands theologisch tijdschrift*
NHS	Nag Hammadi Studies
NICNT	New International Commentary on the New Testament
NovT	*Novum Testamentum*
NovTSup	*Novum Testamentum* Supplements
NTD	Das Neue Testament Deutsch
NTS	*New Testament Studies*
PGM	K. Preisendanz (ed.), *Papyri graecae magicae*
RNT	Regensburger Neues Testament
SBLDS	SBL Dissertation Series
SBM	Stuttgarter biblische Monographien
SBS	Stuttgarter Bibelstudien
SBT	Studies in Biblical Theology
SE	*Studia Evangelica*
SJT	*Scottish Journal of Theology*
SNTSMS	Society for New Testament Studies Monograph Series
ST	*Studia theologica*
SUNT	Studien zur Umwelt des Neuen Testaments
TDNT	G. Kittel and G. Friedrich (eds.), *Theological Dictionary of the New Testament*
TF	*Theologische Forschung*
THKNT	Theologischer Handkommentar zum Neuen Testament
TZ	*Theologische Zeitschrift*
USQR	*Union Seminary Quarterly Review*
WBC	Word Biblical Commentary
WTJ	*Westminster Theological Journal*
ZNW	*Zeitschrift für die neutestamentliche Wissenschaft*
ZTK	*Zeitschrift für Theologie und Kirche*

Chapter 1

INTRODUCTION

'In some ways, this shortest of the gospels is also the strangest and most difficult to grasp.'[1] So begins a recent introduction to the New Testament in its chapter on the gospel of Mark. The comment is insightful. Anyone who looks seriously and in depth at the shortest gospel can readily note its compelling drama and masterful artistry. Yet there is another aspect of Mark which is often overlooked, namely its mysterious presentation. The gospel meets the reader with ambiguity and mystery in many places.

Recently, W. Telford has suggested that the 'way forward' in Markan studies is toward further research on individual passages, coordinating the results of analysis of the text at various levels, and moving toward more synthetic constructions.[2] The question of the motif of wonder in Mark meets such criteria. Wonder, according to G. Theissen, comprises all of the narrative elements which express astonishment, fear, terror and amazement. It may be expressed by a verb: θαυμάζω, ἐξίστημι, φοβέομαι, ἐκπλήσσω, by an adjective or noun: ἔκστασις, φόβος, θάμβος, or by any description of a reaction or state of awe.[3]

The number of places where reactions of wonder occur in Mark depends on

---

1. L.T. Johnson, *The Writings of the New Testament: An Introduction* (London: SCM Press, 1986), p. 147.
2. W. Telford, ed., *The Interpretation of Mark* (Philadelphia: Fortress Press; London: SPCK, 1985), p. 27.
3. G. Theissen, *The Miracle Stories of Early Christian Tradition* (Edinburgh: T. & T. Clark, 1983), pp. 69-71. I will accept the definition of Theissen in this work, and would emphasize that the study of wonder is not merely a lexical study seeking words like θαυμάζω or ἐκπλήσσμαι, but seeks all indications of astonishment, amazement or awe in the text. For this reason, reactions like that of 1 Kgs 18.39 will be taken into account, because a reaction of awe is present, even though none of the usual lexical terms are used. Consequently, searches in texts will not be concordance searches for selected words, but will involve the reading of whole texts seeking such reactions.

the way one counts. Pesch has 34 occurrences,[4] but I will combine some of his references and suggest 32 occurrences, which will be detailed in Chapters 5 and 6.

Of course, wonder in Mark has not been completely overlooked, but it is a true gap in scholarship. Most scholars have come across it in Mark when researching something else, and commented on it in passing. Often, writers will refer back to the three page excursus on the *Admirationsmotive* by Pesch, who takes what might be called an 'epiphanic' view of wonder in Mark.[5] Also, frequently referred to are the articles by Bertram in *TDNT*.[6] K. Tagawa has about twenty-five pages of remarks on the motif in his Strasbourg dissertation which was written under E. Trocmé, and focuses on christological elements of wonder in Mark.[7] Many take note of wonder in the course of examination of miracle stories in Mark, and some make it a constituent part of miracle stories.[8]

4. R. Pesch, *Das Markusevangelium*, (HTKNT; 2 vols; Freiburg: Herder, 1976, 1977), II, pp. 150-52.
5. Pesch, *Markusevangelium*, II, pp. 150-52. Pesch's 'epiphanic' view of wonder in the gospel is similar to that of E. Lohmeyer, *Das Evangelium des Markus* (MeyerK; Göttingen: Vandenhoeck & Ruprecht, 1963), p. 34; and J. Gnilka, *Das Evangelium nach Markus* (EKKNT; 2 vols.; Zürich: Benzinger Verlag, 1978, 1979), I, pp. 216, 218, 269-70, 2, pp. 46, 344, as the miracles, teaching, death and resurrection are being presented as epiphanies of the divine presence in Jesus.
6. G. Bertram, 'θάμβος, θαμβέω, ἔκθαμβος, ἐκθαμβέομαι' in *TDNT*, III, pp. 4-7, and also his article 'θαῦμα, θαυμάζω, θαυμάσιος, θαυμαστός' in the same volume, pp. 27-42. Bertram sees wonder in Mark as the evangelist's method of underlining the revelation-content of that which he is recording.
7. K. Tagawa, *Miracles et Evangile* (Paris: Presses Universitaires de France, 1966). Tagawa would distinguish between Greek literature in its language of wonder and Jewish texts. Fear serves in the recitation of divine epiphanies in Greek literature, but in the Old Testament and Qumran it generally expresses fear of God as an element of Israelite faith. Mark is closer to Hellenistic literature, but Tagawa ties this up to the christology of the gospel, for it is the events and the existence of the life of Jesus which are amazing, not the occasional attitude of the people. This is to continue in the faith of the Christian, for whom faith is the direct experience of an encounter with the living Jesus (see pp. 100-16, 121). Tagawa seems to follow E. Trocmé, 'Is There A Markan Christology?', in *Christ and the Spirit in the New Testament: Studies in Honour of C.F.D. Moule* (ed B. Lindars and S.S. Smalley; Cambridge: Cambridge University Press, 1973), pp. 3-13.
8. A recent example of this is E.K. Broadhead, *Teaching with Authority: Miracles and Christology in the Gospel of Mark* (JSNTSup, 74; Sheffield: Sheffield Academic Press, 1992). Broadhead develops a 'narrative grammar' of the miracle stories in Mark, and sees wonder as part of the 'responses' of crowds, victims, opponents and representatives (see

1. Introduction

Almost completely overlooked, though quoted with some approval in the recent study of E.K. Broadhead, is the full study on the topic undertaken in the unpublished doctoral thesis of R. Stacy, who takes a negative view of reactions of wonder in Mark, a view which follows many others.[9] It is timely to push beyond these studies and undertake a full study of wonder in Mark. Two introductory

---

pp. 54, 56). One wonders if the crowd gathering at the door in 1.33 should not be separated from 'responses' like wonder in 1.22 and 27, and if greater differentiation to fit the actual language of the gospel would not be helpful. Perhaps a 'narrative grammar' over-schematizes the gospel. Others who link wonder with miracle stories include Theissen, *Stories*, pp. 47-72, where wonder is one of the 33 motifs that are typical elements of miracle stories; R. Bultmann, *History of the Synoptic Tradition* (Oxford: Basil Blackwell, 1968), p. 226; M. Dibelius, *From Tradition to Gospel* (London: Ivor, Nicholson & Watson, 1934), p. 97; and T.A. Burkill, *Mysterious Revelation: An Examination of the Philosophy of St. Mark's Gospel* (Ithaca, NY: Cornell University Press, 1963), p. 73. A major problem with this view is that if wonder is a constituent element of a miracle story, one would expect to find it commonly in extra-biblical miracle stories as well, and Theissen is forced to admit that parallels from outside the New Testament are not very common and lists only seven (*Stories*, p. 70). He quotes Tagawa to the effect that in pre-Christian parallels the motif is not so frequent as to allow one to speak of a stereotyped motif in ancient miracle stories (p. 70). A further problem is that Mark, for example, uses more reactions of wonder *outside* of miracle stories than in them!

9. R.W. Stacy, *Fear in the Gospel of Mark*, (Doctoral thesis; Louisville: Southern Baptist Theological Seminary, 1979. Stacy's work goes far beyond wonder to include such items as references to 'tumults' and words like σκανδαλίζω. He finds 63 references in Mark! Stacy works from the perspective that wonder or fear is a defective reaction, saying that fear is the ultimate antithesis of faith, and fear is entirely defective (p. 256). Stacy follows some who have seen a 'corrective christology' at work in Mark. The lack of background material hinders Stacy, and methodologically he does not make use of redaction or narrative criticism. These problems limit the examination of Markan nuances of wonder. Further, Stacy's work suffers from a failure to limit his examination based on form-critical considerations. Also, his exegesis on verses like 7.37 (see ch. 5 of the present study) does not allow for the unique texture of each verse. Others who have seen wonder as defective include W. Kelber, *The Kingdom in Mark: A New Place and A New Time* (Philadelphia: Fortress Press, 1974), especially p. 49, and W. Wrede, *The Messianic Secret* (Cambridge, MA: James Clarks, 1971 [1901]), pp. 97, 103; J.D. Kingsbury, *Conflict in Mark* (Philadelphia: Fortress Press, 1989), pp. 23, 98, 100. Fear or wonder as defective seems to overlook the possibility that the reaction is a necessary response to the numinous. The prime exponent of a 'corrective christology' in Mark (denied by Kingsbury) has been T.J. Weeden, *Mark: Traditions in Conflict* (Philadelphia: Fortress Press, 1971). For a solid critique of a 'corrective christology' in Mark, see Broadhead, *Teaching*, pp. 210-13.

issues must be surveyed, however. The first surrounds an appropriate method in a time of methodological diversity in gospel studies, and the second wonders why one should look at Mark and not the other synoptics?

Method and the Evangelist

Within the last forty years there have been two clear turning points in Markan methodology. The first was the appearance in 1956 of Willi Marxsen's work applying redaction criticism to Mark (*Der Evangelist Markus: Studien zur Redaktionsgeschichte des Evangeliums*[10]). The second was the seminal article by one of the foremost practitioners of redaction criticism in Mark, Norman Perrin, in 1976.[11] Perrin had defined redaction criticism as 'concerned with studying the theological motivation of an author as this is revealed in the collection, arrangement, editing and modification of traditional material, and in the composition of new material or the creation of new forms within the traditions of early Christianity'.[12] Yet, seven years later, Perrin would say that this methodology is not adequate to the interpretation of Mark because it defines the literary activity of the evangelist too narrowly and *does not do justice to the full range of the text he has created.*[13] Perrin went on to say regarding redaction criticism in Mark, 'Less than justice is being done to the text of the Gospel as a coherent text with its own internal dynamics'.[14] Others have given the same evaluation. For example, N. Petersen, in presenting the case that Mark should be read as a narrative rather than a redaction, has stated that Mark created an integral system, and for this reason it is necessary to read the gospel as a narrative. While Petersen believes that there is a place for reading the text as a redaction, he thinks this often hinders one from understanding the narrative world of Mark.[15] The comments of Perrin and Petersen direct us to a special crossroads at which Markan methodology currently stands.[16]

---

10. Translated as *Mark the Evangelist: Studies on the Redaction History of the Gospel* (trans. J. Boyce *et al.*; Nashville, TN: Abingdon Press, 1969).
11. N. Perrin, 'The Interpretation of the Gospel of Mark', *Int* 30 (1976), pp. 115-24.
12. Perrin, *What is Redaction Criticism?* (Philadelphia: Fortress Press, 1969), p. 1.
13. Perrin, 'Interpretation', p. 120, my emphasis.
14. Perrin, 'Interpretation', p. 120.
15. N. Petersen, 'Point of View in Mark's Narrative', *Semeia* 12 (1978), p. 118.
16. The crossroad, however, has several forks in it, and several possible by-ways. A fine guide is S. Moore and J.C. Anderson (eds.) *Mark and Method* (Minneapolis: Augsburg–Fortress, 1992).

1. Introduction

Redaction criticism in Mark must be distinguished from that which is practised in Matthew or Luke. The reason for this is two-fold. First of all, because we do not have the sources Mark used, separation of tradition from redaction in Mark is inevitably somewhat tenuous. Secondly, there is no definite statement of purpose in Mark to guide readers to the author's intentions in shaping the text. These two difficulties have led to a wide diversity of understanding of what is tradition and what is redaction in Mark. Tradition for one scholar is often redaction for another, and vice-versa. This has been well illustrated in the recent work of C. Clifton Black, which has presented the redaction-critical practices in Mark of Meye, Best and Weeden alongside each other and shows the different conceptions about the history of traditions behind Mark.[17] Black recognizes the limits of redactional analysis in Mark because assumptions are made which are unamenable to empirical analysis; Markan redaction criticism is forced to appeal to interpretive clues lying behind the boundaries of the gospel itself; and redaction criticism of Mark attempts to answer questions that its critical apparatus is not always able to handle (such as issues of theology, *Traditionsgeschichte*, literary composition and socio-historical setting).[18]

Black, however, recognizes the benefits of redaction criticism for Markan studies, which I would also want to affirm. Criteria for separation of tradition from redaction in Mark have been greatly clarified since Marxsen.[19] In my

---

17. C.C. Black, *The Disciples According to Mark: Markan Redaction in Current Debate* (JSNTSup, 2; Sheffield: Sheffield Academic Press, 1989), and 'The Quest of Mark the Redactor: Why Has It Been Pursued, and What Has It Taught Us?', *JSNT* 22 (1989), pp. 19-39.

18. Black, 'Quest', pp. 30-32.

19. Especially helpful on redaction-criticism in Mark are E.J. Pryke, *Redactional Style in the Markan Gospel* (SNTSMS, 33; Cambridge: Cambridge University Press, 1978); C.H. Turner, 'Markan Usage: Notes Critical and Exegetical on the Second Gospel', *JTS* 25 (1923), pp. 378-86, 26 (1924/25) 12-20, 145-56, 225-40, 337-46, 27 (1925/26) 58-62, 28 (1926/27) 9-30, 349-62, 29 (1927/28) 275-89, 346-61; R.H. Stein, 'What is Redaktionsgeschichte?', *JBL* 88 (1969), pp. 45-56, and 'The Proper Methodology for Ascertaining a Markan Redaction History', *NovT* 13 (1971), pp. 181-98; F. Neirynck, *Duality in Mark: Contributions to the Study of the Markan Redaction* (Leuven: Leuven University Press, 1972) and 'The Redactional Text of Mark', *ETL* 57 (1981), pp. 144-62; J. Schreiber, 'Die Christologie des Markusevangeliums', *ZTK* 58 (1961), pp. 154-83; Q. Quesnell, *The Mind of Mark: Interpretation and Method through the Exegesis of Mk. 6.52* (AnBib, 38; Rome: Pontifical Biblical Institute, 1969); J.D. Crossan, 'Mark and the Relatives of Jesus', *NovT* 15 (1973), pp. 81-113, esp. pp. 81-82; and D. Peabody, *Mark as Composer* (New Gospel Studies 1; Macon, GA: Mercer University Press, 1987).

examination of the gospel, after surveying wonder in the Greco-Roman, Jewish and early Christian literary worlds, I will seek to examine the form of the various pericopae in which wonder occurs, and then ask if the reactions are from the tradition or are redactional. Here, I will depend on the criteria developed by Pryke, Stein, Neirynck and especially Peabody. Peabody focuses on 'recurring phraseology' which indicates a keen interest on the part of the evangelist, and with this criteria, I will attempt to show that wonder is indeed a keen and repeated interest of the evangelist. Yet, because at issue is something which might be called a motif, we will have to give special care to the plot and flow of the gospel as a whole, something redaction critical methodology is not always suited for, and clarify the indicators of a motif.

Black has observed that although identification of themes or motifs in Mark could be, and indeed have been, incorporated into redaction critical paradigms, *such a determination is not an intrinsically redaction critical criterion but a literary-critical assessment.*[20] He notes that themes and motifs are central to the interpretation of Mark due to the fact that Mark is not in the form of a self-conscious theological treatise, but a narrative and should be treated as such.

It must be made clear that literary criticism, as related to Mark, like redaction criticism, has both its strengths and weaknesses, and carries the additional problem of being an entire field of methods in itself.[21] A strength is close attention to the plot, settings, characters and the flow of the narrative.[22] In short, it

20. Black, 'Quest', p. 31, his italics.
21. The move to reader-oriented methods would bring into question assumptions of the 'unity' of a text, and deconstruction, with its 'warring forces of signification' questions the coherence of any text.
22. Helpful in literary and narrative criticism in Mark, are, in addition to the article of Perrin cited above, D. Rhoads, 'Narrative Criticism and the Gospel of Mark', *JAAR* 50 (1982), pp. 411-34, and D. Rhoads and D. Michie, *Mark as Story* (Philadelphia: Fortress Press, 1982); J. Drury, 'Mark' in *The Literary Guide to the Bible* (ed. R. Alter and F. Kermode, Cambridge, MA: Harvard University Press, 1987), pp. 402-217; Petersen, *Literary Criticism for New Testament Critics* (Guides to Biblical Scholarship; Philadelphia: Fortress Press, 1978); and 'Point', pp. 97-121; R.C. Tannehill, 'The Gospel of Mark as Narrative Christology', *Semeia* 16 (1979), pp. 57-95; J.D. Kingsbury, *The Christology of Mark's Gospel* (Philadelphia: Fortress Press, 1984); R.M. Frye, 'A Literary Perspective for the Criticism of the Gospels' in *Jesus and Man's Hope*, (ed. D. Miller and D. Y. Hadadian; Pittsburgh: Pittsburgh Theological Seminary, 1971), II, pp. 193-221; M. Sternberg, *The Poetics of Biblical Narrative* (Bloomington, IN: Indiana University Press, 1985); and R. Fowler, *Loaves and Fishes* (SBLDS, 54; Chico, CA: Scholars Press, 1981), especially pp. 40-44. A survey of the development and application of literary criticism is found in

can help to view to gospel as a whole. The achilles heel of literary criticism is thought by some to be that the gospels are not novels and should not be treated as such, but literary critics often speak of 'texts' which encompass film, television shows, and the like, not limiting their analysis to novels. A bigger problem may be the avoidance at times of historical questions for the gospels, which are texts which emerge from history and create history. It is likely that the gospel authors did not have the possibility of total creativity, but restraints of the tradition and the outline of Jesus' life (baptism, healing, teaching, crucifixion, resurrection) as presented in the kerygma exercised some control. Interpreters will differ as to the amount of control which was involved, but almost all will agree that some parameters had been set prior to the composition of Mark.

I propose, then, to view Mark with a redaction critical methodology to seek the interests of the evangelist, and to utilize with restraints what might be called a form of narrative criticism (instead of literary criticism, with its numerous options). Each may then serve as a control on the other. The latter pays close attention to the movement of the narrative and the plot of the gospel as a whole. Within the restraints that are recognized, narrative analysis has some special help to offer on wonder because the quest at hand is the discernment and evaluation of a motif. The term 'motif' is used self-consciously here, as usually describing a salient feature of a work. The language of wonder is indeed a salient feature of Mark, and I can here illustrate the unique insights narrative analysis can provide.

William Freedman is one who has contributed mightily to the study of motifs in narratives. In an important article entitled 'The Literary Motif: A Definition and Evaluation',[23] Freedman presents two key factors which are indispensable

---

S. Moore, *Literary Criticism and the Gospels* (New Haven: Yale University Press, 1989), and Moore moves into deconstruction in *Mark and Luke in Post-structuralist Perspectives: Jesus Begins to Write* (New Haven: Yale University Press, 1992), an innovative book, but one that it is hard to know what to do with! Critics relied on tend to include W. Booth, *The Rhetoric of Fiction* (Chicago: University of Chicago Press, 1961); N. Frye, *The Great Code: the Bible and Literature* (New York: Harcourt Brace Javanovich, 1981); S. Chatman, *Story and Discourse: Narrative Structure in Fiction and Film* (Ithaca, NY: Cornell University Press, 1978); F. Kermode, *The Genesis of Secrecy* (Cambridge, MA: Harvard University Press, 1979) and *The Sense of An Ending* (London: Oxford University Press, 1976); and R. Scholes and R. Kellogg, *The Nature of Narrative* (London: Oxford University Press, 1966). The utilization of Barthes and Derrida *et al.* has gained steam in the last decade as some move to post-structuralism, and a helpful guide is The Bible and Culture Collective, *The Postmodern Bible* (New Haven: Yale University Press, 1995).

23. *Novel* 4 (1971), pp. 123-31.

to the establishment of a motif. The first is the frequency with which it recurs. That is, it should occur often enough to indicate that 'purposiveness rather than merely coincidence or necessity is at least occasionally responsible for their presence'. The second key factor in establishing a motif is the avoidability and unlikelihood of the particular uses of the motif. In other words, it should appear in contexts which are unlikely and do not demand references from the field of the motif. In an examination of wonder in Mark, it can be said to meet both criteria. Wonder occurs often enough in Mark (32 times, once in every chapter but two) to indicate that it is intentional. Secondly, wonder appears in unlikely contexts. It might possibly be expected in miracle stories, but the occurrences in relation to the teaching of Jesus, and places like Mk 9.15, 10.32, and 16.8 certainly make it stand out as appearing in places where it could have otherwise been avoided. Thus, wonder in Mark meets Freedman's two main criteria for establishing a motif in a narrative.

Freedman further gives five sub-criteria for determining the efficacy of a motif in a narrative. His secondary criteria are, again, frequency, along with avoidability and unliklihood; the significance of the contexts in which it occurs (that is, if it occurs at climactic points in the narrative, it will have the greatest effect); the degree to which all the instances of the motif are relevant to the principle end of the motif as a whole (in other words, does the motif serve a central point?); and the appropriateness of the motif to its object. Here, again, Mark meets the criteria to a remarkable degree. It will be shown that wonder occurs in unlikely settings, such as Mk 10.32 and 14.33. Wonder certainly meets the third criterion, occurring at climactic points in the narrative (for example, twice in the first miracle story in relation to the *teaching* of Jesus, three times in the empty tomb account of 16.1-8). The fourth criterion, that the occurrences of wonder serve a central point is one which I can propose and test in later exegesis in the chapters on Mark. I will return to this shortly. The fifth criterion, however, fits in light of the following two chapters. Wonder will be seen commonly as the response to divine interventions and as part of Jewish eschatological expectations. Thus, if wonder in Mark is a response to divine, eschatological interventions, this criterion can stand as well. Let me now return to the fourth criterion: Does wonder serve a central point? What might that be in Mark?

It is commonly recognized that, in light of the summary proclamation of 1.14-15, the overarching theme in Mark is the kingdom of God.[24] In exegesis, I

---

24. A.M. Ambrozic, *The Hidden Kingdom: A Redaction-Critical Study on the References to the Kingdom of God in Mark's Gospel* (CBQMS, 2; Washington: The Catholic

will test whether in the gospel the motif of wonder serves the central point of the breaking-in of the kingdom. If it is objected that christology is the point of Mark, I would respond with Dautzenberg that in the gospel the kingdom is the framework of christology.[25] Thus, here narrative and redactional concerns join by aiming our focus at a central issue and interest in the gospel and for the evangelist.

I propose, then, to view Mark in light of the forms of the various pericopae in which wonder occurs, to ask whether wonder is from the tradition or redaction as it is met, and to pay careful attention to see if there is a relation between the breaking-in of the kingdom and wonder. In our case, redaction criticism can help us understand the parts, and the concerns of the evangelist, and narrative analysis can help us understand the whole.

Biblical Association, 1972), p. 247, says that 1.14-15 is the foundation and summary of everything that Mark intends to say in the gospel; Kelber, *Kingdom*, p. 3, says that 1.14-15 has programmatic consequences and is the key to the Markan Jesus' life and death, on p. 11 that all aspects of Jesus' career must be viewed in light of the programmatic kingdom text, and on p. 42 that Mark is in effect writing a history of the kingdom; E. Schweizer, *The Good News According to Mark* (London: SPCK, 1987), p. 44, sees 1.14-15 as a caption to the whole gospel; D. Dormeyer, 'Die Kompositionsmetapher "Evangelium Jesu Christi, des Sohnes Gottes" Mk 1.1. Ihre Theologische und Literarische Aufgabe in der Jesus-Biographie des Markus', *NTS* 33 (1987) p. 466, n. 18, says that the central position of the kingdom proclamation in Mark is 'unbestritten' (undisputed); D.O. Via, *The Ethics of Mark's Gospel: In the Middle of Time* (Philadelphia: Fortress Press, 1985), p. 77, says the kingdom of God is the presiding theological motif of the gospel; B.L. Mack, 'The Kingdom Sayings in Mark', Foundation and Facets Forum 3 (1987) p. 41, notes that scholars have seen 'over and over again' that 1.14-15 is a concise statement of the Markan purpose for the composition of the gospel; F. Müssner, 'Gottesherrschaft und Sendung Jesu Nach Mk 1.14f' in *Praesentia Salutis. Gesammelte Studien zu Fragen und Themen des Neuen Testaments* (Düsseldorf: Patmos Verlag, 1967), pp. 91, 95, 97-98 notes that 1.14-15 is fulfilled in Jesus' messianic work; G. Rau, 'Das Markusevangelium: Komposition und Intention der ersten Darstellung Christlicher Mission' in *Aufstieg und Niedergang der Römischen Welt*, 2.25.3 (Berlin: de Gruyter, 1985), p. 2051, sees the concept of the gospel of God and kingdom expectation the underlying coordinates of Mark's historical understanding, and also, pp. 2135, 2230, where the first half of Mark is seen as 'fulfilled time' and the second half as the 'coming near' of the kingdom; A.Y. Collins 'Narrative, History and Gospel: A General Response', *Semeia* 43 (1988) p. 148, where Mark is said to be writing a narration of the course of eschatological events; and see also Rhoads and Michie, *Story*, p. 73, Pesch, *Markusevangelium* I, p. 72.

25. G. Dautzenberg, 'Die Zeit des Evangeliums: Mk 1.1-15 und die Konzeption des Markusevangeliums', *BZ* 22 (1978) p. 83. Dautzenberg says that the kingdom message and expectation forms the historical framework for the Markan portrait of Jesus.

There is a question which remains to be answered in this introduction. Why focus on Mark instead of the other synoptic gospels in examining the motif of wonder?

Mark and the other Synoptic Gospels

Markan priority may no longer be an axiom in New Testament studies, but one can work on the supposition that it still best fits the evidence. Since this is the case, and noting that Matthew and Luke have reactions of wonder, is Mark unique enough to focus on in a study of wonder? At stake, again, is the keenness of the evangelist to emphasize wonder, *in comparison with the other evangelists*.

I have noted earlier 32 references to wonder in Mark. Of these, in ten cases (almost one third of the instances), the reaction is solely Markan (3.21; 5.20; 6.6, 6.51; 9.15; 10.24, 10.32; 14.33; 15.44 and 16.8). Six times the Markan note is used (or modified) by both Matthew and Luke (1.22; 2.12; 9.6, 32; 12.12, 17). Ten times only Matthew follows Mark (6.2, 20, 50; 7.37; 10.26; 11.18, 32; 12.11; 15.5; 16.6), and six times only Luke follows Mark (1.27; 4.41; 5.15, 33, 42; 16.5). This points out the fact that Mark is quite distinct in many of the places where the gospel uses the motif, and the other synoptics do not follow Mark in any slavish manner.

Of the 32 occasions where Mark uses the motif, eight involve miracles or exorcisms (2.12; 4.41; 5.15, 33, 42; 6.50, 51; 7.37); teaching or passion predictions also have eight occurrences (1.22, 27; 6.2; 9.32; 10.24, 26; 11.18; 12.17); three occurrences are in the empty tomb narrative (16.5, 6, 8); five relate to the fear of various leaders, either Jewish or Gentile (6.20; 11.32; 12.12; 15.5, 44); the remaining eight are difficult to categorize (3.21; 5.20; 6.6; 9.6, 15; 10.32; 12.11; 14.33).

Whereas Mark has 32 places where the motif is used, Matthew (a full third longer, with 18,298 words compared with Mark's 11,078[26]) has only 27 occasions. Matthew does not follow Mark 16 times (Mk 1.27; 3.21; 4.41; 5.15, 20, 33, 42; 6.6, 51; 9.15; 10.24, 32; 11.18; 15.44; 16.5, 6, 8). A pericope in which Matthew uses a Markan pericope as a source adds the motif on three occasions (Mt. 21.20; 22.33; 27.54). A breakdown of Matthew would indicate that eight times wonder is used with miracles or exorcisms (Mt. 8.27; 9.8, 33; 12.23; 14.26; 15.31; 21.5, 20); five times the teaching of Jesus is involved (Mt. 7.28;

---

26. R. Morgenthaler, *Statische Synopse* (Zürich: W. Gotthelf, 1971), p. 89.

1. Introduction

13.54; 19.25; 22.22, 33); four times the death or resurrection is involved (Mt. 27.14, 54; 28.4, 8); ten occurrences might be called miscellaneous (Mt. 2.3, 22; 8.10; 14.5, 26, 30; 17.6; 21.26, 42, 46).

When one compares the vocabulary of the first gospel with the second, several things can be noticed. Matthew prefers forms of φόβος or φοβέω, which are used ten times (2.22; 9.8; 14.5, 30; 17.6; 21.26, 46; 27.54; 28.4, 8) or forms of θαυμάζω or θαυμαστός, which are used nine times (8.10, 27; 9.33; 15.31; 21.15, 20, 42; 22.22; 27.14). In fact, Matthew likes to change other Markan terms to θαυμάζω (Mk 4.41 at Mt. 8.27; Mk 7.37 at Mt. 15.31; Mk 12.17 at Mt. 22.21), and will add it in non-Markan cases in Mt. 8.10; 9.33; 21.15, 20. On the other hand, Matthew does not like the compounds that Mark so often prefers, using ἐκπλήσσομαι only at 7.28; 13.54; 19.25 and 22.33. No less than six terms of Mark are not used by Matthew at all. ἐκθαμβέομαι, θαμβέομαι, ἐκθαύμαζω, τρόμος, ἔκστασις and ἔκφοβος.

Other tendencies can be seen in the Matthean use of Mark. Matthew likes to add subjects to verbs of amazement, adding ὄχλοι in 9.8 to Mk 2.12, and ἄνθρωποι in 8.27 to Mk 4.41 (see also 9.33; 12.23; 21.20).[27] Mark is more content to leave the subject of the verb indefinite. K. Tagawa has also suggested that the form of reactions of fear and amazement in Matthew is much more stereotyped than in Mark, with language like 'The people (or crowd) became amazed and said...' (Mt. 8.27; 9.33; 12.23; 13.54; 21.20) or 'The people became amazed and glorified God' (Mt. 9.8; 15.31).[28] Matthew also likes to use reactions of fear and amazement to lead into a statement or question (Mt. 8.27; 9.33; 13.54; 14.26; 19.25; 21.20) or a christological remark (12.23; 27.54).

Matthew does not use Markan 'double-expressions' (two reactions of wonder in a single pericope), which can be found in Mk 1.22 and 27; 5.15 and 20; 33 and 42; 6.2 and 6, 50 and 51; 10.24 and 26; 16.5, 6 and 8. Neither does Matthew use Markan 'puzzling references', those places where the mystery of the Markan language causes commentators to despair (Mk 3.21; 9.15; 10.32; 14.33; 16.8). It is clear that Matthew prefers to soften, or simply not use the intensity of the Markan language (ἐφοβήθησαν φόβον μέγαν of Mk 4.41 is not used, neither is καὶ ἐξέστησαν ἐκστάσει μεγάλῃ of Mk 5.42, nor is λίαν ἐκ περισσοῦ ἐν ἑαυτοῖς ἐξίσταντο in Mk 6.51, καὶ ὑπερπερισσῶς ἐξεπλήσσοντο in Mk 7.37 is softened, and ἐξεθαύμαζον in Mk 12.17 is also softened). Matthew also changes Mark's fear on occasion (to amazement,

27. Tagawa, *Miracles*, p. 96.
28. Tagawa, *Miracles*, p. 96.

Mk 4.41 par. Mt. 8.27; and to grief, Mk 9.32 par. Mt. 17.23).

This should show that Matthew, a book a full third longer, is simply not like Mark in reactions of wonder. Both use such reactions, but there are crucial differences. Matthew is more stereotyped than Mark, less intensive, less varied and less mysterious. The motif is more frequent in Mark. In Matthew's longer gospel, the motif does not pack the punch that it does in the shorter, faster-moving account of Mark. One must not assume that the synoptics are all alike in reactions of wonder. The evidence shows notable differences.

It is interesting to point out a couple of tendencies of the synoptic tradition at this point. In the category of emotions mentioned, where there is a reference in one gospel but not in another, Mark is quite distinctive. Matthew is more detailed than Mark and Luke three times each, and Luke is more detailed than Matthew four times and more than Mark twice. Mark, however, is more detailed than the longer Matthew 11 times and the lengthier Luke eight times.[29] Mark also is distinctive in the use of miscellaneous details. Matthew includes such details twice each more than Mark or Luke, and Luke includes such details on four occasions more than Matthew and once more than in Mark. Mark, however, has miscellaneous details seventeen times more than Matthew and seven times more than Luke, bringing E.P. Sanders to conclude that Mark is 'very much more detailed' than Matthew, and 'considerably more detailed' than Luke'.[30]

When one compares Luke with Mark, the results are also quite interesting, and show (like Matthew) there are some major differences between the second and third gospels. Luke has 34 reactions of wonder, that is, just two more in a work 8,370 words longer! Luke tends to group such reactions together, with ten occurrences in the birth narratives of Chapters 1 and 2, and five occurrences in the resurrection narrative of the final chapter. Thus, 15 of Luke's 34 occurrences (almost half!) are either in the first two or last chapters of the gospel. What makes this element of Luke even more intriguing is that Luke has eight solid chapters (Chapters 12-19) without a single reaction of wonder. Mark does not group his motif in the unusual fashion that Luke does. Mark has only two chapters where the motif does not occur (Chapters 8 and 13), and, unlike Luke, Mark never loads down a chapter (the most references Mark has in a single chapter are four in Chapter 5 and five in Chapter 6).

---

29. E.P. Sanders, *The Tendencies of the Synoptic Tradition* (SNTSMS,9; Cambridge: Cambridge University Press, 1969), pp. 181-82.

30. Sanders, *Tendencies*, p. 186.

1. Introduction

Luke's use of reactions of wonder can be grouped as follows. 11 times such reactions occur in relation to miracles or exorcisms, a somewhat common element in the New Testament (4.36; 5.9, 26; 7.16; 8.25, 35, 37, 47, 56; 9.43; 11.14), but only four references occur in relation to the teaching of Jesus (2.47; 4.22, 32; 20.26). Eight times reactions of wonder occur in either visionary or revelatory experiences (1.12, 29; 2.9; 9.34; 24.5, 12, 37, 41) and there are 11 occurrences which can be called miscellaneous (1.21, 63, 65; 2.18, 33, 48; 9.45; 11.38; 20.19; 22.2; 24.22). One notices immediately that Luke has many more references relating to miracles than to the teaching of Jesus, in contradistinction to Mark which has the exact same number of reactions of fear and amazement in relation to Jesus' teaching as to Jesus' miracles (eight each), thus achieving a far greater balance in the presentation of Jesus.

Luke does not follow Mark in 18 different places, namely Mk 3.21; 5.20; 6.6, 20, 50, 51; 7.37; 9.15; 10.24, 26, 32; 11.18, 32; 12.11; 15.5, 44; 16.6, and 8. Luke modifies Mk 1.27; 2.12; 4.41; 5.33, 42; 6.2; 9.6; 12.17 and 16.5. Thus, of the 32 occurrences in Mark, Luke follows only five exactly. One can also note at this point that Luke, like Matthew, does not use any of the 'mysterious' references of Mark (3.21; 9.15; 10.32; 14.33; 16.8).

Luke likes doxologies (used only in Mark at 2.12), and adds them to a Markan source at Lk. 5.26 and 7.16, and uses them without references to amazement or fear at 13.13, 17.15 and 18.43. Like Matthew, Luke's favorite term is θαυμάζω, used in Lk. 1.21, 63; 2.18, 33; 4.22; 7.9; 8.25; 9.43; 11.14, 38; 20.26; 24.12 and 41, thirteen times in all. The other favorite term, again like Matthew, is φόβος or φοβέομαι (1.12, 65; 2.9; 7.16; 8.25, 35, 37; 9.34, 45; 20.19 and 22.2, 11 times and note also ἔμφοβος in 24.5 and 37). Thus, those two words account for 26 of Luke's 34 occurrences. Also, like Matthew, Luke does not like to use the intensive compounds that Mark so often prefers. The third gospel does not use the Markan ἐκθαμβέομαι, ἐκθαύμαζω, ἔκφοβος, nor does Luke use θαμβέομαι or τρόμος. Tagawa says that Luke historicizes and psychologizes, noting that Luke adds fear to Mk 2.12 in Lk. 5.26, and to Mk 4.41 in Lk. 8.25 amazement is added.[31] He sees a historicizing process in the Lukan tendency to make the reactions of witnesses at the scene of an event serve as less of a traditional formula (as Matthew), and more of a true reaction.[32] It can be added that Luke shows a theological interest with use of the 'doxological motif'.

Luke does use intensive terms (Lk. 2.9; 8.25; 37), but when Mark is used as

---

31. Tagawa, *Miracles*, pp. 97-98.

a source, there is a tendency to soften and smooth Mark's emphatic speech (for example in Lk. 8.47 par. Mk 5.33 Luke drops φοβηθεῖσα and keeps only τρέμουσα; in Lk. 8.56 par. Mk 5.42 the Markan ἐξεστησαν ἐκστάσει μεγάλῃ becomes ἐξέστησαν; Lk. 9.34 par. Mk 9.6 Mark's ἔκφοβοι becomes ἐφοβήθησαν; and in Lk. 20.26 par. Mk 12.17 ἐξεθαύμαζον becomes θαυμάσαντες). While stylistic reasons may at times be present, the alteration of Mark by Luke remains striking.

To sum up the comparison of Luke with Mark, it can be said that in the longer work of Luke the reactions of wonder and fear do not stand out as much as they do in the more compact Mark. It is interesting to note that a recent study of the narrative of Luke by R. Tannehill takes no special note of the role that such reactions play in the Lukan narrative,[33] whereas a similar study of Mark by Rhoads and Michie does comment on the importance of such reactions in the second gospel.[34] The fact that Luke has only two more references than Mark in a work over 8,000 words longer tells us much about the relative importance of the motif in the gospels.

Luke is also much less balanced than Mark, as the distribution in the birth narratives and in the final chapter shows. Mark has nothing like Luke's huge 'gap' in it. Beyond this, one can safely say that Luke does not have the mystery (the 'puzzling' Markan verses are all left out), the intensity (the Markan language is often softened), the variety (two words are used for the most part in Luke) or the frequency (given the relative lengths of the two books) that Mark does.

In light of the preceding, it can be noted with some certainty that reactions of wonder function in quite a different way in Mark than in the other synoptic gospels. Whatever other similarities there may be between the synoptics, here we have some clearly defined differences. The distinctiveness of Mark here clearly must arrest our attention, especially in light of the terseness of the narrative.

Conclusion

In summary, a thorough and careful study on the motif of wonder in Mark is needed. An attempt will be made to push beyond the earlier treatments of Bertram, Pesch, Tagawa and Stacy. Reactions of wonder do qualify as a motif

32. Tagawa, *Miracles*, pp. 97-98.
33. R.T. Tannehill, *The Unity of Luke–Acts: A Literary Interpretation*. I. *The Gospel According to Luke* (Philadelphia: Fortress Press, 1986).
34. Rhoads and Michie, *Story*, p. 135.

in Mark, have a mystery and a frequency, and a drama which draw us to the text of the gospel. Markan reactions of wonder are quite distinct from such reactions in the other synoptics, justifying an examination of wonder in Mark rather than Matthew or Luke. A modest use of redaction criticism combined with attention to the narrative texture of Mark can be utilized as an appropriate methodology. Following the suggestions of Freedman, it is worth looking at wonder in Mark as relating to the central proclamation of the coming of the kingdom in 1.14-15. First, however, Mark must be set in literary context. Since one naturally is interested how wonder might be used in other texts in the ancient world, I will look at the way wonder works in Greco-Roman literature, the Old Testament and early Jewish literature, and the rest of the New Testament and early Christian literature to see what light may be shed on Mark (Chapters 2 through 4). If there is a specific pattern which may be discerned regarding the use of wonder in the literary world of Mark, it will sharpen the issues I come to the gospel with in the fifth and sixth chapters. In those chapters, my attention will turn to Mark itself for exegesis of the wonder texts. The understanding that will emerge will hopefully lead to a fuller and more comprehensive understanding of the motif, and of the gospel as a whole.

Chapter 2

WONDER IN THE GRECO-ROMAN WORLD

In any examination of parallels, two pitfalls must be avoided. One is the famous 'parallelomania' lamented by Samuel Sandmel.[1] To avoid this, types of literature have been selected for comparison most similar to the gospels, giving the benefit of the doubt (for the moment) to scholars who have suggested sources closest in genre. The other pitfall is the *post hoc, ergo propter hoc* fallacy. Phenomena superficially similar in an earlier culture are not necessarily the cause of a later manifestation.[2]

The issue of genre may be somewhat misleading, and I will only note in passing the comments of G. Kennedy, who says that the question of genre evolved in Alexandria for the purpose of library classification, and that the question of the genre of the gospels is not primary.[3] Instead of endorsing any theory of gospel genre, I will simply apply the question of the use of reactions of wonder to representative and important hypotheses. The use of wonder in inscriptions is difficult due to the fragmentary nature of the remains, so I will stay with literary evidence.[4] Also, reactions of wonder cannot be called in every text a 'motif', since to speak of a motif implies a dominant or salient feature of a work

---

1. S. Sandmel, 'Parallelomania', *JBL* 81 (1962), pp. 1-13.
2. Note here H.C. Kee, *Miracle in the Early Christian World* (New Haven: Yale University Press, 1983), p. 51.
3. Referred to in R.H. Fuller, 'Classics and the Gospels: The Seminar', in *The Relationships Among the Gospels: An Interdisciplinary Dialogue* (San Antonio, TX: Trinity University Press, 1978), p. 189. For a contrary view, see Burridge later in this chapter.
4. An examination of the inscriptions shows that wonder plays virtually no part. For example, see E.J. and L. Edelstein (eds.), *Asclepius: A Collection and Interpretation of the Testimonies* (2 vols.; Baltimore: The Johns Hopkins Press, 1945). Theissen separates wonder from acclamation, which does play a part in the inscriptions (Theissen, *Stories*, pp. 152-73). Another problem is the difference between the literary and inscriptional remains of an ancient culture.

(see the previous chapter), and wonder is not such in every case. Thus I will speak of 'reactions' of wonder.

The 'Divine Man'

One of the liveliest debates surrounding the gospel of Mark in the last 20 years is the question of the possible relation of the so-called 'divine man' (θεῖος ἀνήρ) of the Greco-Roman world (along with the inseparable question of aretalogy) to Mark's portrayal of Jesus. The literature is voluminous.[5] The debate is not all one sided, however, and strong voices have resounded against 'divine man' concepts.[6] Certainly the debate is not over. Yet the controversy is such that

---

5. J.D. Kingsbury, 'The "Divine Man" as the Key to Mark's Christology–The End of an Era?', *Int* 35 (1981) pp. 243-57 asked if the era of applying the θεῖος ἀνήρ question to Mark was over, but E.V. Gallagher, *Divine Man or Magician: Celsus and Origen on Jesus* (SBLDS, 64; Chico, CA: Scholars Press, 1982), and G.P. Corrington, *The Divine-Man: His Origin and Function in Hellenistic Popular Religion*, (AUSS 7; Theology and Religion, vol.17; New York: Peter Lang, 1986), especially p. 301, responded with a resounding 'no'. L. Bieler, ΘΕΙΟΣ ANHP *Das Bild des göttlichen Menschen in Spätantike und Frühchristentum* (2 vols; Vienna: Oskar Hofels, 1935), is a basic source. M. Hadas and M. Smith, *Heroes and Gods: Spiritual Biographies in Antiquity* (Freeport, NY: Books for Libraries Press, 1970), and M. Smith, 'Prolegomena to a Discussion of Aretalogies, Divine Men, The Gospels and Jesus', *JBL* 90 (1971) pp. 174-99, applied the issue to Luke and Mark; H.-W. Kuhn, *Ältere Sammlungen im Markusevangelium* (Göttingen: Vandenhoeck & Ruprecht, 1971), especially pp. 193-225, directly related wonder in the miracle stories of Mk. 4-6 to characteristics of a divine man; S. Schulz, *Die Stunde der Botschaft* (Hamburg: Furche; Zürich: Zwingli, 1970), especially pp. 67-72, related wonder to the epiphany character of the miracle stories; T. Weeden, 'The Heresy that Necessitated Mark's Gospel', *ZNW* 59 (1968) pp. 145-58 and *Traditions*, saw Mark as a correction to a divine-man heresy with the passion story; H.D. Betz, 'Jesus as Divine Man' in *Jesus and the Historian* (ed. F.T. Trotter; Philadelphia: Westminster Press, 1968), pp. 114-33, depicts Mark as criticizing and correcting his sources which present Jesus as the divine man in a 'naive' way; Bultmann, *History*, especially p. 241, and *Theology of the New Testament* (2 vols.; London: SCM Press, 1983), I, pp. 121-32 relates the question directly to Mark; H. Koester, 'One Jesus and Four Primitive Gospels' in *Trajectories through Early Christianity* (Philadelphia: Fortress Press, 1971), pp. 158-204, takes cues from Hadas and Smith; L. Keck, 'Mark 3.7-12 and Mark's Christology', *JBL* 84 (1965) pp. 341-58, refers especially to the miracle stories. Most of these build on Bieler and R. Reitzenstein, *Hellenistische Wundererzählungen* (Leipzig: Teubner, 1910), especially p. 12.

6. W. v. Martitz claims that θεῖος ἀνήρ is not a fixed expression, and θεῖος is not a title, but predicative in 'υἱός' in *TNDT*, VIII, pp. 334-40; M. Hengel bluntly calls θεῖος ἀνήρ

application to our topic is necessary. In the so-called 'divine-man' literature, do reactions of wonder play a part? Is wonder a constituent part of the so-called 'divine-man' stories, and could it have entered Mark from these portraits? I will suspend judgement temporarily and examine the major texts, granting concession also, since the works range from the fourth century BCE to the third century CE, a period of some 700 years![7]

a 'worn out catchphrase' in *Studies in the Gospel of Mark* (London: SCM Press, 1985), p. 41, and also note *The Son of God* (London: SCM Press, 1976), especially p. 31, where he says that almost all of Bieler's sources come from Neo-Platonism and the church's hagiography; K. Berger says θεῖος ἀνήρ is unsuitable as an explanation of individual cases and that the concept must be used with great caution for handling sources in 'Zum Problem der Messianität Jesu', *ZTK* (1974) pp.1-30, especially p. 6; H.C. Kee in *Community of the New Age* (London: SCM Press, 1977), pp. 17-18, and 'Aretalogy and Gospel' *JBL* 92 (1973) pp. 402-22, makes a strong case against aretalogy as a fixed literary form, and argues compellingly that the aim of a miracle story should be a function of the use to which the story is put (in Mark's case to demonstrate that Jesus is the agent for the defeat of demonic powers and the establishment of the divine rule), rather than something that is inherent in the story itself; W.L. Lane makes a good case against Weeden's reconstruction in 'Theios Aner Christology and the Gospel of Mark' in *New Dimensions in New Testament Study* (ed. R. Longenecker and M.C. Tenney; Grand Rapids: Zondervan, 1974), pp.144-61; O. Betz questions whether the type is behind either Mark or 2 Corinthians in 'The Concept of the So-Called "Divine Man" in Mark's Christology' in *Studies in New Testament and Early Christian Literature: Essays in Honor of Allen Wikgren* (ed. D. Aune; NovTSup, 33; Leiden: Brill, 1972), pp. 229-40; E. Schweizer makes the point that Mark is closer to the Old Testament rather than 'Hochliteratur' and that the disciples are not depicted completely negatively in Mark in 'Neuere Markus-Forschung in USA', *EvT* 33 (1973), pp. 533-37; Theissen notes that the miracles must not be separated from eschatology or redemptive action and that θεῖος ἀνήρ is implausible as a theory until comparable lives which inspired Mark are found in *Stories*, especially p.220, n. 43 and pp. 270-94; C. Holladay wants to abandon the preoccupation of focusing on miracles as ways of attesting divinity, as with Greek miracle workers, which obscures the more fundamental continuity of Hellenistic Judaism with the Old Testament understanding of miracles in terms of salvation history in *Theios Aner in Hellenistic Judaism: A Critique of the Use of this Category in New Testament Christology* (SBLDS, 40; Chico, CA: Scholars Press, 1977), especially p. 239; Kingsbury argues against a divine man concept and Mark having a corrective christology in *Christology*, pp. 34-37, 71; B. Blackburn says that virtually none of the supposed θεῖος ἀνήρ elements in the gospels requires an explanation based on such a type in *A Critique of the Theios Aner Concept as an Interpretative Background of the Miracle Traditions used by Mark* (Unpublished Ph.D. thesis; Aberdeen: University of Aberdeen, 1986).

7. I have examined Plato's *Crito, Euthryphro, Apology* and *Phaedo*, since Hadas and Smith have suggested that Socrates is the paradigm and source for all subsequent aretalogies,

2. Wonder in the Greco-Roman World

First of all, it becomes evident that wonder plays little part in the portraits of 'divine-men' and they are not presented as often evoking reactions of wonder. Wonder cannot be said to be a constituent part of the 'divine-man' stories. In the lengthy (and late) *Vit. Ap.*, for example, wonder only occurs 20 times[8] (not always related to Apollonius), much less than in Mark. It rarely occurs in the Socratic dialogues, and occurs in *Vit. Pyth.* (Porphyry) only twice in relation to the hero.[9] In Philo's *Vit. Mos.* it occurs only twice as a reaction to Moses.[10] It is unlikely that the gospel of Mark picked up or follows a pattern for reactions of wonder from these types of stories.

pagan and Christian, in *Heroes*, pp. 49-63; Philostratus' *Life of Apollonius of Tyana*, the writing of the ancient world probably most often compared with the gospels despite the fact that it was composed in the third century CE, is 35 times the length of Mark, and twice the length of all four gospels together (C.W. Votaw, *The Gospels and Contemporary Biographies in the Greco-Roman World* (Philadelphia: Fortress Press, 1979 [1951]); Porphyry's *Life of Pythagoras*, which Smith claims is arranged in a way parallel to the gospels with a great sensation made by the hero on his arrival, his gathering a body of followers, a preliminary account of his daily regime and diet, a fuller account of his teaching, a distinction between what he taught in public and in private, his death, and the survival of his teaching through followers (*Heroes*, p. 107); Iamblichus' *Life of Pythagoras*; Philo's *Life of Moses*, where Hadas and Smith see the influence of aretalogical traditions as greatest other than in the accounts of Apollonius, Pythagoras and Jesus (*Heroes*, p. 101); Josephus' portrait of Moses in *Jewish Antiquities* 2.210-4.331; *4 Maccabees*, which S.E. Johnson has compared to Mark in 'Greek and Jewish Heroes: Fourth Maccabees and the Gospel of Mark' in *Early Christian Literature and the Classical Intellectual Tradition: In Honor of Robert M. Grant* (ed. W.R. Schoedel and R.L. Wilken; Paris: Editions Beauchesne, 1979), pp. 157-75; Plutarch's *Cleomenes*; Diogenes Laertius' *Lives of Eminent Philosophers* (Corrington suggests that philosophers possessed the embodiment of power and divinity to an even greater degree than kings in *Origin*, p.89); Lucian's *Alexander the False Prophet* (Corrington claims that this satire shows that there is really no distinction between philosophy and religion on a popular level, and the picture of a type of person who performs θαυμάστα καὶ τέρατα to win the devotion of people can be seen here, *Origin*, pp. 101-102) and *Heracles*; Euripides' portrait of Heracles in *The Madness of Heracles*. Obviously with *4 Maccabees*, Philo and Josephus I am crossing into Jewish material, anticipating the next chapter, but the content makes grouping these portions here convenient.

8.   Eight times at surprising statements (1.19; 1.27; 3.40; 4.3; 4.21; 4.44; 6.3; 7.36), nine times at Apollonius himself (1.19, 27; 3.40; 4.21; 4.31; 7.32; 8.8; 8.9; 8.30; 8.31), and Apollonius himself is amazed, possibly sarcastically (3.16 twice), and in a statement in 7.22. This would be equivalent to one half reaction in every section the length of Mark.
9.   25.21; 28.12.
10. 1.6.27; 2.14.70.

I should also note that rarely do reactions of wonder occur in miracle stories in these sources, only five times. The only miracle stories where reactions of wonder occurred were in *Vit. Ap.* 9.20, 8.8 and 8.9, *Ant.* 2.280, and *Alex.* 13.1420. It is striking, for example, that in *Vit. Ap.*, twice wonder occurs in relation to the sudden disappearance of Apollonius. It occurs only once in relation to an exorcism (4.20). In *Ant.* 2.280, Aaron and the Hebrew elders are amazed at the astonishing spectacle of the miracles (οἱ δ' ὑπ' ἐκπλήξεως τῶν παρὰ δόξαν). In *Alex.* 13.1420, the people marvel (θαυμάσαντες) at the contrived discovery of an egg with a snake. One immediately sees the problem of claiming that wonder is a stereotyped reaction in Hellenistic miracle stories. It is more frequent in the gospels than in any of these stories. Reactions of wonder, then, are unlikely to have entered the synoptic miracle tradition from these tales, or been patterned after the reactions of wonder in these tales.[11]

Reactions of wonder do occur in response to surprising statements or teachings of individuals. This happens eight times in *Vit. Ap.*,[12] yet only eight times in a work 35 times the length of Mark (which also has eight such reactions) hardly shows it to be a dominant factor or a motif in the book. It is surprising how little these reactions are used in the Socratic dialogues (where it is mostly ironic, for example in *Sym.* 198 B and C. *Prot.* 359 C).

The work in which it is most common here (in frequency related to length, which can indicate intensity) is *4 Maccabees*, with eight references related to the death of the martyrs.[13] In 1.11, for example, it speaks of being amazed (θαυμασθέντες) at the endurance and courage of Eleazer, his brothers and their mother, and in 17.17, the 'tyrant' and council marvel at their endurance (ἐθαύμασεν αὐτῶν τὴν ὑπομονήν). Twice in this text it occurs in relation to the

---

11. Theissen, *Stories*, pp. 60-70, admits that the reactions are not very common outside the NT, and lists only four extra-NT examples (Oxy. 10.1242, where Trajan marvels after the superiority of Serapis to the Jewish God is seen, θεασάσμενος δὲ Τραιανὸς ἀπεθαύμασεν); Lucian *Philops.*12 (after a field is cleared of snakes: οἱ παρόντες δὲ ἐθαύμαζεν); *PGM* 4.245 (θαυμάσας τὸν προφήτην διπλᾶ ὀψωνία αὐτῷ ἐκέλυσε δίδοσθαι); and Apul. Met. 11.13 (after Lucian is turned back into a man: *populi mirantur religiosi venerantur tam evidentem maximi numinis potentiam* ...). Bultmann's examples are all from the NT, *History*, p. 226. Blackburn, *Critique*, p. 282, n. 215, says that most examples are post-NT, and lists Eur. *Bacch.* 449, IG 4^2 1. no. 121 par 5, IG 9.1299, Diod Sic. 4.43.af, Luc. *Abdic.* 5 and Phil. *Vit. Ap.* 4.20.25 in addition to Theissen's references. By all accounts reactions of wonder in miracle stories outside the NT are rare, with just a handful of examples.

12. 1.19, 1.27, 3.40, 4.31, 4.44, 6.3, 7.36.

13. 1.11; 6.13; 7.13; 9.26; 17.16, 2 twice; 17.17; 18.3.

2. Wonder in the Greco-Roman World

countenance of the brothers (8.4, 8.5). In 4.10 there is another occurrence, where Apollonius and his soldiers appear from heaven riding upon horses with lightening flashing from their armor, and great fear and trembling comes upon Apollonius and his soldiers (καὶ πολὺν αὐτοῖς φόβον τε καὶ τρόμον ἐνιέτες). There are two special definitions which we should acknowledge in these texts. In Philo's *Vit. Mos.* 1.38.213 it is stated that the unfamiliar in nature (referring to the plagues in Egypt) is regarded with amazement (ξέναις φαντασίαις ἐνδιδόντες καταπληττόμεθα τῷ φιλοκαίνῳ). Also, in *Vit. Ap.* 7.22, Apollonius speaks of wisdom amazing all that are sensible of her, but not being amazed by anything (σοφία μὲν τὰ ξυνιέντα ἑαυτῆς ἐκπλήττει πάντα, αὐτὴ δ' ὑπ' οὐδενὸς ἐκπλήττεται).

The most common source of wonder seems at this point to be acts or interventions of God (or gods), especially in the Hellenistic Jewish sources I have examined. I would separate these from miracles performed by unique individuals. One can note eight references in Philo's *Vit. Mos.*[14] All of these relate to the acts of God at the exodus. For example, in 1.14.78 Moses marvels at the double change of the serpent to the staff and back (ὡς θαυμάζειν μὲν τὰς μεταβολὰς ἀμφοτέρας), and in 1.32.177 Moses marvels (θαυμάσας) at the parting of the sea. In the section of *Antiquities* surveyed, there are nine examples of reactions of wonder at acts of God.[15] The interesting discovery here is that when the so-called 'divine man' stories were surveyed to see if these individuals were portrayed with reactions of wonder, it happened very seldom. I did find, however, that in the accounts of Moses (often said to be presented as a 'divine man'), that reactions of wonder do not often occur at Moses himself (twice in Philo, four times in Josephus), but instead at interventions of God. These are seen as distinct from the miracles of the individuals.

Another point needs to be made here. Often, wonder is said to be indicative of an epiphany, and so is in the gospel of Mark. It must be noted that the reactions, as noted in Philo's *Vit. Mos.* 1.32.177 for example, are better constituted as responses to 'divine interventions' than 'divine epiphanies'.

All in all, it is interesting how small a part wonder plays in this literature. The sources that have it most are *Life of Apollonius of Tyana*, *Jewish Antiquities*, *The Life of Moses*, and *4 Maccabees*. Lucian uses it satirically at times. These lengthy texts (the section of *Antiquities* was 190 pages of Greek text, for example) simply do not emphasize wonder like Mark. It seems safe to

14. 1.14.78 twice; 1.14.81; 1.16.91; 1.32.177; 1.32.180; 1.36.200; 2.48.264.
15. 2.267 twice; 2.270; 2.274; 2.280; 3.38; 3.82; 4.66; 4.111.

say that it is difficult to see the reactions of wonder as in any way stereotyped or as a motif in these texts. As stated earlier, it is rare in miracle stories in these texts. It is most common, however, in divine interventions in Hellenistic Jewish sources surveyed under this rubric.

Greco-Roman Biography

In 1915, Clyde Weber Votaw proposed that the gospels are of a common genre with Greco-Roman biographies.[16] In recent years this thesis has been revived by C. Talbert (who basically is arguing against Bultmann's contention that there are not generic links between the canonical gospels and Greco-Roman biographies by attempting to show that Greco-Roman biographies are indeed cultic, mythic and world-negating, as are the gospels),[17] and P.L. Shuler (who says that Talbert has failed to demonstrate that those conventions shared by the gospels are common to ancient biographical narratives and attempts to show that there is a *bios* narrative pattern where the person presented stands in the center of the literary stage.[18]

A very notable contribution on the relation of the gospels to ancient biographies comes recently from R.A. Burridge.[19] Burridge believes previous attempts to classify the gospels as biographies have floundered on limitations in understanding of both classical literature and contemporary literary theory. He sees ancient biography to be a flexible genre which has strong relationships with history, encomium and rhetoric, and moral philosophy with its concern for character. Burridge's method of comparison is unique, for he analyzes suggestions of genre through first, the opening feature of a text or its title; secondly, the identification of subjects of verbs by a numerical analysis; thirdly, external features of representation; and fourthly, internal features of content.[20]

---

16. Votaw, *Gospels*.

17. C. Talbert, *What is a Gospel? The Genre of the Canonical Gospels* (Philadelphia: Fortress Press, 1977)

18. P.L. Shuler, *A Genre for the Gospels: The Biographical Character of Matthew* (Philadelphia: Fortress Press, 1982). Also, D. Aune, *The New Testament in its Literary Environment* (Philadelphia: Westminster, 1987), p. 46, says that an analysis of the constituent literary features of the gospels places them comfortably within the parameters of ancient biographical conventions in form and function.

19. R.A. Burridge, *What are the Gospels?* (SNTSMS, 70; Cambridge: Cambridge University Press, 1992).

20. Burridge, *What?*, p. 126.

2. Wonder in the Greco-Roman World

Consequently, the gospels begin with a preface with the subject's (Jesus) name, Jesus is the subject of a large number of the verbs in the gospels, the mode of representation in size, structure and scale is similar in the gospels to biographies, and internal features of the gospels are roughly comparable to biographies.[21] Burridge suggests that Matthew and Luke recognized Mark's genre and brought it closer to other Greco-Roman βίοι.[22] Burridge does not discuss wonder as a possible formal characteristic of ancient biography, either as a feature of representation or an internal feature of content.

An important presentation of the difficulty of the views of Votaw, Talbert, Shuler and Burridge was written before any of them. This is the 1903 work of Johannes Weiss on Mark, *Das älteste Evangelium*. Weiss shows that the interest in birth, descent, childhood, character development and depiction, chronological outline and personal description common to ancient biographies is lacking in Mark.[23] Any comparison of the gospels with ancient biography must take these problems into account, yet Talbert, for example, does not refer to Weiss. To be fair, one must also say that not every Greco-Roman biography had the elements Weiss suggests. Burridge would contend that biography was more flexible than Weiss presents, but here is the heart of the problem: whether or not one sees the gospels as biographies in genre depends on *how one constructs the genre of biography*. Certainly anyone looking to classical texts with one eye on the gospels will tend to place features of the gospels in the foreground, shading everything that follows. The boundaries of a 'genre' are certainly constructable in different ways, either to include or exclude the canonical gospels. No one, to my knowledge, has suggested that wonder is a common feature or motif of both gospels and biographies.

Biography gained prestige during the Roman Imperial age. It was the natural way to tell the story of a Caesar, and also, in contrast, a vehicle for unorthodox political and philosophical ideas.[24] Momigliano suggests that the fact that the Hellenistic and Roman biographers wrote about men of the same type (generals, philosophers and demagogues) indicates that the type was more important than the individual.[25] Yet this was only one of the directions that the literature

---

21. Burridge, *What?*, p. 218.
22. Burridge, *What?*, p. 249.
23. J. Weiss, *Das älteste Evangelium* (Göttingen: Vandenhoeck & Ruprecht, 1903), pp. 11-15.
24. A. Momigliano, *The Development of Greek Biography* (Cambridge, MA: Harvard University Press, 1972), p.99.
25. Momigliano, *Development*, p. 13.

tended to follow. Besides studies of commanding figures who played a great part in some major domain of human life, biographies also served to bring information to readers in quest of specialized knowledge.[26] Biographies provided education for learned individuals who wanted to know something of the lives of poets, philosophers and kings.[27] Yet it must not be overlooked that biographies were also created to sway or create opinion about certain political or philosophical principles.[28] P. Cox points out that by the first century CE the philosopher (either a roving preacher, magician-prophet or acknowledged leader of a particular school of thought) had become a holy man in the eyes of his followers and this process brought the development of the biographical genre into close association with holy sages.[29] For our purposes it is important to keep in mind that biographies often used material similar in form to serve different purposes, that is, different authors will have adapted related motifs and styles for their own philosophical or theological ends. Motifs do not necessarily define the structure of texts which happen to include them.[30] Thus care must be observed in the examination of texts for motifs, with no assumptions made as to the particular use that a motif might be given in an individual text.[31] With this in mind, we have evaluated the way in which reactions of wonder are used in representative and notable biographical works.[32]

I have found that in Greco-Roman biography, wonder at the individual

---

26. D.S. Reed, *Epochs of Greek and Roman Biography* (New York: Biblio & Tanner, 1967 [1928]), pp. 157-58.
27. Momigliano, *Development*, p. 84.
28. P. Cox, *Biography in Late Antiquity: A Quest for the Holy Man* (Berkley: University of California Press, 1983), p.16.
29. Cox, *Biography*, pp. 19-20.
30. Cox, *Biography*, p. 49.
31. It is recognized that the distinctions between what is 'divine man' literature and what is biography are not always clear, with the same sources often cited for both genres. Perhaps this in itself shows the tenuous nature of such classification.
32. The texts we have examined are Isocrates' *Helen, Busiris, Evangoris* (which Shuler calls 'laudatory biographies', a variation of epideictic oratory or encomium, *Genre*, p. 58); Xenophon's *Agesilaus* (another 'laudatory biography', according to Shuler, *Genre*, p. 58) and *Cyropaedia* (Momigliano calls this 'the most accomplished biography we have in classical Greek literature' and 'Xenophon's greatest contribution to biography', *Development*, p. 28); Lucian's *Demonax* (a further example of Shuler's 'laudatory biography'); Josephus's *Life of Josephus*; Porphyry's *Life of Plotinus*; Plutarch's *Parallel Lives*. These give us a representative sampling of over fifty works. In each case I have sought to pay attention to the likely purpose and situation of each writing.

2. Wonder in the Greco-Roman World 35

depicted plays little part. Many of the sources have few or no examples. In *Helen, Busiris, Agesilaus, Life of Plotinus,* and in Plutarch's *Cimon, Tiberius Gracchus, Philopoemen, Otho* and in all his *Comparisons,* wonder does not occur. Many of the examples do not refer to the individual portrayed. There are more examples of a general admiration (θαυμάζειν) than specific reactions of wonder. Thus reactions of wonder are not a constituent part in the representative biographies examined.

Wonder does occur at times in response to surprising statements of individuals. This can be seen, for example, 11 times in Plutarch.[33] Even here, 11 times in a work that is 11 volumes in the Loeb edition is hardly a dominant theme, and often surprise rather than wonder is involved. There is no work I have surveyed where wonder is a reaction to statements of speeches as frequently as in Mark. In this connection one should not overlook the statement of *Hel.* 7 that young rhetoricians were inclined to that which is extraordinary and astounding (πρὸς τὰς περιττότητας καὶ τὰς θαυματοποιίας).

The most common occurrence is wonder as a response to divine interventions, portents or dreams. For example, in *Cyrop.* 4.2.15, a light from heaven shines on Cyrus and his army, filling them with awe (ὥστε πᾶσι μὲν φρίκην ἐγγίγεσθαι πρὸς Θεῖον). Plutarch has a special interest here, probably because he was a priest at Delphi, and the fulfillment of signs or omens was important to his moral purpose in writing.[34] He was setting forth examples of virtue or attainment of virtue (ἀρετή) as an aid to the good life in his readers.[35] His characters can be distinguished by their possession of ἀρετή, or their partial or total lack of it. He also wanted to set forth examples of men who have done fine things (καλός) and whose lives can be seen to have been controlled by choice.[36] Wonder in Plutarch is most often the reaction to some divine intervention.

I can illustrate this with some examples. In *Rom.* 2.6, the cowherd who spots the twins Romulus and Remus must overcome his amazement (θαυμάσαντα) at spotting a she-wolf giving them suck, and birds bringing food to them. In *Them.* 30.3, Themistocles is amazed at an epiphany (θαυμάσας τὴν ἐπιφάνειαν) of the Goddess Rhea (Cybele) who appears to him in a dream and tells him to 'shun a head of lions'). Themistocles avoids a village called Lion's

---

33. *Lyc.* 16.10, *Them.* 13.3, *Pomp.* 14.3, *Dion.* 6.4, *Demos.* 5.3, *Cic.* 4.5, *Alex.* 12.3, 14.3, 49.3, and *Mar.* 17.2 and 31.3.
34. A.D. Nock, 'Religious Attitudes of the Ancient Greeks', in *Essays on Religion and the Ancient World* (2 vols.; Oxford: Clarendon Press, 1972), II, p. 538.
35. A. Wardman, *Plutarch's Lives* (London: Paul Elek, 1974), p. 19.
36. Wardman, *Lives,* p. 116.

Head, where it turns out that the Pisidians seek to attract and kill him. In *Cam.* 5.5, the bystanders are confounded (διαταραχθέντων δὲ τῶν παρόντων) when Camillus stumbles and falls after a prayer, and the stumbling is regarded as the answer to the prayer. In *Luc.* 8.7, as a battle is about to take place between Marius and Lucullus, the sky 'bursts asunder' and a 'huge, flame-like body' falls between the two armies. Both sides are astonished (δείσαντας ἀμφοτέρους) and separate. In *Per.* 35.2, Pericles is about to go to sea with 150 ships, but an eclipse occurs. All are frightened (ἐκπλαγῆναι) and look upon the eclipse as a portent. Pericles is able to overcome their fear, however. Similarly, in *Nic.* 23.1, there is an eclipse of the moon which causes some superstitious ones to quake (ἐκπεπληγμένοις). In *Ages.* 24.5, the soldiers of Agesilaus see a light streaming from some sanctuaries of Eleusis and are filled with shuddering fear (φρῖξαι καὶ περιφόβους γενέσθαι τοὺς στρατιώτας). In *Tim.* 12.6, the people of Adranum report to Timolean with terror and amazement (μετὰ φρίκης καὶ θαύματος) that the sacred portals of their temple have opened of their own accord and that the faces of the god ran down with seat while his spear trembled. Further, in *Alex.* 74.4, it is noted that Cassander, years after the death of Alexander, saw an image of Alexander at Delphi which caused him to be struck with shuddering awe and trembling (πληγέντα φρῖξαι καὶ κραδανθῆναι τὸ σῶμα). Finally, in *Caes.* 67.2, the bystanders are amazed (ἐκπλαγέντων δὲ τῶν παρατυχόντων) when Caius Cornelius, sitting in the place of augury, springs up and cries 'Thou art victorious, O Caesar', as Caesar goes to battle against Pompey (according to a lost book by Livy).

These reactions go beyond epiphanies and include signs, portents and general interventions of the gods. For Plutarch, unusual phenomena of any kind can be portentous, and the unusual events are not portrayed as miracles so much as events in which the deity is present to an exceptional degree.[37] It is expected that humans will be astounded when the divine intervenes. In *Lys.* 25.2, where Lysander fabricates various signs in an attempt to terrify (προεκπλήξας) his countrymen by 'vague religious fear and superstition' in order to be given a voice in ruling Sparta, the implication is that he knows people will react with wonder to signs.

The developing pattern seems to be reactions of wonder respond to various divine interventions, such as portents and signs, as was also seen in the previous section on 'divine man' literature. These reactions can be distinguished

---

37. B.S. MacKay, 'Plutarch and the Miraculous', in *Miracles: Cambridge Studies in Their Philosophy and History* (ed. C.F.D. Moule; London: Mowbrays, 1965), pp. 98, 103.

2. Wonder in the Greco-Roman World

from reactions to frightening 'natural' sights, such as a large invading army. Biographies, however, like 'divine man' literature, do not have wonder as a constituent part.

Esteemed Teachers

Vernon Robbins has recently observed that both exorcisms and healing are a part of Jesus' role as teacher in Mark.[38] There was a fusion of religious traditions, folklore and ethical pronouncements in some Jewish and Greco-Roman literature of the first century which has parallels in Mark, and Robbins proposes that the integration of Greco-Roman literature and its religio-ethical teachers with Jewish influences provided the overall integration point for the Jesus traditions in Mark. Mark modified the conventional repetitive and progressive forms of expression in prophetic biblical literature by adopting a socio-rhetorical pattern associated in contemporary culture with Greco-Roman religious teachers who gathered disciples or companions. Since both exorcisms and healing in Mark are a part of Jesus' role as teacher, it is fitting to compare this function in Mark to Xenophon's *Memorabilia*, which Robbins does in great detail. The fact that both Xenophon's work and the gospels were called *apomnemoneumata* in the second century strengthens the comparison. Although Robbins recognizes some differences in these texts, he claims that these do not annul the basic similarities between the two works.[39]

Comparisons between Jesus and Socrates are nothing new, of course. Votaw did this back in 1915.[40] A question arises: did reactions of wonder play a dominant part in the literature of esteemed teachers in the Greco-Roman world? In light of the fact that there are eight places in Mark where the motif occurs in relation to the teaching of Jesus, the question becomes quite relevant.[41]

Unfortunately, the results are largely negative. After a survey of 11 basic and important portraits of esteemed teachers, it can be said that reactions of wonder are not used to any degree to draw attention to these famous teachers,

---

38. V.K. Robbins, *Jesus the Teacher* (Philadelphia: Fortress Press, 1984), p.66.
39. Robbins, *Teacher*, p. 207.
40. Votaw, *Gospels*, pp. 35-62.
41. The texts I have surveyed in this category are Xenophon's *Memorabilia*; Plato's *Protagoras, Menexenus, Symposium, Alcibiades 1* and *2, Phaedrus, The Lovers,* and *Hipparchus* (*Alcibiades 1* and *2* and *Hipparchus* are probably not true works of Plato, though they are included in the Platonic corpus); Dionysius of Halicarnassus' *Isaeus, Isocrates, Demosthenes, Lysias* and *Thucydides*; and Lucian's *Nigrinus*.

philosophers or rhetoricians. For example, there are no examples to be found in *Menexenus, Alcibiades 1* and *2, Phaedrus, Hipparchus, Isaeus* or *Thucydides*. The places where it is a factor in these tales of esteemed teachers relates to the oratory of the teachers. There are a couple of points where the oratory or rhetoric has dramatic effects on those listening, and certain speakers had the ability to induce this (which is not always viewed positively). For example, in *Prot*. 328 D, Socrates speaks, in an ironic way, of being under the spell of Protagoras after a speech (καὶ ἐγὼ ἐπὶ πολὺν χρόνον κεκλημένος). There is a remark in *Demos*. 4 by Dionysius that when Isocrates (he often refers to other orators instead of focusing on the individual at hand) wished to astound his hearers (εἰς δὲ τὸ καραπλήξασθαι) he could use a more elaborate and artificial style. In the same work, in 22, Dionysius notes that when he reads one of the speeches of Demosthenes (who is the idea orator), 'I am transported; I am led hither and thither, feeling one emotion after another—disbelief, anguish, terror, contempt, hatred, pity, goodwill, anger, envy—every emotion in turn that can sway the human mind'. He goes on to say that he feels like those participating in the Corybantic dances and the rites of Cybele.

A further example of this dramatic effect produced on a listener is in *Nig*. 35, where the narrator says upon completion of a discourse of Nigrinus, 'until then I had listened to him in awe' (ἐγὼ δὲ τέως μὲν ἤκουον αὐτοῦ τεθηπώς), fearing he would stop. When he does stop, the narrator looks on spellbound (ἀπέβλεπον κεκηλμμένος) and afterward has a fit of confusion and giddiness and drips with sweat. It is then stated in *Nig*. 37 that not all who listen to philosophers are enraptured (ἔνθεοι), but the reaction is only for those who have a previous bond with philosophy. One can take into consideration the satirical interests of Lucian here, but satire must have a faint ring of truth to be effective, and thus it is safe to say that there must have been those who reacted in dramatic ways to the teaching of certain philosophers.

In summary, reactions of wonder play little part as a response to esteemed teachers. At times, however, the oratory or rhetoric has a dramatic effect on some listeners, though this is not always viewed positively and at times may result from rhetorical manipulation. This is quite different from Mark, where it is the authority of Jesus, not the theatrical presentation, which strikes the listeners with wonder.

Ancient Drama

There have been a number of scholars who have related Mark to ancient drama, either tragedy or comedy, or in one case the hybrid tragi-comedy. As early as

1931, E.W. Burch called Mark a 'closet drama', that is, a drama whose power is felt by the reader without stage presentation, but which has a well-constructed plot within prose narrative corresponding to the demands of Greek dramatic action.[42] More recently, F.G. Lang has written a stimulating article in which he unveils an elaborate symmetry in the construction of Mark.[43] Dan O. Via believes that Mark exceeds the genre of tragedy and suggests that it is a tragicomedy.[44] G. Bilezikian also has compared Mark to tragedy.[45] B.H. Standaert compares Mark to both drama and rhetoric.[46] Let us note for purposes of comparison, the kind of comparison suggested here, taking Lang as representative.

Lang sees Mark not as 'Kleinliterature', but as the *Gattung* of epic where the portrayal is narrated. In particular, there are five acts in Mark. After a salvation-historical prologue in 1.1-13, 1.14-3.6 is the first 'act', a rhetorical *propositio*. The second 'act' is 3.7-8.26, and the third is 8.27-10.52, which achieves the *peripateia* (a complete change or reversal of situation within a single scene).[47] Here also is the *anagnorisis* (the 'recognition'), in Mark the sudden shift to misfortune. The fourth 'act' is 11.1-13.37, which brings the *lusis* or *katastrophe*, the violent breaking of the knot which has been tied. The fifth 'act' is 14.1-15.39, the *pathos* proper, which ends with the confession that the crucified man is the son of God. Alternatively, there may be a three part scheme (1.14-8.26,

---

42. E.W. Burch, 'Tragic Action in the Second Gospel: A Study in the Narrative of Mark', *JR* 11 (1931) pp. 346-58.

43. F.G. Lang, 'Kompositionsanalyse des Markusevangeliums', *ZTK* 74 (1977), pp. 1-24. Lang sees five acts in Mark: a rhetorical *propositio*, a *peripeteia*, an *anagnorisis*, a *lusis* or *katastrophe*, and the *pathos* proper. Lang relates the effects of tragedy (ἔλεος καὶ φόβος, Aristotle, *Poet.* 6.2).

44. D.O. Via, *Kerygma and Comedy in the New Testament* (Philadelphia: Fortress Press, 1975), see p. 100.

45. G.G. Bilezikian, *The Liberated Gospel: A Comparison of the Gospel of Mark and Greek Tragedy* (Grand Rapids: Baker, 1977).

46. B.H. Standaert, *L'Evangile Selon Marc: Composition et Genre Litteraire* (Nijmegen: Stichting Studentenpress, 1978), see p. 9. Standaert relates 16.5-8 to sentiments fitting for a tragedy, and refers to the suggestion of Aristotle for silence at the beginning and end of a drama (pp. 97-104). Another who relates 16.1-8 as appropriate for drama is A. Stock, *Call to Discipleship* (Wilmington. DE: Michael Glazier, 1982), pp. 51, 53, 57.

47. One wonders how sudden this change or reversal is. In 1.21-28, the synagogue harbours an unclean man, and teachers without authority. As early as 3.6, the conflict, which has already been building, explodes to a point where the Herodians and Pharisees are conspiring to destroy Jesus.

8.27-10.52, and 11.1-15.39) which preserves the tying of the knot, the *peripateia* and the resolution. The scheme is related to our motif of wonder, because Lang relates the effects of tragedy (ἔλεος καὶ φόβος, Aristotle, *Poet.* 6.2) to the ending of Mk 16.8.[48]

Another who has related the 'pity and fear' of tragedy to Mark is Bilezikian. He is careful to point out that there are differences between ancient tragedy and the gospel, such as religious content, inherent world-view, intended function and literary character, but suggests that both Mark and tragedy have a preoccupation with the serious and profound questions of life. Both propose answers that take for granted a moral order issuing from transcendence, and both have a plot revolving around a central figure.[49] The effects of 'pity and fear' are achieved in Mark by the elements of discovery, reversal and suffering.[50] Though wonder is not related to this, it is said to be the reactions of undiscerning disciples. Is there a relation between the ἔλεος καὶ φόβος of drama and wonder in the gospel?

In tragedy, fear comes from the feeling that one might suffer a fate like that of the character portrayed, and pity is from the undeserved evil that comes on the main character (not Aristotle's *Poetics* 9.1452.22-3, and *The Art of Rhetoric* 2.8. 1-2). It is suggested by Aristotle that the incidents arousing pity and fear should occur suddenly, and in relation to other incidents, either by the spectacle (presentation), or by the very structure and incidents in the play (which is the better way and shows the better poet). In *Poetics* 14.1453.3-6 it is suggested that the plot should be so framed that one simply hearing the account of the things which have taken place should be filled with 'horror and pity'. Pity is produced by undeserved misfortune. A catharsis for the audience is produced.

In Mark, the issue is not catharsis but expectation and preparation. Rather than seeking to produce a fear that the reader or hearer might be crucified as Jesus, 8.34-37 may seek to produce an understanding of what following Jesus entails. The passion is necessary (δεῖ, 8.31). It is the cup Jesus must drink and the baptism he must undergo (10.39, 14.36), in fulfillment of the scriptures (14.49). When the crucifixion comes, it is open and public. It is not presented as bad fortune, but as the will of God, even foretold by the scriptures. Pity and fear are aroused by unexpected misfortune in drama, but in Mark the passion is not unexpected (see 3.6).

48. Lang, 'Kompositionsanalyse', p. 20.
49. Bilizekian, *Liberated*, p. 28.
50. Bilizekian, *Liberated*, pp. 101-102.

2. Wonder in the Greco-Roman World

A distinction must be made between the effect sought in the end of a drama, and continued reactions in the gospel. Amazement seems to belong to different categories than pity for one undergoing misfortune. Again, unfortunately, our results are negative. Fear and pity in drama do not apply to the motif of wonder in Mark.

Rhetoric

In the mid-1970s, H.D. Betz[51] and W. Wuellner[52] used Hellenistic-Roman rhetoric in analysis of Pauline texts. The classicist G. Kennedy has also written an important book on rhetoric in the New Testament.[53] The evaluation of texts in light of ancient rhetorical conventions is at a kind of crossroads at the present time, with one fork involving 'discovering' rhetorical patterns in New Testament texts (Betz and his students), and another fork moving towards post-structuralism (Wuellner). In other words, differing methodologies are attempting to be classified under the rubric of rhetorical criticism.[54]

The authors of the New Testament would have been hard pressed to escape an awareness of rhetoric as practiced in the Greco-Roman culture surrounding them. Rhetorical theory found immediate application in every form of oral and written communication. Indeed, all writing was embraced in the field of rhetoric in the classical world.[55] Rhetoric influenced oratory in the three main categories of oratory: judicial; deliberative and epideictic; though as time progressed, pure categories were not always preserved. In the second century BCE, the Romans became aware of Greek culture on a large scale, and within a century rhetorical studies were as at home in Rome as they were in Athens.[56]

---

51. H.D. Betz, 'The Literary Composition and Function of Paul's Letter to the Galatians', *NTS* 21 (1975), pp. 353-79; 'The Problem of Rhetoric and Theology According to the Apostle Paul' in *L'Apôtre Paul* (ed. A. Vanhoye; Leuven: Peeters–Leuven University Press, 1986), pp. 16-48; and *Galatians: A Commentary on Paul's Letter to the Churches in Galatia* (Hermenia Commentaries; Philadelphia: Fortress Press, 1979).

52. W. Wuellner, 'Paul's Rhetoric of Argumentation in Romans', *CBQ* 38 (1976), pp. 330-51 and 'Greek Rhetoric and Pauline Argumentation' in *Grant*, pp. 177-88.

53. G. Kennedy, *New Testament Interpretation through Rhetorical Criticism* (Chapel Hill, NC: University of North Carolina Press, 1984).

54. See W. Wuellner, 'Where is Rhetorical Criticism Taking Us?', *CBQ* 49 (1987), pp. 448-63; and Bible, *Postmodern*, pp. 149-86.

55. G. Kennedy, *The Art of Persuasion in Greece* (London: Routledge and Kegan Paul, 1963), p. 10.

56. Kennedy, *Persuasion*, p. 336.

Rhetorical handbooks were utilized mostly for the inexperienced, while professionals learned from each other and from experience.[57] Soon, rhetoric would be the centerpiece of all education.

Education for Romans in the first century was dominated by the discipline of rhetoric. Grammar prepared for it, law and philosophy might give it a background or capstone, and the forum and law courts were the major places where it found expression.[58] In rhetoric, there were only three internal modes of persuasion, *ethos*, *pathos* and *logos*. Here, it is *pathos* which interests us most. Kennedy defines *pathos* as reactions which the hearers undergo as the orator 'plays upon their feelings'.[59] This gives us pause, since reactions of hearers are at issue. Further cause for pause is given since the influential works of Cicero give special attention to *pathos*.[60] Roman oratory was emotional almost from the start, according to Kennedy, and in contrast to Greek oratory which mostly left emotional appeal to the peroration, the Romans wove it throughout the entire speech.[61] As one moves into the empire, it became more important.

This concern must be linked with the appropriate classification. In judicial rhetoric, the author or speaker seeks to persuade an audience to make a judgment about events occurring in the past. In deliberative rhetoric, the focus is on persuading the audience to take some action in the future. This often found expression in political debates. Epideictic was used for praise and censure in the present, most commonly at funeral orations.[62]

Here a problem must be faced. Mark does not easily fit any of these categories and probably should not be forced. However, since epideictic concerned individuals, sought to bring to memory an individual after death for the purposes of praise, and was used to persuade an audience to reaffirm or hold fast a viewpoint in the present, there may be some link with Mark. Though one hesitates to classify Mark as epideictic rhetoric, these similarities do give one

---

57. Kennedy, *Persuasion*, p. 262.
58. G. Kennedy, *The Art of Rhetoric in the Roman World 300 BC – AD 300* (Princeton: Princeton University Press, 1972), p. 138.
59. Kennedy, *Interpretation*, p. 15.
60. M.L. Clarke, *Rhetoric at Rome* (London: Cohen and West, 1953), p. 72, where it is stated that 'the characteristic feature of Cicero's oratory is the appeal to the emotions'.
61. Kennedy, *Rhetoric*, p. 101.
62. W.R. Roberts, *Greek Rhetoric and Literary Criticism* (London: George G. Harrup, 1928), p. 27. Kennedy doubts whether Greek judicial rhetoric ever found much application at Rome (*Rhetoric*, p. 10.).

2. Wonder in the Greco-Roman World

pause.[63] Might reactions of wonder in Mark be a rhetorical convention, playing on appeal to the emotions (*pathos*) in epideictic rhetoric?[64]

One must be cautious because there are no known analogies where repeated reactions of amazement are used in a speech to create *pathos* as a persuasive tool.[65] As a persuasive tool, there was a lingering concern to use *pathos* in conclusions (*Rhet. Her.* 2.30.47, 3.14.24; *De Inv.* 1.3.98; *Top.* 36.98-99; *De Or.* 2.77.311). However, the focus of most of those texts is judicial situations and the emotion sought is pity (for the one on trial), and this is certainly not the same situation as Mk 16.1-8. Further, a narrative is not a persuasive speech. Also, emotional appeals were not always viewed positively, especially by philosophical schools.

To say that Mark used wonder as an emotional appeal comes close to saying that the form shaped the content. Though Mark is dramatic and captures hearers in a way which has remained strong through generations, it must be said that evidence is simply lacking to be able to contend that rhetorical conventions concerning wonder were followed by Mark (though rhetorical conventions seem to play a part with Romans or Galatians), since we do not have any analogy where repeated reactions of amazement are used in a narrative speech to appeal to *pathos* as a persuasive tool. Unfortunately, again, the conclusion must be negative, that rhetorical convention is unlikely to be the source of wonder in Mark. It seems better to focus on the divine interventions we have seen as evoking wonder, than to suggest that wonder in Mark is driven by a rhetorical convention.

---

63. This idea has been picked up by C. Bryan, *A Preface to Mark: Notes on the Gospel in its Cultural and Literary Setting* (Cambridge: Cambridge University Press, 1993), p. 60, with deliberative elements in 8.35-38, 10.42-45 and 13.5-37.

64. I have examined Aristotle's *The Art of Rhetoric*, Dionysius of Halicarnassus's *On Literary Composition*; *On the Sublime* (attributed to Longinus, but the author is unknown); *Rhetorica Ad Herennium*; Cicero's *de Inventione, Orator, Topica, De Oratore*; *On Style* attributed to Demetrius, but the authorship is uncertain); Quintillian's *Institutio Oratia*.

65. In *Ar. Rh.* 3.14.7 it is stated that hearers pay attention to things that are important, concern their own interests, which are astonishing (τοῖς θαυμαστοῖς) or are agreeable, and the speaker should deal with such subjects. *On the Sublime* 35.5 states that unusual things inspire wonder (θαυμαστὸν δ' ὅμως ἀεὶ παράδοξον). However, one must differentiate between a speech to persuade in a legal case, for example, and a narrative.

The 'Marvelous' in Ancient Literature

There is a collection of interesting (and sometimes obscure) works in ancient literature which deal with 'marvelous' occurrences. These are rarely discussed in relation to the New Testament, but are worth examination here because of some common elements.[66] Unfortunately, these works focus on 'wonders' rather than reactions of wonder. For example, these 'wonders' include a lake in Cyme which has thick trees surrounding it, but never has any leaves in the water (*On Marvelous Things Heard*, p. 102); the floating tale of Theopompus, who fell asleep for 57 years (in Apollonius, 1); and various tales of hermaphrodites (recounted by Phlegon in 6-8 and 10). Herodotus is an exception, however, and regularly makes use of reactions of wonder.

Herodotus has reactions of wonder most commonly at interventions of the gods of various types (such as dreams, portents and signs). For example, 1.24 tells of the sailors who threw Arion from the ship after being amazed (καὶ τοὺς ἐκπλαγέντας) at seeing him well after a dolphin has carried him to land and not being able to deny it. In 1.34, Croesus was greatly frightened by a dream (καταρρωδήσας τὸν ὄνειρον). Cyrus and his companions are greatly astonished (ἀπεθώμαζέ τε ὀρέων) seeing Croesus after rain quenched a fire which was about to burn him, in 1.88. Astyages is terrified (ἐφοβήθη) when the magi interpret a dream of his about his daughter. In 3.3, the wives of Cyrus marvel (ἐν θώματι γενέσθαι) at a statement of the ten year old Cambyses that one day he would turn Egypt upside down (Herodotus does not believe this story). In 7.38, a certain rich man named Pythius is frightened (Πύθιος ὁ Λυδος καταρρωδήσας τὸ ἐκ οὐρανοῦ φάσμα) by an eclipse, something traditionally taken as a sign or portent. Also relating to portents is the incident in 8.37-38, where everyone in Delphi leaves town at the threat of an attack, except 60 people and a prophet. A miracle takes place when the prophet sees certain sacred weapons (which no one may touch without sacrilege) brought out of the chamber within and laid before the shrine in the temple of Athene Pronaea. Herodotus calls this marvelous (θῶμα), but says that a second visitation was more marvelous. This

---

66. These texts include *On Marvelous Things Heard* (which is included in the corpus of Aristotle, but is probably not an authentic work of his); ΙΣΤΟΡΙΩΝ ΠΑΡΑΔΟΞΩΝ by Antigonus of Carystese (fl. 240 BCE); ΙΣΤΟΡΙΑΙ ΘΑΥΜΑΣΙΑΙ (from an obscure Apollonios, perhaps from the second century BCE); Phlegon of Trelles' ΠΕΡΙ ΘΑΥΜΑΣΙΩΝ (likely written by a freedman of Hadrian, c.140 CE); Herodotus' *Histories* (which is included here due to his special interest in the marvelous).

came when foreigners came near the temple, and they were struck with thunderbolts and two peaks of Mount Parnassus broke off and crushed many. At this, a shout and cry were heard from the temple of Athene. These events struck terror (φόβος) into the foreigners. Also involving a threat by an enemy, in 8.65 a certain Dicaeus tells of seeing a great cloud of dust coming from Eleusis, as if raised by an army of about 30,000 men, but no one is there; Dicaeus and Demartus marvel greatly (ἀποθωμάζειν) at the dust, and hear a cry, which Dicaeus identifies as heaven sending aid to the Athenians. In both of the last cases, the wonder is at a divine intervention which may be distinguished from an epiphany.

In a similar way, Herodotus marvels (θῶμα δέ μοι) in 9.65 that when the Persians were being routed by the Lacedaemonians at Plataeae, there was no sign that any Persian had been slain or had entered the precinct of Demeter, even though the battle was near it. Herodotus suggests that the goddess herself denied them entry because they burned her temple at Eleusis. There is the story of fish being fried by a Persian guard in 9.120: while the guard is frying dried fish, they begin to leap and writhe, as if newly caught, amazing (ἐθώμαζον) those nearby. This is also taken as a portent. In 4.28, it is stated that people are accustomed to be amazed at portents such as thunderstorms (ὡς τέρας νενόμισται θωμάζεσθαι). This is crucial for understanding reactions of wonder, and the thought is similar to what we have seen in *Jewish Antiquities*, *4 Maccabees* and Plutarch's *Lives*. In summary, though the 'marvelous' literature goes in a different direction, Herodotus commonly has reactions of wonder in response to divine interventions, portents and signs. Let me now sum up what has been seen and draw some conclusions regarding wonder in Greco-Roman literature.

Conclusion

E. Peterson has written in a brief excursus on wonder that the testimony of astonishment in reports of miracles in Christianity was already found in heathen aretalogies, and gives five examples, four of which are either from inscriptions or papyri.[67] He suggests that acclamation in the miracle stories had a 'religious' sense, that is, in demonstrating the power and truthfulness of what is recorded,

---

67. E. Peterson, ΕΙΣ ΘΕΟΣ: *Epigraphische, formgeschichtliche und religionsgeschichtliche Untersuchungen* (FRLANT, 41; Göttingen:Vandenhoeck & Ruprecht, 1926), p. 194. It is necessary, however, to make a distinction between wonder and acclamation, as Theissen does. Peterson's examples are acclamation, see n. 70.

even though he says that in the New Testament, acclamation itself within the miracle story is missing.[68] Fr. Pfister has given a rather comprehensive examination, but ranges far beyond our interests into music, dance and other mediums which produce ecstasy.[69] One must be careful to distinguish different senses of the term ἔκστασις, as Dodds does.[70] In this sense the present survey is broader than that of Peterson and more focused than that of Pfister. Although wonder in the classical world can be a full monograph in itself, the purpose at hand is to bring it to bear on Mark.

Wonder plays a rather small part in Greco-Roman miracle stories. It is a somewhat common reaction to statements or speeches of individuals. Sometimes this is because the things said is unusual or surprising, and surprise more than wonder may be present. The most common place that reactions of wonder are to be found is in reference to signs, portents and dreams, or divine interventions in general. A classic example is in Xenophon's *Cyropaedia* 4.10, where a light from heaven fills Cyrus and his men with awe. Divine interventions can also be seen in texts like the *Iliad* and the *Odyssey*. For example, in *Il.* 8.77, the Achaeans are seized with wonder and fear as Zeus thunders and sends a 'blazing flash' among them. Thus in Greco-Roman literature, divine interventions are extraordinary and unusual, and the individuals present react with wonder. This needs now to be linked with the use of wonder in Jewish literature, and will be important to keep in mind as the study moves finally to examine the things in Mark which evoke wonder.

---

68. Peterson, ΕΙΣ ΘΕΟΣ, pp. 194-95. This is questionable in light of Mk 2.12; 7.37; Lk. 7.16 and others.

69. Fr. Pfister, 'Ekstase', in *Reallexikon für Antike und Christentum* (17 vols.; Stuttgart: Anton Hiersemann, 1959), IV, pp. 944-87.

70. E.R. Dodds, *Pagans and Christians in an Age of Anxiety* (Cambridge: Cambridge University Press, 1965), pp. 70-71. In *Who is the Heir*, pp. 249-52, 257-60, Philo distinguishes four kinds of ecstasy (see the following chapter).

2. Wonder in the Greco-Roman World

Excursus: The Magical Papyri

The Greek Magical Papyri are a collection of magic spells and formulae, hymns and rituals, for which the extant texts date from the second century BCE to the fifth century CE. Contained within are elements from Egyptian, Babylonian, Greek, Jewish and Christian religions. Reactions of amazement occur at several points within these manuscripts.[1]

Here, after the magical spell is cast, the unusual event occurs, which amazes those involved. A few examples can suffice. We see this in *PGM* 4.161: 'and after you have tested it, you too will be amazed at the miraculous nature of the magical operation' (θαυμάσεις τὸ παράδοξον τῆς οἰκονομίας); *PGM* 4.775: 'and he will see so clearly it will amaze you' (καὶ ὄψεται δηλαυγῶς ὥστε σε θαυμάζειν, referring to a potion to put on the eyes of a person which results in clear vision); *PGM* 4.791: 'many times I have used this spell and marvelled greatly' (πολλάκις δὲ πραγματείᾳ χρησάμενος ὑπερεθαύμασα). The powers invoked by these spells are thought to intervene in the desired ways, and this is often expected to evoke a response of wonder.

---

71. K. Preisendanz (ed.), *Papyri Graecae Magicae: Die Griechischen Zauberpapyri* (2 vols.; Leipzig: Teubner, 1928), and H.D. Betz (ed.), *The Greek Magical Papyri in Translation* (Chicago: University of Chicago Press, 1986).

Chapter 3

WONDER IN EARLY JEWISH LITERATURE

Judaism at the beginning of the Christian era has been called 'a complex and variegated phenomenon' by one of its most eminent modern interpreters.[1] That interpreter went on to state that this complexity was true culturally, socially and theologically. Modern studies in the field have found a diversity among the Jewish people of the Greco-Roman period that was previously unsuspected.[2] Paradigms which identified Judaism as a unified set of beliefs in the period up to 100 CE are now obsolete.[3] The factors involved in this radical shift in understanding include the discovery of the Dead Sea Scrolls, renewed scholarly interest in the Old Testament Psuedepigrapha, recognition of the hellenisation of Palestine, and a revised assessment of rabbinic writings. Daniel J. Harrington writes that 'a good deal more is known about Palestinian Judaism in Jesus' day than was known years ago. But in another sense *we know less* [his italics].' Or at least we are less confident about simple and neat pictures. What emerges from all this research is a variety of Judaisms and some doubt about whether one can speak of any center or core.[4]

As one looks at early Jewish literature to see how wonder might function, one must keep in mind this diversity of early Judaism (Harrington's term is 'Judaisms'). One must also take care not to work on the basis of 'comfortable theories'[5] which make a neat distinction between Palestinian and Hellenistic

1. G.W.E. Nickelsburg, 'Introduction: The Modern Study of Early Judaism', in *Early Judaism and its Modern Interpreters* (ed. G. Nickelsburg and R. Kraft; Philadelphia: Fortress Press, Atlanta: Scholars Press, 1986), p. 3.
2. Nickelsburg, 'Introduction', p. 20.
3. M.E. Stone, 'Judaism at the Time of Christ', American Schools of Oriental Research Newsletter 1 (1973/4), pp. 1-6.
4. D.J. Harrington, 'The Jewishness of Jesus: Facing Some Problems', *CBQ* 49 (1987), p. 7. One might say, however, that Torah was core amidst a wide variety of interpretations.
5. S. Sandmel, 'Palestinian and Hellenistic Judaism and Christianity: The Question of the Comfortable Theory', *HUCA* 50 (1979), pp. 137-48.

3. Wonder in Early Jewish Literature

(diaspora) Judaism. Universal statements must be avoided at all costs. New Testament scholars have been criticized for examining early Jewish literature with New Testament issues in view, and rightly so. The interests of the sources are not the same. Recognition of this from the outset may not totally avoid the problem, but at least it can limit the false paths which might be taken.[6] One must also remember that the diversity of the writings and so context must be continually in view. Finally, one must remember that parallels do not necessarily signify influence.[7]

The term 'early Jewish literature' can be elusive. Generally, it is used to include the writings of the Second Temple period (including those works which respond to the fall of the temple, such as *4 Ezra* and *2 Baruch*). In any event, the formation of the Mishnah, c. 200 CE, is often seen as the solidification of a single movement (rabbinic Judaism) from within the diversity of 'early Judaisms'. This is beyond our scope, except for evidence regarding charismatics of first century Galilee, some of which is enshrined in rabbinic materials.

The Septuagint

The scripture of the early church, following the usage of the Hellenistic synagogue, was the Septuagint.[8] More specifically, an examination of the use of the scripture in Mark yields the information that for the author of the gospel, the 'Bible' was the Septuagint (or a closely kindred Greek recension).[9] A number of scholars have sought to compare Mark to the Old Testament.[10] The

---

6. J.H. Charlesworth, *The Old Testament Pseudepigrapha and the New Testament* (SNTSMS, 54; Cambridge: Cambridge University Press, 1985), p. 50, says that motif research and the study of parallels between Judaism and Christianity must not be abandoned for fear of the charge of parallelomania, but comparisons must take careful cognizance of the whole and of the function and the context of the comparisons.

7. S. Sandmel, *The First Christian Century in Judaism and Christianity: Certainties and Uncertainties* (New York: Oxford University Press, 1969), p. 84.

8. H. Koester, *Introduction to the New Testament*. I. *The History, Literature and Culture of the Hellenistic Age* (Philadelphia: Fortress Press; Berlin: de Gruyter, 1982), p. 253.

9. H.C. Kee, 'The Function of Scriptural Quotations and Allusions in Mark 11-16', in *Jesus und Paulus: Festschrift für Werner Georg Kümmel zum 70. Geburtstag* (ed. E.E. Ellis and E. Grässer; Göttingen: Vandenhoeck & Ruprecht, 1975), p. 174.

10. For example, G. Hartman, *Der Aufbau des Markusevangeliums* (Neutestamentliche Abhandlungen 17; Münster: Aschendorff, 1936); R.E. Brown, 'Jesus and Elisha', *Perspective* 12 (1971), pp. 85-104; B. Lindars, 'Elijah, Elisha and the Gospel Miracles' in *Miracles: Cambridge Studies in their Philosophy and History* (ed. C.F.D. Moule; London:

Septuagint, however, is not limited to the canon later recognized by rabbinic Judaism, and some books which would later be considered non-canonical (at least by Judaism and Protestant Christianity) are also involved when one speaks of the Septuagint.[11] One must also recognize the heterogeneity of the Septuagint. Contained within it are translations of various types, early and late, relatively original and significantly revised, official and private, literal and free.[12] At least

Mowbray, 1965), pp. 63-79; W. Roth, *Hebrew Gospel: Cracking the Code of Mark* (Bloomington, IN: Meyer-Stone, 1988); E.C. Hobbs, in 'Norman Perrin on Methodology in the Interpretation of Mark: A Critique of "The Christology of Mark" and 'Toward an Interpretation of the Gospel of Mark" in *Christology and a Modern Pilgrimage: A Discussion with Norman Perrin* (ed. H.D. Betz; Claremont, CA: The New Testament Colloquium, 1971), especially pp. 85-87; M. Kline, 'The Old Testament Origins of the Gospel Genre', *WTJ* 38 (1975), pp. 1-27; Schweizer, *Good News*, especially p. 24; S. Schultz, 'Markus und das Alte Testament', *ZTK* 58 (1961), pp. 184-97; A. Suhl, *Die Function der alttestamentlichen Zitaten und Anspielungen im Markusevangelium* (Gütersloh: Mohn, 1965); H.-J. Steichele, *Der leidende Sohn Gottes: Eine Untersuchung einiger alttestamentlicher Motive in der Christologie des Markusevangeliums* (Münchner Universitäts Schriften; Munich: Friedrich Pustet Revensburg, 1980); J.D.M. Derrett, *The Making of Mark* (2 vols; Shipston-on-Stour: P. Drinkwater, 1985); R. Meye, 'Psalm 107 as Horizon for Interpreting the Miracle Stories of Mark 4.35 to 8.26', in *Unity and Diversity in New Testament Theology: Essays in Honor of George E. Ladd* (ed. R. Guelich; Grand Rapids: Eerdmans, 1978), pp. 1-13; S. Freyne, 'The Disciples in Mark and the *Maskilim* in Daniel: A Comparison', *JSNT* 16 (1982), pp. 7-23; G.W.E. Nickelsburg, 'The Genre and Function of the Markan Passion Narrative', *HTR* 73 (1980), pp. 153-84; Kee, *Community*, especially pp. 64-70; N. Perrin, *The New Testament, An Introduction: Proclamation and Parenesis, Myth and History* (New York: Harcourt Brace Jovanovich, 1974), pp. 144-65; J. Jeremias and W. Zimmerli, *The Servant of God* (SBT, 20; London: SCM Press, 1957); C. Maurer, 'Knecht Gottes und Sohn Gottes im Passionsbericht des Markusevangeliums', *ZTK* 50 (1982), pp. 1-38; H.L. Chronis, 'The Torn Veil: Cultus and Christology in mark 15.37-39', *JBL* 101 (1982), pp. 97-114; J.G. Williams, *Gospel Against Parable: Mark's Language of Mystery* (Sheffield: JSOT Press, 1985); J. Marcus, *The Way of the Lord: Christological Exegesis of the Old Testament in the Gospel of Mark* (Louisville, KY: Westminster John Knox, 1992). There is no suggestion in these works that wonder in Mark is rooted in the OT or LXX, except for Maurer, who raises the possibility that Pilate's amazement at Jesus' silence in Mk. 15.5 and at Jesus' quick death in Mk. 15.44 might be related to Isa. 52.15 (LXX: οὕτως θαυμάσονται ἔθνη πολλὰ ἐπ' αὐτῷ). See Maurer, 'Knecht', p. 10, assuming a misprint of Isa. 52.15.

11. *4 Maccabees* was examined in the previous chapter.
12. E. Tov, 'Jewish Greek Scriptures', in G.W.E. Nickelsburg and R. Kraft (eds.), *Early Judaism and its Modern Interpreters* (Philadelphia: Fortress Press; Atlanta, CA: Scholars Press), p. 225.

3. *Wonder in Early Jewish Literature* 51

five basic recensions may be involved (the Old Greek, Kaige-Theodotion, Ur-Theodotion, Proto-Lucian and Lucian). Thus when one examines the Septuagint to see how wonder is used, the task is more difficult than merely sitting down and looking at a Greek text. In light of this, how do reactions of wonder function in the Septuagint?

Reactions of wonder do not necessarily use the language that we find in Mark. There are many Septuagint references to people 'falling on their faces' before God or an angel, which we certainly regard as a response of wonder (Gen. 17.3; Exod. 3.6, where Moses 'hides his face'; Lev. 9.24; Num. 14.5; 16.4, 22, 45; 20.6; Josh. 5.14; Judg. 13.20; 3 Kgdms. 18.39; 2 Chron. 6.13; 7.3; 20.18; Tob. 12.16; Ezek. 1.28; 9.8; 11.13; Dan. 8.17). In Dan. 2.46, Nebuchadnezzer falls on his face as a response to the interpretation of the dream that Daniel gives. Certainly Isa. 6.5 is a reaction of wonder, though it is not specifically stated that Isaiah was astounded by the vision or fell on his face.

It is common to find language of wonder as reactions to dreams, visionary experiences or epiphanies. In Gen. 15.12, Abraham receives a vision (περὶ δὲ ἡλίου δυσμὰς ἔκστασις ἐπέσεν τῷ Αβραμ καὶ ἰδοὺ φόβος σκοτεινὸς μέγας ἐπιπίπτει αὐτῷ). After the vision of Jacob in Gen. 28.17, it is noted καὶ ἐφοβήθη καὶ εἶπεν Ὡς φοβερὸς οὗτος... In *2 Macc.* 12.22, terror and fear come upon the opposition (δέους ἐπὶ τοὺς πολεμίους φόβου) due to a manifestation of 'The One who beholds all things'. In 2 Esd. 2.43 (*4 Ezra*), Esdras awakens from a revelatory dream with an extreme trembling through his body and with a troubled mind. Other places where reactions of this type occur in relation to dreams, visionary experiences or epiphanies are in Gen. 41.8; Tob. 12.16; 2 Macc. 3.24; Ps. 47.6; Job 4.14; 7.14. The book where this use is most common is Daniel (4.19 κγ; 8.27 θ; 5.9 θ; 7.15 θ; 28 κγ; 10.7 θ).[13] A most interesting place where the language is found, though not in a narrative but in a prayer, is Wis. 17.3, where it is requested that foes be 'stricken with terrible awe and sore troubled by spectral forms'(ἐσκορπίσθησαν θαμβούμενοι δεινῶς καὶ ἰνδάλμασιν ἐκταρασσόμενοι).

In this category I have noted two places in *2 Maccabees* where epiphanies or visions cause awe (3.24 and 12.22). There is another incident in *2 Maccabees*, in 1.22, which deserves some thought and which might be better called a divine

---

13. Freyne, 'Disciples', notes the repeated awe and fear in Daniel, but compares with Mark the privacy of the experiences and the inability of those receiving the revelation to understand rather than the reactions as such. Mk. 9.2-9 is the only reaction of wonder in Mark compared with Daniel. See pp. 14-15.

intervention rather than an epiphany. There is the recounting of what happened to the fire from the temple altar which the priests before the exile had saved. It seems to have turned into a thick liquid, which Nehemiah orders to be sprinkled on wood and on the sacrifice laid on it. Some time passes, and then when the sun comes out, a great fire blazes up, so that all marveled (ὥστε θαυμάσας πάντας). This account may be constructed with a view to the fire falling on Mount Carmel during the days of Elijah.[14] In addition to these incidents, there is a prayer in *2 Macc.* 15.23 for God to send a good angel to cause 'terror and trembling' (εἰς δέος καὶ τρόμον). *Second Maccabees* has a strong bias as 'temple propaganda', and the book may be structured by three attacks on the Jerusalem temple which ruin the plunderers. In ch. 3 Heliodorus seeks to plunder the temple; in 4.1-10.9, Antiochus IV Epiphanes along with Jason bring an extreme Hellenisation to the temple, but the account ends with Judas's capture of the temple and its purification; and in 10.10-15.36, Nicanor is eventually killed when carrying out the orders of Antiochus V Eupator. The account in Chapter 3 may be stylized to proclaim the greatness of the God of Israel who protects the temple, a common motif in the Greco-Roman world (for example, Herodotus 8.35-39).[15] We will see this theme again in the *Letter of Aristeas* which, along with *2 Maccabees*, was likely written c.124 BCE in Egypt to try and keep the Jews there within the sphere of influence of the temple of Jerusalem rather than the sphere of influence of the competing temple at Leontopolis.[16]

Another category of reactions of wonder in the Septuagint is in relation to divine acts. There are at least three places in the Exodus account where this occurs. In Exod. 15.14-16, the song of Moses, the text reads:

ἤκουσαω ἔθνη καὶ ὠργίσθησαν
ὠδῖνες ἔλαβον κατοικοῦντας φυλιστιιμ
τότε ἔσπευσαν ἡγεμόνες Εδωμ

---

14. J.A. Goldstein, *2 Maccabees: A New Translation with Introduction and Commentary* (AB; Garden City, NY: Doubleday, 1984), p. 177.

15. R. Doran, *Temple Propaganda: the Purpose and Character of 2 Maccabees* (CBQMS, 12; Washington DC: Catholic Bible Association, 1981), pp. 48-52.

16. A. Momigliano, 'The Second Book of Maccabees'. *Classical Philology* 70 (1975), p. 83. H. Attridge also believes that *2 Macc.* was directed polemically against the claims of the rival temple at Leontopolis in 'Jewish Historiography' in Nickelsburg and Kraft (eds.), *Judaism*, p. 322. This view is not unanimous, however. Doran sees no evidence of such a polemic (p. 11).

3. Wonder in Early Jewish Literature 53

καὶ ἄρχοντες Μωσαβιτῶν, ἔλαβεν αὐτοὺς τρόμος
ἐτάκησαν πάντες οἱ κατοικοῦντες χανααν
ἐπιπέσοι ἐπ' αὐτοὺς φόβος καὶ τρόμος
μεγέθει βραχίονός σου ἀπολιθωθήτωσαν
ἕως ἂν παρέλθῃ ὁ λαός σου, κύριε
ἕως ἂν παρέλθῃ ὁ λαός σου οὗτος, ὃν ἐκτήσω.

Although this is poetic, it suggests an expect reaction of wonder at a mighty deed of God. Also in the Exodus account, Jethro is amazed at the good things God has done for Israel in Exod. 18.9 (ἐξέστη δὲ Ιοθορ ἐπὶ πᾶσι τοῖς ἀγαθοῖς). All of the people are in awe at the sight of Sinai in 19.18 (καὶ ἐξέστη πᾶς ὁ λαὸς σφόδρα ...), and Exod. 20.19 again relates to Sinai (φοβηθέντες δὲ πᾶς ὁ λαὸς ἔστησαν μακρόθεν ...). In a similar way, reactions of wonder to divine acts can be found in Lev. 9.24 (fire falls from heaven); 2 Kgdms. 6.9 (David has a special fear of the Lord after the Lord strikes Uzzah for touching the ark); 3 Kgdms. 18.39 (the people fall on their faces and proclaim that the Lord is God after God answers Elijah's request for fire from heaven); *3 Macc.* 2.23 (the people present are struck with fear when God strikes Ptolemy so that he is paralyzed and unable to speak); Job 42.11 (all marvel at what God has done for Job); and Jon. 1.16 (the sailors greatly fear the Lord after the sudden calming of the sea after Jonah has been thrown in).

Another category of reactions of wonder in the Septuagint that is quite relevant to our study is that there is an expectation of such reactions in the coming age of salvation. It can be said that there was an eschatological expectation that God would astound people. This can be seen in Hos. 3.5: καὶ μετὰ ταῦτα ἐπιστρέψουσιν οἱ υἱοί Ισραηλ καὶ ἐπιζητήσουσιν κύριον τὸν θεὸν αὐτῶν καὶ Δαυιδ τὸν βασιλέα αὐτῶν; καὶ ἐκστήσονται ἐπὶ τῷ κυρίῳ καὶ ἐπὶ τοῖς ἀγαθοῖς αὐτοῦ ἐπ' ἐσχάτων τῶν ἡμερῶν. This important verse links eschatological expectation, messianic hope and wonder. Also important here is Mic. 7.15 and 17. Mic. 17.15 reads: καὶ κατὰ τὰς ἡμέρας ἐξοδίας σου ἐξ Αἰγύπτου ὄψεσθε θαυμαστά and 7.17 reads: ἐπὶ τῷ κυρίῳ θεῷ ἡμῶν ἐκστήσονται καὶ φοβηθήσονται ἀπὸ σοῦ. Here there is a link between eschatological expectation and wonder. One should also note Zech. 14.13: καὶ ἔσται ἐν τῇ ἡμέρᾳ ἐκείνῃ ἔκστασις κυρίου ἐπ' αὐτοῖς μεγάλη... Here again is a link between eschatological expectation and wonder.[17] Perhaps one should relate Wis. 5.2

---

17. This may be especially important since Mark. often uses the apocalyptic section of Zech. 9-14. See R.M. Grant, 'The Coming of the Kingdom of God', *JBL* 67 (1948), pp. 297-303.

ἰδόντες ταραχθήσονται φόβῳ δεινῷ καὶ ἐκστήσονται ἐπὶ τῷ παραδόξῳ τῆς σωτηρίας. This is in the context of 5.2-23, a passage about the wicked after the judgment, followed by a refutation of the wicked which develops into an apocalyptic description.[18] While it has been noted that there is a clear expectation in Wisdom of some type of consummation (note the references to the visitation in 2.20, 3.7, 9, 13, 4.15, 14.11, 19.15 and the day of decision in 3.18), Sweet believes that the expectation is not a future universal intervention, but a continuous renewal and refashioning of the universe by God or wisdom (which represents God's immanent control of the world).[19] Winston, however, notes in his commentary that the entire section of 5.1-23 is colored by the language of Isa. 52.13-20, as well as the motif that the wicked will be astounded at the unexpected deliverance of the just man.[20]

One other place where there is an eschatological expectation linked with the theme of wonder is in the later 2 Esdras 13.30. In the interpretation of a messianic vision, Esdras is told that when the Most High begins to deliver those upon the earth, 'there shall come astonishment of mind upon them that dwell upon the earth'. While 2 Esdras is, in its present form, a Christian writing which contains (chs. 3-14) the Jewish apocalypse known as *4 Ezra*,[21] one can again note Jewish eschatological expectation of wonder.

One also finds the language of wonder in messianic predictions. I might refer to Isa. 52.15 (οὕτως θαυμάσονται ἔθνη πολλὰ ἐπ' αὐτῷ ...), but one must not overlook the preceding verse: ὃν τρόπον ἐκστήσονται ἐπὶ σὲ πολλοί... Ps. 2.11 calls for fear and trembling before the Davidic ruler: δουλεύσατε τῷ κυρίῳ, καὶ ἀγαλλιᾶσθε αὐτῷ ἐν τρόμῳ. It is interesting that there is a reaction of awe to the preceding vision in Dan. 7.15, the vision of the 'son of man' figure. We can also note Ps. 117.13 (Septuagint): καὶ ἔστιν θαυμαστὴ ἐν ὀφθαλμοῖς ἡμῶν, which follows the 'rejected stone' image that was used messianically in early Christian communities. Such language is striking, but the

---

18. J.M. Reese, 'Plan and Structure in the Book of Wisdom', *CBQ* 27 (1965), p. 395.
19. J.P.M. Sweet, 'The Theory of Miracles in the Wisdom of Solomon', in Moule (ed.), *Miracles*, pp. 119-20.
20. D. Winston, *The Wisdom of Solomon: A New Translation with Introduction and Commentary* (AB; Garden City, NY: Doubleday, 1981), p. 146. For a connection to Mark see J. Donahue, 'Temple, Trial and Royal Christology (Mark 14.53-65)', in *The Passion in Mark: Studies in Mark 14-16* (ed. W. Kelber; Philadelphia: Fortress Press, 1976), p. 66.
21. G.W.E. Nickelsburg, *Jewish Literature between the Bible and the Mishnah* (Philadelphia: Fortress Press, 1981), p. 287.

3. Wonder in Early Jewish Literature

question of Mark's use of Psalm 2 and Isa. 52.13-53.12 is much disputed.[22] Yet the fact that these texts were indisputably used among early Christian communities in a messianic sense (see Acts 4.25-26, 8.32-33, 13.33) leads one to hesitate to deny that these verses were at least conceptually at work in Mark.

There are a number of scattered references to wonder in the Septuagint that also draw our attention. I have noted Jethro in Exod. 18.9 being amazed at the good things which Yahweh had done for Israel, and this idea of people marveling at hearing of Yahweh's deeds is present elsewhere (for example, Josh. 5.1: καὶ ἐτάκησαν αὐτῶν αά διάνοιαι καὶ κατεπλάγησαν, and Judith 11.16, where Judith speaks of the expectation that the earth will be astounded at God's preservation: ἐφ' οἷς ἐκστήσεται πᾶσα ἡ γῆ). In Sir. 47.17, people marveled at the wisdom of Solomon evident in his songs, proverbs and parables (ἀπεθαύμασάν σε χῶραι).

We have seen in the Septuagint that reactions of wonder are common as a response to dreams, visions or epiphanies. This is expected (Wis. 17.3). Such reactions also occur in response to divine interventions. Also, there is an eschatological expectation of wonder, linked with the messiah at points. One must not preclude the possibility that such conceptions resource or inform the Markan construction of the gospel, especially in light of the Septuagint being the 'source text' for Mark. As we continue to look at early Jewish literature, let us now move on to Philo and Josephus.

Philo and Josephus

The voluminous works of these two first century Jewish writers are grouped together out of convenience rather than any specific similarity. It is best, as

---

22. V. Taylor saw a definite allusion to Ps. 2.7 in Mk. 1.11 in *The Gospel According to St. Mark* (London: Macmillan, 1953), p. 162, and I.H. Marshall states that a denial of the presence of ideas from Ps. 2.7 and Isa. 42.1 in Mk. 1.11 is to be rejected, in 'Son of God or Servant of Yahweh?: A Reconsideration of Mark 1.11', *NTS* 15 (1968/9), p. 335. We have already noted the position of Maurer. Williams has said that the primary narrative 'seed' of the suffering son of man is the servant of Isa. 52.13-53.12 (*Gospel*, p. 132). Chronis extends the case beyond the servant to Deutero-Isaiah in general, and cites many possible 'linguistic and literary relationships', 'Veil', p. 104, n. 38. However B.D. Chilton's study of the use of the Isaiah Targum leads him to conclude that the Targum offers no support for anything like a 'suffering servant' motif in early Judaism which Jesus may have used, but he does allow for a 'messianic servant' commissioned by God whose ministry involves the risk of death. See *A Galilean Rabbi and His Bible* (Wilmington, DE: Michael Glazier, 1984), pp. 199-200. The Targum of Isa. 52.15 speaks of the silence of kings, rather than their amazement.

before, to give a distillation of the results of an examination of the corpus of each writer.

Philo (c. 10 BCE to 45 CE) was a devotee of what Sandmel calls a 'book religion'. For Philo, that book goes under the name νόμος and virtually everything he writes is in some way dependent on or related to the centrality of νόμος.[23] The aim of Philo's writings was definitely practical. He wanted to bring his readers to follow the law of the Pentateuch.[24] Philo uses his allegories to make the νόμος intelligible to a Hellenistic reader, and to exalt wisdom. He is a biblical exegete above all, but for him biblical exegesis and philosophy are inseparable.[25]

Many of the writings of Philo contain not a single element of the language of wonder. This is because his works are, for the most part, not narrative but commentary. There are some important uses, however, and perhaps the two most important references in all of Philo's works are in *Who is the Heir?* 249-51; 257-60; and *Questions and Answers on Genesis* 3.9. In the text of *Who is the Heir?*, one in which Philo discusses creation as a technical philosopher with definite influences of Pythagorean Platonism,[26] he refers to Gen. 15.12 and speaks of four kinds of ecstacy (ἔκστασις). One type is a mad fury, producing mental delusions because of old age, or melancholy, or other 'similar causes'. An example of this is Deut. 28.28-29. A second type is extreme amazement (ἡ δὲ σφοδρὰ κατάπληξις) at events which happen suddenly and unexpectedly. Examples given for this are Gen. 27.33; 45.26; Exod. 19-18 and Lev. 9.24. Philo says that 'ecstacy' in this sense produces great agitation and terrible consternation. The third form of ecstacy is passivity of mind, 'if indeed the mind can ever be at rest'. Genesis 2.21 is given as an example of this. Philo says that the fourth type is the best, and this is divine possession or frenzy (ἔνθεος κατοκωχή τε καὶ μανία). This is what happens with the prophets, and Gen. 15.12 is given as an example. We have here an important definition of the range of ways in which the word ἔκστασις (Mk 2.12; 5.42; 16.8) can work, and Philo's second division is the closest to the use in the gospels. Acts 10.10, 11.5 and 22.17 are probably New Testament examples of the fourth division, but Acts 3.10 may use the term more like Mark does.

23. Sandmel, *First*, p. 117.
24. P. Borgen, 'Philo of Alexandria', in *Jewish Writings of the Second Temple Period* (ed. M. Stone; CRINT, 2; Assen: Van Gorcum, Philadelphia: Fortress Press, 1984), p. 233.
25. Borgen, 'Philo', p. 264.
26. E. Goodenough, *An Introduction to Philo Judaeus* (London: Basil Blackwell, 1962), p. 107.

3. Wonder in Early Jewish Literature 57

Questions and Answers on Genesis is a commentary in the form of questions and answers, as the name implies, which has many points of contact with the *Allegorical Interpretation of Genesis*, but is not as complex.[27] Most of the Greek original is lost, and we are mainly dependent on the Armenian version. In 3.9, on Gen. 15.12, Philo asks, 'What is the meaning of the words, "At sunset an ecstacy fell upon Abram and behold a great dark fear fell upon him"?' The answer is that a 'divine tranquility' came upon the man of virtue. (Armenian *artakacout' ium*, different from *tardemah*, which renders the Septuagint ἔκστασις) is nothing else than the departing and going out of the understanding. This happens often with the prophets, who became divinely possessed and 'filled with God'. The mind is then no longer within itself, but has received the divine spirit to dwell within it. This is a sudden attack rather than something that comes upon one gently and softly. The mention of fear is understandable, because the one who is in fear is not oneself. The greater the darkness is, the duller the mind. Philo concludes by saying that these things are evidence of the clear knowledge of prophecy, by which oracles and laws are legislated by God.

There is some evidence here of the mystical side of Philo, something that Goodenough among Philonic scholars has especially emphasised. Both of the citations given refer to ecstacy, and both are in the case of Abraham. This is in keeping with the general thought of Philo that Abraham, as well as Isaac, Jacob and Moses, have come through their experiences with the help of the Powers to the end of the mystic road, and have been given the final vision of reality.[28] It can be gathered from this that in some segments of early Judaism there was a link in thought between ἔκστασις and mysticism. While it would be difficult to apply the mystical speculations of Philo to the narrative of Mark crudely, it is indeed important to keep in mind that some of the language of amazement which the gospel uses had quite a different background in philosophical and exegetical discussions of the first century. This may be especially important in Mk 16.8, and it should not be discounted too quickly that in the message of the resurrection, the women could be understood to be seized with the fitting reaction to the 'final vision of reality'. Mark 3.21 and 14.33 are also potentially important here.

There are some categories which might be used to arrange reactions of wonder in Philo. It should be kept in mind, however, that such reactions are not very

27. Borgen, 'Philo', pp. 241-43.
28. Goodenough, *Introduction*, p. 141.

frequent in the Philonic corpus. Philo does emphasize reactions of wonder at God, however. It is stated in *On the Account of the World's Creation Given by Moses* 2.7 that instead of holding the world in admiration rather than its maker, as some do, we ought to be astonished (καταπλαγῆναι) at God's powers as maker and father. In *Who is the Heir?* 23, Philo speaks of God being able to inspire fear and terror. In *Decalogue* 46, there is reference to the voice of God coming from the fire to the utter amazement of the Israelites. In fragment 2.10 of *On Providence*, Philo speaks of being awestruck by divine revelation. In *Questions and Answers on Exodus* 2.47, God shows 'what he wished to seem to be' rather than his essence, to the amazement of the spectators. Philo adds a special note in *On the Migration of Abraham* 34, when he speaks of being filled with amazement (καταπλαγείς) at God's might at times when it was difficult for him to write.

Philo also uses reactions of wonder in response to dreams. This can be seen in *On Dreams* 1, where Jacob is 'rightly afraid and awestruck' (δικαίως οὖν ἐφοβήθη καὶ εἶπε θαυμαστικῶς) at his dream. The second dream of Jacob is called 'more astounding' than the first in *On Joseph* 8, and the dream is said to amaze his father (ὡς τὸν πατέρα θαυμάσαντα).

There is also an understandable emphasis on the virtue of various people causing reactions of wonder. In *On Joseph* 80, Joseph is said to have displayed such virtue to awe and astound (τεθηπέναι καὶ καταπλήττεσθαι) even the most vile of inmates while he was in the Egyptian jail. In the tract *On Virtues* 217, it is stated that people were awestruck (καταπληττόμενοι) at the all embracing sweetness of the nature of Abraham. In *On Rewards and Punishments* 164, there is a telling comment about conversion to virtue striking awe (κατάπληξιν ἐργασαμένης) in those observing.

It should perhaps also be noted that there are a couple of references where there are reactions of wonder in relation to the law, which would be expected since the law is Philo's central concern. One might note *On Special Laws* 1.186 and the Armenian fragment of *Questions and Answers on Exodus* 3.117 (on Exod. 28.27). Thus, Philo seems to cluster wonder around his most important concerns (God, mystical experiences, virtue, the law).

Though Philo's corpus is not narrative like the gospel of Mark, it does reveal some interesting things. There is a special Jewish interest in ἔκστασις and indeed wonder becomes an item of speculation in Philo. Perhaps the thought in *On the Account of the World's Creation Given by Moses* 2.17 (that people ought to be astonished at God's powers as maker and father) crystallizes Philonic thought. Once again, it is God and God's acts which inspire wonder.

3. Wonder in Early Jewish Literature

There are two central themes throughout Josephus's work. Firstly, history is a series of examples substantiating the belief that God provides providential concern that justice be done. Secondly, morals are important because of their religious foundation and function.[29] Josephus is much maligned as a historian, not always without cause. There are distinct elements of self-promotion in his works which need to be recognized and expected. For example, one of the main motives of *War* is to defame John of Gischala, and Josephus often congratulates himself for battle strategies which were standard practices of the time.[30] We should not be surprised that the winners, or in this case the survivors, have written the history.

The sources which Josephus used must be kept in mind when looking at his works. He likely used Esdras, Aristeas and *1 Maccabees* in direct ways, and was on the whole faithful to them (though not slavishly imitating them, but adapting them to suit his own aims).[31] Yet one sees in Josephus an illustration of a portion of Hellenistic Judaism which did not think primarily in terms of law or ethical practices as Philo did, but found an identity in the often fantastic stories of ancestral heroes who outshone the best of the Greeks, Babylonians and Egyptians.[32]

Josephus has a special interest in miracles and portents. If John Mark is the author of the gospel of Mark, and the gospel emerges from Rome,[33] it is interesting to compare two Jews who lived as young men in Jerusalem, migrated to Rome and were engaged in writing for a Roman audience within the 25 year period, 65-90 CE, and who wrote about messianic portents in their native land. This interest of Josephus in portents has been recognised in several fine studies, including those by Betz,[34] Delling,[35] McCasland,[36] and MacRae.[37] Betz has

---

29. D.J.Harrington, 'Palestinian Adaptions of Biblical Narratives and Prophesies' in Nickelsburg and Kraft (eds.), *Judaism*, p. 245.

30. S.J.D. Cohen, *Josephus in Galilee and Rome: His Vita and Development as a Historian* (Leiden: Brill, 1979), see especially pp. 90, 95-95.

31. Cohen, *Josephus*, p. 47.

32. J.J. Collins, *Between Athens and Jerusalem* (New York: Crossroad, 1983), p. 51.

33. See Hengel, *Studies*, pp. 1-30. For the view that Mark emerged from Syria, see Kee, *Community*, pp. 100-105.

34. O. Betz, 'Das Problem des Wunders bei Flavius Josephus im Verbleich zum Wunderproblem bei den Rabbinen und im Johnnesevangelium' in *Josephus-Studien: Untersuchungen zu Josephus, dem antiken Judentum und dem Neuen Testament. Otto Michael zum 70 Geburtstag gewidmet* (ed. O. Betz, K. Haacker and M. Hengel; Göttingen: Vandenhoeck & Ruprecht, 1974), pp. 23-44.

35. G. Delling, 'Josephus und das Wunderbare', *NovT* 2 (1958), pp. 291-309.

emphasised two primary functions of miracles in Josephus: as historical acts of God, and to legitimate prophets (except in the Jewish war when they were a false sign). It is important to distinguish between works of God (in which the miracle worker has an unselfish attitude, and passes up praise and honor), and deceiving works of magic.[38] True miracles were signs (σημεῖον rather than παράδοξα, which is rarely used), which were meant to awaken belief in the miracle worker. Both Delling and MacRae point to the use of the term ἐπιφάνεια in Josephus (*Ant.* 2.339 for the parting of the Red Sea, or 1.255 for the way in which Abraham's servant found Rebecca, and 18.286 for the rain which fell when Petronius, governor of Syria, interceded with Caligula on behalf of the Jews).[39] This is not the visible appearance of God, but rather the manifestation of God's works, as Delling points out. This sense of the term is not common in Hellenistic Judaism (mostly in *2* and *3 Maccabees* and not in the New Testament), but more frequent in the literature of the Hellenistic world.[40]

Another element which Josephus shares with the Greco-Roman world is his almost unbroken belief in foretelling and omens, even in heathen prophesies.[41] McCasland has examined the seven portents which foretold the fall of Jerusalem in *The Jewish War* 6.288-309, and concludes at this point that Josephus 'sounds like a page from almost any one of a half-dozen of his contemporaries in the Greco-Roman world'.[42] Given the special interest of Josephus in miracles and portents, one might expect to find the language of wonder as common in his narratives and this is indeed the case.

Reactions of wonder are quite common in the various events related to the Jewish war in *War* (for example, 2.553; 2.613; 3.237; 5.472; 6.180). Reactions of wonder are also common as a response to portents, dreams and predictions, as might be expected. In *War* 1.328, Herod has a dream of his brother's death

---

36. S.V. McCasland, 'Portents in Josephus and in the Gospels', *JBL* 51 (1932), pp. 323-35.
37. G. MacRae, 'Miracles in the *Antiquities* of Josephus' in Moule (ed.), *Miracles*, pp. 127-47.
38. Betz, 'Problem', p. 24.
39. MacRae, 'Miracles', pp. 143-44, and Delling, 'Josephus', pp. 307-308.
40. See F. Pfister, 'Epiphanie', in *Paulys Real-Encyclopädie des Classischen Altertums-Wissenschaft*, Supp. 4 (Stuttgart: J.B. Metziersche Verlagsbuch-handlung, 1924), pp. 277-323.
41. Delling, 'Josephus', p. 294.
42. McCasland, 'Portents', p. 329.

3. Wonder in Early Jewish Literature 61

which causes him to spring up from his bed in horror (μετὰ ταραχῆς). In *War* 3.188, the Romans are filled with dismay (κατάπληξις ἦν) at the sight of a wall streaming with water. When Pharoah has his dreams, *Ant.* 2.82 says that the second dream was 'more wondrous than the first', and this dream terrified and disquieted him more than before (ὅ με καὶ μᾶλλον ἐδφορεῖ καὶ ταράττει). In *Ant.* 2.83, the king states that these dreams caused him consternation (ἔκπληξίν μοι παρέσχον). In *Ant*.2.206, Pharoah reacts with alarm (δείσας δ' ὁ Βασιλεὺς) at the prediction of an Egyptian scribe that a great Israelite leader is to be born.

Another category in Josephus where repeated reactions of wonder can be seen is in response to divine interventions. In *Ant.* 9.58, in the story of Elisha, the Syrians come to be in dire consternation (ἐν ἐκπλήξει) at the divine and marvelous event' (there are two uses here of the rare παραδόξος), which occurs as they are blinded and surrounded in Samaria. In regard to the same event, it is stated that the Syrian king Adados was amazed at the marvel (θαυμάσος ὁ Ἄδαδος τὸ παράδοξον) in *Ant.* 9.60. Both of these cases, it should be noted, are additions to the source text of 2 Kings 6. The combination of biblical and Hellenistic elements has led to a new synthesis in the story. In another case, Josephus states in *Ant.* 11.268 that he himself is moved to marvel at God's dealings with Esther.

An interesting place where reactions of wonder occur is in response to God's legislation, as in Philo and in the *Letter of Aristeas* which we will examine later. Here there is a likely apologetic interest. In his polemic with Apion, Josephus states in 2.221 that a Greek would be astonished (θαυμάσαι) upon hearing of the practices taking place in an obscure nation. In *Ant.* 8.168-70, there are constant references to the wonder of the Queen of Sheba as she visits Solomon: the temple is called 'wonderful'; the Queen is amazed at Solomon's wisdom; she marvels at the beauty of his palace, but is more amazed at the hall called the Forest of Libanos. (See 3 Kgdms. 10.5). It is stated in 8.170 that she marveled beyond measure (ὑπερεθαύμαζε) at the sacrificial system, was not able to contain her amazement (τὴν ἔκπληξιν) at what she saw, and showed her admiration (θαυμαστικῶς). Later in the *Antiquities* there are several reactions of wonder by King Ptolemy to various elements of the Jewish legislation (for example, 12.90; 12.101; 12.110).

There is also wonder at the temple. In *Ant.* 15.388, a presentation of the plan of Herod to rebuild the temple in Jerusalem in a speech astonished (ἐξέπληξε) many. After the temple is rebuilt, in 15.414, the carvings of the column capitals in the temple cause amazement (ἔκπληξιν ἐμποιούσαις). In 15.416, the structure of the walls and columns in the temple were beheld with amazement by all who saw them. I have already spoken of the language of wonder used in connection with the visit of the Queen of Sheba to the first temple.

In light of the two central themes of Josephus's work, stated earlier, one is not surprised to find that there are some places where the providence of God causes amazement. In *Ant.* 18.286, Petronius of Syria is amazed (ὅ τε Πετρώνιος κατεπέπληκτο) after seeing God's providence is over the Jews, as is evidenced by a much needed heavy rainfall. The same individual marvels (ἐξεθαύμασεν) at the providence of God again in *Ant.* 18.309, when a letter comes reporting Gaius's (Caligula) death before one from Gaius ordering Petronius to commit suicide (sparing him from the act).

In summary, Josephus uses wonder most frequently as a response to portents (including dreams), divine interventions, Jewish legislation, the war and the temple. Philo's language of wonder is less common, but still striking, especially in two interesting cases. He is interested in explicating concepts of ecstasy, which may be important for understanding Mark's use of ἔκστασις. Both Philo and Josephus wed biblical and Hellenistic elements, and both share the idea that the intervention of God is awe-inspiring. Whether attaching it to a biblical narrative like 2 Kings 6, or narrating the relief of Petronius with it, or relating it to Abraham's dream, one sees that reactions of wonder so common in Greco-Roman narrative literature like Herodotus and Plutarch could certainly be a response to the God of the Jews as well.

The Dead Sea Scrolls

Any discussion of the Dead Sea Scrolls is hampered by the controversy surrounding the group the scrolls emerged from, the relation of the scrolls to the building remains near the caves where many of the scrolls were found, the fragmentary nature of many of the scrolls, and the wide variety of documents found among the caves and at other related sites. It is still probably best to relate the scrolls to the main periods of occupation of the building site at Qumran. Itwas inhabited between 150 BCE and 68 CE, with the first period of occupation ending with a great fire and earthquake in 31 BCE and the second period terminating with the war.[43]

Many of the available scrolls contain no language of wonder at all. In the *Manual of Discipline*, there are references to God's 'marvels' (11.3; 11.9), but this is different than the narrative reactions of wonder we have seen. There are

---

43. D. Dimant, 'Qumran Sectarian Literature', in *Writings*, ed. Stone, pp. 483-84.

3. *Wonder in Early Jewish Literature* 63

also a number of references to the marvelous deeds or mysteries of God (for example, *Manual of Discipline* 11.21; *War Scroll* 8.9; *Hymn Scroll* 1.21, 2.13). Again, this is not the same as the reactions of wonder I am examining. For these, I can note two examples in the Genesis Apocryphon (20.9 and a parallel story in the *Book of Enoch* 106-107 which is badly mutilated in col.2). In that text, Lamech is seized with fear before his infant son (Noah) as he speaks to the 'Lord of Righteousness'. The other case has Pharoah marvel at the beauty of Sarah. All in all, the scrolls are not very fruitful for an examination of reactions of wonder.

One element that should be underscored, however, is the expectation of a 'marvelous salvation' and a 'marvelous intervention' in an eschatological framework in the *War Scroll*. Here, as in the Old Testament, is the expectation that God would act marvelously in the last days. If wonder in Mark is related to the breaking-in of the kingdom or rule of God, in light of the literary world from which the gospel emerged one would expect wonder to be the reaction in the gospel.

Pseudepigrapha

Study of the Pseudepigrapha[44] has revolutionized biblical studies in the last 20 years. The new translations edited by Charlesworth[45] have spurred this interest. The category 'pseudepigrapha' is somewhat flexible, and texts like *Joseph and Asenath* are grouped with the pseudepigrapha in Charlesworth's edition and here.

There is a common theme of reactions of wonder at God in these texts. For example, in *1 En.* 14.24, Enoch is covered with trembling while prostrate on his face before God. In 60.3-4, Enoch is seized with a great trembling and fear, loses control of his loins and kidneys and falls on his face when he sees a vision of God sitting on a throne surrounded by angels and 'righteous ones'. In *Jub.* 18.10, Abraham is terrified when God suddenly calls out to him, as he is about

---

44. There is some obvious overlap here with the Dead Sea Scrolls, since Pseudepigrapha such as *Jubilees* and *1 Enoch* have been among the scrolls. The Pseudepigrapha I have examined included *1 Enoch, 2 Enoch, Jubilees, Testament of Moses, Testament of Job, Letter of Aristeas, Joseph and Asenath, Sybylline Oracles, Testament of Twelve Patriarchs, Psalms of Solomon, Biblical Antiquities, Apocalypse of Abraham* and *2 Baruch*.

45. J.H. Charlesworth, ed., *The Old Testament Pseudepigrapha* (2 vols; Garden City, NY: Doubleday, 1983, 1985).

46. A recent argument against this position was by R.G. Hall in 'The "Christian

to sacrifice Isaac, which is a development of Genesis 22. This addition to the biblical source text is something we have seen Josephus do with 2 Kings 6 and other places. I would also note here *2 En.* 22.4 and 39.8 in recension J, where Enoch falls on his face before God in the first case, and in the second case Enoch tells his children how terrifying it is to stand before God and the heavenly armies. In the *Apocalypse of Abraham*, a work written as a response to the fall of the temple like *2 Baruch* and *4 Ezra*, which may have Christian interpolations and possibly a couple of glosses by the mediaeval dualist sect the Bogomils,[46] there is only amazement at God. In 10.2, Abraham's spirit is amazed, his soul flees from him, he becomes like a stone and falls on the ground after hearing God's voice. In 17.1-3, Abraham receives a vision of God as a bright light with a fire burning in it. He wants to fall face down on the earth, but has been carried off the ground by an angel, so he bows down instead. In *2 En.* 69.16, the people tremble and glorify God when they watch the altar shake and a knife leap up into Methusalam's hand (this was the sign that God had chosen him to be a priest). In *2 En.* 71.18, Noe and Nir are terrified with a 'great fear' when they spot a child, as developed as a three year old and fully clothed, sitting beside the dead wife of Noe, who had been pregnant. In *Biblical Antiquities* 27.12, the servants of Kenaz are amazed when they awake and find a field full of bodies after Kenaz has killed 45,000 Amorites. Kenaz proceeds to ask them why they are amazed, since God is able to do whatever God wants.

There is an important theme in the pseudepigrapha that God with cause amazement in the last days. This was already seen in Septuagint *Hos.* 3.5; *Zech.* 14.13 and *Mic.* 7.15 and 17. In *2 Baruch* 70.2, Baruch is told (in the explanation of a dream vision) that God will cause confusion of spirit and amazement of heart to come over rulers and inhabitants of the earth when the harvest of the seeds of the good and evil ones comes. This is a time of tribulation before all is delivered into the hands of God's servant, the anointed one. Similarly, in *Testament of Moses* 10.4, the appearance of the kingdom of God is portrayed. It is stated that the earth trembles, and 'even to its ends shall be shaken'.[47] Further, in *1 En.* 1.4-5 there is a reference to an eschatological revelation of God. When God comes forth from his dwelling, and marches upon Mount Sinai, 'everything shall be afraid, and watchers shall quiver. And great fear and

Interpolation" in the *Apocalypse of Abraham'*, *JBL* 107 (1988), pp. 107-10.
47. It is debatable whether this refers to the inhabitants of the earth, or the earth itself, as in an earthquake.
48. Momigliano, 'Maccabees', p. 83.

trembling shall seize them unto the ends of the earth'. *4 Ezra* 13.30 (LXX 2 Esdras) says that when the Most High begins to deliver them that are on the earth, 'there shall come astonishment of mind upon them that dwell on the earth. The pseudepigrapha clearly continue the Old Testament tradition of an eschatological expectation of wonder.

Another important way in which wonder is used in the pseudepigrapha is as an element of propaganda. One way of showing the effect of the true God is to have people amazed at God's actions. Amazement shows that God is present. This can be quite clearly seen in *Joseph and Asenath* and the *Letter of Aristeas*. In the *Ep. Arist.* 96-99, the propaganda relates to the temple. The reader is told that a general silence reigns in the temple and that everything is carried out in a reverent manner befitting God. It was supposedly an occasion of great amazement (Μεγάλην δὲ ἔκπληξιν ἡμῖν παρέσχεν) to the author when he saw Eleazer the priest engaged in his ministry (especially in light of his vestments, which are explained in detail). It is stated that the appearance of the vestments makes one awe-struck and dumbfounded, so that one would think one had gone out of this world into another one (ἡ δὲ συμφάνεια τούτων ἐμποιεῖ φόβον καὶ ταραχήν ὥστε νομίζειν εἰς ἕτερον ἐληλυθέναι ἐκτὸς τοῦ κόσμου). The author goes on to say that everyone who comes near this spectacle will experience astonishment and amazement beyond words (εἰς ἔκπληξιν ἥχειν καὶ θαυμασμόν ἀδιήγητον).

I noted earlier in this chapter the thesis that the *Letter* and *2 Maccabees* were written to try and keep the Jews in Egypt within the sphere of the temple in Jerusalem, instead of the competing temple at Leontopolis, c. 124 BCE.[48] Philo and Josephus also used reactions of wonder in relation to the God of Israel. It would seem that in early Jewish literature, if one wanted to convince that God was involved, manifest or intervening in something, a reaction of amazement was one key way to do it.

In *Joseph and Asenath*, reactions of wonder underscore the two elements of romance and proselytism. In regards to Asenath as the prototypical proselyte, one sees, in 9.1, Asenath fall on her bed exhausted, in distress, fearing and trembling, and continuously sweating after Joseph speaks to her in the name of God. As Asenath is watching the sky after her prayer of penitence in 14.3, she sees a morning star arise, and close to it the heavens are 'torn apart', and a great and unutterable light appears, which causes her to fall on her face. This is certainly a sign from God, and is followed by an angelic messenger. In 14.10 she

---

49. G. Vermes, *Jesus the Jew* (London: Collins, 1983), originally published in JSS 23

falls down at the feet of the angel and prostrates herself. Later in the text, the sons of Bilhah and Zilpah are afraid and fall to the ground and prostrate themselves before Asenath in 28.1, when God reduces their swords to ashes. A proof that God is involved in something is that people react with wonder, and a convert to the God of Israel (Asenath) can have reactions of wonder as she turns to God, and as God is intervening in her life. Like Petronius in Josephus, gentiles can be amazed at the God of Israel. I will have occasion to return to these ideas when I focus on Mark.

The wide and sometimes unknown provenance of the pseudepigrapha, as well as the likely sectarian nature of many of the documents, must keep one from overstating any thesis. Little here is unarguably 'mainstream'. In summary, however, I can note some general trends, such as the way in which reactions of wonder in the pseudepigrapha tend to focus on God, miracles, an eschatological expectation of wonder, and as propaganda for God's true presence.

Charismatic Miracle-Workers

The comparison between Jesus and first century Galilean miracle-workers Hanina ben Dosa and Honi the Circle-Drawer by G. Vermes[49] raises the issue of reactions of wonder in the accounts of those miracle workers. An examination of the relevant texts, however, reveals no reactions of wonder.

Conclusion

In an examination of the Septuagint, Josephus, Philo, the Dead Sea Scrolls, thirteen relevant pseudepigraphical texts and traditions surrounding early Jewish miracle workers, four conclusions can be drawn regarding reactions of wonder. First, reactions of wonder are common as a response to God or God's acts.

(1972), pp. 28-50 and JSS 24 (1973), pp. 51-64. Not all have accepted the comparison. Chilton objects to the attempt to understand Jesus in the later context of Talmudic Judaism (*Galilean*, p. 23), and S. Freyne questions the possibility of the charismatic as a religious type within Palestinian life in the early centuries of the common ear, in 'The Charismatic' in *Ideal Figures in Ancient Judaism* (ed. Nickelsburg and Collins; Chico, CA: Scholars Press, 1980), pp. 247-49. The relevant texts for Honi the Circle-Drawer are Josephus *Ant.* 14.22-24; MTa'an 3.8; bTa'an 23a; and Genesis Rabbah 13.7. For Hanina ben Dosa, the texts are MBer. 5.5; MSot. 9.15; MAboth. 3.10-11; bBer. 34b; bBk. 50a; bTa'an 24b, 25a; yBer. 9d and tBer. 3.20.

This tends to be visions of God in apocalyptic texts and saving deeds of God in narratives. The reactions in LXX *Exod.* 15.14-16, 18.9, 19.18 and 20.19 are good examples. They can be quite intense, as for example in *1 En.* 60.3-4.

Second, there is a theme of an expectation of reactions of wonder in the eschatological age. This begins with Hosea, Micah and Zechariah and can be seen in later works such as the *Testament of Moses* and *Second Baruch*. We have seen in *1 En.* 1.45 that the eschatological march of God upon Mount Sinai will cause fear and trembling to the ends of the earth.

Third, reactions of wonder are related to the expected messiah at several points. In *Isa.* 52.15 the language of the Septuagint is quite different from that of the Hebrew (and the targum). *Hos.* 3.5 also fits this category.

Fourth, reactions of wonder are used in propagandistic texts. Particularly in *2 Maccabees*, *Joseph and Asenath* and the *Letter of Aristeas*, there is a demonstration that the God of Israel is the true God by the way God does things to astound people. This is potentially very important for Mark, and one must keep in mind the possibility that Mark uses reactions of wonder in such a way to let his readers or hearers know that one proof that God was revealed in the ministry of Jesus is that people responded with wonder and awe at what took place. For those who may have begun to doubt the ministry of Jesus, or the presence of God in a period in the ministry of Jesus like the passion, this would be a striking affirmation. At this point, I will turn to early Christian writings, including the New Testament, gnostic and apocryphal texts, to continue our search.

Chapter 4

WONDER IN EARLY CHRISTIAN LITERATURE

Scholars are increasingly recognizing that it is anachronistic to speak of the New Testament when describing a period when there was not yet a settled or canonized New Testament. There is a trend related to this to date certain apocryphal or gnostic texts as contemporary with books that would become canonical. Among those who have done so are Koester, Crossan and Cameron. Koester would place at least five apocryphal gospels to be as old and as valuable as the canonical gospels as sources for the earliest developments of the traditions about Jesus (*Gospel of Thomas*, *Unknown Gospel* of Papyrus Egerton 2, the *Apocryphon of James*, *Dialogue of the Saviour* and the *Gospel of Peter*).[1] Crossan says that canonical Mark is possibly a revision of Secret Mark, that the canonical gospels may depend on the *Gospel of Peter*, that the *Gospel of Thomas* is a 'separate and parallel stream of the Jesus tradition', and that the *Unknown Gospel* is depended on by Mark.[2] Cameron says, for example, that the *Gospel of Peter* antedates the canonical gospels and was possibly used as a source by them.[3] These scholars are not alone, though others are more cautious.[4]

1. H. Koester, 'Apocryphal and Canonical Gospels', *HTR* 73 (1980), pp. 105-30. He places these apocryphal gospels at the stage of sources in the development of the canonical gospel literature, actually earlier than the gospels that would become canonical. However the evidence Koester produces says merely that the five apocryphal gospels in question are dependent on older traditions that the canonical gospels, not actually pre-dating them. He would later claim that Secret Mark preceded canonical Mark in 'History and Development of Mark's Gospel (from Mark to *Secret Mark* and "Canonical" Mark)' in *Colloquy on New Testament Studies* (ed. B.C. Corley; Macon, CA: Mercer University Press, 1983), pp. 35-57.
2. J.D. Crossan, *Four Other Gospels: Shadows on the Contours of Canon* (New York: Winston Press, 1985), pp. 108, 133, 183.
3. R. Cameron, ed., *The Other Gospels* (Philadelphia: Westminster Press, 1982), pp. 76-78. For a clear statement in opposition, see R. Brown, 'The Gospel of Peter and Canonical Gospel Priority', *NTS* 33 (1987), pp. 321-43, and note also, Brown, 'The Relation of the "Secret Gospel of Mark" to the Fourth Gospel', *CBQ* 36 (1974), pp. 466-85.

4. Wonder in Early Christian Literature

The tendency to remove the canonical 'fence' in the study of early Christian literature is welcome and is evident in the introductions of Vielhauer[5] and Koester.[6] In light of this, in this chapter I have surveyed not only the canonical New Testament, but also gnostic texts, ten early apocryphal gospels (some of which, like the *Gospel of Peter*, are fragmentary), and seven other early apocryphal texts relating to the apostles. Again, rather than citing every example, I will focus on key texts including John, Acts and Revelation in the New Testament, an important text in the *Gospel of Thomas*, and several apocryphal gospels and Acts.

New Testament

Within the canonical New Testament (other than Matthew and Luke which were looked at in the first chapter, and Mark itself which will follow), the three most notable texts with reactions of wonder are John, Acts and the Apocalypse. Let me look at these in their canonical order, and then proceed to some miscellaneous citations in the New Testament.

John is especially important here, because it has been suggested by Barrett[7],

---

4. For example, S.L. Davies in *The Gospel of Thomas and Christian Wisdom* (New York: Seabury Press, 1983) says that the evidence for a mid-first century date for *Gos. Thom.* is considerable but not conclusive. *Gos. Thom.* did have access to very early oral and perhaps written tradition which was 'independent of and occasionally superior to the traditions in the synoptics' (see p. 16). Also, W.D. Stroker, in 'Extra Canonical Parables and the Historical Jesus', *Semeia* 44 (1988), pp. 95-120, says that *Gos. Thom.* is independent and preserves a stage of tradition in several passages earlier than the synoptic gospels due to, first, the very different sequence of materials in *Gos. Thom.* 2; secondly, the presence of materials which may be considered earlier on the basis of form-critical considerations; and thirdly, the absence of elements attributed to the redactional activity of the evangelists. While he says that a first century date must not be excluded, even if the form in which we have *Gos. Thom.* is established as second century or later, the fact that it preserves traditions independent of the synoptics allows for the possibility that 'some of the parables not paralleled in the synoptic tradition may be genuine and that others with parallels may contain elements of a stage of tradition earlier than that contained in the canonical gospels'. See pp. 98-99.
5. P. Vielhauer, *Geschichte der Urchristlichen Literatur* (Berlin: de Gruyter, 1975).
6. Koester, *Introduction*.
7. Barrett, *Gospel*, pp. 42-54. On p. 45, Barrett says that it is plausible that John used Mark, thought it contained a suitable gospel outline and often (perhaps involuntarily) echoed Mark's phrases when writing about the same events.

Kümmel,[8] de Solages[9] and others[10] that John knew Mark (or the synoptics in general). If this were the case, one might expect to see Mark's reactions of wonder emerging in the fourth gospel. Some commentators, however, such as Bultmann and Haenchen, do not believe that John used the synoptics. A solid middle view would be that of Smith, who conceives of a situation where John originated in 'somewhat independent' Christian circles in which the synagogue controversy and a dispute over christology (doceticism) became the dominant issues. Matthew and Mark became known to the members of the Johannine community without having been fully appropriated into its traditions. The life, interests and controversies of the community provided inspiration and primary material for the author of John, while the influence of the synoptics were 'at best secondary and perhaps in some cases secondhand'. John did not use the synoptics as a source, but neither did he write in complete isolation from them.[11]

This question is important for the topic at hand, since one would expect to see Markan reactions of wonder emerging in the fourth gospel if John knew Mark. Yet the only reaction of wonder common to both is the incident of the sea walking, which both portray. In John 6.19, καὶ ἐφοβήθησαν differs from the Mark's καὶ ἐταράχθησαν, and John does not use καὶ λίαν [ἐκ περισσοῦ] ἐν ἑαυτοῖς ἐξίσταντο (Mk 6.51).[12] One should note that in the schemes of five

---

8. W.G. Kümmel, *Introduction to the New Testament* (London: SCM Press, 1984), pp. 201-204. Kümmel says that John knew Mark and Luke and utilized them as seemed appropriate.

9. M. de Solages, *Jean et les Synoptiques* (Leiden: Brill, 1979). The thesis here is that John knew the synoptics, but did not use them.

10. For example, F. Neirynck *et al.*, *Jean et les synoptiques: Examen critique de l'exégèse de M.E. Boismard* (BETL, 49; Leuven: Leuven University Press, 1979). Also, J.M. Robinson, 'On the Gattung of Mark (and John)', in *Jesus and Man's Hope* (ed. D.C. Miller and D.Y. Hadidian; Pittsburgh: Pittsburgh Theological Seminary, 1970), pp. 99-129. Another possibility is that John used synoptic-like traditions, either oral or written.

11. D.M. Smith, 'John and the Synoptics: Some Dimensions of the Problem', in *Johannine Christianity: Essays on Its Setting, Sources and Theology* (Columbia, SC: University of South Carolina Press, 1984), pp. 170-71.

12. W. Nicol, *The Semeia in the Fourth Gospel* (NovTSup, 32; Leiden: Brill, 1972), relates the fear of Jn. 6.19 to Mk. 6.49, 51, and says that it is different than the shouting and astonishment of the Markan account. He remarks on reactions of amazement and says that these are the reactions to miracles in Hellenistic literature, but that the reaction in John is Jewish because in Jewish literature fear is the normal reaction when God appears (Gen. 28.17; Exod. 3.6, 34.30).

4. *Wonder in Early Christian Literature* 71

leading advocates of a 'signs source' (Fortna,[13] Teeple,[14] Nicol,[15] Becker[16] and Schnackenburg[17]), 6.19 is the only place where the wonder language is found to be the pre-Johannine source postulated (although Teeple does find 4.27, καὶ ἐθαύμαζον, in his source). It is important, however, to keep in mind the comment of Lindars that whatever the sources behind the fourth gospel, they have been so creatively employed, so reworked, that their original form is nearly lost to the redaction of the evangelist.[18]

In general in John, one is struck by three things in regard to the way in which reactions of wonder function. The first is that it is usually the opponents of Jesus who marvel (with the exceptions of 4.27 and 6.19). Often it is explicitly 'the Jews'. The second factor of interest is that twice there is the command not to be amazed (μὴ θαυμάσῃς in 3.6 and μὴ θαυμάζετε in 5.28; see 1 Jn 3.13). This command is never given in Mark. Thirdly, amazement is never the reaction to specific miracles, as in the synoptics. The closest to this in John is 7.21, which refers to the miracles of Chapter 5, but there is no such reaction in Chapter 5 itself. Rather than wonder being the reaction to specific miracles in John, it is instead primarily the reaction of unbelieving opponents of Jesus and people are told not to be amazed. In John, those who believe in Jesus should not marvel (for example, 2.11),[19] and it can be noted that disciples are not struck with the awesome terror that befalls the opponents of Jesus in 18.6 and 19.8. Let me fill out this summary a bit.

In Jn 4.27, the imperfect (καὶ ἐθαύμαζον ὅτι μετὰ γυναικὸς ἐλάλει ...) suggests more than a momentary surprise.[20] Culpepper finds a note of awe in the amazement of the disciples that Jesus would speak with a woman, but would not question Jesus.[21] The amazement may be understandable in light of the

---

13. R.T. Fortna, *The Gospel of Signs* (SNTSMS, 11; Place: Publisher, 1970), and *The Fourth Gospel and Its Predecessor* (Philadelphia: Fortress Press, 1988).

14. H. Teeple, *The Literary Origins of the Gospel of John* (Evanston: Religion and Ethics Institute, 1974).

15. Nicol, *Semeia*.

16. J. Becker, 'Wunder und Christologie', *NTS* 19 (11969/70), pp. 130-48.

17. R. Schnackenburg, *The Gospel According to St. John* (3 vols.; New York: Seabury Press, 1980, 1980, 1982).

18. B. Lindars, *Behind the Fourth Gospel* (London: SPCK, 1971), p. 54.

19. This is recognised by Bertram, *TDNT*, III, p. 40.

20. R.E. Brown, *The Gospel According to John* (AB; 2 vols.; Garden City, NY: Doubleday, 1966), I, p. 173.

21. R.A. Culpepper, *Anatomy of the Fourth Gospel* (Philadelphia: Fortress Press, 1983), p. 116.

traditional warning against Jewish men speaking to women in public (for example, Sir. 9.1-9, *Pirqe Aboth* 1.5). Bultmann notes that the evangelist draws out the idea that the disciples cannot understand why the Revealer chooses certain men or women to speak with, and it is not permissible to ask why those individuals are chosen.[22]

John 5.20 is important for understanding wonder in the fourth gospel: ὁ γὰρ πατὴρ φιλεῖ υἱὸν καὶ πάντα δείκνυσιν αὐτῷ ἃ αὐτὸς ποιεῖ, καὶ μείζονα τούτων δείξει αὐτῷ ἔργα, ἵνα ὑμεῖς θαυμάζητε. In 5.18 the Jews (John's opponents of Jesus) are seeking to kill Jesus, and 5.19 begins a speech of Jesus to the Jews. The greater works will make the Jews marvel. The ὑμεῖς is clearly emphatic, and Brown suggests it may be derogatory ('people like you').[23] This verse must not be isolated from the command μὴ θαυμάζετε τοῦτο ... of verse 28, and these three factors (the speech directed at the opponents, the emphatic ὑμεῖς, and the warning of verse 28) point to a negative connotation of amazement here, as Schnackenburg,[24] Calvin,[25] Schlatter[26] and Riedl[27] have seen.

It has already been noted that Jn 6.19 (καὶ ἐφοβήθησαν) is parallel to Mk 6.50. Gnilka notes that the threat of the epiphany scene is the cause of the fear.[28] Here, one should note that in John the disciples are never afraid of Jesus, not even after the resurrection (see 20.19-20 for fear of the Jews by the disciples, but joy at Jesus' presence). Apart from the quotation in Jn 12.15 (Isa. 40.9), the fear is almost always fear of the Jews (7.13; 9.22; 19.38; 20.19)[29] with the exception being 19.8 where Pilate is 'even more afraid' when he hears that Jesus has made himself the Son of God. According to Schnackenburg, numinous awe is present at this point.[30]

22. R. Bultmann, *The Gospel of John: A Commentary* (Oxford: Basil Blackwell, 1971), p. 193.
23. R.E. Brown, *The Gospel According to John* (2 vols.; AB; Garden City, NY: Doubleday, 1966), p. 214.
24. Schnackenburg, *Gospel*, I, p. 104.
25. J. Calvin, *The Gospel According to St. John* (2 vols.; Edinburgh: Oliver & Boyd, 1959), I, p.126.
26. A. Schlatter, *Der Evangelist Johannes* (Stuttgart: Calwer Verlag, 1948), p. 148.
27. J. Riedl, *Das Heilwerk Jesu nach Johannes* (Freiburg: Herder, 1973), pp. 226-27.
28. J. Gnilka, *Johannesevangelium* (Die neue Echter-Bibel; Würzburg: Echter Verlag, 1983), p. 48.
29. There is increasing agreement that the author of the fourth gospel was related to a community of believers engaged in a serious dispute with a synagogue. See R. Kysar, *The Fourth Evangelist and His Gospel* (Minneapolis: Augsburg, 1975), p. 149.
30. Schnackenburg, *Gospel*, II, pp. 26-27.

4. Wonder in Early Christian Literature 73

In Jn 7.15, it is again the opponents, the Jews, who marvel: ἐθαύμαζον οὖν οἱ Ἰουδαῖοι λέγοντες, Πῶς οὗτος γράμματες οἶδεν μὴ μεμαθηκώς. There have been numerous reconstructions of this chapter,[31] but as the text stands it fits with the synoptic witness to the effect of Jesus' teaching on his contemporaries (Mk 1.22; 6.2; Lk. 4.22), as Beasley-Murray has noted.[32] Perhaps more pronounced than in the synoptics, however, is the note of derision in θαυμάζειν. Martyn[33] follows Bultmann[34] in seeing the sense both here and in 7.21 (ἓν ἔργον ἐποίησα καὶ πάντες θαυμάζετε) is a reference back to the Sabbath healing in Chapter 5 (though no wonder is mentioned there). The explanation of Jesus in verses 22-24 indeed indicates that the reaction of the Jews was skeptical unbelief out of concern for the sanctity of the Sabbath rather than compassion for the individual in deed. By this point in the fourth gospel, the opposition of the Jews has been clearly defined, so one is hard pressed to see 7.15 as merely neutral. Also, the amazement at Jesus in 7.15 for teaching without formal training in the Torah reminds one of the disdain shown for those who do not know the law in 7.49. In 7.21, Jesus is speaking to 'the crowd'. This group had accused him of having a demon in 7.20, and in 7.12 the crowd was grumbling about Jesus, with some claiming that he was deceiving the people. Thus there are several contextual factors which give a hard negative connotation to θαυμάζειν in 7.15 and 21. It is not necessary, however, to alter the sense of θαυμάζειν to something like σκανδαλίζειν as Bultmann and Martyn would do. In general, then, there is a strong negative connotation to wonder in the gospel of John.

In Jn 9.30 there is a related instance, where the man Jesus had healed of blindness tells the Pharisees: Ἐν τούτῳ γὰρ τὸ θαυμαστόν ἐστιν ὅτι ὑμεῖς οὐκ οἴδατε πόθεν ἐστίν, καὶ ἤνοιξέν μου τοὺς ὀφθαλμούς. The surprise of the

---

31. Schnackenburg would insert verse 25 after verse 14 (II, pp. 145-56) and place 7.15-24 as the conclusion to the argument following the Sabbath healing in Chapter 5 (II, p. 134). Bultmann would move 7.15-24 to follow 5.28 (p. 237-38). J. Becker, *Das Evangelium des Johannes* (OTKNT; Würzburg: Gütersloher Verlaghaus, 1979), II, pp. 248-51, would place 7.15-24 after 5.31-47. The reasons of Schnackenburg for his shift of 7.15-24 should be noted, since he claims that since θαυμάζειν occurs only in 5.20, 28 and 7.15, 21, there is a direct contextual fit into Chapter 5. Yet there is no textual evidence for such a translocation, nor do all uses of a word in a book require a single context.
32. G. Beasley-Murray, *John* (WBC; Waco,TX: Word Books, 1987), p.108.
33. J.L. Martyn, *History and Theology in the Fourth Gospel* (New York: Harper & Row, 1968), p. 111.
34. Bultmann, *Gospel*, p. 273.

man at the ignorance of the Pharisees (who should have known) is similar to that of Jesus at Nicodemus in 3.10.[35] Morris says that the article τό preceding θαυμαστόν may signify 'this is the truly marvelous thing: your unbelief in the face of evidence that is more of a miracle than my cure'.[36] One could add that the emphatic ὑμεῖς also points to the thought that the focus is on those who should understand but are ignorant. There is a strong note of irony present here.[37]

It should also be noted that there may be a reaction of wonder involved in the response of the healed man in 9.38: καὶ προσεκύνησεν αὐτῷ. This is the only place in John where such a response occurs. This does not warrant its exclusion on textual grounds, however.[38]

A reaction of wonder which does not contain the usual lexical terms is clearly found in Jn 18.6: ὡς οὖν εἶπεν αὐτοῖς, Ἐγώ εἰμι, ἀπῆλθον εἰς τα ὀπίσω καὶ ἔπεσαν χαμαί. This is not, as Hingston proposed, those with Judas slipping behind him to push him forward to give the identifying sign.[39] Neither is there an indication in this verse that those who came to arrest Jesus stumbled and fell.[40] One must also be careful in understanding this verse in light of parallels of people falling to the ground before the appearance of a heavenly being.[41] While some see various Psalmic materials providing the basis of this

---

35. Brown, *John*, I, p. 375, and B. Lindars, *The Gospel of John* (NCB; London: Oliphants, 1972), p. 348.

36. L. Morris, *The Gospel According to St. John* (NICNT; Grand Rapids: Eerdmans, 1972), p.492

37. P.D. Duke, *Irony in the Fourth Gospel* (Atlanta, CA: John Knox Press, 1985), p.69.

38. C.A. Porter, 'John 9.38-39a: A Liturgical Addition to the Text', *NTS* 13 (1966/67), pp. 387-94, notes that these verses are missing in X, W, Q, P[75], and on the evidence that ἔφη is rare in John, the use of πιστεύω (the form of which occurs nowhere else in John), and the assertion that προσκυνεῖν occurs nowhere else in John would omit 9.38-39a from the text.

39. J. Hingston, 'John 18.5, 6', *ExpTim* 32 (1920/21), p. 232. His theory depends on αὐτοῦ having dropped out in transmission, for which there is no evidence.

40. P. Mein, 'A Note on John 18.6', *ExpTim* 65 (1953/54), pp. 286-87. If there is a cryptic reference to the 'stone of stumbling' of Isa. 28.14, as Mein suggests, it is cryptic beyond recognition.

41. An incisive note is given by A. Dauer in *Die Passionsgeschichte im Johannesevangelium: Eine traditionsgeschichtliche und theologische Untersuchung zu Joh. 18.1-19.30* (Munich: Kösel, 1972) in an excursus entitled 'Religionsgeschichtliche Parallelen zu Joh. 18.6', pp. 41-43, points out that John 18.6 is not parallel with an appearance with a heavenly being due to the fact that not all fall to the ground before Jesus, only his enemies. The motif is similar to *1 En.* 52.6, for example, but such epiphanies cannot definitively be called *vorlagen*.

4. Wonder in Early Christian Literature 75

verse, Haenchen sees Ps. 27 (26). 2 LXX and Ps. 35 (34). 4 LXX as the originator of this tradition,[42] and Barrett sees Ps.55 (56). 10,[43] others focus on the divine name I AM.[44] Brown suggests that if the story Eusebius relates of Pharaoh falling speechless to the ground when Moses uttered the divine name (*Praep. Ev.* 9.27.24-26) has been available, this would have been excellent background for John.[45]

In addition to these insights, it is helpful to keep some additional factors in mind when looking at John 18.6. First, in light of the reality of the experience of *mysterium tremendum* before the presence of God in general religious experience (see the excursus to this chapter), one should not exclude the possibility that such a reaction is is being conveyed by the text. Also, the fact that the opponents fall to the ground, rather than all present, indicates that this is a demonstration that no one would take Jesus' life from him, but that he would give it up (10.18). Then, if it is the I AM that is seen as causing the reaction, the ancient world had no lack of confidence in the effects of the pronunciation of divine names (note the uses in the magical papyri). It seems to be the effect of the divine name which causes those arresting Jesus to fall to the ground. As such this links with the other I AM statements of Jesus in John and the self-revelation of the Word. The presence of the Word become flesh causes even armed enemies to fall in awed terror.

Finally, in John one should note 19.8, when Pilate finds out that Jesus has made himself out to be the son of God: ὅτε οὖν ἤκουσεν ὁ Πιλᾶτος τοῦτον λόγον, μᾶλλον ἐφοβήθη. The comparative μᾶλλον here may have elative force ('He was very much afraid').[46] The combination of the term 'son of God' and the reactions may lead beyond ordinary fear to what Schnackenburg calls 'numinous terror before the divine.'[47] Pilate was moved by the presence of a son of God, possessing supernatural powers, who might bring havoc on him.[48] A reaction of wonder is normal before a divine being.

In John, then, reactions of wonder are usually those of opponents of Jesus

---

42. E. Haenchen, *A Commentary on the Gospel of John* (2 vols.; Philadelphia: Westminster Press, 1984), II, p. 165.
43. Barrett, *Gospel*, p. 520.
44. Brown, *John*, II, p. 818.
45. Brown, *John*, II, p. 818.
46. Brown, *John*, II, p. 877, and Barrett, *Gospel*, p. 542.
47. Schnackenburg, *Gospel*, III, p. 260.
48. C.H. Dodd, *Historical Tradition in the Fourth Gospel* (Cambridge: Cambridge University Press, 1963), p. 114, and Bultmann, *Gospel*, p. 661.

(with exceptions in 4.27 and 6.19). There is the command not to be amazed given in 3.6; see also 5.28 and 1 John 3.13. Reactions of wonder are never reactions to specific miracles. If the author of the fourth gospel knew Mark, he certainly used reactions of wonder in a very different way.

There are a variety of nuances to reactions of wonder in Acts. At times, people are disposed to belief or obedience (8.13; 13.12; 16.29; 19.17).[49] At other times, it predisposes people to following a magician (8.9, 11). At yet other times, there is unbelief involved (the quote of Hab. 1.5 in 13.41). The fact that awe falls on the community of believers (as well as unbelievers, 19.17; 24.25) at times increases the variety of ways wonder functions in Acts. As would be expected, divine interventions and manifestations cause wonder (miracles, the falling of the Holy Spirit). Perhaps the superstitiousness of the ancient world makes necessary the warnings. One must look beyond human vehicles (3.12) and not be deceived by magicians performing astonishing feats (8.9, 11). A dose of discernment is always needed.

There are 28 reactions of wonder in Acts. Three are at the falling of the Holy Spirit (2.7, 12; 10.45), and eight as a response to miracles (3.10, 11; 5.5, 11; 8.13; 9.7; 12.16; 16.29). It occurs in the call or conversion of Saul in 9.7 and in his account of this event in 26.14 (and at his preaching in 9.21). The vision of Cornelius in 10.4 brings the remark ὁ δὲ ἀτενίσας αὐτῷ καὶ ἔμφοβος γενόμενος ... There is awe in the community at 2.43 and possibly 5.5 and 11, and at the message proclaimed in 4.13 and 24.25. Twice a reaction of wonder occurs in a reference to the Old Testament in a speech (7.31, 32), and once in an Old Testament quotation (Hab. 1.5 in 13.41). There are four special occasions when wonder leads to following someone: 8.9 and 11 where the Samaritans follow Simon because he has amazed them with his magic; 8.13 where Simon then believes and is baptized because of his amazement at the signs and wonders of Philip; 13.12 where the proconsul Sergius Paulus believes when he sees how God struck the magician, 'being amazed at the teaching of the Lord'; and 16.29 where the jailer rushes into the jail trembling as he asks 'What must I do to be saved?'

The favourite word in Acts to describe these reactions is ἐξίστημι (2.7, 12;

---

49. J.C. O'Neill, *The Theology of Acts in Its Historical Setting* (London: SPCK, 1970), p. 143, suggests that the theology of conversion in Acts makes it similar to Hellenistic Jewish missionary propaganda such as *Joseph and Asenath*. The reactions of wonder we have seen in that work are indeed similar to those of some converts in Acts.

8.9, 11, 13; 9.21; 10.45; 12.16).⁵⁰ This word was used three times in Luke (2.47; 8.56; 24.22) and four times in Mark. A common construction is ἐξίστημι leading to a question: 2.7 ἐξίσταντο δὲ καὶ ἐθαύμαζον and question; 2.12 ἐξίσταντο δὲ πάντες καὶ διηπόρουν and question; 9.21 ἐξίσταντο δὲ πάντες οἱ ἀκούοντες and question; (see also 16.29, where wonder leads to a question; Lk. 1.65-66; 4.22, 36; 8.25). Forms of ἐξίστημι and ἐξιστάνω are used for disbelieving reactions upon hearing God's witnesses in Lk. 24.22 and Acts 9.21, as well as for the hearers of the young Jesus in Lk. 2.47.

Another common construction is φόβος with γίνομαι: 2.43 Ἐγίνετο δὲ πάσῃ ψυχῇ φόβος; 5.5 ἐγένετο φόβος μέγας ἐπὶ πάντας τοὺς ἀκούοντας; 5.11 ἐγένετο φόβος μέγας ἐφ᾽ ὅλην τὴν ἐκκλησίαν; (for ἐπέπεσεν φόβος ἐπὶ πάντας αὐτούς in 19.17, see Lk. 1.12, 65; 8.37). The use of θαυμάζω as the reaction to the words of the 'uneducated' witnesses in Acts 4.13 has parallels in Lk. 2.18 and 4.22.

Other parallels between the use of reactions of wonder in Luke and Acts include fear coming on all involved with the initial event (Lk. 1.65; Acts 2.43); amazement occurring after the hearing of the first utterances of the anointed messengers (Lk. 4.22; Acts 2.7, 12); and the initial healing and exorcism which is not detailed (not general signs and wonders, Acts 2.43) has a reaction of amazement with θάμβος: Lk. 4.36 ἐγένετο θάμβος ἐπὶ πάντες, Acts 3.10 καὶ ἐπλήσθησαν θάμβους καὶ ἐκστάσεως ἐπὶ τῷ συμβεβηκότι αὐτῷ; see 3.11 συνέδραμεν πᾶς ὁ λαὸς ... ἔκθαμβοι.

The reactions of 2.7 (ἐξίσταντο δὲ καὶ ἐθαύμαζον λέγοντες, Οὐχ ἰδοὺ ἅπαντες οὗτοί εἰσιν οἱ λαλοῦντες Γαλιλαῖοι) and 2.12 (ἐξίσταντο δὲ πάντες καὶ διηπόρουν, ἄλλος πρὸς ἄλλον λέγοντες, Τί θέλει τοῦτο εἶναι;) are related by the linking word ἐξίσταντο, and Pesch believes that the repetition of the terms shows a strain from layers of text which are not uniform.⁵¹ As he points out, there is a shift from the singular to the plural in 6a-6b. The introduction of the diaspora Jews in verse 5 shifts to the 'multitude' of verse 6, and then includes the people of the city in verse 14. It is thus possible that the list of names in verses 7-11 is secondary,⁵² in which case ἐξίσταντο would indeed be a linking word. Conzelmann sees verses 12-13 as a variant of

---

50. G. Schneider, *Die Apostelgeschichte* (HTKNT; 2 vols.; Freiburg: Herder, 1980, 1982), I, p. 252, notes that 11 of the 17 NT occurrences of this term are in Luke and Acts.
51. R. Pesch, *Die Apostelgeschichte* (EKKNT; 2 vols.; Zürich: Benzinger Verlag, 1986), I, p. 100.
52. Pesch, *Apostelgeschichte*, I, p. 100.

verse 7, a redactional account of the effect on the audience.[53]

Acts 2.43 is similar to 5.5, 11, as was noted earlier. The φόβος is religious awe due to the miraculously manifested power of God.[54] The imperfect ἐγίνετο denotes a fear which continued to be a feature of the following days rather than a momentary panic.[55] A similar reference is 1 QH 4.26 ('But Thou will put their fear upon Thy people').[56] In Acts 5.5 it is curious that the fear (a fright from the *mysterium tremendum*) is said to come on those present who 'hear the report'.[57] This is expanded in 5.11 to all the church. The word ἐκκλησία occurs here for the first time in Acts.

An important cluster of reactions of wonder occur in 8.9, 11 and 13. In 8.9 the text shifts to the Hellenistic ἐξιστάνω, and the participles μαγεύων and ἐξιστάντων are probably both to be taken with προϋπῆρχεν.[58] The interplay here between the effect which Simon has on the people of Samaria, and the fact that the signs and miracles of Philip then have the same effect on Simon is striking. Here one finds that amazement leads to allegiance or following (see Acts 13.12), but that amazement must not be uncritical, for it can lead to attachment to a magician, or to belief that a human is the source of the miracle (3.12). Also the amazement of Simon at the miracles of Philip was no guarantee that his belief was genuine or lasting.

Acts 16.29 is an example where a reaction of wonder leads to belief, as opposed to Hab. 1.5 in Acts 13.41, where wonder is no guarantee that one will perceive the work of God. The reaction of Felix should perhaps be noted here. In Acts 24.25, when Paul is speaking to him about righteousness, self-control and the judgment to come, Felix becomes terrified (ἔμφοβος γενόμενος ὁ φῆλιξ). Perhaps the guilt of Felix in having illicit relations with Priscilla, combined with Paul's speech on coming judgment strikes the governor with awe, but there is no indication of an attempt to remedy the situation.

Acts is different from John in that the predominantly negative connotations of wonder in John are not present, but rather there is a sense that God astounds

---

53. H. Conzelmann, *The Acts of the Apostles* (Hermeneia Commentaries; Philadelphia: Fortress Press, 1987), p. 15.

54. Schneider, *Apostelgeschichte*, I, p. 287, and E. Haenchen, *The Acts of the Apostles* (Oxford: Basil Blackwell, 1971), p.192.

55. F.F. Bruce, *The Acts of the Apostles* (London: Tyndale Press, 1952), p. 100.

56. G.Schille, *Die Apostelgeschichte des Lukas* (THKNT; Berlin: Evangelische Verlaganstalt, 1984), p. 121.

57. Pesch, *Apostelgeschichte*, I, p. 200.

58. Conzelmann, *Acts*, pp. 62-63.

believers and unbelievers alike. Wonder is a step on the way to either belief or disbelief. As expected, divine manifestations evoke wonder, but also the proclamation of the message carries a divine power to evoke wonder. There is evidence, then, in John and Acts, for a variety of nuances of wonder in the New Testament.

As we turn to Revelation, it can be noted that the Apocalypse is close to the fourth gospel in its use of reactions of wonder. While it is apocalyptic in genre the book differs from Jewish apocalypses in that it is not pseudonymous, does not indulge in lengthy *ex eventu* prophesies, and is presented as a circular letter to the churches rather than a secret book.[59] The common elements with Jewish apocalypses are the form in which the revelation is presented (a heavenly vision with an angelic interpreter), the eschatological content, and the hope of both a cosmic transformation and a personal afterlife.[60] While there has been some debate regarding the sources of the Apocalypse,[61] there has been more emphasis of late on the present form of Revelation as the composition of a single author who made use of some sources of limited scope as well as of apocalyptic tradition in oral form.[62]

It should be remembered that in the third chapter I noted that in Jewish apocalypses, reactions of wonder were common when the seer receives a vision (for example, Dan. 10.7-8, *1 En.* 60.3-4), and it has been recognized that terror and fainting commonly characterise the responses of visionaries to a vision or the voice of God, but also to other kinds of visionary phenomena (Dan. 5.6; 7.15, 28; 8.27; *1 En.* 14.9, 13-15, 24; 2 Esd. 10.30).[63] There are two types of reactions to angelophanies, according to Bauckham, both of which include fear and prostration. In the first type the fear is extreme and the prostration is involuntary (here the visionary falls on the ground 'as one dead'), and in the second type

---

59. J.J. Collins, 'Pseudonymity, Historical Reviews and the Genre of the Revelation of John', *CBQ* 39 (1977), p. 330.

60. Collins, 'Pseudonymity', p. 329-30.

61. J.M. Ford, *Revelation: A New Translation with Introduction and Commentary* (AB; Garden City, NY: Doubleday, 1975) discusses the possible taking over of Jewish sources. The classic form of this theory is E. Vischer, *Die Offenbarung Johannes: Eine jüdische Apokelypse in christlicher Beararbeitung* (Leipzig: Hinrich, 1886).

62. A.Y. Collins, 'The Political Perspective of the Revelation to John', *CBQ* 96 (1977), pp. 241-56, and *Crisis and Catharsis: The Power of the Apocalypse* (Philadelphia: Westminster Press, 1986).

63. R. Bauckham, 'The Worship of Jesus in Apocalyptic Christianity', *NTS* 27 (1980/81), p. 324.

the fear is less extreme, but the prostration again occurs (for example, 2 *En.* 2.7).[64] Bauckham claims that the fear involved in both of these types of angelophanies is very close to the essential religious experience to the numinous which Rudolph Otto[65] has described as a mixture of fascination and terror (see the excursus).[66] It becomes important in Jewish texts because of the need for the angels involved to safeguard against a threat to monotheism, by declaring that the seer must only worship God. This can be seen in Rev. 19.10 and 22.8-9. Here, then, the reactions of wonder are somewhat inevitable in view of the angelophany, but these reactions must not lead to worship. This is important for understanding reactions of wonder throughout Revelation. Wonder can be misleading if it moves one to worship the beast.

In Rev. 1.17, John has a reaction of wonder at his vision of Christ: καὶ ὅτε εἶδον αὐτόν, ἔπεσα πρὸς πόδας αὐτοῦ ὡς νεκρός. There are visionary comparisons which may be made (Dan. 8,18; 10.7-9; 15-19; Ezek. 1.28; *1 En.* 1.5; 14.14; Mt. 16.6),[67] and the following command not to fear is most like that of Dan. 10.12.[68] The idea that one must fall before the divine holiness (Gen. 32.31; Exod. 33.20; Judg. 13.7; Isa. 6.5) brings about the dramatic response,[69] and should lead one to hesitate to call this 'stereotyped behaviour in apocalyptic trances'.[70]

The responses of Rev. 4.10 and 5.8 should perhaps be noted. In these places, the 24 elders fall before the throne and worship (in 5.8 the four living creatures and the 24 elders do this). It has been noted that falling down may precede worship (Jn 9.38), but the response involved here is probably more humility than

64. Bauckham, 'Worship', p. 323.
65. R. Otto, *The Idea of the Holy* (London: Oxford University Press, 1923).
66. Bauckham, 'Worship', p. 324.
67. A. Wikenhauser, *Die Offenbarung des Johannes*, (RNT; Regensburg: Pustet, 1959), p. 33; E. Lohmeyer, *Die Offenbarung des Johannes* (HNT; Tübingen: Mohr, 1971), p. 18.
68. P. Prigent, *L'Apocalypse de Saint Jean* (CNT; Paris: Delachaux & Niestlé, 1981), p. 31.
69. E. Lohse, *Die Offenbarung des Johannes* (NTD; Göttingen: Vandenhoeck & Ruprecht, 1971), p. 21.
70. R. Mounce, *The Book of Revelation* (London: Marshall, Morgan & Scott, 1977), p. 80 and also C. Rowland, *The Open Heaven: A Study of Apocalyptic in Judaism and Early Christianity* (London: SPCK, 1982), pp. 231-32. Rowland believes that there may be relics of actual experience involved. The evaluation of S. Niditch, 'The Visionary', in *Ideal Figures*, (eds.; Nickelsburg and Collins), p. 161, is interesting as the description of the emotional and physical state of seers such as Daniel and Esdras is said to recall the trance state of shamanism.

4. Wonder in Early Christian Literature 81

astonishment or awe.[71] This is also likely the case in Rev. 7.11.

Though the typical language of wonder is not present in Rev. 6.15-17, it is certain that the reaction of the various strata of society hiding themselves from the presence of God and the lamb is a reaction of fearful awe. There is a strong scriptural background to these verses with traditional elements of the depiction of the end of times and the terror which causes people to flee and hide from God (Isa. 2.10; 19.21; Hosa. 10.8; Lk. 21.25).[72] There is also the element found in Gen. 3.8 of guilty individuals hiding 'from the face of the Lord', with perhaps an *Urzeit–Endzeit* schema.[73] Ford notes that the ancients spoke of the awe-inspiring glamor of kingship which blinded and terrified people.[74] Here, the fearful initial display of the wrath of God terrifies people who fear the divine judgment.

The reaction of those observing the resurrection of the two witnesses in Rev. 11.11 is certainly a reaction of wonder: ...καὶ φόβος μέγας ἐπέσεν ἐπὶ τοὺς θεωροῦντας αὐτούς. This is followed in 11.13 by the response of those who survive the great earthquake which kills 7000: ...καὶ οἱ λοιποὶ ἔμφοβοι ἐγένοντο καὶ ἔδωκαν δόξαν τῷ θεῷ τοῦ οὐρανοῦ. The language φόβος... ἐπέσεν ἐπὶ is surprisingly similar to that of Acts 19.17 (see Lk. 1.12; Acts 5.5, 11), but Charles notes that the phrase is also found in the Old Testament (Exod. 15.16; Ps. 54 (55).5).[75] The language ἔμφοβοι ἐγένοντο of 11.13 is much like that of Acts 24.25 (ἔμφοβος γενόμενος ὁ Φῆλιξ). Thus, the language in these two verses is quite similar to Lukan style. The result of this awe is that the people 'gave glory to the God of heaven'. Many commentators recognise that repentance is involved in this (note the proclamation of the angel in 14.7 to fear God and give God glory, and in 16.9 that giving God glory follows repentance).[76] It must be said that the text does not say that the signs performed by the witnesses astonished the people (verse 6), but that their resurrection did. The awe which falls following the judgments of verse 13 remind one of Acts 5.5, 11.

If a reaction of wonder leads to repentance in Rev. 11.11, 13, the danger that a reaction of wonder can lead to is depicted in 13.3. The whole earth marvels after the beast when his head wound is healed (καὶ ἐθαυμάσθη ὅλη ἡ γῆ ὀπίσω

---

71. Note the casting of the crowns in 4.10. Falling to one's feet is an act of reverence, Wikenhauser, *Offenbarung*, p. 53, rather than an act of awe such as in Lk. 6.8.
72. Wikenhauser, *Offenbarung*, p. 65.
73. Lohmeyer, *Offenbarung*, p. 66.
74. Ford, *Revelation*, p. 101.
75. R.H. Charles, *A Critical and Exegetical Commentary on the Revelation of St. John* (ICC; 2 vols.; Edinburgh: T & T Clark, 1920), I, p. 290.

τοῦ θηρίου). This immediately leads to worship of the dragon and the beast in v. 4. The supernatural brings wonder, but in this case it is a deception of Satan. The verb ἐθαυμάσθη, passive voice, signals here a 'disconcerted awe', according to Lohmeyer.[76] The picture of the world wondering or gaping after the beast can be compared with the graphic picture of Josephus of the enthusiasm with which the people received Vespasian after the restoration of peace to the empire (*War* 7.63-74).[77] It is crucial to note here that Satanic deception, as well as divine intervention, can lead people to marvel. This, in turn, can lead to the worshipping of Satan and his agents. It would seem clear that here a negative sense attaches to the reaction of wonder. It is the wonder of those deceived.

In a similar way to 13.3, a negative pall is cast over reactions of wonder in 17.6 and 17.8. In 17.6 John marvels when he sees the woman who is drunk with the blood of the saints and of the witnesses of Jesus (Καὶ ἐθαύμασα ἰδὼν αὐτὴν θαῦμα μέγα). This reaction is given an immediate negative response by the angel (Διὰ τί ἐθαύμσας, 17.7).[78] Then, in 17.8, those who dwell on the earth, whose names are not written in the Book of Life, marvel after the beast, again with the passive voice (καὶ θαυμασθήσονται οἱ κατοικοῦντες ἐπὶ τῆς γῆς ...). The seer is not to marvel after the beast, for this is the response of those who are not believers. Prigent notes that θαυμάζειν can have a large semantic range ('émerveiller'), and has the sense of the attitude of the human before the marvelous (which in this case is the supernatural manifested at Satan's inspiration).[79] There is a strong Johannine note here (see Jn 3.7; 5.28; 1 Jn 3.13).

As in the book of Acts, wonder may be the first step to following someone. This is not unequivocally positive in either case, however (remember Acts 8.9-11). Supernatural manifestations must be discerned. Wonder can be said to have a negative cast at times in Acts, John and Revelation. In Acts and Revelation, it may also be part of coming to believe. Both Revelation and the fourth gospel emphasise that wonder can characterize undiscerning believers, though in Revelation it is a response to counterfeit acts of power, and in John it is commonly a response to Jesus prompted by unbelief. Both John and Revelation ask those who marvel why they do so (Jn 3.7; 5.28; Rev. 17.7). Rev. 1.7 is an

---

76. Wikenhauser, *Offenbarung*, pp. 87-88; Charles, *Commentary*, I, pp. 291-92; and I.T. Beckwith, *The Apocalypse of John* (repr.; Grand Rapids: Baker, 1967, [1919]), p. 604.

76. Lohmeyer, *Offenbarung*, p. 111.

77. Ford, *Revelation*, pp. 221-22.

78. Lohmeyer, *Offenbarung*, p. 142, correctly notes that this is a literary style reminiscent of the fourth gospel.

79. Prigent, *Apocalypse*, p. 259.

4. Wonder in Early Christian Literature

exception to the negative cast generally given in Revelation. It is important to note here that though amazement can lead to following the wrong person as well as the right person, it is the response by those touched by powers beyond this world.

Outside of the gospels, Acts and Revelation, the language of wonder is not common in the New Testament. This is not surprising, since the rest of the New Testament contains letters of various forms, not narratives. Two places do deserve note.

In 2 Thess. 1.10, there is a remarkable use of θαυμάζειν in connection with the return of Jesus: ὅταν ἔλθῃ ἐνδοξασθῆναι ἐν τοῖς ἁγίοις αὐτοῦ καὶ θαυμασθῆναι ἐν πᾶσιν τοῖς πιστεύσασιν, ὅτι ἐπιστεύθη τὸ μαρτύριον ἡμῶν ἐφ᾽ ὑμᾶς, ἐν τῇ ἐκείνῃ. One finds here that amazement is expected and approved of in believers, in connection with the parousia. In this verse the infinitives ἐνδοξασθῆναι and θαυμασθῆναι, both passive, are parallel. Whether the parallelism implies a single sense, however, is questionable.[80] Parallelism may add to the sense of the previous unit. In light of the spectacular accompanying events of 2 Thess. 1.7-8, 'to be marveled at' would be much more understandable as a reaction than 'to be admired', and therefore justified as a rendering in verse 10.[81] The sight of the Lord coming from heaven with his mighty angels in flaming fire, to give punishment to those who did not know God or obey the gospel, is more likely to adduce marveling than mere admiration. The passives indicate that believers are acted upon by the sight to produce the reaction. In this case, wonder is entirely appropriate.

The second place which deserves note is in James 2.19. The dramatic reaction of demons to God is stated: καὶ τὰ δαιμόνια πιστεύουσιν καὶ φρίσσουσιν. The idea of demons shuddering is present in the gospels (Mk 1.24; 5.27, and others), and there are numerous references in Jewish literature to this response.[82] The thought is that of hair standing up on end, and is used of awe at

---

80. C. Masson, *Les deux épîtres de Saint Paul aux thessaloniens* (CNT; Paris: Delachaux & Niestlé, 1957), p. 88, believes that both verbs have one sense. He uses the sense 'to admire' for θαυμάζω . B. Rigaux, *Saint Paul: Les épîtres aux thessaloniens* (Paris: Gabalda, 1956), pp. 634-35 also has a similar sense.

81. R.A. Ward, *Commentary on 1 and 2 Thessalonians* (Waco, TX: Word Books, 1975), pp. 148-49.

82. P.H. Davids, *The Epistle of James* (NIGTC; Exeter: Paternoster Press, 1982), p. 125, provides a list and S. Laws, *A Commentary on the Epistle of James* (BNTC; London: A. & C. Black, 1980), p. 127, cites the reference in MM where φρίσσω refers to the response the sorcerer wishes to bring about by magic.

a mysterious divine power (Plato, *Phaedra* 251a), but depicts an idea more distant and terrifying than that of worship.[83] The thought in James is that demons not only believe that God is one, but go beyond this and shudder. While this is not a reaction of wonder at a specific miracle or teaching, it indicates the important concept of the continual (present tense) terrifying awe which the demons have before God. Certainly this would help explain the response of the demons to Jesus in the gospels. Also, this points to the inevitable nature of such responses.

In summary, there is a polyvalence to reactions of wonder in the New Testament. Though not always viewed in a positive light, at times such reactions are fully appropriate, such as at the return of Christ. Other things beyond miracles can convey the divine presence and power which evokes wonder, such as the word being preached. Though imitations of the divine power are presented in Revelation, at other times the necessity of amazement seems quite marked, such as when the Spirit falls in Acts. One should not be surprised if the same polyvalence found in the New Testament in general is in the gospel of Mark.

Gnostic Writings

There is a single logion that is important for our topic in gnostic writings. It has turned up in several places, but because it is included in the *Gospel of Thomas*,[84] we will look at it here.

Gospel of Thomas Logion 2 reads: 'Jesus said, "Let one who seeks not stop seeking until that person finds, and upon finding, the person will be disturbed, and being disturbed will be astonished, and will reign over the entirety"'.[85] Prior to the discovery of the only extant Coptic translation at Nag Hammadi in 1945, this logion was already known, in Oxyrhynchus Papyri 654.7, which Grenfall and Hunt assigned, in 1904, to the middle or end of the third century.[86] It was only with the discovery of *Thomas* at Nag Hammadi that it became certain that three of the Oxyrhynchus fragments (1, 654 and 655) were all part of the same

83. F.J.A. Hort, *The Epistle of St. James* (London: Macmillan, 1909), p. 61.
84. The view of Davies, *Gospel*, p. 3, that Thomas is in no meaningful sense gnostic is by far the minority view.
85. This is the translation of B. Layton, *The Gnostic Scriptures: A New Translation with Annotations and Introductions* (Garden City, NY: Doubleday, 1987).
86. *The Oxyrhynchus Papyri* (ed. H. Grenfall and R. Hunt; London: Oxford University Press, 1904).

4. Wonder in Early Christian Literature

work. The Greek of Isaiah 2 is shorter than the Coptic, has a different ending, and has been restored as:

[λέγει 'Iη(σοῦ)ς
μὴ παυσάσθω ὁ ζη[τῶν τοῦ ζητεῖν
ἕως ἂν] εὕρῃ, καὶ ὅταν εὕρῃ
[θαμβηθήσεται καὶ θαμ]βηθεὶς
βασιλεύσῃ κα[ὶ βασιλεύσας ἀναπα]ήσεται[87]

The complicating factor with this saying is that Clement of Alexandria quoted it as being from the *Gospel According to the Hebrews* in Strom. 2.9.45 and 5.14.96 (the extant portions of *Gospel According to the Hebrews* do not contain this saying). The latter has this version of the saying:

οὐ παύσεται ὁ ζητῶν
ἕως ἂν εὕρῃ
εὑρὼν δὲ θαμβηθήσεται
θαμβηθεὶς δὲ βασιλεύσει
βασιλεύσας δὲ ἐπαναπαύσεται

The words θαμβηθήσεται and θαμβηθεὶς immediately catch our attention. Fitzmyer finds the meaning of these words in question, although it is clear that the statement is quoted by Clement of Alexandria as a way of showing that the beginning of true philosophy is wonder.[88] It has been related by Swete to the similar terms in the New Testament we have observed in Mark, and to ecstasy 'which attends the unexpected, especially when it belongs to the region of the supernatural or the Divine'. In this logion, it indicates the rush of mingled fear and joy which ought to follow the great εὕρηκα of life, the discovery of God, according to Swete.[89] Harnack interpreted the wonder in the sense of joyful surprise which he sees in Mt. 13.24.[90] Jeremias, on the other hand, says the terms such as 'marvel' and 'rest' compare to the mystery religions in thought.[91]

---

87. This is the restoration of J.A. Fitzmyer, 'The Oxyrhynchus *logoi* of Jesus and the Coptic Gospel According to Thomas', in *Essays on the Semitic Background of the New Testament* (London: Geoffrey Chapman, 1971), p. 372.
88. Fitzmyer, 'Oxyrhynchus', p. 373.
89. H.B. Swete, 'The New Oxyrhynchus Sayings', *ExpTim* 15 (1903/4), p. 491.
90. Referred to in Fitzmyer, 'Oxyrhynchus', p. 373.
91. J. Jeremias, *Unknown Sayings of Jesus* (London: SPCK, 1957), pp. 14-15. He says that the 'step-parallelism' is not in accordance with Jesus' actual words, nor is the 'artificial description' of the way to salvation. It is suggested that it is a secondary expansion of the logion, 'seek and you shall find'.

Davies discusses the logion more thoroughly, and notes that logion 2 is not randomly placed at the beginning of *Thomas*, but is the definite expression of a theme 'permeating and unifying the whole text'. This theme, seeking and finding, is frequent in *Thomas* (38, 92, 94, 107, with reflections in such sayings as 76, 80, 49, 24, 27). It is also a common feature in wisdom literature in general (Sir. 6.18; 4.11; Prov. 1.28; 8.17).[92] He claims that the idea of marveling has no overt theological overtones, although it is worth noticing that the one who is amazed does not enjoy the instantaneous awakening and immediate recognition and joy that is a prominent motif in *Thomas*.[93] 'Rest' and 'reign' are theologically loaded terms, however ('rest': Wis. 4.7; 8.13, 16; Mt. 11.29-30; 'reign': Prov. 8.15) but reigning is a metaphor for discovering wisdom and should not be taken literally,[94] while rest is a goal in *Gospel of Thomas* (50, 51, 86, 90).[95]

It would help our understanding if there were other logia in the sayings traditions which had similar remarks about marveling.[96] This is not the case, however. The only other place in *Thomas* where there is a reference to wonder is in 29, where Jesus is said to have stated that it would be amazing if it was for the spirit that the flesh came into existence, and amazing indeed if the spirit came into existence for the sake of the body. He is then amazed as to how 'this great wealth' (the spirit) has come to dwell in this poverty (the body). The only other possible statement which might help us is in *Hymn of the Pearl* 98, where the writer arises into the realm of peace, 'belonging to reverential awe'. This is different from *Thomas* 2, however, for it is awe existing in the realm of peace, not awe leading to rest. Neither is there any logion in the apocryphal or canonical gospels which can help us understand the words about amazement in *Gospel of Thomas* 2.

92. Davies, *Gospel*, pp. 36-37.
93. Davies, *Gospel*, p. 139.
94. Davies, *Gospel*, pp. 39-40.
95. J.D. Crossan, 'Aphorism in Discourse and Narrative', *Semeia* 43 (1988), p. 130. He regards *Thomas* 2 as an expansion of the 'ask, seek, knock' aphorism, as does Jeremias above.
96. Crossan, 'Aphorism', p. 131, says that *Thomas* 2 is the structural *ordo salutis* for *Dialogue of the Saviour* (seek, 9-10; seek–find, 19-20; marvel, 37; rule, 49-50; rest, 64-68), as does E. Pagels, 'Report on the Dialogue of the Saviour' in *Nag Hammadi and Gnosis* (ed. R.McL. Wilson; Leiden: Brill, 1978), pp. 66-72. Both believe that the insertion of the apocalyptic vision is to allow for the marveling. Since the only reaction of wonder in the *Dialogue* occurs after the saying (136.2) in the midst of the vision (134.24-137.3), not after the vision itself, I would question this understanding.

It is important to note that the locations where this logion appears are geographically diverse. Thomas is seen as originating in Syria by Crossan,[97] Koester[98] and Vielhauer.[99] The *Gospel According to the Hebrews*, on the other hand, has its likely origin in Egypt.[100] Since *Thomas* obviously made its way to Egypt, it would first appear that *Thomas* was simply a source for *Gospel According to the Hebrews* and subsequently Clement in Egypt. The complicating factor, however, is the recognition that the Greek and Coptic versions of *Thomas* are not of the same recension.[101] There are also form-critical reasons (shorter statements usually become longer, though this is not always the case) why it is possible that *Gospel According to the Hebrews* was a source for *Thomas*, rather than the other way around.[102] Although it is unnecessary for us to solve this literary puzzle, even if possible, we can note that in more than one group in early Christianity, amazement was seen as the first step to spiritual life. It was not negative, as in John and at times in Revelation. Another interesting possibility is that the precursor of *Thomas* was Mark 4 rather than Q.[103] Whether

---

97. Crossan, *Four*, p. 26. He claims that the Abgar legend and other Syrian traditions prove that the original provenance of *Thomas* was eastern Syria, near Edessa.

98. Koester, *Introduction*, II, pp. 150-53.

99. Vielhauer, *Geschichte*, pp. 620-21, though he would place *Thomas* in the middle of the second century.

100. Koester, *Introduction*, II, p. 224.

101. Vielhauer, *Geschichte*, p. 620, notes that the Greek version was not the direct vorlage of the Coptic due to the fact that the oldest Oxyrhynchus papyri date c.200, while *Thomas* was already in existence at that time, and there are individual differences in the versions. Fitzmyer, 'Oxyrhynchus', p. 416, also notes that the two versions are actually of different lengths. He says we do not have the same recension in two languages, but rather the variants prior to two recensions.

102. See the discussion of G. Quispel, '"The Gospel of Thomas" and 'The Gospel of the Hebrews"', *NTS* 12 (1965/66), pp. 371-82. This would mean that *Gospel According to the Hebrews* was known in Syria at an early date!

103. This is suggested by J. Robinson, 'Gnosticism and the New Testament', in *Gnosis: Festschrift für Hans Jonas* (ed. H. Bianchi *et al.*; Göttingen: Vandenhoeck & Ruprecht, 1978), pp. 125-43. Many believe that *Thomas* was dependent on a source distinct from the synoptic gospels, for example Crossan, *Four,* p. 37; R.McL. Wilson, '"Thomas" and the Growth of the Gospels', *HTR* 53 (1960), pp. 231-50 and 'Thomas and the Synoptic Gospels', *ExpTim* 72 (1960/61), pp. 36-39; H. Koester, '*Gnomai Diaphoroi*: The Origin and Nature of Diversification in the History of Early Christianity', *HTR* 61 (1968), pp. 203-47; J. Robinson, '*Logoi Sophoi*: On the *Gattung* of Q'. in *Trajectories* (eds., Koester and Robinson), pp. 114-15, 158-204.

or not this is the case, it is apparent that wonder played a wide and diverse function in early Christianity, as we will continue to see with the apocryphal gospels and acts.

Apocryphal Gospels and Acts

Research in the apocryphal gospels and acts has been lively and interesting of late.[104] Reactions of wonder can be found quite commonly in the miracle stories of the young Jesus in the gospels, and also in the miracle stories of the acts. For example, in the *Infancy Story of Thomas*, the Jews are amazed in 2.5 when they see the clay sparrows the young Jesus made fly away. Joseph is amazed in 13.2 when Jesus lengthens a beam for him. The people marvel in 17.7 when Jesus raises a dead child. In *Acts of John* 61, John's companions are amazed at the collection of bugs which obey John and do not bother him at an inn. In *Acts of Peter* 5.12, the crowd which sees a speaking dog tell Simon Magus to come out is amazed.

A clear distinction can be seen, however, in that in the apocryphal texts surveyed, the only examples of amazement at the teaching of Jesus are in *Infancy Story of Thomas* 6.1 and 19.2, and 19.2 is much the same as the probable source, Lk. 2.47.[105] The common element of amazement at Jesus' teaching

---

104. For example, D.R. MacDonald, *The Legend and the Apostle: The Battle for Paul in Story and Canon* (Philadelphia: Westminster Press, 1983); S.L. Davies, *The Revolt of the Widows: The Social World of the Apocryphal Acts* (Carbondale, IL: Southern Illinois University Press, 1980); V. Burns, 'Chastity as Autonomy: Women in the Stories of the Apocryphal Acts', *Semeia* 38 (1986), pp. 101-17; F. Bovon *et al.*, *Les Actes Apocryphes des Apôtres: christianisme et monde païen* (Geneva: Laber, 1981); and early influential works include E.v. Dobschütz, 'Der Roman in der altchristlichen Literatur', Deutsche Rundschau 111 (1902), pp. 87-106, and R. Söder, *Die apokryphen Apostelgeschichten und die romanhafte Literature der Antike* (Stuttgart: Kohlhammer, 1979 [1932]). I have examined here *The Gospel of the Nazaraeans, The Gospel of the Ebionites, The Gospel According to the Hebrews, The Gospel of the Egyptians, The Gospel of Peter, Epistula Apostolorum, The Protoevangelium of James, The Infancy Story of Thomas, The Arabic Infancy Gospel, The Gospel of Pseudo-Matthew, The Gospel of Bartholemew, Acts of Pilate, Kerygmata Petrou, Acts of John, Acts of Paul, Acts of Andrew* and *Acts of Thomas*.

105. Luke is recognized as one of the sources of *Infancy Story of Thomas*, along with oral tradition. This text likely originated in Syria, home of many Thomas traditions, and was very esteemed, as can be seen from the number of translations (it exists in Greek, Latin, Syriac, Ethopic, Georgian and Old Slavonic, with a variety of recensions. It was used by the Marcosians, according to Iranaeus (*Adv. Haer.* 1.20.1), see Vielhauer, *Geschichte*, p. 673, and Cameron, *Other*, pp. 122-24.

has greatly receded in the apocryphal gospels.

At times, the reaction follows the biblical account (*Gos. Pet.* 6.21 and 13.57 follows Mt. 27.51-54, 28.8; *Ep. Apos.* 5 follows Mk 5.33, but has the disciples rather than the woman amazed). Sometimes the apocryphal gospels add to the biblical account (*Prot. Jas.* 11.18; *Acts Pil.* 8.1)[106]. At times, great drama is added. An example of this is in the *Latin Infancy Gospel* 71, where the midwife stands stupefied and amazed, and is seized with fear at the shining light emanating from the baby Jesus. She takes him in her arms with great fear and terror because he has no weight like other infants. She also wonders greatly because he does not cry as other infants do. In *The Gospel of Bartholemew* 4.9, Bartholemew becomes frightened and falls on his face when Jesus tells him that he has asked for what he cannot see (he asked to see the devil, 'the adversary of men').

While no text has the intensity of reactions of wonder that Mark does, there are enough reactions of wonder in the apocryphal texts to tell us that 'popular' literature which was enlivened by wonderous phenomena often depicted the impression that these wonders evoked by reactions of amazement. Those producing such texts in the second and third centuries saw amazement as a natural corollary of the feats depicted. This was widespread, from Asia Minor (*Acts of Peter*, *Acts of Paul*) to Syria (much of the literature associated with Thomas) to Egypt (*Epistula Apostolorum*). Wonder was the response to divine intervention and contact by mortals with the supernatural.

Conclusion

I can note five things from the examination of various types of early Christian literature in relation to wonder. First, reactions of wonder can have either strong negative or strong positive connotations and can have both in the same text, as in Acts and Revelation. It can be the reaction of skeptical opponents of Jesus, as in John, or it can characterize a community of believers (Acts 2.43; 5.5; 11).

Secondly, a reaction of wonder can lead to faith, or it can lead to deception. The proconsul in Acts 13.12 and the Philippian jailer in Acts 16.29 believe after being struck with wonder, but Simon the magician is able to deceive people because he amazes them (Acts 8.9-11), as is the beast of the Apocalypse (Rev. 13.3, 17.8). It can be said that often one struck with amazement is on the point

---

106. *Acts of Pilate* had all four canonical gospels as sources, and had an apologetic function; see Cameron, *Other*, pp. 163-65.

of decision. It is the way in which the supernatural powers confront people, with implications that then alter one's way of life.

Thirdly, there is a strong existential and experiential aspect running throughout these texts. Our examination of Greco-Roman and early Jewish literature identified this as a common factor in the ancient world. We can assume that this is not simply a literary phenomenon, but also a vital part of the experience of people in Greco-Roman antiquity.

Fourthly, when one undergoes this supernatural experience, one enters a realm beyond the natural. Some of the terms used readily denote this: ἔκστασις, ἐξίστημι. One is 'out of one's self'. There is a movement beyond that which is normal or natural into the realm of the supernatural.

Fifthly, reactions of amazement were important enough to play an important part in many narrative texts in early Christianity, canonical and non-canonical, 'orthodox' and 'heretical' (to use later categories). It can be suggested that this shows the way in which experience with the supernatural played a vital role in early Christianity. The powers that were beyond this earth were continually confronting people, and bringing them to a point of decision. Within the various streams of early Christianity, there was a continual sense of being lifted into another realm, at least in the narrative worlds created.

All of this has implications for Mark, to which I will shortly turn. Mark may use wonder either negatively or positively, or a combination of both. Mark may be using wonder to denote confrontation by God, with a subsequent decision open to various possibilities. People may be brought into a realm beyond the natural with wonder, and it will be important to note exactly *what* is seen as being imbued with the divine. There may be a strong theological purpose for Mark's use of wonder. Wonder may be casting the divine over something not previously recognized, or questioned, as divine.

Excursus: The Numinous and Religious Experience

There have been a number of significant studies on religious experience which relate to wonder. Among these are studies by R. Otto,[107] W. James,[108] G.v.d. Leeuw,[109] J. Wach,[110] A. Maslow[111] and A. Greeley.[112] Otto is the best known, and called the essential religious

107. Otto, *Holy*.
108. W. James, *The Varieties of Religious Experience*, (New York: Random House, 1902).
109. G.v.d. Leeuw, *Religion in Essence and Manifestation* (2 vols.; New York: Harper & Row, 1963).
110. J. Wach, *Types of Religious Experience: Christian and Non-Christian* (Chicago: University of Chicago Press, 1972).
111. A.H. Maslow, *Religions, Values and Peak-Experiences* (New York: Viking Press, 1973).
112. A. Greeley, *Ecstacy: A Way of Knowing* (Englewood Cliffs, NJ: Prentice-Hall, 1974).

4. Wonder in Early Christian Literature

experience the *mysterium tremendum*. Three elements are involved in the *tremendum*: the element of awefulness (*Erschauern*), in which religious dread or awe is present; the element of 'overpoweringness' or *majestas*; and the element of 'energy' or 'urgency', which encompasses vitality, passion, movement, excitement and force.[113] One is filled with wonder and astonishment when facing the dauntingly 'other' and the incomprehensible. Otto relates this to the gospels, but it is important for our purposes to note that wonder is a necessary part of our experience of the holy.

James described the center of personal religious experience as in mystical states of consciousness, of which there are a great variety. Mystical experience is described in turn as being surrounded with truths one cannot grasp amounting to indescribable awe.[114] Van der Leeuw spoke of a primary fear, involving both avoidance and attraction, not based on any rational set of conditions, as prior to every religious experience. Dread was the 'primeval experience in religion'.[115] Wach noted that the *sensus numinis* was not a response to a phenomenon, object or person in which power manifests itself, but is the response to the power which transcends it.[116] Wonder is an aspect of Maslow's peak experiences.[117] Greeley sees ecstasy as 'a powerful spiritual force that draws me out of myself'.[118]

Wonder in Mark must clearly be related to broader religious experience. It is a part of experience with the uncanny, the Wholly Other, which brings one out of the sphere of the usual, the intelligible, the familiar and the mortal. One is submerged in an experience with the divine and struck with religious dread, 'out of one's self'. Wonder seems a *necessary* part of such encounters, as was hinted at earlier in this chapter. The places where Mark plots such encounters is where we now turn, which is bound to shed light on the whole of the gospel.

---

113. Otto, *Holy*, pp. 12-24.
114. James, *Varieties*, pp. 370, 375.
115. v.d. Leeuw, *Religion*, II, p. 465.
116. Wach, *Types*, p. 36.
117. Maslow, *Religions*, pp. 59-68.
118. Greeley, *Ecstasy*, p. 11.

Chapter 5

MARK I

In this chapter, it is my intention to examine the places in Mark where the language of wonder occurs. My methodology will be that which was discussed in the first chapter. I will examine consecutively the verses in question.

As was noted in the first chapter, in light of the summary proclamation of 1.14-15, it is commonly recognized that the overarching theme of Mark is the kingdom or rule of God.[1] It is only fitting, then, following the definition of a motif in Chapter 1, to ask if the texts in question may relate to this central theme.

Mark 1.22, 27

In the pericope of Mk 1.21-28 there are two places where wonder occurs: in v. 22 (καὶ ἐξεπλήσσοντο ἐπι τῇ διδαχῇ αὐτοῦ, ἦν γὰρ διδάσκων αὐτοὺς ὡς ἐξουσίαν ἔχων καὶ οὐχ ὡς οἱ γραμματεῖς) and v. 27 (καὶ ἐθαμβήθησαν ἅπαντες, ὥστε συζητεῖν πρὸς ἑαυτοὺς λέγοντας, Τί ἐστιν τοῦτο; διδαχὴ καινὴ κατ' ἐξουσίαν. καὶ τοῖς πνεύμασι τοῖς ἀκαθάρτοις ἐπιτάσσει, καὶ ὑπακούουσιν αὐτῷ).[2] The pericope is thus framed by the language of wonder, which emphasises the motif. In addition to this emphasis, this is a crucial pericope in the construction of Mark. After the summary proclamation of Jesus about the nearness of the kingdom of God in 1.14-15, there follows the calling of the four disciples to be 'fishers of men' in vv. 16-20. The emphasis is on the gathering of the kingdom community and the summoning of the eschatological

---

1. In addition to the studies noted in Chapter 1, see C.S. Mann, *Mark: A New Translation with Introduction and Commentary* (AB; Garden City, NY: Doubleday, 1986), pp. 140, 154; and Gnilka, *Evangelium*, I, p. 64-69.

2. For the ways in which Matthew and Luke develop and alter this and the other Markan pericopae with wonder, see Chapter 1.

fisherman.³ The pericope at hand follows, which sets forth the first miracle, presented by the author specifically as an exorcism. As such it must be seen to have paradigmatic force. This has been seen by several writers. Tagawa notes that the exorcism takes a programmatic aspect, which is why the evangelist placed it at the beginning of the gospel.⁴ Achtemeier believes that there is great emphasis on 1.21-28 in the context of the gospel: it is the first story Mark records of Jesus' public activity, it is the first miracle story, and it is carefully introduced and concluded.⁵ Ambrozic also says that the pericope ought to be viewed paradigmatically and programmatically, and notes that the context of ch. 1 is full of eschatological overtones such as Old Testament prophesies in vv. 2-3, apocalyptic imagery at the baptism, kingdom proclamation, victory over Satan in the wilderness and Jesus' teaching as an eschatological activity bringing about the kingdom of God.⁶ Thus it will reward us to pay careful attention to the way and context in which this programmatic miracle is presented, and these elements ought to give us special insight into the language of amazement in Mark, and into the content of the gospel itself.

One should especially note that there is a direct relation between this pericope and Jesus' proclamation of the kingdom of God. The pericope itself does not record the content of Jesus' teaching which amazed the listeners in 1.22. Since 1.14-15 is to be seen as a summary of Jesus' teaching, the reader is directed to understand that the thrust of the teaching (whose authority brings wonder) is the kingdom of God.⁷ The issue of how the teaching is 'new' (v. 27) can be explained by the note that the 'time has been fulfilled' in v. 14.⁸ The authority of the teaching, unlike that of the scribes (v. 22) may be seen as a result of Jesus' baptismal anointing in 1.9-11. Also, there must be a clear relationship

3. W.H. Wuellner, *The Meaning of 'Fishers of Men'* (Philadelphia: Westminster Press, 1967), pp. 226-27, 229.
4. Tagawa, *Miracles*, p. 88.
5. P. Achtemeier, '"He Taught Them Many Things": Reflections on Markan Christology', *CBQ* 42 (1980), p. 478.
6. A.M. Ambrozic, 'New Teaching with Power (Mk. 1.27)', in *Word and Spirit: Essays in Honor of David Michael Stanley on his 60th Birthday* (ed. J. Plevnik; Willowdale, Ont.: Regis College, 1975), pp. 114, 124.
7. W. Grundmann, *Das Evangelium nach Markus* (THKNT; Leipzig: Deichart, 1968), p. 42; and E. Klostermann, *Das Markusevangelium*, HNT (1971), p. 14.
8. Gnilka, *Evangelium*, I, p. 82, says that Mark portrays the 'newness' as the breaking-in of the kingdom, and Ambrozic, 'Teaching', p. 137, says the linking of 'new' and 'teaching' depicts it as an eschatological activity, since in the OT newness is the quality belonging to God's saving action (Isa. 42.9; 43.18-19; 65.17; 1 En. 45.4; 72.1; Targum Micah 7.14).

between the announcement of the nearness of the kingdom of God and the victory over Satan described in the pericope. Kee has focused on the term ἐπιτιμᾶν in v. 25, and says that the term shows that Satan's rule is being overcome. His evidence centers on the Hebrew parallel גער, which is a technical term for the commanding word by God or God's spokesmen, by which evil powers are brought into submission, and the way prepared for the establishment of God's righteous rule in the world. It is not a 'rebuke', but a wresting of power from evil forces (1 QM 14.9-15; Ps. 5.6; 68.31; 76.7; 80.16; Isa. 17.3; Zech. 3.2).[9] Kee says that in Mk 1.21-28 there can be no mistaking Mark's intention: it is in the exorcisms that Jesus' authority is supremely manifest, and through the exorcisms that the kingdom has drawn near.[10] If it is now clear that the pericope is specifically related to the kingdom, it remains to see how the wonder language ties in with this.

The word ἐξεπλήσσοντο is used in 1.22 with ἐπὶ τῇ διδαχῇ αὐτοῦ (par. Mt. 7.28 ἐξεπλήσσοντο οἱ ὄχλος ἐπὶ τῇ διδαχῇ αὐτοῦ; par. Lk. 4.32 ἐξεπλήσσοντο ἐπὶ τῇ διδαχῇ αὐτοῦ ; comp. Mk 11.18 πᾶς γὰρ ὁ ὄχλος ἐξεπλήσσοντο ἐπὶ τῇ διδαχῇ αὐτοῦ; Mt. 22.33 οἱ ὄχλοι ἐξεπλήσσοντο ἐπὶ τῇ διδαχῇ αὐτοῦ; Acts 13.12 ἐκπληττόμενος ἐπὶ τῇ διδαχῇ τοῦ κυρίου). It is not uncommon to find ἐπὶ with ἐκπλήσσομαι (Xen. *Cyr.* 1.4.27; Dio Chrysostom 29 [46] 1; Aelian *V.H.* 12.41; Barnabas 7.10, 16.10). The meaning is literally 'to be struck out of one's senses'.[11] This is the first use in Mark of διδαχῇ (1.27; 4.2; 11.18; 12.38), and it is a particular Markan emphasis to see Jesus as the διδάσκαλος (4.38; 5.35' 9.17, 38; 10.17, 20, 35; 13.14, 19, 32; 13.1; 14.14, of which only 5.35, 12.32 and 14.14 are not vocative addresses to Jesus). Also common is διδάσκω (1.21, 22; 2.13; 4.1, 2; 6.2, 6, 30, 34; 7.7; 8.31; 9.31; 10.1; 11.17; 12.14, 35; 14.49, of which only 6.30 and 7.7 do not refer to Jesus). The language of teaching has special Markan (redactional) emphasis.[12]

9. H.C. Kee, 'The Terminology of Mark's Exorcism Stories', *NTS* 14 (1967/68), p. 243.
10. Kee, 'Terminology', p. 242. E. Best, in *The Temptation and the Passion* (SNTSMS, 2; Cambridge: Cambridge University Press, 1965), p. 116, relates the fact that Jesus has won victory in his conflict with Satan to the pericope at hand in which Satan's subordinates are now also conquered.
11. W. Bauer *et al.*, *A Greek-English Lexicon of the New Testament and Other Early Christian Literature* (Chicago: University of Chicago Press, 1979), p. 244.
12. See especially E. Schweizer, 'Anmerkung zur Theologie des Markus', in *Neotestamentica et Patristica: Eine Freundesgabe Herrn Professor Dr Oscar Cullman zu seinem 60. Geburtstag überreicht* (NovTSup, 6; Leiden: Brill, 1962), pp. 35-46; Robbins, *Teacher*; Achtmeier, 'Reflections'.

1.27 uses the term ἐθαμβήθησαν, with the preceding καὶ linking it to the exorcism in verse 26. θαμβέομαι is specifically Markan in the New Testament (also 10.24, 32), and this is the only place in Mark where a form of ἅπας is used with amazement (2.12; 5.20; 6.50; 9.15; 11.18 πᾶς). The definition of θαμβέομαι given by BAGD is 'be astonished' or 'be amazed', and occurs most commonly in the transitive or passive (for example, Plut. *Brut.* 20.9 has Caesar amazed at a dream, καὶ τεθαμβημένον ἔπεσθαι; *PGM* 13.527 has amazement as a reaction to a statement of Hermes, καὶ πάντα ἐθαμβήθη; and *1 Macc.* 6.8 has the king amazed when he hears his armies are put to flight ἐθαμβήθη καὶ ἐσαλεύθη σφόδρα).[13] This is the only place in Mark or the New Testament where a clause introduced by ὥστε follows a reaction of wonder. However, Mark uses also uses a form of λέγω following amazement in 2.12 (a doxology), 4.41 (a question), 6.2 (a question), 7.37 (an acclamation) and 10.26 (a question). Thus there is a Markan pattern of amazement leading to a question or statement pointing to Jesus' identity. The reader, of course, knows the identity in light of 1.1.

Both terms are rare in the Septuagint (ἐκπλήσσομαι: Qoh. 7.16; Wis. 13.4; *2 Macc.* 7.12; *4 Macc.* 8.4; 17.16; Aq. Gen. 27.33; 1 Kgs. 4.13; 13.7; 16.4; 21.1; 28.5; Dan. 4.16; Sym. Gen. 27.33; 1 Kgs. 16.14; Ps. 47 (48) .6; Ezek. 30.9; θαμβέομαι : Judg. 9.4; 1 Kgs. 16.14; 23.26; Ps. 47 (48) .6; 115 (116) .2; Sym. Job. 8.11; Th. Ps. 52 (53) .6; Isa. 44.8; Al. 1 Ch. 21.31). Mark relates both of the terms to Jesus' teaching (wonder is related to Jesus' teaching or passion predictions eight times in the gospel). As might be expected, there are other places outside the New Testament where amazement in general is related to unusual statements or teaching (for example, five times in Philostratus's *Vit. Ap.*, and *Nig.* 35; Dion. of Hal. *Lysias* 3; *Demos.* 4.22; Plut. *Cic.* 4.5; *Alex.* 64.3; *Ca. Ma.* 31.3; Sir. 47.17 [where people marvel at the wisdom of Solomon, ἀπεθαύμασάν σε χῶραι]; Judith 11.20 [where Holofernes and his servants marveled, ἐθαύμασεν, at the wisdom of Judith] and note that 'Longinus', *On the Sublime* 1.4, speaks of genius in composition not as to persuade audiences, but to transport them out of themselves, εἰς ἔκστασιν ἄγει τὰ ὑπερφυᾶ). It is especially notable here, however, that although a miraculous exorcism has taken place, the amazement is not directed towards it, *but rather to Jesus' authoritative teaching.*

The form of the story has been seen as typical of an exorcism by Pesch: first, the encounter of the exorcist with the demon (vv. 21b, 23a); second, the defense

13. BAGD, p. 350.

of the demon (vv. 23b-24); third, the threat of the exorcist (v. 25a); fourth, the command to silence (v. 25a); fifth, the command to depart (v. 25b); sixth, the departure of the demon (v. 26); seventh, the amazement of onlookers (v. 27a); eighth, *Chorschluss* (v. 27b); ninth, notice of spreading of news (v. 28).[14] Within this schema, there is a common agreement that v.22 is redactional.[15] The reasons for this view are that v. 22 is part of the 'seam'; διδαχή is a Markan term; the verse is not essential to the pericope and that there is Markan style and vocabulary as well as Markan amazement.[16] These reasons apply to v. 21b as well as v. 22. The redactional or traditional nature of the language of amazement in v. 27 is less clear, however.

Those who would see 1.27a as part of the tradition[17] in general would base their conclusion on the perception that amazement is supposedly a stylistic element at the conclusion of a miracle or exorcism.[18] Yet in light of my examination of the motif of wonder in Greco-Roman and early Jewish literature, the 'stylistic' use of amazement at the end of these stories can be called into question. I have noted that it occurs very infrequently in this way in the literature outside the New Testament. Since this is the case, the gospel of Mark, as the first gospel written, may be responsible to a large degree for developing the 'form' one sees in the other gospels and Acts, and in the apocryphyal Christian literature. Thus one would hesitate to uncritically ascribe 1.27a to the tradition

14. Pesch, *Markusevangelium*, I, p. 119.
15. L. Schenke, *Die Wundererzählungen des Markusevangeliums* (Stuttgart: Katholisches Bibelwerk, 1974), pp. 96-97; D.-A. Koch, *Die Bedeutung der Wundererzählungen für die Christologie des Markusevangeliums* (ZNW 42; Berlin: de Gruyter, (1968), p. 43; K. Kertelge, *Die Wunder Jesu im Markus-Evangelium* (Munich: Kösel, 1970), p. 50; Ambrozic, 'Teaching', p. 129; Pesch, *Markusevangelium*, I, p. 117; B.D. Chilton, 'Exorcism and History: Mark 1.21-28' (*Gospel Perspectives*, VI; ed. D. Wenham and C. Blomberg; Sheffield: JSOT Press, 1986), p. 254; R.H. Stein, 'The Redaktionsgeschichtliche Investigation of a Markan Seam (Mk 1.21ff)', *ZNW* 61 (1970), p. 89; P. Guillemette, 'Un enseignment nouveau, plein d'autorité', *NovT* 22 (1980), p. 226; Gnilka, *Evangelium*, I, p. 72; Pryke, *Redactional Style*, p. 10.
16. Stein, 'Investigation', p. 89.
17. Kertelge, *Wunder*, p. 52; Schenke, *Wundererzählungen*, p. 99, n. 325; Pesch, *Markusevangelium*, I, p. 119; Guillemette, 'Einseignment', p. 232; and Klostermann, *Markusevangelium*, p. 14, are examples.
18. Klostermann, *Markusevangelium*, p. 17, says that 1.27 is a stylistic expression of amazement, and the scheme devised by Pesch demonstrates his understanding of this, p. 119 and also p. 124, where the admiration motif is called a typical closing motif in Christian miracle stories.

on the basis of a supposed pre-existing miracle-exorcism form. Also, the amazement in v. 27 is not directed to the exorcism as such, but to the 'new teaching with authority'.

Some have seen v. 27a as redactional, but have not always explained their reasoning. Schweizer says that in vv. 22 and 27-28. Mark is giving the message that he wants to convey, namely that the miracle is evidence of the authority of Jesus' teaching.[19] Tagawa says that the application of the amazement to Jesus' teaching (without indicating the content) and the repetitive use of amazement is surely intentional, and shows both 1.22 and 27 to be redactional.[20] Crossan is unambiguous when he says that the amazement in 1.27 is redactional since in the traditional form of the miracle story it is expected as a reaction to the miracle, but here it is directed to the 'new teaching with authority', stressing Jesus as teacher, and because the par. Lk. 4.36 polishes the verse.[21] I would agree with Schweizer, Tagawa and Crossan, but want to make the reasoning clearer.

First of all, there is the use of the rare Markan word, θαμβέομαι,[22] and the fact that only here is it joined with ἅπαντες. Secondly, there is the factor already mentioned of the relation of the amazement to teaching in 27b. This is highly unusual in light of the narration that an exorcism took place,[23] and it is difficult to avoid the conclusion that διδαχὴ καινὴ κατ' ἐξουσίαν picks up ἐπὶ τῇ διδαχῇ αὐτοῦ ... ὡς ἐξουσίαν ἔχων in v. 22. If these are by the same hand, should not the language of amazement also be from this hand in both verses? Thirdly, v. 27a is part of the seam of v. 27-28, and the story could have ended at v. 26 in the tradition and made good sense.[24] Fourthly, once the criterion of amazement in the form of a miracle story is dropped, there is no reason left for regarding it as traditional.

19. Schweizer, *Good News*, p. 50.
20. Tagawa, *Miracles*, pp. 89, 92.
21. Crossan, 'Relatives', p. 100.
22. R. Stein, 'The Proper Methodology for Ascertaining a Markan Redaction History', *NovT* 13 (1971), p. 197, lists θαμβέομαι as a Markan term, and Gnilka, *Evangelium*, I, p. 82, notes that this is the only place in the NT where it occurs in a miracle story.
23. Best, *Temptation*, p. 68, says that v. 27 takes up v. 22, so if v. 22 is not part of the traditional material, then the same should be said of v. 27. He would evidently prefer, however, to see vv. 21b-22 as a fragment of traditional material which Mark has introduced at this point as a preliminary to v. 27. In regards to the teaching, Stein, 'Investigation', pp. 86, 89, sees the phrase 'new teaching with authority' in v. 27b as a redactional emphasis on Jesus as teacher, but wants to leave v. 27a as traditional.
24. I agree here with D. Lührmann, *Das Markusevangelium* (HNT; Tübingen: Mohr, 1987), p. 49, who sees the seams of vv. 21b-22 and 27-28 as redactional.

The thought of the pericope can be summed up as follows. Mark is describing the effects of the breaking-in of the kingdom through the victory over the forces of evil. The point is made redactionally that the miracle of Jesus must be seen only in light of the teaching.[25] The authority of the teaching is present in the miracle. This in turn directs the reader back to 1.14-15 to find out the content of that teaching and source of the authority. In this process, Jesus' teaching is of itself portrayed by Mark as a 'divine eschatological irruption into the world'.[26] It is then this eschatological breaking-in of the kingdom, manifested in authoritative teaching and subsequent exorcism, which is the cause of wonder, and this again is a redactional point of Mark. This coheres with the Jewish expectation of wonder in the last days which has been noted earlier in Chapter 3.

A question which has been raised on the basis of this pericope is whether reactions of wonder in Mark imply negative connotations or insufficient understanding on the part of those involved. Lohmeyer, for example, says that the effect of the *chorschluss* in 1.27 is not understanding and belief, but rather dull amazement with a question.[27] Chilton sees the reaction in 1.27 as necessary, but insufficient, and not a guarantee that one has correctly understood.[28] Also, Ambrozic believes that here amazement is imperfect as a response, for although it is positive to a degree, it is also aligned with misunderstanding.[29] Yet what indication is there in the pericope itself that these reactions of wonder at the teaching of Jesus indicate a lack or understanding, or a lack of faith? Is not the question of 1.27 natural since those in the synagogue do not have the information of 1.1, 9-11 as to the identity of Jesus? It is probably better at this point to agree with Cranfield that the amazement in 1.27 *may* be the first step towards either faith or stumbling,[30] but only as one follows the progress of the motif throughout the gospel will one be able to make a more complete determination.

---

25. E. Schweizer, 'Mark's Contribution to the Question of the Historical Jesus', *NTS* 10 (1963/64), p. 423, says that the teaching of Jesus in authority is even more important for Mark than his miracles.

26. Ambrozic, 'Teaching', p. 137. Achtemeier, 'Reflections', p. 478, says that by virtue of v. 27 Mark wants the reader to be clear that the power inherent in Jesus' teaching is the same power that enabled him to overcome demonic forces.

27. Lohmeyer, *Evangelium*, p. 35.

28. Chilton, 'Exorcism', p. 267, n. 18.

29. Ambrozic, 'Teaching', pp. 130-31.

30. C.E.B. Cranfield, *The Gospel According to St. Mark* (CGTC; Cambridge: Cambridge University Press, 1979), p. 73.

One can clearly see here, however, a link between eschatological power in Jesus' teaching and reactions of amazement as part of the redactional shaping of the tradition in the programmatic miracle of the second gospel.

Mark 2.12

The next reaction of wonder in Mark is in 2.12: καὶ ἠγέρθη καὶ εὐθὺς ἄρας τὸν κράβαττον ἐξῆλθεν ἔμπροσθεν πάντων, ὥστε ἐξίστασθαι πάντας καὶ δοξάζειν τὸν θεὸν λέγοντας ὅτι οὕτως οὐδέποτε εἴδομεν. 2.1-12 contains the account of a healing of a lame man and the pericope is close related to the Markan context of ch.1. The pericope centers on the ἐξουσία of Jesus to forgive sins in 2.10, and the word draws us back to 1.22 and 27 and the words, ἦν γὰρ διδάσκων αὐτοὺς ὡς ἐξουσίαν ἔχων...and διδαχὴ καινὴ κατ' ἐξουσίαν. Kertelge has even stated that Mark clearly has the thought of 1.22, 27 in mind in the healing of the lame man.[31] The fact that 1.22 and 27 both have reactions of wonder, as does this pericope, and that in both pericopae teaching situations give rise to miracles, causes us to probe further relations with Mark 1.

Other textual connections include the remark that Jesus sees τὴν πίστιν of the men carrying the lame man, which draws one back to the summons to repentance and faith at the advent of the kingdom in 1.15, the time element in the acclamation οὕτως οὐδέποτε εἴδομεν of 2.12 which draws one back to the 'fulfilled time' of 1.14 and the 'new teaching' of 1.27, and the note that Jesus forgives the sins of the lame man in 2.5 connects with the forgiveness preached by John in 1.4-5. The opposition of τινὲς τῶν γραμματέων in v. 6 is striking in light of the notion that we have already been told, that Jesus taught with authority: οὐχ ὡς οἱ γραμματεῖς, in 1.22. The question of 2.7, τί οὗτος οὕτως λαλεῖ, is reminiscent of 1.27, τί ἐστιν τοῦτο. The combination of these elements, and connections to 1.21-28 leads one to see this pericope as related also to the breaking-in of the kingdom of God in Jesus' authority to forgive and heal. In the Markan framework, the ἐξουσία of Jesus is a sign of the beginning of the kingdom of God.[32] Goppelt notes that since in the Old Testament God forgave (2 Sam. 12.13, Isa. 44.22), this story leads to the conclusion that in the person of Jesus it was God who was becoming involved with people and now establishing the eschatological rule.[33] It is perhaps appropriate to note again here the

---

31. Kertelge, *Wunder*, p. 82.
32. Gnilka, *Evangelium*, I, p. 102.
33. L. Goppelt, *Theology of the New Testament* (2 vols.; Grand Rapids: Eerdmans,

expectation of Hos. 3.5: καὶ ἐκστήσονται ἐπὶ τῷ καὶ ἐπὶ τοῖς ἀγαθοῖς αὐτοῦ ἐπ' ἐσχάτων τῶν ἡμερῶν.

One meets here the verb ἐξίστημι, which only occurs as a reaction only for miracles in Mark (5.42; 6.51; and also 3.21 where it is not a reaction), and only here in the infinitive. The literal meaning is to 'drive out of one's senses'.[34] The combination of a form of πᾶς with ἐξίστημι occurs in Mt. 12.33 (ἐξίσταντο πάντες οἱ ὄχλοι); Lk. 2.47 (ἐξίσταντο δὲ πάντες οἱ ἀκούοντες αὐτοῦ); Acts 2.7 (ἐξίσταντο δὲ πάντες καὶ διηπόρουν); and Acts 9.21 (ἐξίσταντο δὲ πάντες οἱ ἀκούοντες); but not elsewhere in Mark. A clause with ὥστε with 'amazement' occurs also in Mk 15.5 par. Mt. 27.14, and in Mt. 13.54 and 15.31. This is the only place in Mark where a doxology is joined with a reaction of amazement, and in fact the only place in the gospel where a doxology occurs (however note 7.37, an acclamation rather than a doxology).

The story follows the scheme of a miracle story, according to Pesch, with the following elements: first, the appearance of the miracle worker (1.2); second, an encounter with a sick person (3); third, a difficulty to be overcome (4); fourth, healing (11); fifth, the establishment of healing (12a); sixth, a demonstration of healing (12a); seventh, wonder (12b); eighth, *Chorschluss* (12b).[35] As can be seen with this scheme, vv. 5b-10 appear superfluous. Thus many have seen vv. 5b-10 as a separate piece of tradition or an addition.[36] This view relies on tensions in the account, such as a break in the narrative in 10b; the expression λέγει τῷ παραλυτικῷ repeated in vv. 5 and 10b; the repetition of the expression in vv. 9 and 11: Ἔγειρε καὶ ἆρον τὸν κράβαττόν σου; the idea that 'all' in v. 12 supposedly cannot refer also to the scribes introduced in v. 6; and

1981), I, p. 132; W. Lane, *The Gospel of Mark* (NICNT; Grand Rapids: Eerdmans, 1979), p. 99, also notes this connection, and points out that the announcement and presentation of radical healing to a man in his entire person was a sign of the kingdom of God drawing near (Isa. 35.6; Jer. 31.8).

34. BAGD, p. 276.
35. Pesch, *Markusevangelium*, I, pp. 152-53.
36. J. Gnilka, 'Das Elend vor dem Menschensohn', in *Jesus und der Menschensohn: Für Anton Vögtle* (ed. R. Pesch and R. Schnackenburg; Freiburg: Herder, 1975), p. 200; Gnilka, *Evangelium*, I, p. 96; Bultmann, *History*, pp. 14-16; Taylor, *Gospel*, pp. 191-92; D.J. Doughty, 'The Authority of the Son of Man (Mk. 2.1-3.6)', *ZNW* 74 (1983), p. 162; M.d. Tillesse, *Le secret messianique dans l'Evangile de Marc* (Paris: Cerf, 1968), pp. 116-17; Koch, *Bedeutung*, pp. 46-47; Kertelge, *Wunder*, p. 77; Schweizer, *Good News*, p. 60; Kuhn, *Ältere*, p. 53; Lohmeyer, *Das Evangelium*, p. 50; Grundmann, *Evangelium*, p. 54; Pesch, *Markusevangelium*, I, p.151.

the supposition that v. 12 in its totality refers to the healing, but not to the controversy. One should also add that the accusation of blasphemy in v. 7 seems to be odd in a unified pericope, since nothing said in v. 5 is strictly speaking blasphemous. The transition to v. 6 is therefore rough, since there is no self-evident reason why the scribes should be introduced at this point. Other reasons given include the supposed form of a miracle story in vv. 3-5 and 11-12; the fact that τὴν πίστιν αὐτῶν in v. 5a disappears in vv. 6-10; 'Son of Man' is deemed a later title and could well be used generically in v. 10 (meaning 'a human'); the supposed blasphemy of v. 7 was not brought up at Jesus' trial; and a supposed apologetic interest in legitimating the practice of the church's forgiving sins is served by vv. 5b-10.

A strong criticism of such a division in the pericope has been produced by H. Simonsen. He says that unexpected developments in a pericope must not be seen as having as their only explanation differing pieces of tradition, and that one must not overestimate the needs of the early community in the formation of pericopae (that is, there is a possibility that the community formed vv. 5b-10 as a basis for granting forgiveness of sins).[37] Daube also argues against a dissection of the pericope on the basis of a common three-part scheme (revolutionary action, protest, silencing of remonstrants).[38] Cranfield contents for a unity, claiming that those who divide the pericope into sources fail to see the real and close connection between the healing of sickness and the forgiveness of sins.[39] Maisch gives 24 reasons for the unity of the passage.[40] I would also

---

37. H. Simonsen, 'Zur Frage der Grundlegenden Problematik in form-und redactionsgeschichtlicher Evangeliensforschung', *ST* 26 (1972), pp. 1-23, esp. p. 6. Interestingly enough, the view Simonsen argues against overestimating would fit quite well with the notion that 'son of man' in v. 10 can refer to a 'human' and need not always be a title, since the notion that the community forgives sins would find more continuity with 'a human' who forgave sins than it could with an exalted 'Son of Man' figure who acts by virtue of his authority. At any rate, the inclusion of vv. 5b-10 in a unified pericope certainly does not negate the possibility that it pointed to the community practice of forgiving sins. Such a possibility fits a unified pericope as well as the possibility that vv. 5b-10 are a separate piece of tradition.

38. D. Daube, *The New Testament and Rabbinic Judaism* (London: Athlone Press, 1956), pp. 172-74.

39. Cranfield, *Gospel*, p. 96. Also arguing for a unity are J. Dewey, 'The Literary Structure of the Controversy Stories of Mk. 2.1-3.6', *JBL* 92 (1973), pp. 397-401; and R.T. Mead, 'The Healing of the Paralytic: A Unit?', *JBL* 80 (1961), pp. 350-52, but Dewey and Mead argue on the basis of a creation of the entire pericope. Mead agrees with the pattern Daube has given.

hesitate to separate vv. 5b-10 for the reasons given, and also since Old Testament eschatological expectation included both forgiveness of sins (Isa. 43.25, 44.22)[41] and healing (Isa. 35.5-6), there is no reason why they could not have been joined in this pericope or in the ministry of the historical Jesus in the context of the kingdom proclamation. Also, we do know of a real connection between sickness and sin in Jewish deuteronomistic thought (2 Kgs. 6.20-27; 15.1-5; 2 Chron. 7.14; Ps. 103.3; Isa. 19.22; 38.17; 57.18-19; Jn 9.2; Jas. 5.15), which need not have been joined only at the level of composition. Miracle stories do not always have an exact, 'pure' form, but there is almost unlimited variability of the compositional elements.[42] 'Son of Man' need not be a later title for Jesus,[43] and there seems to be a true continuity between v. 9 and v. 11.

As with 1.27, there is a tendency of some to see 2.12 as traditional solely because it is supposedly stylistic at the end of the miracle story.[44] Yet there are reasons for seeing Markan redaction here: ὥστε with the infinitive has been identified as a recurring feature of the gospel having the highest probability of

40. I. Maisch, *Die Heilung des Gelähmten: Eine exegetisch traditions-geschichtliche Untersuchung zu Mk. 2.1-12* (SBS 52; Stuttgart: Katholisches Bibelwerk, 1971), pp. 22-24. She notes, for example, that all three synoptics have the story without division, and a controversy story (vv. 5b-10) cannot be without an introduction; and that the table fellowship of Jesus with sinners also understands forgiveness as a constituent part of Jesus' ministry. Also, since thought in Palestine linked sin and sickness, a solution to one of these problems must include the other.

41. This is not limited in the OT or early Jewish tradition to a divinely anointed 'Son of Man' figure.

42. See H.D. Betz, 'The Early Christian Miracle Stories: Some Observations on the Form-Critical Problem', in *Semeia* 11 (1978), p. 71.

43. G. Vermes, *Jesus*, pp. 188-89. This can fit either a unified pericope or two roughly fitted pieces of tradition. Some support for this reading of Mark can be found in the way Matthew read the pericope, for in Mt. 9.1-7, Matthew's reading of Mark concludes, after the reaction of wonder in v. 8a, καὶ ἐδόξασαν τὸν θεὸν τὸν δόντα ἐξουσίαν τοιαύτην τοῖς ἀνθρώποις.

44. Pesch, *Markusevangelium*, I, p. 157; Gnilka, *Evangelium*, I, pp. 101-102; Koch, *Bedeutung*, pp. 46-47; Kertelge, *Wunder*, p. 81; Doughty, 'Authority', p. 162. The view of Klostermann, *Markusevangelium*, p. 25, when he describes v. 12a as having a typical ending, is common to all. Maisch, *Heilung*, pp. 62-64, claims to find three parallel stories with the healing of someone lame and a reaction of wonder: Cicero, *De div.*, 1.26.55; Livy, 2.36 and Plutarch, *Cor.*, 24.3. An examination of these stories, however, shows no wonder in the Cicero story, and that the story of Livy is the same as that of Plutarch. Titus Latinus is palsied when he fails to tell the senate a dream which Jupiter had revealed to him, and has his strength return when he tells the dream. The senate is amazed.

being redactional,[45] the singular acclamation which follows the wonder, and the structural similarities with 1.27 (καὶ ἐθαμβήθησαν...ὥστε λέγοντας and καὶ ἠγέρθη...ὥστε...λέγοντας).[46] Also, 2.12 in the text as it stands adds an eschatological and christological ('We have never seen anything like this') coloring[47] to the passage *as a whole*. The onlookers are amazed at *both* the healing and the forgiveness.[48] Further, the onlookers are all (πάντας) amazed, and since this interesting usage occurs (in contrast to the possible ὁ ὄχλος), it may well be that πάντας includes even the scribes![49] Mark does not limit amazement to those sympathetic to Jesus in the rest of the gospel,[50] though the obvious problem with this is that the scribes, given their role later in the gospel would seem to be included in the latter part of v. 12 (glorifying God as a result of the miracle of Jesus) only with difficulty. Perhaps it is simple best to say that πάντας is ambiguous here. For the reasons given above, although it is fair to say that v. 12 may possibly have come from the tradition,[51] it also seems that there is Markan coloring and possible rewriting in the verse.

Part of the curiosity of reactions of wonder in Mark is that there are such differences of opinion as to whether they should be seen as positive or negative. Here, for example, Mead sees the crowd in 2.12 as unbelievers, and claims that they overlook the forgiveness and marvel at the healing,[52] while Kertelge believes that the statement that glory was given to God indicates that the

---

45. Peabody, *Composer*, pp. 45, 163, and Pryke, *Redactional Style*, p. 115; both see 2.12 as redactional for this reason.

46. J. Kiilunen, *Die Vollmacht im Widerstreit: Untersuchungen zum Werdegang von Mk. 2.1-3.6* (Helsinki: Suomalainen Tiedeakatemia, 1985), p. 93. Kiilunen says that while vv. 11-12 are usually reckoned as part of the tradition, which can seem correct if the verses are taken to be the end of a pericope, this is difficult to sustain in the context of Mark. He feels that vv. 11-12 are redactional mission propaganda, and that v. 12bc makes sense in light of the entire pericope as the reaction to the authority of Jesus in healing and the forgiveness of sins. The fact that the theme of the novelty and authority of Jesus is Markan points against this coming from the *vorlage*. See pp. 92, 100-101.

47. Tillesse, *Secret*, pp. 120-21.

48. A. Pohl, *Das Evangelium des Markus* (Wuppertaler Studien Bibel, Ergänzungsband; Wuppertal: R. Broachaus, 1986), p. 124.

49. The passage is read this way by Bryan, *Preface*, p. 90.

50. It is an interesting feature of Mark that even opponents of Jesus can be amazed, as 12.17 and 15.5 show.

51. E. Best, *Disciples and Discipleship: Studies in the Gospel According to Mark* (Edinburgh: T & T Clark, 1986), p. 118.

52. Mead, 'Healing', pp. 353-54.

onlookers understand that the uncommon act which they have witnessed goes back to God.⁵³ Against these antitheses it is perhaps better to say that there is neither approval nor disapproval of the amazement in 2.12. Although there is approval by the narrator and Jesus at the faith of those who brought the paralytic, and disapproval of the skepticism of the scribes, the amazement is related without specific approval or disapproval.⁵⁴

Here, then, a pericope relates the eschatological authority of Jesus with many similar features of the previous pericope. The onlookers, perhaps even opponents, are struck 'out of themselves' at the new actions of forgiveness (which take place apart from the temple cultus) and healing. Mark has again likely coloured the reaction of wonder in a way to emphasize the novelty and power which God (δοξάζειν τὸν θεὸν) has activated in the ministry of Jesus.

Mark 3.21

One of the most puzzling and disputed verses in Mark is 3.21: καὶ ἀκούσαντες οἱ παρ' αὐτοῦ ἐξῆλθον κρατῆσαι αὐτόν, ἔλεγον γὰρ ὅτι ἐξέστη.⁵⁵ Perhaps the scandalous nature of the verse is seen in the development that the other synoptics did not use it. Here we have the surprising switch that the language of wonder describes not the crowds, but (probably) Jesus, who is said to be mad. This is the traditional view of the verse, which follows the Vulgate *in furorem uersus est*. Another view on the verse has also been voiced lately, that the subject of ἐξέστη is not Jesus, but the crowd.⁵⁶ The interpretation of the verse depends on the meaning and subject of ἐξέστη (is it Jesus or the crowd?), the identity of οἱ παρ' αὐτοῦ (disciples, family or friends of Jesus?), the subject of ἔλεγον in v. 21 (is it the same as the οἱ παρ' αὐτοῦ or someone else?), and the

53. Kertelge, *Wunder*, p. 81.
54. Petersen, 'Point', p. 100.
55. There are variant textual readings in W, which attributes the remarks about madness to the 'scribes and others around him', changing ἐξέστη to ἐξήρτηνται αὐτούς. θ makes the verb transitive, and D has ἐξέσταται αὐτούς, but the textual evidence here is slight and explainable as alterations.
56. H. Wansbrough, 'Mark 3.21: Was Jesus Out of His Mind?', *NTS* 18 (1972), pp. 233-35; D. Wenham, 'The Meaning of Mark 3.21', *NTS* 21 (1975), pp. 295-300, following G. Hartmann, 'Mk. 3.20f', *BZ* 11 (1913), pp. 249-79; J.E. Steinmueller, 'Jesus and the οἱ παρ' αὐτοῦ', *CBQ* 4 (1942), pp. 355-59; and H.-H. Schroeder, *Eltern und Kinder in der Verkündigung Jesu*, *TF* 53 (1972). A further possibility has been suggested by Roth, *Hebrew*, pp. 42-44, who relates 3.21 to the 'madness' of Jehu in 2 Kgs. 9.20, but this interesting possibility suffers from locating the meaning of the verse outside of the text itself.

meaning of κρατῆσαι αὐτόν (to 'seize' or to 'calm down' Jesus or the crowd?). The alternative suggestion presents the possibility that those around Jesus went to calm (κρατῆσαι) the crowd down (αὐτόν in this reading), since the crowd was 'awe-struck', taking ὁ ὄχλος in v. 20, the last masculine noun, as the referent of αὐτόν.

There is, however, a meaning for the word ἐξίστημι other than that which was seen in 2.12. It can also mean to be out of one's senses, or to lose one's mind.[57] The thought is similar in both cases: to be out of one's sense with amazement or out of one's senses with madness. In 2 Cor. 5.13, it is the opposite of σωφρονέω: εἴτε ἐξέστημεν...εἴτε σωφρονοῦμεν. A good example of this is in Josephus Ant. 10.114, when Jeremiah is ridiculed by the leaders and the ungodly as if he were out of his mind: οἱ δὲ ἡγεμόνες καὶ οἱ ἀσεβεῖς ὡς ἐξεστηκότα τῶν φρενῶν αὐτοῦ οὕτως ἐξεφαύλιζον. It is often used with μαίνομαι.[58] One sees this, for example, in Arist. Hist. An. 622.12: ἐξίσταται καὶ μαίνεται (a scent drives a hippopotamus out of his mind and mad; see Euripides, Bacc. 850; Testament of Job, 39.13). A clear link between the two terms is in Aristotle's Nic. Eth. 7.7.1149b35: ἐξέστηκε τῆς φύσεως ὥσπερ οἱ μαινόμενοι τῶν ἀνθρώπων. A clue to the meaning of ἐξίστημι in the context of Mark is given by the parallel accusation in v. 22: ἔλεγον ὅτι Βεελζεβοὺλ ἔχει. The use of ἔλεγον...ὅτι (v. 21) and ἔλεγον ὅτι (v. 22) points to a parallel construction and leads us to ask what similarities there might be in the other parts of the parallel, between ἐξέστη and Βεελζεβοὺλ ἔχει. I would note that the ideas of being possessed by a spirit and being out of one's senses go together. In Herodotus 4.79, for example, there is the idea of being taken hold of by a spirit and being mad (the Scythian king, Scylas). This idea is also in Eurip. Bacc. 291-310; 1 Cor. 14.23 has those coming into the assembly seeing the spirit-possessed speaker in tongues and Paul asks οὐκ ἐροῦσιν ὅτι μαίνεσθε. One can also see this thought in the accusation of Jn 10.20: ἔλεγον δὲ πολλοὶ ἐξ αὐτῶν, Δαιμόνιον ἔχει καὶ μαίνεται. Here is a concept very similar to the accusations of Mk 3.21-22, namely of being mad and being possessed by a spirit. In fact it is clear that one of the overriding issues in 3.7-30 is the activity of spirits. In 3.11-12, demons recognize Jesus as the Son of God. In 3.15, authority to cast out demons is stated as part of the purpose for the

---

57. BAGD, p. 276. This would be the fourth type of ἔκστασις listed by Philo in *Who is the Heir?* 249-52, 257-60. See Chapter 3 above on Philo.

58. Pohl, *Evangelium*, p. 164, says that μαίνομαι has the same sense as ἐξίστημι when used in this way.

selection of the twelve. In 3.23-20, the discussion revolves around the thought that Jesus does not cast out demons by Beelzebul because Satan does not cast himself out, but is bound and his goods plundered. To charge Jesus with possession by an unclean spirit is to blaspheme the Holy Spirit who truly indwells in Jesus (1.10). Thus I would suggest that the similarities of thought of ἐξίστημι and μαίνομαι, both of which are the understood result of spirit-possession, would argue here for the meaning of ἐξέστη as 'he is out of his senses'.

The possible group designated by οἱ παρ' αὐτοῦ may be either the disciples, friends or family of Jesus. Mark uses παρά with the genitive in 5.26 (τὰ παρ' αὐτῆς πάντα) with the sense of 'her belongings'. However, it is also used in 14.43 in the sense of 'with' (παρὰ τῶν ἀρχιερέων), and in 8.11 and 12.2, 11, with the sense of 'from'. Perhaps the simplest way to identify the οἱ παρ' αὐτοῦ is to relate it to those mentioned in v. 31, the family of Jesus. There seems to be a sequence in 3.21: ἐξῆλθον κρατῆσαι...and 3.31: ἔρχεται ἡ μήτηρ αὐτοῦ καὶ οἱ ἀδελφοὶ ἔξω στήκοντες ἀπέστειλαν...καλοῦντες αὐτόν. Also, οἱ παρά has the meaning of parents and other relatives in Susanna 33; *1 Macc.* 9.44, 58; Prov. 31.21; see Josephus *Ant.* 1.10.5.[59] The disciples, on the other hand, are described in 4.10 as οἱ παρ' αὐτόν. They would be more likely to 'see' an unruly crowd than to 'hear' of one. At any rate, there is no precedent for the disciples calming a crowd. The understanding of οἱ παρ' αὐτοῦ as the relatives of Jesus also gives a vivid contrast to the preceding pericope of the choosing of the twelve in 3.13-19 while Jesus' own family thinks him to be mad.

The subject of ἔλεγον is easier to clarify now, and I would agree with Cranfield that the natural assumption would be that οἱ παρ' αὐτοῦ is the subject of ἔλεγον. A plural verb need not be seen as indefinite when there is a plural subject in the immediate context.[60] One is thus drawn to the interpretation that the family of Jesus goes out to restrain him because they think he is mad.

This view has not been universally accepted. H. Wansbrough, as mentioned above, says that the understood subject of ἔλεγον is not Jesus but the crowd, ὁ ὄχλος. His reasoning is that ὁ ὄχλος is that the most recently mentioned masculine noun, ἐξίστημι, is used in the gospels only of the reaction of awe and

---

59. F. Blass and A. Debrunner, *A Greek Grammar of the New Testament and Other Early Christian Literature* (trans. and rev., R. Funk; Chicago: University of Chicago Press, 1961 [1896]), p. 124, and Taylor, *Gospel*, p. 236.

60. Cranfield, *Gospel*, pp. 133-34.

wonder to Jesus, never of madness, and οἱ παρ' αὐτοῦ refers to those with Jesus (not the family), who go out to restrain the crowd.[61] Wenham identifies the difficulties of Wansbrough's view: it is odd to make ἀκούσαντες refer to the disciples since they were with Jesus; κρατῆσαι does not mean 'to calm down'; αὐτοῦ with different meanings is rough, and ἔλεγον loses its parallelism; and there is no Markan parallel where a singular pronoun refers to a collective noun.[62] Wenham also seeks to strengthen the case of Wansbrough by the following three arguments. 3.31 is too far removed from the context to define οἱ παρ' αὐτοῦ. The uncontrolled crowd corresponds to the depiction in 3.8-9, 4.1-2. The parallels in Mt. 12.23 and Lk. 11.14-15 precede the Beelzebul accusation with a reference to the crowd's astonishment. Wenham seems to think that Mark worked from a Q tradition, but is hesitant whether this view outweighs the arguments against it.[63]

I would simply respond that the greatest problem with the view of Wansbrough, Wenham and others is over-ingenuity. The parallel concepts of madness and spirit-possession are overlooked by them, and the meaning of ἐξίστημι should not be determined by statistics of usage, but by the immediate context. Mark 3.31 is not far from the immediate context, and indeed is left hanging without a reason why the relatives come to Jesus if οἱ παρ' αὐτοῦ does not refer to the family. Also, the possibility that Matthew and Luke are polishing Mark is greater than the other way around (or the possibility of Mark using Q, though that can be left open). Best points out that the traditional view also fits Mark's sandwich style, and was understood in some areas of the church, since D and W amend it.[64]

There is clear evidence of Markan redaction in 3.21. One finds here the avoidance of direct speech, a parenthetical clause, a γάρ explanatory clause,[65] and the Markan terms ἀκούσαντες, οἱ παρ' αὐτο, κρατῆσαι, and ἐξέστη[66] and the editorial 'sandwich style.'[67]

It remains now to ask how the accusation that Jesus was mad fits into the context of the gospel as a whole, and why the language of wonder was used. I would observe that there is a clear connection between the passage at hand and

61. Wansbrough, 'Mark', pp. 233-35.
62. Wenham, 'Meaning', pp. 295-96.
63. Wenham, 'Meaning', pp. 296-300.
64. Best, *Disciples*, pp. 55-56.
65. Pryke, *Redactional Style*, pp. 73-74, 126-34, 155.
66. Crossan, 'Relatives', pp. 83-84.

the kingdom announcement in 1.14-15. The discussion here speaks of a βασιλεία in v. 24, which in the context would be Satan's. Satan is mentioned here specifically in 3.23, 26, for the first time since 1.13: πειραζόμενος ὑπὸ τοῦ Σατανᾶ. 3.26 (τέλος ἔχει) may be a result of the fulfilled time of 1.15. The mention of the Spirit by whom Jesus casts out demons (since to attribute the activity to Beelzebub is to blaspheme the Holy Spirit) in 3.29 draws us back to the baptism in 1.10. The parallel Mt. 12.28 makes clear the connections between exorcisms, the Spirit of God, and the kingdom of God, and Matthew may have read Mark that way. As in ch. 1, the Spirit and the coming of the kingdom overthrow the power of evil. Jesus, the anointed one whom God uses to vanquish Satan, is thought mad as a 'man of spirit'. It may be that the aura of 'otherness' (the numinous presence felt by those around charismatic figures) around Jesus could explain the reaction of Jesus' family in 3.21.[68] The wonder terminology is used here as an accusation of madness which comes upon Jesus as the one in whom God has placed the Holy Spirit and by whom the kingdom of Satan is overthrown because 'the time is fulfilled' and the reign of Satan is at an end, τέλος ἔχει. Once again, then, our motif is related to the breaking-in of the kingdom, here as an accusation of its Spirit-anointed messenger.

Mark 4.41

The next occurrence of the motif of wonder is in 4.41: καὶ ἐφοβήθησαν φόβον μέγαν, καὶ ἔλεγον πρὸς ἀλλήλους, Τίς ἄρα οὗτός ἐστιν ὅτι καὶ ὁ ἄνεμος καὶ ἡ θάλασσα ὑπακούει αὐτῷ. The pericope is about the calming of a storm, and has again several textual connections with 1.12-28. The disciples address Jesus with the redactional Διδάσκαλε in v. 38 (compare Mt. 8.25: κύριε; Lk. 8.24: ἐπιστάτα, ἐπιστάτα). One is again drawn back to the authority of Jesus the teacher as in 1.27. Jesus 'rebukes' the wind, ἐπετίμησεν, which reminds one of the use of the same term in 1.25. In 4.29, πεφίμωσο reminds us of 1.25 φιμώθητι. Also, 4.41's ὑπακούει αὐτῷ is like 1.27's καὶ ὑπακούουσιν αὐτῷ.

---

67. Best, *Disciples*, p. 56, though Best may well be correct in saying that v. 21b is rewritten tradition. Others seeing redaction in v. 21 are Schweizer, *Good News*, p. 83, and Gnilka, *Evangelium*, I, p. 145.

68. M. Borg, *Jesus: A New Vision* (San Francisco: Harper & Row, 1987), p. 46, and also J.D.G. Dunn, *Jesus and the Spirit: A Study of the Religious and Charismatic Experience of Jesus and the First Christians as Reflected in the New Testament* (London: SCM Press, 1975), p. 87, who suggests that the charges of madness and demon-possession are both prompted by Jesus' exorcisms and authority.

It is hard to avoid seeing the calming of the storm portrayed like the exorcism of 1.21-28. When one adds the element, οὔπω (A reading) ἔχετε πίστιν, one is drawn back to the call for faith in 1.15 in light of the 'fulfilled time'.

In view of this, I am led to see the pericope 4.35-41 in the framework of the victory of God over evil. The historic roots are in the Old Testament concept of the movement from chaos to cosmos in Ps. 89.9, 93.3-4 and 107.28-29, and the victory of God over the evil force of the sea as at creation and the exodus. In light of the study of Kee on the concepts behind ἐπιτιμᾶν – נער, the parallel with 1 QM 14.9-15 is unmistakable. Mark 4.35-41 shows Jesus speaking the word of command by which an evil πνεῦμα is overcome, as the forces of evil have power wrested from them. The hostile and estranged creation, under subjugation to Satan, is brought under the rulership of God.[69] This fits with the context of ch. 4 as well, for in 4.1-34 Jesus' teaching interprets the nearness of the kingdom by words (especially the mystery of the kingdom, vv. 10-12), and 4.35-41 shows the victory of the kingdom in Jesus' deeds.[70]

The emphatic ἐφοβήθησαν φόβον μέγαν is an example of the accusative of content or cognate accusative, where the accusative is a cognate of the verb in meaning or etymology. It serves a purpose when a qualifying word or phrase in the form of an attributive is used (μέγαν).[71] It occurs in the Septuagint with φοβέομαι in *1 Macc.* 10.8: καὶ ἐφοβήθησαν φόβον μέγαν (when the people heard that the king had given them authority to gather an army), and Ps. 52.6: ἐκεῖ φοβηθήσονται φόβον, οὗ οὐκ ἦν φόβος. The clearest parallel to Mk 4.41, however, is Jon. 1.16: καὶ ἐφοβήθησαν οἱ ἄνδρες φόβῳ μεγάλῳ τὸν κύριον... (Hebrew: וייראו האנשים יראה גדולה). I would translate 4.41 'they were greatly terrified'. The allusion to Jon. 1.16, where the fear is the reaction of the sailors in recognition of Yahweh, now shows Jesus as the one in whom Yahweh is manifested.[72] Yet Mk 4.41 is also the inverse of Jon. 1.16, in that while Jonah is fleeing from the presence of the Lord which leads to the storm on the sea, Jesus manifests the presence of the Lord in calming the storm on the sea.[73] In both

---

69. Kee, 'Terminology', pp. 244, 246.
70. Lührmann, *Markusevangelium*, p. 97.
71. Blass and Debrunner, *Grammar*, pp. 84-85. See Plato *Prot.* 360b: οἱ ἀνδρεῖοι οὐκ αἰσχροὺς φόβους φοβοῦντα. This is also a semitic construction as in Hebrew Gen. 27.34; Ps. 14.5; Prov. 15.27; Lam. 1.8; 1 Sam. 1.6; 1 Kgs. 1.12. See E. Kautzsch and A.E. Cowley, *Gesenius' Hebrew Grammar* (Oxford: Oxford University Press, 1980), pp. 366-67.
72. Pesch, *Markusevangelium*, I, p. 273.
73. E.S. Malbon, 'The Jesus of Mark and the Sea of Galilee', *JBL* 103 (1984), p. 306, n. 11.

cases, the sudden calming of the sea terrifies those present.

The general form of vv. 35-41 is that of a rescue miracle: the introduction of the scene (vv. 35-36); the need (v.37); the cry for help (v. 38c); the rescue with miracle-working word (v. 39ab); the demonstration of the miracle (v. 39c); wonder (v. 41a); and acclamation (v. 41bc).[74]

Mark 4.41a is probably part of the tradition.[75] I would point to the semitic coloring of the language, the thought that this story would seem incomplete without such a reaction (in contrast to 1.27), and to the way in which the more common φόβος and φοβέομαι are used here. Yet even though it is not likely redactional, the motif of wonder plays a crucial part in the pericope. There is a contrast between the response (δειλός, adj. cowardly, Rev. 21.8; see 2 Tim. 1.17) of the disciples *during* the storm (οὐ μέλει σοι... only in Mark) and the terror of the disciples *after* the calming of the storm. The terror then leads to the question, Τίς ἄρα οὗτός ἐστιν..., which is similar to 1.27, Τί ἐστιν τοῦτο and 2.7, Τί οὗτός οὕτως λαλεῖ. The reader, of course, knows the answer, because of 1.1, 9-11. Mark 4.41 is the terror of men in the presence of the supernatural. While the storm is frightening, the calming of the story is terrifying. The uncanny power of Jesus terrifies the disciples.[76] There is an awestruck

74. Pesch, *Markusevangelium*, I, pp. 269-70.

75. This view is taken by G. Schille, 'Die Seesturmerzählung Markus 4.35-41 als Beispiel neutestamentlicher Aktualisierung', *ZNW* 56 (1965), p. 34; B.M.F.v. Iersel and A.J.M. Linmans, 'The Storm on the Lake, Mk. 4.35-41 and Mt. 8.18-27 in the light of Form-Criticism, "Redaktionsgeschichte" and Structural Analysis', in *Miscellanea Neotestamentica* (NovTSup, 48; Leiden: Brill, 1978), II, p. 20; Schenke, *Wundererzählungen*, p. 58; Schweizer, *Good News*, p. 107; Kertelge, *Wunder*, p. 95; Gnilke, *Evangelium*, I, pp. 1933-94. P.J. Achtemeier, 'The Origin and Function of the Pre-Markan Miracle Catenae', *JBL* 91 (1972), pp. 198-221, sees this as part of a pre-Markan miracle block, 4.35-5.43; 6.34-44, 53. Another pre-Markan block he sees is 6.45-51; 7.24b-30, 32-37; 8.1-10; 8.22-26. He sees a θεῖος ἀνήρ portrayed in these blocks, which Mark proceeds to argue against. The dubiousness of a θεῖος ἀνήρ concept was stated in Chapter 2 above. As a part of his thesis, he says that the epiphanic emphasis of the first catena's miracles is indicated by the repeated use of cognates of φόβος in 4.41; 5.15, 33, 36. We saw in Chapter 2 that these terms actually play little part in what is supposedly θεῖος ἀνήρ literature. Also viewing 4.35-5.43 as a pre-Markan unit is Pesch in *Der Besessene von Gerasa: Entstehung und Überlieferung einer Wundergeschichte* (SBS 56; Stuttgart: Katholisches Biblewerk, 1972), p. 15, and Kertelge, *Die Wunder*, pp. 92-97. The problem with the views of Pesch and Kertelge is that they place the weight of the development of the pericopae in the pre-unitary stage, but yet the compositional unevenness is the same as if developed redactionally. See Gnilka, *Evangelium*, I, p. 200.

76. A.E.J. Rawlinson, *St. Mark* (Westminster Commentaries; London: Methuen, 1925), p. 61.

awareness of being in the presence of the inexplicable.[77] They ask each other whom they are with. Jesus has exhibited the authority of the reign of God once more in overcoming the forces of evil, and the question of the disciples leads us to christology in the framework of victory of the kingdom of God over evil.

The reaction of 4.41 has been seen as negative by some.[78] However, one must question this. The cowardice of the disciples, indicated by Jesus' question, Τί δειλοί ἐστε, appears in a negative light in view of the behaviour and question ('Teacher, do you not care...'), but their terror of 4.41a is not related to the storm, but to the sudden calming of it. To make the terror negative would make it avoidable, and while the cowardice in the storm and doubt of Jesus' care is avoidable, the terror must be seen in a sense as an unavoidable reaction to uncanny power.[79] Small wonder the disciples were terrified, since Jesus does in this pericope what God can do in the Old Testament (Ps. 89.9, 107.28-29).[80] Supernatural powers are at work. Evil is being subdued by the reign of God, the numinous is evident and human terror is expected in such circumstances. Perhaps γάρ explanatory at the beginning of v. 41 would make their terror the source of the cowardice, which in turn could be seen negatively, but καὶ would seem to indicate a further and differing reaction after the calming.

We see, then, in this pericope, the rule of God bringing into submission the forces of evil in the sea, which cause terror in the disciples. In the context of this victory of God, they then ask the identity of the one in whom the kingdom is at work. Wonder is related again to the breaking-in of God's rule, and in light of that the question of Jesus' identity arises. Micah 7.15 gave an expectation that God would again show the people miracles as at the exodus: καὶ κατὰ τὰς ἡμέρας ἐξοδίας σου ἐξ Αἰγύπτου ὄψεσθε θαυμαστά. Here, as at the exodus,

---

77. Mann, *Mark*, p. 276.

78. Kelber, *Kingdom*, pp. 49-50, says that in 4.41a the motif of the disciples' fear is a functional element of Mark's discipleship theology and is associated with a lack of understanding and non-perception rather than being reverential. Also of this view for 4.41a is Kertelge, *Wunder*, p. 100, who says that the disciples have no positive answer to the question of who Jesus is, but only a negative reaction of fear as a deficiency of belief. Also J. Tyson, 'The Blindness of the Disciples in Mark', in *The Messianic Secret* (ed. C. Tuckett; Philadelphia: Fortress Press, London: SCM Press, 1983), p. 36, sees the fear as evidence of the disciples' blindness in 4.41.

79. Pohl, *Evangelium*, p. 217, says the fear is that which all people feel in the recognition of the holy.

80. P.J. Achtemeier, 'Person and Deed: Jesus and the Storm-Tossed Sea', *Int* 16 (1962), p. 174.

God overruled the sea. Micah went on to say that when the Lord did those miracles, ἐπὶ τῷ κυρίῳ θεῷ ἡμῶν ἐκστήσονται καὶ φοβηθήσονται ἀπὸ σοῦ (7.17). Though there is no direct quotation here of Micah, the similarity in thought does not allow us to pass over without a comment. In the submission of the sea to the reign of God, those watching are struck with terror.[81]

Mark 5.15, 20

One meets the next two occurrences of the motif of wonder in the following pericope, 5.1-20. 5.15 reads, καὶ ἔρχονται πρὸς τὸν ᾽Ιησοῦν καὶ θεωροῦσιν τὸν δαιμονιζόμενον καθήμενον ἱματισμένον καὶ σωφρονοῦντα, τὸν ἐσχηκότα τὸν λεγιῶνα, καὶ ἐφοβήθησαν, and 5.20 says, καὶ ἀπῆλθεν καὶ ἤρξατο κηρύσσειν ἐν τῇ Δεκαπόλει ὅσα ἐποίησεν αὐτῷ ὁ ᾽Ιησοῦς, καὶ πάντες ἐθαύμαζον. This pericope again portrays the victory over the realm of Satan by the rule of God as manifested in Jesus. The location is now Gentile territory, the land of the Gerasenes (or Gadarenes, or Gergasenes). Again, common elements with the programmatic miracle of 1.21-8 are present: a man, ἐν πνεύματι ἀκαθάρτῳ (1.23; 5.2); the question Τί ἐμοὶ καὶ σοί (5.7; Τί ἡμῖν καὶ σοί in 1.24); the command, ἔξελθε (1.25; 5.8); and amazement following each exorcism. Yet the elements in this story are in no way schematicized, as the details of the man's agony, the dialogue between Jesus and the demon and the interaction with the herdsmen and townspeople make clear. Taylor makes the point that the unevenness of the narrative makes it nearer the record of an eyewitness than the rounded form of a miracle story.[82] I would, however, note the general thrust of the pericope as showing how the coming of Jesus is putting an end to the rule of Satan, and that 1.21-28 and 5.1-20 should not be seen as a struggle between Jesus and the demons, but rather that the demons are in forced submission to Jesus.[83]

This is the third of four stories presented as exorcisms in Mark. (1.21-28, 4.35-41, and 9.14-29 are the others). All of these contain the motif of wonder, but each shapes the language in differing ways. Three of the four exorcism stories in *Vit. Ap.* do not contain reactions of wonder (3.38; 4.10; 4.43; but 4.20 has ὡς ἐκράτησαν ὑπὸ θαύματος). It does not occur in the stories in Josephus's

---

81. Other than the affinities mentioned to Jon. 1.16 and Mic. 7.15, 17, Meye, 'Psalm 107', p. 7, has noted that the deliverance from peril at sea in Ps. 107.23-32 may help in interpreting Mk. 4.35-41 and 6.45-52. There is no language of wonder in Ps. 107, however.

82. Taylor, *Gospel*, p. 277.

83. Tillesse, *Secret*, p. 85; Koch, *Bedeutung*, p. 57.

Ant. 8.48, or Lucian, *Philop.* 31.16. When one adds to this the view that there is probable Markan redaction in 1.22, 27; 5.15, 20; 9.15; we see that it is part of the intention of the evangelist to relate wonder to the overthrow of Satan in a specific and non-stereotyped way.

Although the form of the pericope has elements of its structure in common with other exorcism stories (first, an encounter between the demonic and the exorcist, vv. 1-2; second, the defensive reaction of the demon, vv. 6-7; third, *apopompe*, or the command to depart, v. 8; fourth, the exit of the demon, v. 13; fifth, the amazement of onlookers, vv. 15, 20, and the spread of the fame of the exorcist, vv. 14a, 18-20, according to Pesch[84]), there are enough other diverse elements in this pericope to defy schematicization in all but the barest elements. There is a lengthy description of the state of the demonic (possibly to recall Isa. 65.3-4, Ps. 68.6[85]), the singular element of the name of the demons in v. 9, the destruction of the pigs in v. 13, the restoration of the demonic in v. 15, and the resulting proclamation in vv. 18-20. These diverse narrative elements would direct us not to quickly assume a stock form of the story,[86] but to allow for elements beyond the barest essentials to be part of the tradition. Also one should look closely to see how the motif of wonder may work.

The reaction in 5.15, καὶ ἐφοβήθησαν, is one of many uses of the verb φοβέομαι in Mark (also in 4.41; 5.33, 36; 6.20, 50; 9.32; 10.32; 11.18, 32; 12.12; 16.8). All except 5.36 and 6.50 are in reactions of wonder, and as with 4.41 it refers to the awe which attends the supernatural.[87] Here there is a recognized Markan term, φοβέομαι,[88] which is presented as an 'impersonal plural',

---

84. Pesch, *Besessene*, p. 21; and also see Koch, *Bedeutung*, pp. 55-56 for a similar scheme.

85. F.J. Craghan, 'The Gerasene Demoniac', *CBQ* 30 (1968), p. 529; J.D.M. Derrett, 'Contributions to the Study of the Gerasene Demoniac', *JSNT* 3 (1979), pp. 2-17; and also H. Salin, 'Die Perikope von Gerasenischen Besessenen und der Plan des Markusevangeliums', *ST* 18 (1964), p. 160, who sees 5.1-20 as a Christian midrash on Isa. 65.1-5, with the demonic representing heathen people as a whole, where Jesus going to the Gerasenes is god stretching out his hand to the Gentiles (Isa. 65.1). Reactions of wonder do not occur in these OT references, nor in Ps. 107.10-16, which Meye suggests as the 'horizon' for interpreting 5.1-20. See Meye, 'Psalm 107', p. 7.

86. As does Craghan, 'Contributions', p. 527, for example, who says the original account could be terminated 'almost any place after v. 15', or J. Bligh, 'The Gerasene Demoniac and the Resurrection of Christ', *CBQ* 31 (1969), pp. 383-84, who follows Craghan in seeing vv. 2-6, 8-10 and 18-20 as secondary.

87. H.B. Swete, *Commentary on Mark* (repr.; Grand Rapids: Kregel, 1977 [1913]), p. 98.

88. Pryke, *Redactional Style*, p. 157.

another Markan feature.[89] In spite of these two Markan features, there has been a tendency to see this reaction as traditional.[90] The general reason has been that it is 'a typical conclusion to a healing pericope'.[91] However, a close reading of vv. 14-15 indicates that the flight of the herdsmen in v. 14 is the reaction to the exorcism, and the fear of the locals in v. 15 is a response to the restoration of the former demoniac (καὶ θεωροῦσιν τὸν δαιμονιζόμενον καθήμενον ἱματισμένον καὶ σωφρονοῦντα, τὸν ἐσχηκότα τὸν λεγιῶνα). It occurs *before* they have even heard about the loss of the pigs (v. 16). This can in no way be seen as typical. Each of the three participles contrasts with the previous condition of the man. The opposite of the unfettered wandering is καθήμενον; ἱματισμένον may suggest a prior state of undress; and σωφρονοῦντα is the opposite of the 'crying aloud' and 'cutting himself with stones'.[92] These three traits show a reintegration of the man into society.[93] Since this is the case, the reaction of fear is not at the exorcism as such, but to the restoration of the man into a whole state. In Jesus, God has brought a man under the dominion of evil back into society, and this is frightening to the locals. The kingdom breaking in does not only vanquish Satan, but it also restores God's creation. The numinous power of the divine has been encountered in the restoration, which makes humans feel their transitoriness, and they fear before the uncanny as it has restored the person.[94']

89. C.H. Turner, 'Markan Usage: Notes, Critical and Exegetical, on the Second Gospel', *JTS* 25 (1924), pp. 378-83.

90. So Craghan, 'Gerasene', p. 527, although he sees τὸν ἐσχηκότα τὸν λεγιῶνα as redactional in v. 15; C.H. Cave, 'The Obedience of the Unclean Spirits', *NTS* 11 (1964), pp. 94-96; Koch, *Bedeutung*, pp. 55-62; Kertelge, *Wunder*, pp. 102-107; Schenke, *Wundererzählungen*, pp. 179-81; Bligh, 'Gerasene', pp. 383-84; F. Annan, *Heil für die Heiden: Zur Bedeutung und Geschichte der Tradition vom Besessenen Gerasener (Mk. 5.1-20 par)*, (Frankfurter Theologisches Studien 20; Frankfurt: Josef Knecht, 1976), p. 61 (he sees v. 15 as redactional until θεωροῦσιν, with καθήμενον); Gnilka, *Evangelium*, I, pp. 200-203. For redactional language, Pryke, *Redactional Style*, pp. 157-58.

91. D. Nineham, *The Gospel of St. Mark* (Penguin Gospel Commentaries; Harmondsworth: Penguin, 1986), p. 154. He says that vv. 16-17 and 18-20 were added later.

92. J. Starobinski, 'An Essay in Literary Analysis: Mk. 5.1-20', *EcumRev* 23 (1971), p. 392.

93. F.J. Leenhardt, 'An Exegetical Essay: Mk. 5.1-20', in *Structural Analysis and Biblical Exegesis: Interpretation Essays* (ed. R. Barthes *et al.*; Pittsburgh: Pickwick Press, 1974), p. 104.

94. W. Schmithals, *Das Evangelium nach Markus* (Ökumenischer Taschenbuch Kommentar zum Neuen Testament; Würzburg: Gerd Mohn; Gütersloh: Gütersloh & Echter Verlag, 1979), I, p. 278; Grundmann, *Evangelium*, p. 111.

There has been a general tendency to see καὶ πάντες ἐθαύμαζον in 5.20 as redactional.[95] The verb θαυμάζω occurs four times in Mark (in 6.6; 15.5 and 44, all for reactions of wonder). Here alone in Mark it is combined with a form of πᾶς, but Mark uses πᾶς with amazement elsewhere, in 2.12, 9.15 and 11.18. It is used in Luke five times other than in Markan parallels, of which four are in the birth narratives; and in Matthew twice, one of which is the only Q parallel with amazement (Mt. 12.23; Lk. 11.14). I would also note the similarity with the redacational 1.27: καὶ ἐθαμβήθησαν ἅπαντες compares with καὶ πάντες ἐθαύμαζον.[96] The phrase, καὶ πάντες ἐθαύμαζον is solely Markan, though the pericope is a triple tradition. Matthew does not even include the preaching of the former demoniac. Here is what seems to be a Markan special emphasis, namely that a message proclaiming that which God has done can astound (16.6-8; see also 6.20).[97] Mark alone places the extent of the preaching as 'in the Decapolis', where Luke localizes it, 'through all the city' (Lk. 8.39). In other words, the Gentiles marvel at what Jesus has done (ὅσα ὁ κύριός σοι πεπεοίηκεν...ὅσα ἐποίησεν αὐτῷ ὁ Ἰησοῦς). A negative local reaction in v. 17 becomes a positive reaction in the surrounding territory.

In 5.1-20 then, neither reaction of wonder is directed at the exorcism itself. One is the response to the power released in restoring the man, and the other responds to the testimony of the man. The Markan emphasis is that the uncanny operates in the restoration of the creation and the preaching of what God has done. As with 1.22, 27, where the wonder was at the forgiveness and healing, Mark is not using simple wonder at miracles or exorcisms. The exorcism was placed in the context of the authoritative teaching in 1.21-28, and here the exorcism is placed in the context of the restoration and re-integration into society of the individual involved, as well as the subsequent witness to that restoration. It appears that the reader is being directed to notice that eschatological power is released in more than the naked miracle or exorcism, but that God's intervention is evident in the amazement at the total process of the restoration, including the verbal witness to that intervention. For the Christian community, this may be a startling reminder that God's power was not released only in the

---

95. Schweizer, *Good News*, pp. 111-13; Schenke, *Wundererzählungen*, pp. 174, 179; Annen, *Heil*, pp. 69-70; Nineham, *Gospel*, pp. 154-55; Gnilka, *Evangelium*, I, p. 207; Pryke, *Redactional Style*, pp. 157-58. Verses 18-20 are often seen as an expansion for missionary purposes.

96. Pointed out by Kertelege, *Wunder*, p. 104.

97. Gnilka, *Evangelium*, I, p. 207, says that the epiphany presented in the miracle becomes present in the proclamation.

miracles of the historical Jesus, but also in the ongoing witness and evangelization of the community as the outcasts of society were restored and integrated into the church.

Mark 5.33, 42

The next two places where the motif of wonder occurs is in the pericope 5.21-43, where we meet another Markan 'sandwich', one incident placed inside the account of another. It is a common technique in the gospel to use insertions to fill in time lapses (3.22-30; 6.14-29; 11.15-19; 14.3-9).[98] A synagogue official named Jairus requests Jesus to come and help his daughter who is near death in vv. 21-24a. In vv. 24b-34 a woman afflicted by a continual menstrual uncleanness touches Jesus, and is healed. When Jesus looks to see who touched him, ἡ γυνὴ φοβηθεῖσα καὶ τρέμουσα, εἰδυῖα ὃ γέγονεν αὐτῇ, ἦλθεν καὶ προσέπεσεν αὐτῷ καὶ εἶπεν πᾶσιν τὴν ἀλήθειαν (v. 33), he sends her away with a word of peace and salvation. Jesus journeys on to Jairus's house and raises his daughter who has now died, which leads to this reaction: καὶ ἐξέστησαν ἐκστάσει μεγάλῃ (v. 42b).[99]

A number of elements serve to bind the two stories together and located them in the broader context of the gospel. Salvation links the two incidents, in 5.23: ἵνα σωθῇ καὶ ζήσῃ; v. 28: σωθήσομαι; and v. 34: σέσωκέν σε. Both emphasize faith, in v. 34: ἡ πίστις σέσωκέν σε; and v. 36: μόνον πίστευε. Both involve touching: the woman touches Jesus, and he grasps the hand of Jairus's daughter. As Jairus falls before Jesus' feet, the woman also falls before Jesus (πίπτει, προσέπεσεν). The woman and the girl were both 'unclean' (by blood, and by death). The woman had a flow of blood for 12 years (v. 25), and the girl is 12 years old (v. 42). Each was beyond the help of doctors (v. 26). Jesus addresses the woman as θυγάτηρ (v. 34), which is also the designation of the girl (v. 23:

---

98. Schweizer, *Good News*, p.116.

99. Some MSS, ℵ, B, C, L, Δ, 33, 892, cop^bo, and eth contain ἐξέστησαν εὐθύς, but this is probably inserted by copyists in imitation of εὐθύς in the previous sentence. B. Metzger says it must be considered because of the excellence of the Alexandrian text, but admits that it is very uncertain, in *A Textual Commentary on the Greek New Testament* (London: United Bible Societies, 1971), pp. 87-88. The UBS committee gave it a D rating, and along with Taylor (*St. Mark*, p. 297) I would omit it. There is no precedent in Mark for εὐθύς directly preceding a reaction of amazement. The textual evidence for omission includes P[45], A, K, W, Θ, Π, f[1], f[13], 28, 565, 700, 1009, 1010, 1071, 1079, 1195, 1230, 1241, 1242 and 1253. There are minor readings for ἐξέστησαν πάντες and ἐξέστησαν οἱ γονεῖς αὐτῆς.

Τὸ θυγάτηρ μου; and v. 35: Ἡ θυγάτηρ σοῦ). With these linking themes, we can see that the story-sandwich emphasises salvation and faith, again showing that the reign of God is breaking in and restoring the creation from the physical and social barriers of sickness, death and uncleanness.[100] Also, the reference to Jesus in v. 35 as τὸν διδάσκαλον seems a clear indication of the Markan emphasis we saw in 1.22, 27. Jesus is the teacher through whose words and actions the power of God is defeating hostile forces (sickness and death) and restoring the creation.

Pesch has schematized the two stories. The resurrection of the daughter follows the miracle story pattern: first, the appearance of the one seeking help (v. 22a); second, the request for help (vv. 22b, 23); third, healing or resurrection through touch and miracle-working word (v. 41); fourth, the establishment of healing or resurrection (v. 42a); fifth, a double demonstration (vv. 42b, 43b); and sixth, admiration (v. 42d). The healing of the woman has a different scheme: first the appearance of the miracle worker (vv. 21c, 24bc); second, the appearance of the sick person (v. 25); third, characterization of the need (vv. 25, 26); fourth, the healing touch (v. 27b); fifth, the results (v. 29a); and sixth, the demonstration (v. 29b).[101] We will look at the reactions of wonder in the order they occur in the text.

The story of the woman with the continuous flow of blood is the story of the re-integration of a social outcast. Both ἐν ῥύσει αἵματος (5.25) and ἡ πηγὴ τοῦ αἵματος (5.29; compare Lev. 12.7, 20.18) are employed as euphemisms for abnormal gynecological conditions associated with menstruation. In Lev. 15.21, a menstruating woman was said to be unclean, and banished for seven days. Lev. 15.25 indicates that any irregularity lengthens the ban, and Lev. 15.21 says that anything touching the menstruating woman is banished until evening. Since the ancient purity laws were by all accounts in force in the first century, Mark here shatters the legal purity system and its restrictive social condition when Jesus does not reprimand the woman for being in the middle of the crowd,

---

100. J.D.M. Derrett, 'Mark's Technique: The Haemorrhaging Woman and Jairus' Daughter', *Bib* 63 (1982), pp. 474-505, may overstate the connections when he relates the passage to Hab. 2.4; Cant. 2, 4.15, 5.1; Ruth 2.8, 3.9; Hos. 2.19-20; and Zeph. 3.17-29, as a midrashic interpretation. It seems tenuous, for example, to say that the girl was laid as a corpse on the couch that was to be the scene of her betrothal to a bridegroom, and that Jesus taking her by the (right?) hand was a symbol of marriage (p. 487).

101. Pesch, *Markusevangelium*, I, pp. 297, 298-99. Pesch, along with Achtemeier and Kertelge views this pericope as part of the pre-Markan unit. See n.71 above.

or for touching him.[102] Theissen believes that the act of touching Jesus might have been understood as an attempt to get rid of the disease by passing it on (*Epidaurus* 7),[103] but a gynecological problem could not have been passed on to a man.

Jesus looks to see the one who has touched him, and the woman makes herself known with fear and trembling. Mark here is unique in ascribing the reaction to her knowledge of her healing (Lk. 8.47: ἰδοῦσα δὲ ἡ γυνὴ ὅτι οὐκ ἔλαθεν). The participles φοβηθεῖσα καὶ τρόμος catch our attention since the more usual expression would be φόβος καὶ τρόμος (1 Cor. 2.3; 2 Cor. 7.15; Eph. 6.5; Phil. 2.12). Also noteworthy is the sequence of an aorist passive participle followed by a present active participle. They, along with the clause εἰδυῖα ὃ γέγονεν αὐτῇ, describe the actions denoted by ἦλθεν, προσέπεσεν, εἶπεν.[104] The woman was seized with fear and begins to tremble when she thinks of what has happened to her.[105] The reaction is not because she knew that she had rendered Jesus unclean,[106] nor due to guilt that she has made use of Jesus' power without his willingness,[107] nor does Mark indicate the reason for the reaction.[108] I would take the participle εἰδυῖα as causal here.[109] She is struck with fear and begins to tremble, because she *knew* what had happened to her. Since fear and trembling are an Old Testament expression for the human attitude before the nearness of God (Jud. 2.28; Dan. 5.19 ; *4 Macc.* 4.10),[110] and we are directed to the δύναμις which had left Jesus in v. 29, the meaning here is clear. The experience of the woman encountering divine power strikes her with fear and trembling.[111]

---

102. For this, see M.J. Selvidge, 'Mark 5.25-34 and Leviticus 15.19-20: A Reaction to Restrictive Purity Regulations', *JBL* 103 (1984), pp. 619-23.
103. Theissen, *Stories*, p. 134. He points out that the touch of a menstruating woman in any event was considered harmful (Pliny, *Nat. Hist.* 7.64).
104. Cranfield, *Gospel*, p. 186.
105. Taylor, *Gospel*, p. 292.
106. Mann, *Mark*, p. 286.
107. E. Klostermann, *Das Markusevangelium* (HNT; Tübingen: Mohr, 1971), p. 52.
108. Cranfield, *Gospel*, p. 186.
109. R.C.H. Lenski, *The Interpretation of St. Mark's Gospel* (Minneapolis: Augsburg, 1964), p. 224.
110. Lohmeyer, *Evangelium*, p. 103.
111. This may be a good place to note that although some would separate the reactions of fear in the gospel from those of amazement (W.C. Allen, '"Fear" in St. Mark', *JTS* 48 (1947), pp. 201-203), this is questionable since the results do not differ significantly. See also

It should be noted here that it is not the crowd who are said to have the reaction, but the individual who experience the power. Schenke notes that the reaction of epiphany fear is not present.[112] Instead, an individual is struck with a sense of the uncanny, and there is no negative view of the reaction. Jesus tells her Θυγάτηρ, ἡ πίστις σου σέσωκέν σε. ὕπαγε εἰς εἰρήνην, καὶ ἴσθι ὑγιὴς ἀπὸ τῆς μάστιγός σου. The motif of wonder here co-exists with belief, just as it co-existed with the praise of God in 2.12.[113] This becomes especially important when it is noted that the woman functions in the gospel narrative as one of the 'little people' whose faith constantly exemplifies the values of the reign of God and who serve as foils for the disciples.[114]

I would consider the expression in 5.33 redactional for the following reasons. It is one of 57 occurrences in Mark of double participles, making it an example of a favorite grammatical expression in the gospel.[115] The verse also contains a double use of αὐτός, and the identifiable Markan terms προσέπεσεν and φοβηθεῖσα.[116] There is also the unusual use of participles to describe the reaction. The story does not need the reaction, as the deletion of it by Matthew shows. It is likely a redactional addition to show the reaction of wonder at the experience of divine power co-existing with belief.

One should also note that the fear-trembling complex here is similar to that which occurs in 16.8. As I will deal with that verse in due course, it suffices to say at this point that 5.33 gives an early indication in the gospel of a co-existence of fear and trembling with faith by a woman.

The reaction in 5.42 again makes use of the cognate accusative which was observed in 4.41.[117] That construction with ἔκστασις can also be seen in Gen. 27.33: ἐξέστη δὲ Ισαακ ἔκστασιν μεγάλην σφόδρα καὶ εἶπεν Τίς οὖν ὁ θρεύσας μου θήραν καὶ εἰσενέγκας μοι. This is the only place in the New Testament where the verb ἐξίστημι is used with the cognate accusative. The

E.S. Malbon, 'Disciples, Crowds, Whoever: Markan Characters and Readers', *NovT* 28 (1986), p. 115.
112. Schenke, *Wundererzählungen*, p. 207.
113. Rau, 'Komposition', p. 2223.
114. Rhoads and Michie, *Story*, pp. 129-36.
115. Neirynck, *Duality*, pp. 82-84.
116. Pryke, *Redactional Style*, p. 158. 5.33 is part of Pryke's redactional text. Also viewing it as redactional are Best, *Temptation*, p. 173; Schweizer, *Good News*, p. 116; and Tillesse, *Secret*, p. 54.
117. Pohl, *Evangelium*, p. 240, says the expression is as strong as in 4.41. In Christ, God is experienced.

indefinite plural would refer most likely to the three select disciples along with Jairus and his wife. They are out of their senses with wonder. The noun ἔκστασις is met here for the first time in Mark (it also occurs for the reaction of the women at the news of the resurrection in 16.8) and in combination with the verb ἐξίστημι it signifies displacement, astonishment and bewilderment to the strongest degree.[118] Once more, it is the reaction to the experience of divine power[119] which has raised the girl from the dead. The expected psychological reaction might be gratitude or joy, but the power of God is overwhelmingly present.[120] The power of death has been defeated and life has been restored.

I would take the reaction of wonder in v. 42c to be from the tradition. The textual uncertainty of εὐθὺς, which would indicate redaction, and the fact that the final clause does not need to stand with the redactional γάρ clause in v. 42b or the redactional command to silence in v. 43, leaves us without redactional features in v. 42c. The semitic coloring of the expression of amazement,[121] and the fact that it is directly related to the raising of the girl, would indicate traditional features.

The motif of wonder in the pericope 5.21-43 has some remarkable nuances. We see fear and trembling co-existing with faith in a redactional verse as a woman experiences the power of the Lord and re-integration into the community. A young girl is raised from the dead and re-integration into the community presumably follows. In both cases heroic 'little people' react with wonder as God's rule breaks-in to defeat sickness and death. The woman, in fact, becomes a model of bold faith in the gospel, as her faith leads to the only miracle in the gospel which takes place solely at the supplicant's initiative.[122] In both of these 'model' cases, the only possible reaction to the uncanny eschatological power is awe.

Mark 6.2, 6a

In the pericope immediately following, the rejection of Jesus at Nazareth, there is this statement in v.2: καὶ γενομένου σαββάτου ἤρξατο διδάσκειν ἐν τῇ

118. Taylor, *Gospel*, p. 297.
119. Kertelge, *Wunder*, p. 119.
120. Gnilka, *Evangelium*, I, p. 2218.
121. Taylor, *Gospel*, p. 297, suggests a Palestinian source, and J. Schmid, in *The Gospel According to Mark* (RNT; Staten Island, NY: Mercier Press, 1968), p. 112, says that the two stories are so closely and naturally joined that they must go back to eyewitnesses.
122. E.S. Malbon, 'Fallible Followers: Women and Men in the Gospel of Mark', *Semeia* 28 (1983), p. 36.

συναγωγῇ καὶ πολλοὶ ἀκούοντες ἐξεπλήσσοντο λέγοντες. Πόθεν τούτῳ ταῦτα, καὶ τίς ἡ σοφία ἡ δοθεῖσα τούτῳ καὶ αἱ δυνάμεις τοιαῦται διὰ τῶν χειρῶν αὐτοῦ γινόμεναι.[123] The pericope ends with 6a: καὶ ἐθαύμαζεν διὰ τὴν ἀπιστίαν αὐτῶν. This section connects to the context of the gospel in several ways. Verse 6.6a links back with the call to believe in 1.15, and contrasts with the faith of the woman in 5.34: ἡ πίστις σου σέσωκέν σε, and μόνον πίστευε in 5.36. We have seen faith as a theme in 2.5 and 4.40 previously. The reference to the miracles which came through Jesus' hands in 6.2 reminds of the way in which Jesus grasped the hand of the child in 5.41. In fact the miracles of 4.35-5.43 may be in view in the question of 6.2c. The setting of this pericope is very similar to 1.21-28, with the common themes of Jesus teaching, the synagogue, the sabbath and amazement. One should understand the ἤρξατο διδάσκειν of v. 2 as relating to the διδαχὴ καινὴ κατ' ἐξουσίαν of 1.27.[124] The question πόθεν τούτῳ ταῦτα in 6.2 reminds of the questions, τί ἐστιν τοῦτο in 1.27 and τίς ἄρα οὗτός ἐστιν in 4.41, and the reader is directed to the progression 'what is this?' followed by 'who is this?' followed by 'where did this one get these things?'. The answer has been given in 1.1-15: this is the breaking-in of the rule of God, as mediated by the spirit-anointed son of God, and the source is heaven itself.

On first glance, 6.1-6a may not seem to have much to do with the breaking-in of God's rule, especially since it is a passage describing rejection and Jesus healing 'only a few'. However, one must note the nuances of the kingdom within the context of the gospel.

Consideration must be given to 4.10-12, and to the Markan concept of the mystery of the kingdom of God. Recent discussion has suggested that one may understand the mystery expresses that though God has broken into the human sphere in kingly power, this does not exclude opposition or defection (note the fate of various seeds in the parable in 4.1-20). The co-existence of the kingly rule and resistance is 'the mystery'. This tension is in itself actually a sign of

---

123. This is textually a C reading, in reference to αἱ δυνάμει... The other readings replace ἵνα καὶ δυνάμεις...γίνωνται (D K 11, 1079, 1195) or replace ἵνα for καὶ and change φινόμαι to γίνονται (A, C², W, f¹), or place ὅτι before καὶ and change to γίνονται (1242, 1²⁹⁹). The chosen reading follows ℵ. Also, πολλοὶ ἀκούοντες is the strongest reading, following ℵ, AA, C, K, W f¹, 33, 700, 1009 and 1071.

124. E. Grässer, 'Jesus in Nazareth (Mk. 6.1-6a): Notes on the Redaction and Theology of St. Mark', *NTS* 16 (1969), p. 14.

the breaking-in,[125] especially since the rule is not yet absolute. In light of this, the relation of 6.1-6a to the kingdom may become clearer. Both divine power and opposition are at work in the pericope, and this is the paradigmatic mystery of the breaking-in of the rule of God as Mark understands it. Just as one of the seeds in the parable of the mystery of the kingdom is said to be σκανδαλίζονται (4.17), so the crowd in the synagogue is said to be ἐσκανδαλίζοντο (6.3). Also, the question in v. 2 as noted above directs one back to previous questions in the gospel, which in turn moves one back to 1.1-15, namely that God is asserting kingly power in his son Jesus. The opposition in the synagogue may be, then, a test case of a 'scandalized' group and of resistance to the miracles and teaching of the kingdom. This is the 'mystery' spoken of in 4.1-20, especially vv. 10-12.

This is the only place in Mark where πολλοί is used with ἐξεπλήσσοντο, or with any verb of amazement (1.27: ἅπαντες; 2.12: πάντας; 5.20: πάντες; 11.18: πᾶς). It is probably best to understand πολλοί not as 'the many', but as 'the great majority', or 'the known crowd', in an inclusive sense.[126] The people are overcome with a 'shocked numbness' as they hear the authoritative new teaching, resplendent with divine power.[127] The verb, ἐκπλήσσομαι is used with in 1.22 and 11.18 (compare 10.26), and 7.37 is the only place in Mark where it is not related to Jesus' teaching. The construction ἐξεπλήσσοντο λέγοντες also appears in 7.37 and 10.26, and shows Mark has used wonder to lead to a discussion of the identity of Jesus or the source of Jesus' power (ἐξεπλήσσοντο λέγοντες is most likely a redactional construction). We thus have indications that Mark has used wonder in a way closely related to his understanding of Jesus as the Son of God exercising kingly power.

There has been some discussion of the possiblity that the reaction in v. 2 is inconsistent with the rejection which follows in the pericope.[128] There is sometimes an inconsistency suggested between the term ἐξεπλήσσοντο and ἐσκανδαλίζοντο in v. 3. This is usually attributed to redaction in v. 2a and tradition

125. The best recent discussion is J. Marcus, *The Mystery of the Kingdom of God* (SBLDS; Chico, CA: Scholars Press, 1986), especially pp. 49, 57, 73-123.
126. Lohmeyer, *Evangelium*, p. 111 (see 10.48); Klostermann, *Markusevangelium*, p. 55; Lane, *Gospel*, p. 201, n.3.
127. Grässer, 'Jesus', p. 6.
128. This thought has been suggested by Grässer, 'Jesus', pp. 5-6; Crossan, ' Relatives', p. 99; W. Knox, *The Sources of the Synoptic Gospels* (2 vols.; Cambridge: Cambridge University Press, 1953), I, p.49; B.H Branscomb, *The Gospel of Mark* (London: Hodder & Stoughton, 1948), pp. 98-99.

in vv. 2b-3 or 3. However when one understands the mystery of the kingdom in Mark, amazement is not inconsistent with a subsequent rejection. While it can co-exist with faith, as was seen in 5.33-34, it can also co-exist with lack of faith, as v. 6a indicates here. Kingly power is evident in the 'new teaching with authority' which is so powerful that people are struck with wonder, but this does not always lead to faith and repentance. The breaking-in of kingly power does not exclude unbelief or hardness of heart or a 'scandalized' crowd. It is thus unnecessary to posit a contradiction in thought between vv. 2a and 2b-3.

The construction καὶ πολλοὶ ἀκούοντες ἐξεπλήσσοντο λέγοντες in v. 2 is most likely redactional, as is the preceding καὶ γενομένου σαββάτου ἤρξατο διδάσκειν ἐν τῇ συναγωγῇ.[129] We can note here the Markan ἄρχομαι plus infinitive, genitive absolute, the joining of favorite terms ἐκπλήσσεσθαι and διδασκεῖν,[130] along with the Markan λέγειν and συναγωγή.[131] Similarities to the redactional 1.21b-22, 27 have already been mentioned. Thus it is a Markan emphasis here to link a reaction of amazement with subsequent rejection.[132]

The statement of v. 6a is very interesting, for here Jesus marvels (ἐθαύμαζεν) at the unbelief of the townspeople. We saw θαυμάζω in 5.20, and it also occurs in 15.5, 44. It is far more common in Matthew (seven times) and Luke (13 times) than Mark. Here alone in the New Testament is it followed by διά (but compare Rev. 17.7), and usually in the New Testament it is followed by ἐπί with the dative (Lk. 4.22; 20.26; Acts 3.12), περί with the genitive (Lk. 2.18), or an accusative of the object (Lk. 7.9; 24.12; Acts 7.31.)[133] There is another place in the gospel where the language of amazement is attributed to Jesus (Mk 14.33, see also 3.21). Jesus is not astonished at being as a prophet in his home-

129. So Knox, *Sources*, p. 49; Grässer, 'Jesus', p. 12; Pryke, *Redactional Style*, pp. 158-59; Gnilka, *Evangelium*, I, pp. 228-29; Best, *Temptation*, p. 75; Crossan, 'Relatives', p. 99; Branscomb, *Gospel*, pp. 98-99; B. Mayer, 'Überlieferungs- und redaktionsgeschichtliche Überlegungen zu Mk. 6.1-6a', *BZ* 22 (1978), pp. 190, 197.

130. As redactional in 1.22; 6.2; 11.18. Schenke, *Wundererzählungen*, p. 96.

131. Pryke, *Redactional Style*, p. 142.

132. I would agree with Best, *Temptation*, p. 75, Gnilka, *Evangelium*, I, pp. 228-29 and Grässer, 'Jesus', p. 16, that the rejection at Nazareth is traditional material, with perhaps two separate pieces of material joined, over against Bultmann, *History*, p. 3, who sees the pericope as a creation springing from the saying in v. 4. Supposed tensions in the pericope, such as between οὐδεμίαν and εἰ μὴ ὀλίγοις, ἐξεπλήσσοντο and ἐσκανδαλίζοντο, or οὐκ ἐδύνατο and ἐθαύμαζεν may be counted for by the progress of the narrative of the pericope, and must not be dissected to the point that there is no unity of thought. Surely Mark could have seen contradictions also!

133. Swete, *Commentary*, p. 115.

town, but he is astonished not to find faith.[134] In light of the great works of 4.35-5.43, this is indeed amazing.

I would attribute v. 6a to the tradition.[135] The sentence lacks identifiable redactional features, and θαυμάζω is not a favorite Markan term.

In summary, there can be seen vv. 6.1-6a an example where the mystery of the kingdom is at work. The question, 'where did this one get these things?', has been answered in 1.1-15. The wisdom and the miracles are from God, and the exercise of authoritative kingly power in the teaching of Jesus strikes the hearers with wonder. In contrast to the 'little people' of the previous chapter, however, this reaction now develops into opposition. Though the kingdom is at work, some are 'scandalized' and fail to believe. Jesus himself marvels at this disbelief, the very opposite reaction than the breaking-in of the kingdom calls for in 1.14-15. Here is the mystery of the kingdom: the juxtaposition of authoritative kingly power and human opposition. It may well be that the point of this pericope is to impress the necessity of faith on the reader or hearer.[136]

It must also be noted that reactions of amazement in the gospel cannot always be seen as negative,[137] since Jesus himself marvels. The special twist is that while people marvel at the presence of the supernatural, Jesus marvels at resistance which hinders the supernatural. With the advent of the kingdom, the uncanny presses upon people, which amazes them, but it is also amazing when the uncanny does not necessarily lead to faith. We are again drawn back to 1.1-15, but now in light of 4.10-12.

Mark 6.20

The motif of wonder occurs again in 6.20, this time as the response of Herod to John the Baptist. Mk 6.14-29 is an interlude between the sending of the twelve in 6.6b-13 and their return in 6.30. In 6.20 the text reads: ὁ γὰρ Ἡρῴδης ἐφοβεῖτο τὸν Ἰωάννην, εἰδὼς αὐτὸν ἄνδρα δίκαιον καὶ ἅγιον, καὶ συνετήρει αὐτόν, καὶ ἀκούσας αὐτοῦ πολλὰ ἠπόρει, καὶ ἡδέως αὐτοῦ

134. Grässer, 'Jesus', p. 18.
135. So Pesch, *Markusevangelium*, I, p. 315; Best, *Temptation*, p. 75; Gnilka, *Evangelium*, I, pp. 228-29; Mayer, 'Überlieferungs-', p. 197.
136. Grässer, 'Jesus', p. 22.
137. This view has been presented by many, including Kelber, *Kingdom*, pp. 49-50; Kertelge, *Wunder*, p. 100; F. Watson, 'The Social Function of Mark's Secrecy Theme', *JSNT* 24 (1985), p. 52; Rhoads and Michie, *Story*, p. 135; W. Wrede, *The Messianic Secret* (rev. ed.; Cambridge, MA: James Clarks, 1971 [1901]), pp. 97, 103.

ἤκουεν.¹³⁸ There is a strong connection between this pericope and the context of Mark. This is one of two passion narratives in the gospel, with the other being that of Jesus. In fact, in the course of the narrative of the gospel, John is the forerunner (1.2-3) of Jesus in a very specific way. John goes ahead of Jesus by anticipating the pattern of Jesus' life: he is sent by God, preaches, is 'handed over', and is put to death. In turn, the disciples are also to follow this pattern of being sent, preaching, being 'handed over' (13.9, 11), and being put to death (13.12).¹³⁹

There are specific connections between the passion of John and that of Jesus which may be observed in the gospel as well. Herod seized John (ἐκράτησεν), as the soldiers seized Jesus (6.17; 14.46; compare 14.1, 44, 49; 12.12); Herod bound John (ἔδησεν), as the soldiers bound Jesus (15.1) there was an intention to put John to death (6.19), as there was with Jesus (14.1); John was separated from his disciples (6.29) as was Jesus (14.50).¹⁴⁰ One can also note the similarities between 6.20 (ἐφοβεῖτο τὸν Ἰωάννην) and 11.18 (Jesus: ἐφοβοῦντο γὰρ αὐτόν). Both John and Jesus were feared by those who had earthly authority over them (Herod and Jewish leaders). Herod, however, planned to keep John safe because of his fear, where the Jewish leaders planned to kill Jesus because

---

138. The main textual problem in this verse centers around ἠπόρει, καὶ. Although this is not the majority reading, it is supported by some strong witnesses: ℵ, B, L, Θ, I¹⁰⁴³, cop^sa, bo. and W have ἠπορεῖτο, καὶ, and ἐποίει, καὶ has the strong support of the majority of MSS, such as A, C, D, K, Π, f¹, f¹³, 28, 33, 565, 700, 892, 1009, 1071, 1195, 1216, 1230, 1241, 1242, 1253, 1344, 1365, 1546, 1646, 2148, 2174 and many versions. A strong advocate for ἐποίει, καὶ is D.A. Black, 'The Text of Mk. 6.20'. *NTS* 34 (1988), pp. 141-45. Black acknowledges that the UBS editors chose ἠπόρει for its strong support by important MSS, and its internally superior meaning, but says that ἐποίει should be chosen due to its large external support (unless one follows automatically the Alexandrian uncials), and because ἐποίει is the *lectio difficilior*, and the sense is that Herod acknowledged John's righteous character and 'did many things' which John required or recommended. In his reconstruction of the text, however, Black has Herod fearing the people, as Josephus's *Ant.* 18.5.2, and Mt. 14.5, but this is not Mark's statement. We would instead follow the reasoning of Cranfield, *Gospel*, p. 210, who says that the support for ἠπόρει, though numerically weak, is strong in quality, and is intrinsically most likely, since after ἐποίει, the following words would be a weak repetition, but after ἠπόρει they make good sense. To this we would add that ἠπόρει seems to be more consonant with the picture Mark is presenting of a king before a holy man of God.

139. Rhoads and Michie, *Story*, p. 65.

140. J. Gnilka, 'Das Martyrium Johannes des Taufers (Mk. 6.17-29)', in *Orientierung an Jesus: Für J. Schmid* (ed. P. Hoffmann; Freiburg: Herder, 1973), pp. 80-81.

of theirs (11.18). The verb φοβέομαι is used as a response to Jesus in 4.41, 9.6 and 10.32 as well as in 11.18. Compare 16.8. There is also a parallel element to the thought of ἡδέως αὐτοῦ ἤκουεν in 6.20 in 12.37: καὶ ὁ πολὺς ὄχλος ἤκουεν αὐτοῦ ἡδέως. Thus the motif of wonder as a response to John is the same as the responses to Jesus in Mark. Both are held in awe by those who eventually see to their death. Mark is relating that even the enemies of God's agents are struck with awe at the holy messengers who have been sent.

It should be noted that the death of John is also recounted in Josephus's *Ant.* 18.5.2. Josephus, however, relates the fear of Herod to John's extensive influence over the people, which might lead to an uprising (as Mt. 14.5). John is called an ἀγαθὸς ἀνήρ rather than an ἄνδρα δίκαιον καὶ ἅγιον. It is not necessary to attempt to harmonize the accounts.[141]

Similarity has been detected between the stories of John's death and Jewish martyr stories such as those of *2 Macc.* 6.18-31; *4 Macc.* 5.1-6.30; Rabbi Akiba; Elijah and Jezebel–Ahab.[142] There are also various Hellenistic themes such as the soothsayer, prophet or wise man associated with a king,[143] and the appearance of the daughter of a king at a feast to make a request.[144] Since our concern is with reactions of wonder, there are also external examples of a holy man causing the king or governmental authorities to marvel. One can note how in *4 Macc.* 6.13 the torturers are struck with wonder (ἐν θαυμαστῷ, other texts -ασμῷ) at the courage of Eleazer; how all wonder (θαυμασάντων) in 9.26 at the constancy of one of the brothers; and the 'tyrant' and his counsel marvel in 17.17 at the endurance (ἐξεθαύμασεν αὐτῶν τὴν ὑπομονήν) of the martyrs. Within the New Testament itself, one can note Acts 24.25: ἔμφοβος γενόμενος ὁ Φῆλιξ. Also important is Jn 19.8: μᾶλλον ἐφοβήθη, when Pilate heard that Jesus claimed to be the son of God.

The imperfect tense of ἐφοβεῖτο should probably be given durative force in 6.20,[145] and it is perhaps better to give the stronger sense of the verb, namely

---

141. As does H. Hoehner, *Herod Antipas* (SNTSMS, 17; Cambridge: Cambridge University Press, 1972), p. 163.
142. Pesch, *Markusevangelium*, I, p. 339; Klostermann, *Markusevangelium*, pp. 58-59; Gnilka, ' Martyrium', pp. 86-88.
143. C. Bonner, 'Note on Mark 6.20', *HTR* 37 (1944), p. 42.
144. H. Windisch, 'Kleine Beiträge zur evangelischen Überlieferung: 1: Zum Gastmahl des Antipas', *ZNW* 18 (1917/18), pp. 73-78.
145. Lenski, *Interpretation*, p. 252.

the meaning here of 'be terrified', or 'be frightened' (Isa. 8.12; 1 Pet. 3.14).[162] This is the only use of the verb in Mark. Present here are some 'typical Markan' elements, including the explanatory γάρ clause and the impersonal plural with no subject expressed.[163] Verse 50b follows with the Markan εὐθύς, and the response to the fear of v. 50a with θαρσεῖτε, ἐγώ εἰμι, μὴ φοβεῖσθε. Jesus wants to calm their terror because they think φάντασμά ἐστιν. They are afraid because they have encountered a ghost or water-spirit.[164] θαρσεῖτε...μὴ φοβεῖσθε are tautological.[165] Only twice in Mark are people told not to fear: here, and 5.36 (see also 16.6 Μὴ ἐκθαμβεῖσθε). The reaction of terror is a response to an epiphany (here thought to be a ghost), as is commonly suggested,[166] and the command not to fear often follows (Dan. 10.12, 19; Mt. 28.5; Lk. 1.13, 30). θαρσεῖτε occurs only here and in 10.49. Thus the reaction of fright at the night vision, mistakenly identified, is what Jesus seeks to calm.

The sequence continues with v. 51a, as Jesus enters the boat and the storm ceases. The reaction to this is in v. 51b: καὶ λίαν ἐκ περισσοῦ ἐν ἑαυτοῖς ἐξίσταντο. This is the only place in the gospel where λίαν is used with amazement, but the intensity of λίαν ἐκ περισσοῦ is not at all unusual (compare 7.37: καὶ ὑπερπερισσῶς ἐξέπλησσοντο...; 10.26: οἱ δὲ περισσῶς ἐξεπλήσσοντο...). The imperfect ἐξίσταντο indicates a continuing state of being 'out of themselves'. We have seen the verb related to the miraculous in 2.12 (healing with forgiveness), and with the cognate noun in 5.42. In the Old Testament it is often used at acts of God (Gen. 42.28: καὶ ἐξέστη ἡ καρδία αὐτῶν, καὶ ἐταράχθησαν πρὸς ἀλλήλους λέγοντες τί τοῦτο ἐποιήσεν ὁ θεὸς ἡμῖν; Exod. 19.18: καὶ ἐξέστη πᾶς ὁ λαὸς σφόδρα; Exod. 18.9: ἐξέστη δὲ Ιοθορ; Lev. 9.24: καὶ εἶδεν πᾶς ὁ λαὸς καὶ ἐξέστη...; Wis. 5.2: καὶ ἐκστήσονται ἐπὶ τῷ παραδόξῳ τῆς σωτηρίας). Here there is the expression ἐν ἑαυτοῖς with ἐξίσταντο, not used elsewhere in Mark with amazement. The amazement was inward, and was not expressed in words.[167] The disciples are frightened at the sight of what they think was a spirit, and Jesus calms this fear. When Jesus enters the boat and the wind stops, they are then out of themselves almost beyond words as Mark loads

---

162. BAGD, p. 805.
163. Turner, 'Usage', pp. 378-83, on the impersonal plural; Pryke, *Redactional Style*, p. 160.
164. Lane, *Gospel*, p. 236; Taylor, *Gospel*, p. 326.
165. Lohmeyer, *Evangelium*, p. 131.
166. Lohmeyer, *Evangelium*, p. 134; Kertelge, *Wunder*, p. 145; Schmithals, *Evangelium*, p. 352.
167. Swete, *Mark*, p. 139. BAGD, p. 212 contrasts ἐν ἑαυτῷ with audible expression.

on λίαν and ἐκ περισσοῦ to express the reaction, but this second, continuing reaction is internal. Is it negative or inappropriate? Many think so.[168]

The understanding of the reaction of amazement in 6.51b depends to a great extent on how one understands the γὰρ of 6.52.[169] Weeden, for example, says that the original tone of the reaction in 6.51b is thoroughly positive, but Mark appended the story with 6.52 to make the original hospitible, ecstatic response a psychologically negative reaction.[170] Heil says that the excessive amazement registers the extraordinary and marvelous character of the epiphany, and serves as an admiration-motif which is an appropriate conclusion, but v. 52 has elevated the problem of the understanding of Jesus' true identity to non-understanding.[171] Schenke believes that v. 51b is an expression of unbelief when understood in connection with v. 52.[172] All of these interpretations assume a redactional γὰρ explanatory in v. 52, that the dramatic reaction is explained by their lack of understanding and hardness of heart, but do not even consider that there might be other possibilities.

Tagawa focuses on the use of γὰρ and notes that in Mark it is not always used to introduce an explanation of the preceding phrase. In a number of cases the evangelist uses γὰρ as the beginning of a parenthetical statement, where he gives his personal explanation for what he has recounted.[173] This has been documented in an article on γὰρ in Mark by C.H. Bird.[174] Tagawa suggests that 6.52

168. Pesch, *Markusevangelium*, I, p. 363; Lane, *Gospel*, p. 238; Nineham, *Gospel*, p. 180; Alexander, *Gospel*, p. 175; Klostermann, *Markusevangelium*, p. 51; Tyson, 'Blindness', p. 36; Kertelge, *Wunder*, p. 145; J.P. Heil, *Jesus Walking on the Sea: Meaning and Gospel Functions of Mt. 14.22-33, Mk. 6.45-52 and Jn. 6.15b-21* (AnBib, 87; Rome: Biblical Institute Press, 1981), pp. 60-67.

169. Verse 52 is uncontested as redactional, as is stated by Schenke, *Wundererzählungen*, p. 241, and Koch, *Bedeutung*, p. 107. See also Pesch, *Markusevangelium*, I, p. 357; Schmithals, *Evangelium*, I, p. 332; Lohmeyer, *Evangelium*, p. 133; Kertelge, *Wunder*, p. 145.

170. Weeden, *Traditions*, p. 49.

171. Heil, *Jesus*, pp. 73-74, 127.

172. Schenke, *Wundererzählungen*, p. 241.

173. Tagawa, *Miracles*, p. 115.

174. C.H. Bird, 'Some γὰρ Clauses in St. Mark's Gospel', *JTS* 4 (1953), pp. 171-87. Bird cites 1.16-17; 5.42; 10.45 and 11.13 as places where γὰρ cannot explain the previous sentence. For this understanding, see also A.T. Robinson, *A Grammar of the Greek New Testament in the Light of Historical Research* (Nashville, TN: Broadman Press, 1934), p. 1190, where he notes that sometimes the explanation γὰρ may introduce can come in by way of an appendix to the train of thought, so Mt. 4.18; Mk. 2.15; Rom. 7.2.

contains more of a commentary on the attitude of the disciples in the entire pericope than the reason for the amazement (the nuance is 'to conclude, I underline the fact that they did not comprehend the sense of the miracle of the bread and their heart was hardened').[175] In a study of 16.8 and the γάρ clause there, Magness has argued that in 6.52 Mark may mean to connect the misunderstanding with the failure of recognition during the storm rather than a failure to appreciate the miracle and reverence the miracle-worker after the storm (which is more in line with the Markan pattern).[176]

Does v. 52 ('for they did not understand about the loaves, but their heart was hardened') best explain v. 51b, or the lack of trust and recognition during the storm? Surely it is a better explanation of the lack of recognition of Jesus and failure to act in faith during the storm than amazement later at the calming of the storm. This was the pattern in 4.35-41. Timidity or cowardice during a storm is rebuked by the question, 'Have you no faith?'. Amazement follows the calming of the storm. Also, readers have been given the use of ἐξίστημι in positive and necessary reactions already in 2.12 and 5.42. Again, one would ask if the reaction was avoidable, or whether, if the disciples' hearts were not hardened, would that mean that they would not react with amazement at the miraculous and supernatural calming of a tempest at sea? In light of the Old Testament uses of the term, such reactions are inevitable at the deeds of God. Finally, we note that as an explanation, v. 52 does not fit the intensity of the amazement in v. 51b. If amazement was being criticized, there would be no need for the intensity of expression preceding, unless one wanted to argue that some amazement was necessary, but excessive amazement was not. In that case, one is quantifying 'appropriate levels' of amazement for which there is no precedent. I would rather conclude that 6.52 is a general statement explaining the lack of faith of the disciples in the storm, and not a specific explanation of 6.51b.

Markan elements in 6.50a were mentioned earlier, namely the γάρ clause and the impersonal plural verb, and for these reasons the verse can be taken as redactional.[177] I would also agree with those who say v. 51b is redactional because of the Markan style of doubling λίαν ἐκ περισσοῦ (περισσῶς is a

---

175. Tagawa, *Miracles*, p. 116.
176. J.L. Magness, *Sense and Absence: Structure and Suspension in the Ending of Mark's Gospel* (SBLDS; Chico, CA: Scholars Press, 1986), p. 97.
177. So Pryke, *Redactional Style*, p. 160; Schmithals, *Evangelium*, I, p. 332; Lohmeyer, *Evangelium*, p. 134.

redactional term), and this level of intensity of amazement is not necessary to the story, though a less intense reaction may have been rewritten here.[178] What we therefore have is a Markan shaping of a response of cowardice and lack of understanding during the storm which is met with a word of comfort by Jesus. This is followed by a more intense reaction at the entire event (Jesus walking on the sea, entering the boat, and the storm ceasing). This is not in itself portrayed as negative, but may just be seen as the natural reaction seeing in Jesus what only God was thought to be able to do. This pattern of fear and comfort followed by greater awe is similar to what was seen in 4.35-41, and must be kept in mind specifically when we come to 16.1-8.

One sees in this pericope, then, the breaking-in of the rule of God over the threats of an unruly creation or watery chaos as Jesus exercises authority which God possessed in the Old Testament. Fear comes when this is not understood, as the result of hardened hearts, but the overwhelming superiority of the creator over the creation and the act of bringing cosmos out of chaos strikes the disciples with a further reaction of awe that almost goes beyond words. The Lord has become king over creation through Jesus, and this strikes deep into the consciousness of people confronted with the uncanny.

Mark 7.37

The motif of wonder occurs next in another intensive verse, 7.37: καὶ ὑπερπερισσῶς ἐξεπλήσσοντο λέγοντες, Καλῶς πάντα πεποίηκεν. καὶ τοὺς κωφοὺς ποιεῖ ἀκούειν καὶ [τοὺς] ἀλάλους λαλεῖν.[179] 7.31-37 is a pericope which is found only in Mark. This is part of the 'great omission' of Mk 6.45-8.26 not in Luke, and Mt. 15.29-31, which follows Mark's sequence between the healing of a Canaanite woman and the feeding of the four thousand is a possible rewriting, though it is a differently shaped pericope, a summary with a different form and a differently named location, but with an expansion of the

---

178. 6.51 is considered redactional by Schweizer, *Good News*, p. 141; Schenke, *Wundererzählungen*, p. 241; Ritt, 'Seewandel', p. 82; P. Lapide, 'A Jewish Exegesis of the Walking on the Water', Concilium 138 (1980), p. 37. Gnilka, *Evangelium*, I, p. 266 says it is difficult to decide with v. 51b.

179. The article τοὺς preceding ἀλάλους is contained in A, D^gr, X, θ, 0131, f¹ and the majority of miniscules, while the article is omitted by ℵ, B, L, D, Δ, 33, 892, 1241 and arm. A number of versions have both readings, and both the article and noun are omitted by W, 28 and syr^c. It is difficult to decide, as shown by the C rating of the article by the UBS committee, and perhaps it is best to include it in brackets.

allusion to Isa. 35.5-6 in Mk 7.37 and in Mt. 15.31. Mk 7.31-37 is in the middle of three miracles among the Gentiles (7.24-30, 31-37, and 8.1-10), and the setting of the Decapolis picks up the location of 5.20. By attributing amazement to the Gentiles, Mark has them experience the intervention of God in the same way as the Jews.

Mark 7.31-31 is very similar to the healing of the blind man at Bethsaida in 8.22-26. One miracle involves a deaf and dumb man, the other a blind man. One is a Gentile, the other a Jew. In both cases a touch is requested (7.32; 8.22). Both are taken apart from others present (in 7.33 from the crowd, and in 8.23 from the village). Both cases involve spitting into the part needing healing (7.33; 8.24). Jesus places his hands on both men (7.33; 8.23). Both are forbidden to tell others (7.36; 8.26). Amazement, however, follows only in 7.37. This has led Gnilka to think that both healing of blind men stories were originally bound together, and the praise of 7.37 was applied at the end to both,[180] but Schenke has suggested that each story had its own acclamation, with 8.27-30 following the other healing of a blind man story, corresponding to 7.37.[181] In 8.27-30, however, the confession is conditioned on a proper understanding of the Messiah by 8.31-33, while the praise in 7.37 is thoroughly positive, as we shall see. The correspondence is not exact. Gnilka may be correct in his suggestion, but it may also be that 7.37 functions as the summary of a number of miracle stories (see below).

Mark 7.31-37 has been called form-critically a classic miracle story, with many parallel elements both within and also beyond the New Testament. One sees, first, the request for help (v. 32); second, the request to place hands on the sick one (v. 32) (Mk 1.31; 5.23 (41); 6.5; 8.23-25; 9.27); third, the separation from the crowd (v. 33) (5.40; 8.23); fourth, spitting (v. 33b) (8.23; Jn 9.6; Vespasian in Tacitus, *Hist*. 4.81.1-3 and Suet. *Ves*. 7; Dio Cassius 66.8); fifth, looking up into heaven (v. 34a) (6.34, connected in Judaism with prayer; Ps. 121.1; 123.1; Lk. 18.13; Jn 17.1; Philo, *Vit. Mos*. 1.190); sixth, groaning (v. 34b) (*PGM* 13.945; Paris Mag. Pap. 2492, suppl. 6k. 574, 1.2441; Leiden Pap. W, col. 21); seventh, use of a foreign word (v. 34c) (5.41; Lucian, *Philop*. 9, 31); eighth, healing (v. 35) (1.31; 2.12; Lucian, *Philop*. 12; Philostratus, *Vit. Ap*. 4.45); ninth, the command to silence (v. 36a) (1.44; 5.43; 8.26; 9.9); tenth,

---

180. Gnilka, *Evangelium*, I, p. 296.
181. Schenke, *Wundererzählungen*, pp. 61-62.

the breaking of the command (v. 36b) (1.45); and eleventh, amazement (v. 37) (2.12; 5.42).[182]

The reaction in 7.37 is quite intense. The preceding adverb ὑπερπερισσῶς, 'beyond all measure', is found only here in Greek literature, and Alexander says that the writer had to coin a word to express the boundlessness of the amazement: a superlative superlative![183] Although Mk 6.51 has ἐκ περισσοῦ ἐν ἑαυτοῖς ἐξίσταντο, and 10.26 has οἱ δὲ περισσῶς ἐξεπλήσσοντο..., this is even more intensive than those verses.

This is the only place in Mark where ἐκπλήσσομαι is used with a miracle (1.22; 6.2; 10.26; and 11.18 all related to teaching, and in Matthew it occurs only for teaching, in 7.38; 13.54; 19.25; and 22.33; while Lk. 9.43 is the only place for a miracle in that gospel). The combination ὑπερπερισσῶς ἐκπλήσσοντο could be translated 'struck out of their senses beyond all measure'.

The participle λέγοντες follows wonder also in 1.27 (ἐθαμβήθησαν ἅπαντες...λέγοντες...); 2.12 (ἐξίστασθαι πάντας...λέγοντες...); 6.2 (ἐξεπλήσσοντο λέγοντες...) and 10.26 (οἱ δὲ περισσῶς ἐξεπλήσσοντο λέγοντες...). It seems by these examples that the gospel is using dramatic reactions of wonder as a bridge to questions or statements regarding Jesus' identity or activity. The statement which follows regarding Jesus' activity here is illuminating.

The text reads Καλῶς πάντα πεποίηκεν. καὶ τοὺς κωφοὺς ποιεῖ ἀκούειν καὶ [τοὺς] ἀλάλους λαλεῖν. There are clear echoes of Gen. 1.31 (καὶ εἶδεν ὁ θεὸς τὰ πάντα, ὅσα ἐποίησεν, καὶ ἰδοὺ καλὰ λίαν); Isa. 35.5-6 (τότε ἀνοιχθήσονται ὀφθαλμοὶ τυφλῶν, καὶ ὦτα κωφῶν ἀκούσονται...καὶ τρανὴ ἔσται γλῶσσα μογιλάλων); and perhaps Sir. 39.16 (τὰ ἔργα κυρίου πάντα ὅτι καλὰ σφόδρα). With this response following the miracle, more than just the miracle of 7.31-36 is in view (πάντα πεποίηκεν). Mark has the Gentile observers say that all the works which Jesus has done in their midst (in the gospel?) are good.[184]

The allusions in the acclamation indicate that the works of Jesus are placed

---

182. See C. Bonner, 'Traces of Thaumaturgic Technique in the Miracles', *HTR* 20 (1927), pp. 171-81; Schenke, *Wundererzählungen*, p. 272; Kertelege, *Wunder*, pp. 157-59; Theissen, *Stories*, pp. 63-66.

183. Alexander, *Gospel*, p. 204. Taylor, *Gospel*, p. 356, says nowhere, even in Mark, is so great astonishment depicted, His translation is 'astonished beyond measure'.

184. Schmithals, *Evangelium*, I, p. 339, says that this response interprets all the miraculous works until now. However, the setting places this in the mouth of Gentiles in the Decapolis (using references to Jewish scripture in their acclamation), and probably should be limited to their recognition of the miracles in their territory. This would include 5.1-20.

in the context of the expected messianic redemption and renewal of the creation.[185] Mark has placed these Jewish concepts in the mouth of Gentiles in the Decapolis, and used their intense reaction of wonder at a healing to lead to this recognition. Amazement again appears in the context of the breaking-in of the rule of God in power to redeem and renew the creation.

It should be noted that the wonder which leads to the acclamation is a thoroughly positive, believing response.[186] There is recognition and understanding of what the reader was told in 1.1, 9-11 and 14-15. Amazement in Mark can hardly be interpreted as indicating a lack of understanding or faith in light of 7.37, where the acclamation produced by the wonder is full of theological awareness as to what is taking place with Jesus' ministry. As in 5.33 where a woman reacts with wonder consonant with her faith, here Gentiles react with wonder co-existent with a true understanding of the theological significance of Jesus' works. In both cases, it is the marginal who are viewed positively, as may be the case in 5.20.

The nature of the acclamation (Καλῶς πάντα πεποίηκεν) has led some, as was noted above, to see 7.37 as being originally the conclusion to a number of miracle stories.[187] There are redactional elements in v. 37, including ἐκπλήσσεσθαι, λαλεῖν, καλῶς,[188] and the contribution of the unique intensity of ὑπερπερισσῶς and the attribution to the Gentiles of an acclamation full of Old Testament allusions certainly betrays a Markan hand. If this was originally the conclusion to a sequence or a series of miracle stories, it has been rewritten with intensity and in the context of Gentile territory.

There is here, then, an example of a recognition of the promised intervention of God being present in all the works of Jesus.[189] That recognition is placed in

---

185. Grundmann, *Evangelium*, p. 157, relates this to the prophetic promises for the end of time, in which the creation will be renewed, beginning the new and final creation which God has promised. Gnilka, *Evangelium*, I, p. 298, says that v. 37 indicates that the fulfillment of the OT eschatological prophesies has come.

186. Lane, *Gospel*, p. 267, calls it a 'response of faith'. Schmithals, *Evangelium*, I, p. 359, calls it a response of 'joyful faith'. Grundmann, *Evangelium*, p. 157, says that the praise was from deep amazement and full of belief.

187. Nineham, *Gospel*, p. 202. He says that the astonishment of v. 37 requires more than one act of healing to provoke it (p. 204). Gnilka, *Evangelium*, I, p. 296, says it applied to both 7.31-36 and 8.22-26. See also Schweizer, *Good News*, p. 154, and Schmithals, *Evangelium*, I, p. 359.

188. 7.37 is described as redactional by Pryke, *Redactional Style*, p. 162; Taylor, *Gospel*, p. 352; and Schweizer, *Good News*, p. 154.

189. Lane, *Gospel*, p. 268.

the mouths of Gentiles. God has broken-in with his kingly rule to restore creation as promised in the Old Testament. This recognition follows the act of being struck with deep, intense wonder. It can be suggested that the intensity here is purposefully made greater (by a redactional insertion or rewriting) than any other place in the gospel, with the possible exception of 16.8, in order to direct the reader or hearer to the understanding that wonder is the response of people to confrontation with the kingly power of God in the deeds of Jesus (as is evidenced in the acclamation). The Old Testament allusions in the acclamation do not allow us to stray to any other understanding. As was expected in the Old Testament, at the time when God came to rule with power, people would react with wonder (Hos. 3.5; Mic. 7.15-17; Zech. 14.13), and Mark specifically makes Gentiles the focus of that response in a positive way. Although some may be struck with amazement and stumble (as 6.2), God has intervened in Jesus and that intervention is experienced and recognized even beyond the borders of Israel. This would be something to which the Gentile Christians address by the second gospel could directly relate.

Mark 9.6

The next place where the motif of wonder occurs is in the account of the transfiguration, 9.2-13.[190] The text in v. 6 reads: οὐ γὰρ ᾔδει τί ἀποκριθῇ, ἔκφοβοι γὰρ ἐγένοντο. The transfiguration story follows the confession of Peter and the first passion prediction in 8.27-9.1. The account centers on the identification of Jesus as the 'beloved Son', which draws the reader back to the same identification at the baptism in 1.11. Along with that identification comes the summons to 'Listen to him'. This must be understood in light of the previous words of Jesus regarding the passion, and the corresponding summons to discipleship in 8.31-9.1. The entire pericope of the transfiguration must in fact be viewed as portraying an original christological setting with the added dimension of discipleship, in keeping with the setting of 8.27-10.45.[191] Although not all will accept

---

190. We should note here that Pesch, *Markusevangelium*, II, pp. 1-27, sees a pre-Markan passion story in 8.27-33; 9.2-13, 30-35; 10.1, 32-34, 46-52; 11.1-23, 27-33; 12.1-12, 13-17, 34c, 35-37, 41-44; 13.11-2; 14.1-16.8. For a good discussion of the strengths and weaknesses of proposed pre-Markan passion blocks, see M.L. Soards, 'The Question of a Pre-Markan Passion Narrative', Biblehashayam 11 (1985), pp. 144-169.

191. E. Best, *Following Jesus: Discipleship in the Gospel of Mark* (JSNTSup, 4; Sheffield: JSOT Press, 1981), p.58, and *Disciples*, pp. 206-25.

9.1 as the key to interpreting the transfiguration (Καὶ ἔλεγεν αὐτοῖς, Ἀμὴν λέγω ὑμῖν ὅτι εἰσίν τινες ὧδε τῶν ἑστηκότων οἵτινες οὐ γεύσωνται θανάτου ἕως ἂν ἴδωσιν τὴν βασιλείαν τοῦ θεοῦ ἐληλυθυῖαν ἐν δυνάμει), making the transfiguration a proleptic view of the kingdom for the three disciples present,[192] the emphasis on discipleship in the transfiguration must at least be seen in light of the summons to appropriate living in light of the breaking-in of the kingdom in 1.14-15.[193]

There are many Old Testament themes from the exodus in the transfiguration, including the 'six days' (see Exod. 24.16), the mountain (Exod. 24.12), transfiguration (Exod. 34.29, 30, 35), tents (Exod. 25.9), Elijah and Moses, the cloud and the voice (Exod. 24.16).[194] Other Jewish parallels include Dan. 12.3; *4 Ezra* 7.97; *2 Bar.* 50.10; *3 En.* 15.48c.[195] Parallel elements have led scholars to seek the genre of the transfiguration story, and suggestions have been many.

Some suggest that the transfiguration is a misplaced resurrection story.[196] This view has been opposed by many, and conclusively, in my view, by Dodd.[197]

192. Lane, *Gospel*, pp. 312-14; Cranfield, *Gospel*, pp. 287-89; and Taylor, *Gospel*, p. 385, say that there is at least a partial fulfillment of 9.1 in the transfiguration, which was the interpretation given by patristic writers such as Chrysostom, Theophylact and Euthymius.

193. Rau, ' Markusevangelium', p. 2230, says that the entire second portion of Mk. 8.27-16.8 is about the beginning of a new collecting of the people of God with the coming near of the kingdom.

194. J.A. Zeisler, 'The Transfiguration Story and the Markan Soteriology', *ExpTim* 81 (1970), pp. 263-68.

195. W. Gerber, 'Die Metamorphose Jesu: Mark 9.2f, par', *TZ* 23 (1967), pp. 385-88.

196. Bultmann, *History*, p. 259; Klostermann, *Markusevangelium*, p. 86; W. Schmithals, 'Der Markusschluss, die Verklärungsgeschichte und die Aussendung der Zwölf', ZTK 69 (1972), pp. 379-411, who believe that the transfiguration was a part of the sequel to 16.1-8 in the source of Mark, along with 3.13-19 and 6.6b-12.

197. C.H. Dodd, 'The Appearances of the Risen Christ: An Essay in Form-Criticism of the Gospels', in *Studies in the Gospels: Essays in Memory of R.H. Lightfoot* (ed. D. Nineham; Oxford: Basil Blackwell, 1955), pp. 9-35. Dodd says that the transfiguration contrasts with the resurrection accounts 'in almost every particular'. He notes that the resurrection appearances start with the disciples orphaned, whereas in the transfiguration they are together with Jesus throughout. In the transfiguration Jesus is silent, but in the resurrection appearances his words receive a significant place. In the transfiguration a voice comes from heaven, which does not occur in the resurrection accounts. In the transfiguration Christ is accompanied by Moses and Elijah, where he is always alone in resurrection appearances. Christ is clothed in visible glory in the transfiguration, which is absent from resurrection accounts. Also standing against the transfiguration as a misplaced resurrection account are Taylor, *Gospel*, p. 367; Cranfield, *Gospel*, pp. 293-94; Schweizer, *Good News*, pp. 180-81;

Other suggestions have included an epiphany story,[198] an enthronement story,[199] a theophany,[200] and a story from the world of magic.[201] Perhaps more fruitful than these suggestions is that of Kee, who says the story is a proleptic vision of the exaltation of Jesus as the kingly Son of Man granted to the disciples as eschatological witnesses. He notes that Mark 9 and Daniel 10 have the same aim: to give assurance to the righteous undergoing suffering that God will bring about vindication in spite of Satanic opposition, and that the rule of God will ultimately triumph. This is an apocalyptic vision similar to Daniel 10 with the background of Jewish kingship.[202] I will come back to this after a look at the terminology used in 9.6.

The verse begins with a γάρ explanatory clause, explaining why Peter said

---

Mann, *Mark*, p. 357; R.H. Stein, 'Is the Transfiguration (Mk. 9.2-8) a Misplaced Resurrection Account?', *JBL* 95 (1976), pp. 79-96; Gnilka, *Evangelium*, II, pp. 30-31; and M. Smith, 'The Origin and History of the Transfiguration Story', *USQR* 36 (1980), p. 41.

198. F.R. McCurley, Jr., 'And After Six Days (Mk. 9.2): A Semitic Literary Device', *JBL* 93 (1974), pp. 67-81; Schmid, *Gospel*, p. 170; Klostermann, *Markusevangelium*, p. 86 (he states both misplaced resurrection story and epiphany story).

199. U.B Müller, 'Die Christologische Absicht des Markusevangeliums und die Verklärungsgeschichte', *ZNW* 64 (1973), p. 190, says it was an original enthronement tradition shaped in light of the suffering Son of Man being proclaimed as the Son of God. See also H. Riesenfeld, *Jésus transfiguré l'arrière du récit évangélique de la transfiguration de notre-Seigneur* (Copenhagen: Ejnar Munksgaard, 1947), pp. 281-88.

200. H.P. Müller, 'Die Verklärung Jesu: Ein motivgeschichtliche Studie', *ZNW* 51 (1960), pp. 61-62, sees Mk. 9.3-6, 8, as originally a theophany story combined with another complex, 9.2a, b, 7, 9.

201. Smith, 'Origin', p. 42, says that the original story exemplified a well-known type of story which involved a magic company or operation or landscape which suddenly vanishes when the wrong word is said or the wrong action performed. Smith claims Jesus practiced magic.

202. H.C. Kee, 'The Transfiguration in Mark: Epiphany or Apocalyptic Vision?', in *Understanding the Sacred Text: Essays in Honor of Morton S. Enslin on the Hebrew Bible and Christian Beginnings* (ed. J. Reumann; Valley Forge, PA: Judson Press, 1972), pp. 135-52. Kee notes that Ἐπιφανεία is the appearance of gods or lesser divinities to men in Hellenistic writers, but in biblical usage it is limited to theophanies or manifestations of divine power coming to someone's aid. He says that in Mark the climax of the story is not the metamorphosis of Jesus, but the heavenly voice, and that there is no manifestation of Jesus' power. Also seeing the transfiguration as an apocalyptically colored vision is Schweizer, *Good News*, pp. 180-81, while M.E. Thrall, 'Elijah and Moses in Mark's Account of the Transfiguration', *NTS* 16 (1970), pp. 310-11, sees the transfiguration as a proleptic view of the resurrection state of Christ.

what he did in v. 5: οὐ γὰρ ᾔδει τί ἀποκριθῇ. Wonder occurs in the ensuing γάρ clause, which shifts to the third-person plural: ἔκφοβοι γὰρ ἐγένοντο. The γάρ–γάρ sequence occurs also in Mk 11.18, and also in 16.8; all have reactions of wonder.[203] The shift to the plural in the second γάρ clause in the verse would then not be a further explanation of why Peter said what he did, but a general explanation of the state of the trio of disciples at the marvelous vision.[204]

The intensive term ἔκφοβος is found only here and Heb. 12.21 (ἔκφοβός εἰμι καὶ ἔντρομος) in the New Testament (but ἔκφοβος is found in Lk. 24.5, 37; Acts 10.4, 24.25; Rev. 11.13). The Septuagint has ἔκφοβος only in *1 Macc.* 13.2 Aq, Sm and Deut. 9.19 (the verb ἐκφοβεῖσθαι is very common, for example Lev. 26.6; Deut. 28.26; Judg. 16.25; Wis. 11.19, 17.6, 9, 19 and others). The adjective is also rare in Greek literature. For example, Plutarch, *Fab.* 6.8: ἀλλ' ἔκφοβοι καὶ περιαλγεῖς οὖσαι δρόμῳ κατὰ τῶν ὀρῶν ἐγένοντο, as 2000 cattle dash down a mountain when torches attached to their horns burn down and the fire begins to burn their skin; and Aristotle, *Physiog.* 812b.29: ὅτι καὶ οἱ ἔκφοβοι γιγνόμενοι φρίσσουσιν, 'for when men are frightened their hair stands up on end'. The kind of terror which the disciples had on the mountain is well explained by the reference from Aristotle. The reaction is not mere fear, but fright enough to make one's hair stand up on end.

Visions were known to bring this kind of reaction. For example, in *4 Macc.* 4.10, the text reads: πολὺν αὐτοῖς φόβον τε καὶ τρόμον ἐνιέντες. Great fear and trembling comes upon Apollonius and his soldiers when they see a vision of angels from heaven riding upon horses with lightning flashing from their armor (Apollonius and his soldiers were attempting to seize the deposits in the temple). I would also note the reaction to the vision of the majestic angel in Dan. 10.7: ἀλλ' ἢ ἔκστασις μεγάλη ἐπέπεσεν ἐπ' αὐτούς, καὶ ἔφυγον ἐν φόβῳ. the thought, as Kee has suggested, is similar. There is a vision of a being

---

203. J.M. Nützel, *Die Verklärungersählung im Markusevangelium* (Würzburg: Echter Verlag, 1973), p. 136, says that 11.18b is redactional since the teaching over which the crowd is amazed can hardly be that of v. 17, and that 18a is likely redactional also, so that the double γάρ clause in 9.6 goes back to the evangelist. He does not want to use 16.8 as evidence, since he says that both γάρ clauses there introduce the reason for the previous main clause (n.254).

204. For this understanding of γάρ in Mark, see n. 173 above.

205. Pryke, *Redactional Style*, p. 163; Stein, 'Transfiguration', p. 86; Weeden, *Traditions*, p. 121; Thrall, 'Elijah', p. 308; Gnilka, *Evangelium*, II, p. 32; McCurley, 'And...', p. 77; Best, *Following*, p. 56, and 'Transfiguration', p. 216. Nützel, *Verklärungserzählung*, p. 136, says there is 'wide unanimity' on v. 6 being redactional.

of supernatural splendor, and those present are struck with terror and run away. It is also a vision of a heavenly being in Acts 10.4 which brings this response from Cornelius: καὶ ἔμφοβος γενόμενος...

It is also of interest to note that the other place in the New Testament where ἔκφοβος is used, Heb. 12.21, is a description of the words of Moses upon seeing the glory of the Lord on Sinai in Deut. 9.19. Thus both heavenly beings and divine glory bring reactions which use terms beyond the simple φόβος. That is precisely what the disciples react to in the transfiguration pericope: two heavenly beings, and Jesus in glory. The invasion of the heavenly into the earthly causes a terror in the disciples as to almost make their hair stand on end.

There is widespread agreement that 9.6 is redactional.[205] The reasons include the verse not furthering the story, but containing a thought of its own; the mention of the fear coming earlier than necessary (Luke has it as the disciples enter the cloud); the double γάρ, the shift to the plural, and the unique ἔκφοβος.[206] The redactional nature of the verse has caused some to postulate that the evangelist added it to give a negative view of the disciples, who are once again without understanding and speak out of turn.[207] However, in light of the traditions that such esteemed men as Moses, Daniel (Dan. 4.19, 7.28) and Cornelius have similar reactions at similar experiences, it would seem unnecessary to read a negative polemic into the standard reaction of the earthly at the heavenly. I would instead suggest that the redactional nature of the verse, along with the redactional ἀκούετε αὐτοῦ, functions in the pericope to emphasize that when people have met with the heavenly and reacted in terror, they must go on and live with obedient discipleship. It has been noted how, in the gospel, amazement can be consonant with faith or lead to a rejection of Jesus. The redactional operation in the transfiguration encourages the readers to proceed to obedient faith and discipleship.

The transfiguration pericope once again shows the intervention of God in the life of Jesus. We see Jesus transfigured with the 'divine passive' verbs, μετεμορφώθη and ὤφθη, along with the cloud and the voice. Throughout the gospel people reacted with wonder when God intervened through Jesus, and

---

206. Nützel, *Verklärungserzählung*, p. 137, suggests, along with Best, 'Transfiguration', p. 216, that it is possible that tradition was rewritten and intensified here by Mark.

207. Bultmann, *History*, p. 259, says that v. 6 is the author's embarrassment at backdating the story. Among those who see v. 6 as redactionally presenting a negative view of the trio of apostles are Weeden, *Traditions*, p. 121; Nützel, *Verklärungserzählung*, p. 245; Kelber, *Kingdom*, p. 49; and Thrall, 'Elijah', p. 315.

here we see three disciples react with wonder when God intervenes with Jesus. Since christology in Mark is in the context of the breaking-in of the kingdom (which means the intervention of God because the 'time is fulfilled'), the transfiguration again shows how the intervention of God with a focus on Jesus brings wonder in a way consistent with what has been seen up to now in the gospel. I again note the added element of an encouragement to obedient discipleship to follow wonder, since the intervention of God is sometimes followed by rejection of Jesus or stumbling.

Summary

I would emphasise two elements in the way amazement works in the first half of Mark. First, it can and must co-exist with obedience rather than rejection (since either may follow). Many who have experienced the intervention of God through Jesus have responded with wonder, but not all undergoing this experience have proceeded to faith and repentance. Secondly, it has been conditioned again and again that wonder follows the acts of God in the breaking-in of the kingdom. This will become vitally important in the second half of the gospel as we will see the saving acts of God in an unexpected way. God was intervening to save people (3.4; 5.23, 28, 34; 6.56), Jews and Gentiles, in the first half. In the second half, God will further act to save people, and that intervention will again bring amazement. The form of that saving intervention, however, will move in a new and unexpected direction, as the Son of Man gives his life as a ransom for many. One way in which this surprising event will be recognized as indeed being the breaking-in of the rule of God is that it will bring amazement, just as the rule of God did in the first half of the gospel. In the totality, God has acted in Jesus to save.

There is also the crucial element in the first half of Mark that amazement is often linked with confessions or questions related to Jesus' identity and mission (1.27; 2.12; 4.41; 7.27). It is surely no accident that the fitting acclamation of 7.37 refers to the eschatological restoration of creation, and is given by Gentiles! In the confession of 2.12, God is seen as acting in the works of Jesus. Wonder is then integrated with Jesus' mission and serves as a vehicle to properly identify it, when followed by faith. The proper identification is that the kingly rule is subduing evil and restoring the creation in Jesus, the spirit-anointed Son of God.

There are remarkable nuances also present in the first half of Mark. Authoritative teaching, healing and forgiveness, and the experience of restoration are all ways in which divine intervention is experienced. The pure miracle or exorcism reaction is rare. God's action to save is shaped in ways to direct one's attention beyond pure acts of power to the integrated ministry of the rule of God in Jesus. Readers or hearers are not seeing pure power displays, but God intervening to rule, save and restore creation in Jesus.

Chapter 6

MARK II

In Mk 9.15 the text reads: καὶ εὐθὺς πᾶς ὁ ὄχλος ἰδόντας αὐτὸν ἐξεθαμβήθησαν, καὶ προστρέχοντες ἠσπάζοντο αὐτόν. This comes near the beginning of the pericope on the healing of a boy with an unclean spirit in 9.14-29. The reason the mere sight of Jesus brings a reaction of wonder has puzzled many interpreters. Although there has been no lack of suggestions, as we shall see, one can gain some insight by observing how wonder has occurred in the gospel previously and comparing it with the present case.

Several themes which we have seen throughout the gospel occur again in the pericope and link it especially to chapter 1. This is the final exorcism in the gospel, and as the vanquishing of Satan is again demonstrated, this once more shows the triumph over evil by the coming of the rule of God.[1] There is here a 'cosmic confrontation with a soteriological center'.[2] This can also be seen in the technical term ἐπετίμησεν in v. 25, which has been discussed in the previous chapter (compare 1.25; 4.39). Along with this, one also sees the theme of faith or lack of faith in the pericope, especially in v. 19: ῏Ω γενεὰ ἄπιστος, and in vv. 23-24: ὁ δὲ Ἰησοῦς εἶπεν αὐτῷ· τὸ εἰ δύνῃ- πάντα δυνατὰ τῷ πιστεύοντι. εὐθὺς κράξας ὁ πατὴρ τοῦ παιδίου ἔλεγεν· πιστεύω· βοήθει μου τῇ ἀπιστίᾳ. The combination of the vanquishing of Satan and the summons to faith recalls 1.14-15 and the programmatic miracle in 1.21-28. Again Jesus is portrayed as teacher, espcially with the address Διδάσκαλε of v. 17 (compare 1.21, 27). A further theme that links the pericope with the early chapters of the gospel is discipleship, especially in the inability of the disciples to cast out the demon, v. 18,

---

1. C.E.B. Cranfield, 'St. Mark 9.14-29', *SJT* 2 (1950), p. 59.
2. F.G. Lang, 'Sola Gratia in Markusevangelium: Die Soteriologie des Markus nach 9.14-29 und 10.17-31', in *Rechtfertigung: Festschrift für Ernst Käsemann zum 70. Geburtstag* (ed. J. Friedrich, W. Pohlmann and P. Stuhlmacher; Göttingen: Vandenhoeck & Ruprecht, 1976), p. 326.

and the private instruction in vv. 28-29. This places the story within the context of the teachings on discipleship in 8.27-10.45,[3] and the initial call in 1.16-20. Other links with ch. 1 of the gospel include a declaration of Jesus as 'beloved son' (1.11; 9.7) preceding a reaction of wonder. Finally, the motif of wonder occurs in the beginning of the pericope, which recalls the way the motif first appeared in the gospel, in 1.22. In both cases it is thrust to the front of a pericope redactionally, as I will note, and in both cases it draws attention away from wonder at the miraculous acts of Jesus to another facet of his activity which the evangelist wants to emphasize.

Some have doubted the unity of this pericope, and have seen two miracle stories combined.[4] The reasons include tensions in the story, such as two descriptions of the sickness (vv. 17-18, 22a); the crowd being present in v. 14, but then assembling in v. 25; the disciples playing a role in vv. 14-19, but then being ignored in vv. 20-27; the dumb spirit of v. 17 is described in v. 25 as deaf and dumb; one motive for the healing is provided in v. 24, but another in v. 25; the symptoms (vv. 18a, 20b, 22a) have nothing to do with the dumbness (vv. 17b, 25) or deafness (v. 25); and v. 18 uses a vocabulary different from vv. 20, 26.[5]

Not all would agree with this analysis.[6] It could be argued that the repetition of the symptoms is an intensification; the doubting plea of v. 22 presupposes disappointment with the disciples, so they are present in vv. 20-27; the idea of faith in v. 23 picks up v. 19; and the regathering of the ὄχλος may be connected with the threat of demonic action.[7] It must be admitted, however, that there are

---

3. Best, *Following*, p. 67; and J. Roloff, *Das Kerygma und der irdische Jesus: Historische Motive in den Jesus-Erzählungen der Evangelien* (Göttingen: Vandenhoeck & Ruprecht, 1973), p. 146, who says Mark understood the pericope as a story of the disciples.

4. Bultmann, *History*, p. 211; P.J. Achtemeier, 'Miracles and the Historical Jesus: A Study of Mark 9.14-29', *CBQ* 37 (1975), p. 476; G. Bornkamm, '*Pneuma alalon*: Einer Studie zum Markusevangelium' in *Gesammelte Aufsätze, Geschichte und Glaube* (Munich: Kaiser, 1971), II, p. 24; Koch, *Bedeutung*, pp. 115-16; Taylor, *Gospel*, p. 395; Schweizer, *Good News*, 1987, p. 187; J. Schniewind, *Das Evangelium nach Markus* (NTD, 4; Göttingen: Vandenhoeck & Ruprecht, 1949), p. 125.

5. Achtemeier, 'Miracles', p. 476. Bultmann, *History*, p. 211, says that one story had a contrast between the master and the disciples in ability to heal, and the other was an apophthegm, describing the paradox of believing faith.

6. Kertelge, *Wunder*, p. 174; Cranfield, *Gospel*, p. 299; Schenke, *Wundererzählungen*, p. 317; Theissen, *Stories*, p. 136; Schmithals, *Evangelium*, II, p. 407-408.

7. Theissen, *Stories*, p. 136. Schmithals, *Evangelium*, pp. 407-408, suggests that the regathering of the crowd may be in anticipation of the healing, as a gathering near the body of the child, and that the descriptions of the illness can be complementary rather than

tensions, but some of these may have to do with redactional expansions, such as the introduction of the crowd in v. 15, and perhaps an intensification of the demonic affliction of the boy.

The reaction in v. 15, which at first glance seems unmotivated, is by all accounts unique. There have been many different suggestions to account for the reaction. It has been suggested that v. 15 is the original conclusion of the miracle story of 8.22-26;[8] the appearance of Jesus is portrayed in the manner of a theophany evoking Exod. 34.29-35;[9] this is typical amazement at the appearance of a miracle worker;[10] there is a similarity to the portrait of a θεῖος ἀνήρ as a result of the transfiguration;[11] wonder is a result of the unexpected appearance of Jesus;[12] the reaction is surprise at Jesus' arrival in the nick of time;[13] wonder is a result of the divine authority and power of Jesus;[14] the reaction is a response to a 'wholly other' nature of Jesus giving the appearance the nature of an epiphany;[15] wonder occurs because Jesus' miracle power is needed;[16] or there is a reaction of wonder simply because Jesus himself is amazing.[17] Before attempting to proceed to an interpretation, it is best first to examine the language of v. 15.

One meets for the first time in Mark the rare and intensive term ἐκθαμβέομαι (14.33, 16.5-6), which is not used outside Mark in the New Testament. The

---

contradictory. He also notes that there is not a NT analogy of a combination of two miracle stories. Schenke, *Wundererzählungen*, p. 318, says the only true stress in the story is the re-gathering of the crowd.

8. W. Schmithals, 'Die Heilung des Epileptischen (Mk. 9.14-29): Ein Beitrag zur notwendigen Revision der Formgeschicht', *Theologia Viatorum* 13 (1975), p. 214, and *Evangelium*, II, p. 15.

9. Tillesse, *Secret*, p. 92.

10. Schenke, *Wundererzählungen*, p. 329.

11. Koch, *Bedeutung*, p. 124, n. 52.

12. Taylor, *Gospel*, p. 396, and Roloff, *Kerygma*, p. 146.

13. Branscomb, *Gospel*, p. 123.

14. Cranfield, 'Mark 9', p. 58; and Schweizer, *Good News*, p. 187, who says that Jesus comes with an authority entirely different from that of the teachers of the law (1.22, 27), which emanates from him before he speaks or acts. Pesch, *Evangelium*, II, p. 87, says that it is amazement at Jesus' numinous presence.

15. Bornkamm, 'Pneuma', p. 26. Gnilka, *Evangelium*, II, p. 46, says that the appearance is presented as an epiphany as Jesus was declared in the transfiguration as the Son of God.

16. Klostermann, *Evangelium*, p. 90.

17. Tagawa, *Miracles*, p. 107, says that it is purely and simply the person of Jesus which provokes amazement: 'Jésus est là!'.

related θαμβέομαι was seen in 1.27, and it will occur again in 10.24 and 32. The preposition ἐκ has the function of intensification,[18] so that the verb has the meaning here of 'utterly astounded'. It is infrequent in all Greek literature (Sir. 30.9 is the only usage in LXX; Orphica, *Arg.* 1217; Galen, 16.493K; P. Grenfell, 1.53.18). There is a sense of fear mixed in with the supreme astonishment in the word as can be shown by the parallelism in Sir. 30.9: Τιθήνησον τέκνον, καὶ ἐκθαμβήσει σε, σύμπαιξον αὐτῷ καὶ λυπήσει σε ('Pamper your child and he shall astonish you [or make you afraid]. Play with him and he will grieve you'). A similar thought in 14.33 is explained in v. 34a: ἐκθαμβεῖσθαι καὶ ἀδημονεῖν...Περίλυπός ἐστιν ἡ ψυχή μου ἕως θανάτου. One can also note the context of 14.32-42 and 16.5-6.

The adverb εὐθύς, so common in Mark, is used with a reaction of amazement only here.[19] The subject πᾶς ὁ ὄχλος is also used with amazement in 11.18, and forms of πᾶς with amazement in 1.27 (ἐθαμβήθησαν ἅπαντες), 2.12 (ὥστε ἐξίστασθαι πάντας) and 5.20 (πάντες ἐθαύμαζον). The emphasis here, as with 2.12, is that 'all', including, one assumes, the scribes mentioned in v. 14, are utterly astonished at the appearance of Jesus.

Attached to the main verb ἐξεθαμβήθησαν is the participle and noun ἰδόντες αὐτόν, probably with a temporal sense, 'when they saw him'. Coordinate verbs of seeing are used with amazement in 5.15 (θεωροῦσιν), 6.50 (εἶδον) and 16.5 (εἶδον). The last example also uses ἐκθαμβέομαι.

As was noted earlier, there is general agreement that 9.15 is redactional.[20] Present here are the redactional terms, καὶ εὐθύς, ὁ ὄχλος, συζητεῖν with γραμματεῖς, and ἐκθαμβέομαι. There seems to be an intensification of 1.27: καὶ ἐθαμβήθησαν ἅπαντες...πᾶς ὁ ὄχλος ἐξεθαμβήθησαν. Verse 14 is not necessary to the narrative; indeed it disturbs its flow by making a crowd present before it gathers in v. 25. The redactional 'Teacher' will come in v. 17. Also, v. 15 fits with the redactional v. 14 as an introduction to the story, which

---

18. C.D.F. Moule, *An Idiom-Book of New Testament Greek* (Cambridge: Cambridge University Press, 1982), pp. 87-88.

19. See the previous chapter for the textual problem in 5.42.

20. Pryke, *Redactional Style*, p. 164; Bultmann, *History*, p. 211; Achtemeier, 'Miracles', p. 475; Koch, *Bedeutung*, p. 120; Tillesse, *Secret*, p. 92; Taylor, *Gospel*, p. 395; Gnilka, *Evangelium*, II, p. 45; Tagawa, *Miracles*, p. 105; Bornkamm, 'Pneuma', p. 25; W. Schenk, 'Tradition und Redaktion in der Epileptiker Pericope Mk. 9.14-29', *ZNW* 63 (1972), p. 82; G. Petzke, 'Die Historische Frage nach den Wundertaten Jesu: Dargestellt am Beispiel des Exorzismus Mk. 9.14-29 par', *NTS* 22 (1976), p. 194; Lührmann, *Markusevangelium*, p. 160.

arranges the pericope to follow a declaration of sonship in 9,2-9 and the note on suffering and the passion in vv. 10-13.

The purpose and meaning of the insertion in v. 15 must be understood in light of the way wonder has worked previously throughout the gospel. It has been noted that throughout the first half of the gospel, reactions of wonder occur in association with the intervention of God as God acts to rule and save. This intervention came not only with miracles and exorcisms, but also with the teaching (1.22), forgiveness of sins (2.12), the witness to the deeds (5.20) and the restoration of individuals (5.15, 33). I suggest that with 9.15, Mark is saying that this intervention has come in a greater way (the added intensity of the word for amazement) than with the mere coming of Jesus with divine authority (1.22, 27). This intervention is now seen in light of the upcoming passion (which has been emphasized in 8.31-9.1; 9.7; 9.9-13). The passion puts the situation of Jesus' ministry in a different light, and may cause one to doubt that God has acted to rule with the coming of Jesus (how could Jesus be rejected and die if God was with him?), but the reader or hearer is directed now to the thought that God has indeed intervened and acted to save in a way even greater than the miracles and exorcisms by the increasing intensity of the reactions of wonder as the narrative moves to the cross and resurrection. In 9.15 this greater wonder comes to disciples, the crowd and scribes by the mere presence of Jesus as he now moves inexorably to the cross. Since the narrative has informed readers and hearers that Jesus is the Christ (8.29) and the Son of God (9.7) shortly before, one may expect a numinous authority to attend him, but with the impending cross now coloring the context, there is a re-affirmation, indeed even a greater confirmation that God is with Jesus.

I would thus agree with Tagawa that it is Jesus himself who is amazing,[21] but want to emphasize the increasing intensity of the amazement (which attends the intervention and salvation of God earlier in the gospel) in light of the upcoming passion. That which, on first glance, might not look at all like a divine intervention, is colored as such by the continued and emphatic wonder.

Mark 9.32

The next place which should be noted is the final verse of the second passion prediction, 9.32: οἱ δὲ ἠγνόουν τὸ ῥῆμα, καὶ ἐφοβοῦντο αὐτὸν ἐπερωτῆσαι. There are the Markan elements of the desire for secrecy (v. 30b) and the ignorance of the disciples (v. 32a) in this prediction. The kernel of the prediction is

21. Tagawa, *Miracles*, p. 107.

v. 31, which Mark may have found as an isolated logion and given a position in Jesus' journey and related to the motifs of secrecy, ignorance and fear.[22] The elements which are the same as the first prediction are the use of son of man, and the reference to being killed and rising after three days. Mark 8.31 ἀποδοκιμασθῆναι ὑπὸ τῶν πρεσβυτέρων καὶ τῶν ἀρχιερέων τῶν γραμματέων becomes εἰς χεῖρας ἀνθρώπων in 9.31, and ἀποκτενοῦσιν αὐτὸν now preceeds ἀποκτανθεὶς/ἀποκτανθῆναι καὶ μετὰ τρεῖς ἡμέρας ἀναστῆναι.

The verb ἐφοβοῦντο (imperfect) is used to describe the disciples' reaction. It has occurred in 4.41; 5.15, 33; 6.20 (imperfect); and will occur in 10.32; 11.18; 16.8 (imperfect) in reactions of wonder. The silence attending it is similar to 16.8, while hesitation to ask Jesus occurs again in 12.34, when no one dares to ask Jesus after an answer to an inquiring scribe about the greatest commandments. Fear has been clearly associated with a rejection of Jesus in 5.15, but was associated with faith in 5.33. It co-exists here with ignorance (οἱ δὲ ἠγνόουν τὸ ῥῆμα). Moreover, amazement or fear will be related to the passion and resurrection in various ways now in 10.32; 14.33; 15.5, 44; 16.5, 6, 8. Ignorance will combine with fear or amazement now as a structural element in this section of Mark (8.27-10.52), as the next passion prediction will also involve fear and amazement, and lack of understanding (10.32-34), while the first passion prediction had only prediction and ignorance (8.31-33).[23]

I would agree with Gnilka[24] that what is being described here is a 'holy terror'. The predominant use of fear in the gospel prior to this occasion has set up such an understanding (the only prior exceptions would be 'fear not' in 5.36 and 6.50), and it will be closely associated in a semantic field of other wonder language in 10.32, 11.18 and 16.8, which in each case is closely related to a passion or resurrection context. Moreover, in light of v. 32 being most likely redactional, the passion is being viewed as evoking the same reaction as such supernatural displays of saving power as the calming of a storm (4.41) or the experiencing of the healing power of Jesus (5.33). The same uncanny sense of the numinous on those occasions is now present as Jesus foretells his death and resurrection.

---

22. Best, *Following*, p. 73; and also see V. Taylor, *The Formation of the Gospel Tradition* (London: Macmillan, 1949), p. 50, on the passion predictions as original forecasts sharpened in light of subsequent events.
23. P. Achtemeier, 'An Exposition of Mk. 9.30-37', *Int* 30 (1976), p. 180.
24. Gnilka, *Evangelium*, II, p. 54.

As stated above, 9.32 has generally been seen as redactional.[25] There is the idea of a failure of understanding of the disciples in view of the passion, along with φοβεῖσθαι. Moreover, it may be that in light of the redactional nature of 5.33 and 5.15, the evangelist is emphasizing that just as wonder could co-exist with belief or rejection of Jesus in his mighty works, so now also that wonder can unfortunately co-exist with ignorance in view of the passion. There is an exhortation not to be unbelieving or ignorant, but to recognize that the reaction of holy terror shows that the power of God is also mightily at work to save as Jesus moves toward the cross, just as it was in the deeds of the first half of the gospel. In other words, holy terror attends both the mighty works and the passion of Jesus because in both the saving and ruling power of God is at work.

Mark 10.24, 26

The next reactions of wonder occur close together in the pericope on the rich man and the question of the relation of riches and the kingdom of God, 10.17-31. In v. 24, the text reads: οἱ δὲ μαθηταὶ ἐθαμβοῦντο ἐπὶ τοῖς λόγοις αὐτοῦ. This follows the statement of Jesus on the difficulty of entering the kingdom of God for those with riches. In v. 24b the difficulty is general, but v. 25 again refers to the rich man, and compares a person with riches entering the kingdom of God to a camel going through the eye of a needle. This statement is met with the following response in v. 26: οἱ δὲ περισσῶς ἐξεπλήσσοντο λέγοντες πρὸς ἑαυτούς, Καὶ τίς δύναται σωθῆναι.[26]

The pericope is related to the gospel as a whole by several important themes. The pericope opens with the way-motif in v. 17, which is a special emphasis in 8.27-10.52. Jesus is addressed twice as Διδάσκαλε (vv. 17, 20), which draws one back to the programmatic miracle of 1.21-28, especially vv. 22, 27. There is the question of entering the kingdom of God in vv. 23, 24 and 25, which draws one back to the summary proclamation in 1.14-15. Along with entry into

---

25. Pryke, *Redactional Style*, p. 164; Gnilka, *Evangelium*, II, p. 53; Lührmann, *Markusevangelium*, p. 163; Schmithals, *Evangelium*, II, p. 425; Best, *Following*, p. 73.

26. Verses 24 and 25 are reversed in the Western text, principally by the 6th and 7th century codex Claromontanus and several Latin MSS of a later date. This can be seen as a scribal attempt to improve the sense and should be rejected, according to Cranfield, *Gospel*, p. 332. See also, Mann, *Mark*, p. 402. The variant in v. 24, ἐστιν τοὺς πεποιθότας ἐπὶ χρήμασιν, though well attested, is an attempt to polish the difficulty that v. 24 generalizes v.23 by the omission of the reference to wealth, while v. 25 then re-introduces the question of wealth. See Best, *Disciples*, p. 20.

the kingdom of God, the question at issue in general involves discipleship and following Jesus (vv. 21, 28-31), which is a major emphasis in 8.27-10.52. The statement in v. 27 that all things are possible with God reaches back to 9.43, 45 and the parallel concepts of eternal life-kingdom of God there (9.45, 47).[27]

Many want to see 10.17-31 as part of a pre-Markan unit.[28] Not all would agree,[29] but it must be admitted that with the discipleship and 'way' themes there is a remarkable link to the context of chapter 10. Also, the pericope 10.13-16 is also directly connected to 10.17-31 with the concepts of receiving and entering the kingdom of God. There are, however, some tensions in 10.23-27 in particular which relate to the two references to the wonder of the disciples.

The verbs used in 10.24 and 26, θαμβέομαι (1.27; 10.32) and ἐκπλήσσομαι (1.22; 6.2; 7.37; 11.18) are the same reactions joined in the pericope 1.21-28, but here they occur in reverse order. 10.24 is the only place in the gospel where οἱ δὲ μαθηταί is specifically used as the subject of a verb of amazement, for it is Mark's preference to leave the subject impersonal, even when it is clearly the disciples who are in view (4.41; 6.51). Also, 10.24 is the only place the prepositional phrase ἐπὶ τοῖς λόγοις αὐτοῦ is joined with a verb of wonder.

27. W. Zimmerli, 'Die Frage des Reichen nach dem ewigen Leben (Mk. 10.17-31 par)', *EvT* 19 (1959), pp. 93-94, relates the question of life to the OT concept, where God is near, there is life (Amos 5.4-7; Isa. 1.10; Ezek. 18), and to the question in the OT of how one may enter the temple gate, the place where God, the source of life is (Mic. 6.8; Ps. 15.1).

28. Pesch, *Markusevangelium*, II, p. 135, sees 10.2-12, 17-27 and 35-45 as a pre-Markan unit. Grundmann, *Evangelium*, p. 208, says it is possible to see 10.13-16, 17-31, as a pre-Markan unit joined under the theme question, 'How may one enter the kingdom of God?'. Best, *Following*, p. 110, sees a pre-Markan association of 10.17-31 with 10.2-12 and 13-16. R. Busemann, *Die Jüngergemeinde nach Markus 10* (Bonn: Peter Hanstein, 1983), pp. 176-77, sees a pre-Markan collection in 10.2-9, 11, 14 (without ἠγανάκτησεν); 16b, 17-20 (without μὴ ἀποστερήσῃς); 21 (without ἠγάπησεν αὐτόν); 22 (without στυγνάσας ἐπὶ τῷ λόγῳ); and in 23b, 25, 26b, 27b, 35-40, 42b, 43-45. Kuhn, *Ältere*, sees 10.1-45 as a pre-Markan complex.

29. For example, Bultmann, *History*, pp. 21-22, sees Mark's hand providing supplements of vv. 24, 26-27, 28-30 to 17-22, 23, 25. Verse 28 may derive from a traditional saying in vv. 29-30, or may be an original introduction to an ancient apophthegm. N. Walter, 'Zur Analyse von Mk. 10.17-31', *ZNW* 53 (1962), p. 217, sees 10.17-31 as two connected stories, 24b-27 and 28-31, which are assimilated with 23-24a and expanded by 28 and 30 b, c. W. Harnisch, 'Die Berufung des Reichen: Zur Analyse von Markus 10.17-27', in *Festschrift für Ernst Fuchs* (ed. E. Ebeling, E. Jürgen and G. Schunak; Tübingen: Mohr [Paul Siebeck], 1973), p. 167, wonders if 17-21, 24c-25 and 27b were linked in a pre-Markan stage. P. Minear, 'The Needle's Eye', *JBL* 61 (1942), p. 165, says that v. 25 is the only real kernel in vv. 23-26 that vv. 23-24 are 'unimaginative explanations of the obvious meaning of the hyperbole', and that vv. 29-30a are the kernel of vv. 28-31 (p. 168).

'stood in awe of' rather than 'feared'.[146] This is supported by the notion that Herod supposes that Jesus is John risen from the dead in 6.14, indicating that John has appeared to the king in a numinous light, righteous and holy.[147] The only person other than John in Mark called ἅγιος is Jesus (by a demon in 1.24). One cannot help but see the irony that is present here, in that the unholy king with earthly power is struck with awe at the holy man without earthly power.[148]

The participle εἰδώς may be taken as causal. Herod stood in awe of John because he knew that John was a righteous and holy man. The participle gives the reason for the awe. Matthew seems to understand it this way in 14.5 when he adapts it to ὅτι ὡς προφήτην αὐτόν εἶχον. I noted in discussing 5.33 that the participle εἰδυῖα functioned as an explanation for a reaction of wonder. 9.6a also uses a γάρ clause as an explanation preceding a statement of a reaction of terror.

Mark further describes the reaction of Herod to John with the expression ἀκούσας αὐτοῦ πολλὰ ἠπόρει. Although the specific verb ἀπορέω is not used as a reaction to Jesus' teaching in Mark (compare Jn 13.22), it is consonant with the misunderstanding in the gospel to translate as 'when he heard him, he was greatly perplexed'. It is common for Mark to use forms of πολύς in the accusative in an adverbial sense (for example, 3.12; 5.10, 43; 9.26; 15.23),[149] and the thought of confusion or uncertainty at the teaching of those sent by God in Mark is better than importing meanings external to the gospel.[150] Just as there was perplexity at the teaching of Jesus (4.13; 8.31-33; 9.32; 10.32), so there is perplexity at the words of the forerunner also sent by God. This does not prohibit, however, a hearing with gladness (v. 20c; 12.37). Mark is saying that a mixture of emotions marked the hearers of God's messengers, as a holy awe surrounded both of them.

---

146. Taylor, *Gospel*, p. 313; Mann, *Gospel*, p. 296; J.A. Alexander, *The Gospel According to Mark* (repr.; Grand Rapids: Baker, 1980 [1858]), p. 156; Bonner, 'Note', p. 42. Pohl, *Evangelium*, p. 258, notes that Mark uses fear as the human reaction to extra-human impressions.

147. Grundmann, *Evangelium*, p. 129.

148. Lohmeyer, *Evangelium*, p. 119.

149. BAGD, p. 688.

150. Bonner, 'Note', p. 42, wants ἀπορεῖν in 6.20 to have the meaning 'raise a question', as in a dialectic, which he says it often means in philosophical contexts (citing Clement, *Strom.* 6.96.1, and Eusebius, *Praep. Ev.* 1.2). However, is this in a philosophical context? I would prefer instead to analyze the tone as that of a prophet or holy man before a fearing king than the cool situation of a philosophic debate.

I would take 6.20 as traditional material,[151] although this is one of the more difficult verses in the gospel to categorize as traditional or redactional.[152] Elements that might be redactional, such as πολλά, along with 'Ηρωδιάς, 'Ιωάννην and φοβεῖσθε can here fit the flow of the narrative, but there may also be a rewriting of the tradition by Mark to make John's picture in the gospel more similar to that of Jesus. The question cannot be decided conclusively.

In the same way that the 'mystery of the kingdom' brought opposition to Jesus (although Satan had been defeated), so John experiences opposition which seems to defeat him. There are similar reactions to him as to Jesus. John plays a part in the eschatological drama as the 'restorer of all things' (9.12-13), and as such the power of God is manifested in his words and person. Although he does not perform miracles, even the king is in awe of him. The association in 6.20-28 of awe that is followed by death will be repeated in the passion of Jesus. Perhaps it is only fitting that the forerunner, as sent by God, also evokes terror in earthly potentates as God brings near the kingdom.

Mark 6.50, 51

The next place where the motif of wonder occurs is in the pericope of the walking on the water, 6.45-52. We read in vv. 50-52: πάντες γὰρ αὐτὸν εἶδον καὶ ἐταράχθησαν. ὁ δὲ εὐθὺς ἐλάλησεν μετ' αὐτῶν, καὶ λέγει αὐτοῖς, θαρσεῖτε, ἐγώ εἰμι. μὴ φοβεῖσθε. καὶ ἀνέβη πρὸς αὐτοὺς εἰς τὸ πλοῖον, καὶ ἐκόπασεν ὁ ἄνεμος. καὶ λίαν ἐκ περισσοῦ ἐν ἑαυτοῖς ἐξίσταντο, οὐ γὰρ συνῆκαν ἐπὶ τοῖς ἄρτοις, ἀλλ' ἦν αὐτῶν ἡ καρδία πεπωρωμένη.[153] The sequence of two reactions of wonder, one while seeing Jesus walking on the sea μὴ φοβεῖσθε, and the other following the calming of the storm as Jesus enters the boat, is

---

151. Along with Schweizer, *Good News*, pp. 132-33; Gnilka, 'Martyrium', pp. 80-81; Pesch, *Markusevangelium*, I, pp. 339-40; Schmithals, *Evangelium*, I, p. 313.

152. Pryke, *Redactional Style*, p. 159, makes it redactional, citing 'Ιωάννης, 'Ηρῴδης, πολλά, φοβεῖσθε, ἀκούειν.

153. There are a couple of textual problems surrounding these verses. Some MSS read ἐξεπλήσσοντο instead of ἐξίσταντο, but the majority of support (א, B, L, Δ, 29 and 892 versions) is with ἐξίσταντο. There is stronger support for ἐξίσταντο καὶ ἐθαύμαζον (A, D, K, W, X, φ, Π, f¹³ and a number of miniscules), but the doubling with καί of the language of amazement is not Markan style, and may have been influenced by Acts 2.7. Also there is some question about ἐκ περισσοῦ by W and HR, but λίαν ἐκ περισσοῦ coheres with Markan style. See Klosterman, *Markusevangelium*, p. 67; Koch, *Bedeutung*, p. 105; Metzger, *Commentary*, p. 92.

critical for understanding this unit, as is the interpretation of the Markan γὰρ clause in v. 52.

This is the second sea-calming in Mark, and there are some common elements with 4.35-41: both incidents took place in the evening; 4.39 and 6.50 both have καὶ ἐκόπασεν ὁ ἄνεμος; and both have a reaction of wonder after the calming, along with an indication of unbelief in the midst of the storm itself. However, there are also differences between the stories. Here it is not called a storm; rather, 'the wind was against them'. Jesus is praying and then walks on the water only here (instead of being with the disciples in the boat). Jesus has supernatural vision to see the disciples harassed while rowing, and wishes to 'pass them by'. He speaks with the disciples, and not to the wind. The wind stops when Jesus enters the boat. There is no actual rebuke from Jesus to the disciples, as in 4.40, but there is the editorial remark in 6.52 (see below). These differences make it difficult to see 6.45-52 as a doublet of 4.35-41, and the pericope was probably originally a self-standing tradition.[154]

The theme of the pericope is the mastery of Jesus over the sea. This reminds of several Old Testament passages which speak of Yahweh's dominance over the sea or chaotic waters, such as Exod. 14.21; Josh. 3.4; Job 9.8; 38.16; Ps. 77.20; Isa. 43.16; and Hab. 3.15.[155] The kingly rule is again exhibited in the gospel as Jesus does what Yahweh does in the Old Testament (compare Job 9.8b: περιπατῶν ὡς ἐπ' ἐδάφους ἐπὶ θαλάσσης).We also see the remarkable words of self-revelation, ἐγώ εἰμι, in v. 50, which are used elsewhere in Mark only twice (13.6 as the claim of false christs, and 14.62 as the answer of Jesus to the Jewish leaders). This is the Old Testament formula of God's self-revelation (Exod. 3.14; Isa. 43.1-3, 10-11). Other Old Testament motifs in the pericope include the 'fourth watch of the night', reflecting the idea that the help of God comes in the morning (Exod. 14.24; Ps. 46.6; 88.14); Jesus praying on the mountain (the place of the revelation of God in Deut. 33.2 and Hab. 3.3), and ἤθελεν παρελθεῖν αὐτούς (Exod. 33.19, 22; 34.6; 1 Kgs 19.11).[156] It can be

---

154. Kertelge, *Wunder*, p. 146, disagrees with Bultmann, *History*, p. 216. I recognize that incidents such as the feeding of the 5000/4000 have differences but may be a true doublet, but in the pericopae in view the differences are in many of the base elements of the stories.

155. Nineham, *Gospel*, p. 180; Schmithals, *Evangelium*, I, p. 333; Kertelge, *Wunder*, p. 145; H. Fleddermann, '"And He Wanted to Pass by Them" (Mk. 6.48a)', *CBQ* 45 (1983), p. 393.

156. H. Ritt, 'Der Seewandel Jesu (Mk. 6.45-52 par): Literarische und Theologische Aspekte', *BZ* 23 (1979), p. 79; Fleddermann, 'Pass', pp. 391-93. Fleddermann notes that 'to

safely said that this pericope, seen in the framework of the gospel, demonstrates the breaking-in of the rule of God, as God saves people and subdues the unruly creation in a way similar to Old Testament precedents.

There has been some discussion as to the unity of the pericope. Some see two stories joined together, namely a rescue miracle with an epiphany.[157] However, we can note that Theissen has demonstrated that comparative parallels show that it is not necessary to separate rescue at sea and epiphany.[158] Also, if two stories were joined, why does John also link this story with the feeding, rather than, say, just one of the traditions?[159] It would seem that the aspects of sea-rescue and epiphany are 'inextricably intertwined'[160] in such a way as to exclude attaching one reaction of wonder only to the rescue miracle and the other to the epiphany.[161] When one grants the rather tenuous nature of separating tradition from redaction in Mark anyway, the division of the pericope into two traditions becomes even less certain.

The pericope as it stands follows the form of separation from Jesus (vv. 45-47); a need and the appearance of Jesus (v. 48); the fear of the disciples (vv. 49-50a); the word of comfort (v. 50b); the rescue (v. 51a); amazement (v. 51b); and editorial comment (v. 52).

In v. 50a one reads: πάντες γὰρ αὐτὸν εἶδον καὶ ἐταράχθησαν. The γὰρ indicates an explanation of v. 49, καὶ ἀνέκραξαν. The passive of ταράσσω has

---

pass through' in the OT means 'to inflict disaster' (Amos 5.16-17), while 'to pass by' means 'to rescue from disaster' or 'save' (Amos 5.16-17). A good translation would be 'and he wanted to save them'. There may be an element of theophany present also, as E. Lohmeyer, 'Und Jesus ging vorüber', NedTTs 23 (1934), pp. 206-24, but it may be stretching the phrase to relate it to the messianic secret, as does T. Snoy, 'Marc 6.48, "...et il voulait les dés passer": Proposition pour la solution d'une énigme', in L'Evangile selon Marc (ed. M. Sabbe; BETL; Leuven: Leuven University Press, 1974), pp. 347-63.

157. For example, Bultmann, History, p. 216, sees the storm motif added secondarily to the walking on the water. Lohmeyer, Evangelium, p. 131, sees two separate stories, with the basic story being Jesus' epiphany on the water, and with the rescue of the disciples added secondarily. See also Pesch, Markusevangelium, I, p. 358, although he sees 6.32-51 as part of a pre-Markan miracle collection; Gnilka, Evangelium, I, p. 266, who also sees the sea walking widened by the sea-rescue; Koch, Bedeutung, p. 105, who sees the rescue miracle in vv. 48a, 51, and the sea walking in vv. 47, 48b-50 as an epiphany.

158. Theissen, Stories, p. 101, citing Hom. Hymns 33.12, Aristides' Hymns to Serapis 33.

159. Grundmann, Evangelium, p. 141.

160. Fleddermann, 'Pass', p. 393.

161. As, for example, Pesch, Markusevangelium, I, p. 358.

The construction in 10.26 is more similar to other places in the gospel. The combination περισσῶς ἐξεπλήσσοντο λέγοντες is reminiscent of the redactional ὑπερπερισσῶς ἐξεπλήσσοντο λέγοντες in 7.37, but an acclamation follows in 7.37 while a question follows in 10.26. Forms of the verb λέγω follow verbs of amazement in 1.27 (ἐθαμβήθησαν...λέγοντας); 2.12 (ἐξίστημι ... λέγοντας); 4.41 (καὶ ἐφοβήθησαν φόβον μέγαν, καὶ ἔλεγον πρὸς ἀλλήλους); 6.2 (ἐξεπλήσσοντο λέγοντες) and 7.37. Questions are involved in 1.22, 2.12, 4.41 and 6.2, but they all relate to Jesus' identity and mission. This may be because the first half of the gospel, between 1.1, 11 and 8.29, 9.7, focuses on Jesus' identity. Here, the question following the wonder relates to the content of the teaching.

The question is asked, πρὸς ἑαυτούς.[30] This is joined with amazement in 1.27 (ὥστε συνζητεῖν πρὸς ἑαυτούς), 6.51 (λίαν ἐν ἑαυτοῖς ἐξίσταντο) and here. Since the question which follows was not directly addressed to Jesus, v. 27, ἐμβλέψας αὐτοῖς (v. 21 also) is necessary to bring the further response of Jesus to bear on the question. There is an awkwardness here which would not be present if the question was asked directly of Jesus.

Within the flow of the pericope, the amazement of v. 24 does not fit smoothly. Jesus has stated, Πῶς δυσκόλως οἱ τὰ χρήματα ἔχοντες εἰς τὴν βασιλείαν τοῦ θεοῦ εἰσελεύσονται, and the disciples respond with amazement. This reaction seems to contradict the assertion of Peter in v. 28, 'Behold, we have left all to follow you'.[31] Since the disciples are not rich and have left everything anyway, how can they be struck with wonder at this statement?[32] It has been suggested that in v. 24a the amazement is because the disciples symbolise the rich, who by the time of writing of Mark are now in the church, so that the astonishment indicates a threat to themselves, or that they are amazed because they assume that wealth is a blessing from God and a sign of righteousness.[33] Other suggestions include that the amazement results from the general emphasis on the

---

30. ℵ, B, C, Δ, Ψ, 892, cop[sa] and [bo] attest πρὸς αὐτόν, but πρὸς ἑαυτούς is Markan (also 1.27; 9.10; 11.31; 12.7; 14.4 and 16.3) and has the vast majority of textual witnesses; see Best, *Disiciples*, p. 19, and Turner, 'Usage', pp. 280-82.

31. Busemann, *Jüngergemeinde*, p. 45. Also S. Légasse, 'Jésus a-t-il annoncé la conversion final d'Israël? (A propos de Marc 10.23-27)', *NTS* 10 (1964), p. 483, notes that the abandonment of goods and relatives which Jesus required of his associates is solidly attested in the tradition, so the amazement is not justified.

32. K.-G. Reploh, *Markus-Lehrer der Gemeinde* (SBM 9; Stuttgart: Katholisches Bibelwerk, 1969), p. 194.

33. Via, *Ethics*, p. 140.

difficulty of salvation,[34] or the alarm shows how fear will seize the man truly confronted by God.[35] By all accounts, v. 24a is awkward.

The verse is most likely redactional.[36] There are Markan terms, μαθητής, θαμβέομαι, πάλιν; the tension with v. 28, and the indication of an artificial insertion of the Markan wonder motif. Also, v. 24b seems to be a clear expansion of v. 23, since now it is difficult for any to enter into the kingdom of heaven. What is the purpose of the expansion in v. 24a?

I noted earlier in the gospel that the teaching of Jesus is redactionally linked with wonder due to the unique authority present in the teaching (1.22; 6.2). Even when an exorcism has taken place, in 1.27, which uses the same word as here, those present are struck by the power of the 'new teaching with authority', not the exorcism itself (in a programmatic pericope). This authority strikes even those who reject it (6.2). Thus it is fruitless here to try and look for a scandalous reason in the content of the teaching as the cause of the wonder. Rather, it is the authoritative power of the teaching itself which excites awe, even when, as here, the teaching does not necessarily contradict something the hearers had already hear Jesus say. In other words, it is not the scandalous nature of the teaching, but the divine authority of the teaching which stuns with wonder. This is especially true when the teaching is regarding the rule of God which has broken-in in the coming of Jesus. In fact, this is indeed the topic of the statement in v. 23. The evangelist, then, has inserted a reaction of wonder at the pure awesome authority of Jesus' pronouncements on the kingdom of God as showing the same power which exorcises demons, forgives sins, restores people to wholeness and works miracles. Since the teaching comes with the same force as the miracles, it is natural that the same reaction should result, especially with an authoritative word on entry into the kingdom. The power inherent in the teaching causes the reaction, not the unusual or scandalous content. Since

---

34. Rawlinson, *Mark*, p. 141.
35. Schweizer, *Good News*, p. 213.
36. So Gnilka, *Evangelium*, II, p. 84; Pesch, *Markusevangelium*, II, p. 136 (by a pre-Markan redactor); Schmithals, *Evangelium*, II, p. 450, Best, *Following*, p. 110; Walter, 'Analyse', p. 209; Pryke, *Redactional Style*, p. 166; S. Légasse, *L'appel du riche (Mc. 110.17-31 et parralléles): Contribution à l'étude des fondements scriptuaires de l'état religieus* (Paris: Beauschesne, 1966), p. 75; W. Egger, *Nachfolge als Weg zum Leben: Chancen neuer exegetischen Methoden dargelegt an Mk. 10.17-31* (Klosterneuberg: Österreichisches Katholisches Bibelwerk, 1979), pp. 191, 217; Tagawa, *Miracles*, p. 103; Busemann, *Jüngergemeinde*, p. 47; Harnisch, 'Berufung', p. 166. Kuhn, *Ältere*, p. 173 says vv. 24, 26 hardly fit the context of the old collection in 10.1-45.

kingdom pronouncements of Jesus contain kingdom authority, the reaction to the pronouncement is the wonder of those experiencing the breaking-in of the kingdom.

The statement in vv. 24b-25 has two parts. In v. 24b is a general statement on the difficulty of entry into the kingdom (πῶς δύσκολόν ἐστιν), and then v. 25 returns to those with riches. After Jesus says that it is easier for a camel to pass through the eye of a needle than for a rich person to enter the kingdom of God, the response is another reaction of wonder: οἱ δὲ περισσῶς ἐξεπλήσσοντο λέγοντες πρὸς ἑαυτούς, Καὶ τίς δύναται σωθῆναι.

The wonder is greater here (περισσῶς) than in v. 24, and the suggested reasons for the greater amazement include the fact that v. 25 is sterner than v. 23, making entrance into the kingdom a virtual impossibility for a rich person;[37] that the disciples did not here understand the meaning of Jesus' teaching;[38] because the statement of the difficulty of entering the kingdom in v. 24b applied to everyone brings the recognition that everyone has something to hold on to;[39] or the recognition that salvation is difficult for all.[40] Harnisch says simply that the repeated amazement of the disciples in vv. 24a and 26a appears unmotivated.[41]

Verse 26 is also most likely redactional.[42] We have in the verse the Markan terms, ἐξεπλήσσοντο λέγοντες πρὸς ἑαυτούς, σωθῆναι, δύναμαι; the intensification of v. 24 with περισσῶς; and the Markan style of amazement followed by a question. The same problem we saw in v. 24a applies here also, since the statement on the impossibility of kingdom participation with riches in v. 25 would not appear to contradict the disciples' understanding in light of v. 28. It would thus seem that the amazement at the impossibility of those with riches entering the kingdom should not shock the disciples in light of their own denial of earthly goods.

---

37. Best, *Disciples*, p. 21. He also adds that the rich man is the one whom it is expected would enjoy God's favor and not rejection, so the point of v. 24 is driven home by v. 25. Reploh, *Markus*, p. 195, remarks on the sharpening of the word about riches in vv. 24b-25.

38. Tagawa, *Miracles*, p. 104.

39. Via, *Ethics*, p. 141.

40. Kuhn, *Ältere*, p. 147.

41. Harnisch, 'Berufung', p. 164.

42. Gnilka, *Evangelium*, II, p. 84; Pesch, *Markusevangelium*, II, p. 136 (pre-Markan redactor); Walter, 'Analyse', p. 211; Harnisch, 'Berufung', p. 167; Busemann, *Jüngergemeinde*, pp. 48-49; Pryke, *Redactional Style*, p. 166; Egger, *Nachfolge*, pp. 191, 217; Schniewind, *Evangelium*, p. 139. Tagawa, *Miracles*, p. 104, says it is not possible to say whether v. 26 is tradition or redaction.

The question in v. 26b begins καὶ τίς, and this may indicate that the statement of vv. 24b-25 was understood as making it difficult for all (anyone in v. 24b; rich in v. 25) to enter the kingdom of God. Is the greater amazement because non-rich are now included in the difficulty? Yet, if the difficulty of the rich is insufficient in itself to provoke amazement, why would difficulty for all explain only the greater *degree* of amazement? Often overlooked is the address of Jesus to the disciples in v. 24, τέκνα, which is especially telling in light of vv. 13-16. Are the disciples shocked because they think that they themselves may be excluded, or are they shocked because anyone outside their circle, rich or poor, may be excluded from the kingdom? I would suggest that neither of these options is the case, and it should be remembered that the reaction is not *surprise* at an unusual statement, but rather *amazement*, for they are 'struck out of their senses' (see my discussion of 1.22 in the previous chapter).

It was suggested earlier that Jesus' pronouncement on the kingdom in v. 23 provoked a reaction of wonder in v. 24 because inherent in kingdom pronouncement was kingdom authority. The further pronouncement in vv. 24b-25 is also about the kingdom, but now the scope has been expanded, and the inherent authority and power in the pronouncement is ineffable. The ways of the kingdom are beyond human compartmentalization (rich-poor) so that the experience of the kingdom now becomes the possibility of the impossible (v. 27). Again, it is not a further scandalous element in the pronouncement which occasions the wonder, but rather a greater experience of the authority of Jesus and the kingdom in its incomprehensibility to human limitations of economic classification. Throughout the gospel there have been periodic occasions where the wonder was greater than at other times (such as 5.42; 6.51; 7.37). It has been seen that the experience of the power can even be limited by unbelief (6.5). One expects kingdom teaching to contain kingdom authority (1.22, 27). It can be suggested here that the kingdom pronouncement itself is uncanny, not in the sense of incomprehensibility, but rather in the sense of being beyond human categorization. Just as the reaction of the woman in 5.33-34 was wonder in her experience of salvation, so now with a pronouncement on salvation the issue, wonder is again experienced. God had acted to rule in the ministry of Jesus, and that intervention was also felt in an authoritative pronouncement regarding the kingdom in which human categories become as nothing before the power present in the possibility of the impossible. Transcendence is experienced in Jesus' authoritative words.

This is, then, another pericope where reactions of wonder are closely associated with the breaking-in of the rule of God. In this case, the rule of God encounters people in a pronouncement of Jesus on entrance into that rule. When the scope of that pronouncement bursts human categorization, the reaction of wonder becomes all the greater, so as to even despair or the possibility of entrance into the kingly rule. Jesus goes on to say, however, that the kingdom is the realm where the impossible is possible (see 9.23-24).

Mark 10.32

The third passion prediction follows in 10.32-34. Mark 10.32a is one of the most unusual verses in Mark, and indeed in all the New Testament: Ἦσαν δὲ ἐν τῇ ὁδῷ ἀναβαίνοντες εἰς Ἱεροσόλυμα, καὶ ἦν προάγων αὐτοὺς ὁ Ἰησοῦς, καὶ ἐθαμβοῦντο, οἱ δὲ ἀκολουθοῦντες ἐφοβοῦντο.[43] Many questions are raised by this verse. Is one group in view or two? Is there a distinction intended by the differing reactions? What is the reason for the wonder and fear? Has Mark edited part of a *Vorlage* which needs to be recovered to understand the reactions?

This pericope is related to the Markan context as the third passion prediction, and this is the second time a reaction of amazement occurs (9.32). Jerusalem is stated as the goal of the journey for the first time in v. 33. We meet in v. 32 the 'way' theme again, which is so important in 8.27-10.52.

It can be seen that wonder relating to events surrounding the passion and resurrection becomes more frequent in the later part of the gospel. The passion is related to the central theme of the kingdom of God in at least three ways. First, in chapter 15 the idea of Jesus as king resounds, as he is addressed by that title six times (15.2, 9, 12, 18, 26, 32).[44] Secondly, when the breaking-in of the kingdom is understood as God coming in power to save through Jesus, the crucifixion can then be seen as the ultimate act of salvation in the gospel. The

---

43. The text here is fairly certain, but there have been attempts at emendation. Wrede, *Secret*, pp. 96, 276, suggests that καὶ ἐθαμβοῦντο should be discarded for text-critical reasons. He believes that this is merely a variant of οἱ δὲ ἀκολοωθοῦντες ἐφοβοῦντο, and cites as his evidence the old Latin codices, ff². The absolute minimum of evidence speaks against this. I agree with Best, *Disciples*, p. 143-44, that the attempts in the textual tradition to omit one group (D, K, it^{ab}), or identify clearly two groups (καὶ replaces οἱ δὲ in A, fam¹³, it^{l.q}, vg and syr^{p.h}) are obvious corrections. See Taylor, *Gospel*, p. 437; Lane, *Gospel*, p. 373.

44. Fine discussions of the way in which the passion brings this title to the forefront have been given by F. Matera, *The Kingship of Jesus* (SBLDS 66; Chico, CA: Scholars Press, 1982), and in less detail by Kingsbury, *Christology*, pp. 120-129.

paradox of Mark is that Jesus' powerlessness is true power![45] Thirdly, in the passion, 'the mystery of the kingdom'[46] has its greatest manifestation, namely how God can come, rule and save, but humans can resist and remain in bondage to sin and Satan (and therefore reject and crucify Jesus). When one understands the passion and resurrection as related to the central theme of the breaking-in of the rule of god, the importance of a reaction of wonder on the way to Jerusalem preceding a passion prediction becomes all the more crucial as one sees a convergence of several main themes of the gospel. It is not overstating the case to say with McKinnis that 10.32 is 'especially revelatory of Mark's intentions in his whole gospel'.[47]

A problem which is particular to the pericope 10.32-34 has been raised by H. Koester.[48] He believes that the edition of the gospel of Mark used by Matthew and Luke is not the Mark which is preserved in the MSS and which is standard today. The earlier version involved a story about the raising of a youth following 10.34, as is indicated in *The Secret Gospel of Mark* found by Morton Smith.[49] Koester claims that the reactions of wonder in 10.32 make no sense, but in the context of *Secret Mark* the reactions were the introduction to the resurrection story following 10.34, much the way the reaction of amazement in 9.15 precedes the miracle story there.[50] Koester calls θαμβεῖσθαι and ἐκθαμβεῖσθαι Hellenistic magical terms which describe the amazement which people experience in view of an extraordinary event, such as the appearance of a god or some supernatural phenomenon.[51] If Koester is correct, the interpretation of 10.32 in the present gospel context has little to do with the original meaning, since it would be the remnant of a prior edition of the gospel.

In response to Koester, I would say that when one reads the letter of Clement

---

45. See the exciting essay by D.A. Lee-Pollard, 'Powerlessness as Power: A Key Emphasis in the Gospel of Mark', *SJT* 40 (1987), pp. 173-88.
46. This is understood along the lines of J. Marcus, *Mystery*.
47. R. McKinnis, 'An Analysis of Mark 10.32-34, *NovT* 18 (1976), p. 82.
48. Koester, 'History and Development of Mark's Gospel (from Mark to Secret Mark and "Canonical" Mark', in *Colloquy on New Testament Studies* (ed. B. Corley; Macon, GA: Mercer University Press, 1983), pp. 35-57.
49. M. Smith, *Clement of Alexandria and a Secret Gospel of Mark* (Cambridge, MA: Harvard University Press, 1973). The discovery was not actually a new gospel, but a letter indicating use of an expansion of Mark by the Carpocratians.
50. Koester, *History*, pp. 36, 52.
51. Koester, *History*, p. 50.

which Smith has discovered containing the indications of a *Secret Mark* existing in Alexandria (assuming the authenticity of the letter), one discovers that the letter states the opposite of what Koester claims. The letter says that *Secret Mark* is an expansion of canonical Mark (by the Carpocratians), not the other way around. Also, to relate the wonder in 10.32 to 9.15 hardly solves the problem of why wonder is placed in the beginning of a miracle story. Further, in light of the way in which Mark uses amazement related to the passion in 9.32; 14.33; 15.5, 44; 16.5, 6, 9; it would seem that another reaction of wonder in a passion prediction in 10.32 can indeed make sense in the context of the gospel. 10.32 is not unusual in Mark as we have it, though it may be hard to understand. Close attention to wonder in the entire gospel can pay dividends in understanding 10.32 without recourse to an improbable source following 10.34.

The first wonder verb of 10.32, ἐθαμβοῦντο, has been met previously in 1.27 and 10.24. The second wonder verb, φοβέομαι, is common in Mark as a reaction of awe (4.41; 5.15, 33; 6.20; 9.32, 11.18; 16.8), and is used in a couple of other ways also (5.36 and 6.50 as 'fear not', and for fear of the crowd by the Jewish leaders in 11.32 and 12.12). The verbs are combined here in an emphatic way with the constructions καὶ ἦν προάγων ὁ Ἰησοῦς and οἱ δὲ ἀκολουθοῦντες ἐφοβοῦντο, and one should not overlook the imperfect tense of both verbs as indicating a continuing rather than momentary reaction while 'on the way'. Jesus is the subject of προάγω also in 14.28 and 16.7. Both προάγω and ἀκολουθέω occur again in 11.9, which can help us understand who is in view in 10.32. Moreover the understanding of the particle δέ (οἱ δὲ ἀκολουθοῦντες ἐφοβοῦντο) is important for interpreting the subjects of these two reactions of wonder.

There are those who would see two groups indicated, namely the disciples (as the subject of ἐθαμβοῦντο), and other followers of Jesus (the subject of ἐφοβοῦντο).[52] I would suggest instead that one indiscriminate group is in mind, and that there is no distinction intended between some being astonished and others fearing. First, I note that in 11.19 οἱ προάγοντες καὶ οἱ ἀκολουθοῦντες are one group who accompany Jesus into Jerusalem. The two participles are general terms describing those around Jesus. Secondly, in the immediate context of ch. 10, ἀκολουθέω is used of both the disciples (v. 28) and also other

---

52. Schmithals, *Evangelium*, II, p. 462; G. Wohlenburg, *Das Evangelium des Markus Kommentar zum Neuen Testament*; Leipzig: Deichert, 1910), p. 281; Cranfield, *Gospel*, p. 335; Taylor, *Gospel*, p. 437; Klostermann, *Markusevangelium*, p. 105; Schweizer, *Good News*, p. 217.

followers of Jesus (the invitation in v. 21, and Bartimaeus in v. 52). Thirdly, δὲ in οἱ δὲ ἀκολουθοῦντες ἐφοβοῦντο need not be taken as adversative, but is used by Mark in a conjunctive rather than disjunctive sense (compare 1.20, 32; 7.24).[53] Fourthly, Mark uses two different terms of amazement together when one person or group is in view at other times (5.33; 16.8), but there is not a case where differing reactions separate groups in the same verse. Fear is very much a part of the wonder language in Mark, and should not be separated from it.[54] For these reason, one can agree with those who say one general group is in view in 10.32, and a separation between disciples and 'others' is not intended here.[55] Astonishment and fear are continually present with those who proceed with Jesus on the journey toward Jerusalem.

Although the text may not seem to make clear the reason for the reactions in 10.32, many suggestions have been produced. It has been thought that a lack of understanding is indicated by the wonder;[56] a fear of what awaited in Jerusalem and amazement that the Galilean ministry was finished so soon;[57] the realization that Jesus was going to immediate peril;[58] and the coloring of the procession with the characteristics of an act of divine revelation.[59] I would suggest instead that the way the motif of wonder has been used in the rest of Mark gives the best help in interpreting this verse.

First, let me note that v. 32a is almost always seen as redactional.[60] There is the 'way' theme; the phrase ἀναβαίνοντες εἰς Ἱεροσόλυμα; ἦσαν with the present participle and ἦν with the present participle;[61] Markan terms ἀκολουθεῖν and θαμβεῖσθαι;[62] along with the impersonal plurals.[63] Verse 32b contains

53. Blass and DeBrunner, *Grammar*, p. 232.
54. I agree here with Malbon, 'Disciples', p. 115, and Best, 'Twelve', p. 147, n. 86.
55. Also R.P. Meye, *Jesus and the Twelve: Discipleship and Revelation in Mark's Gospel* (Grand Rapids: Eerdmans, 1968), pp. 161-64; Busemann, *Jüngergemeinde*, p. 130; Tagawa, *Miracles*, p. 108; Lane, *Gospel*, p. 373, n. 60; Best, 'Twelve', p. 147, *Following*, p. 120.
56. Wrede, *Secret*, p. 103; Schmithals, *Evangelium*, II, p. 462.
57. Mann, *Mark*, p. 408.
58. Cranfield, *Gospel*, p. 335.
59. Schweizer, *Good News*, p. 217.
60. So Weiss, *Älteste*, p. 264, although I do not agree that all of vv. 32-34 is a creation of the evangelist; Busemann, *Jüngergemeinde*, p. 134; Best, *Following*, p. 120; McKinnis, 'Analysis', p. 83; Pryke, *Redactional Style*, p. 166; Gnilka, *Evangelium*, II, p. 95.
61. Turner, 'Usage', pp. 348-51.
62. Stein, 'Methodology', p. 197.
63. Pryke, *Redactional Style*, p. 166.

the Markan πάλιν and ἄρχομαι with the infinitive, and is also most likely redactional. Thus, v. 32 is a clear case of a redactional insertion.

How does the way in which wonder is used in the rest of the gospel help one to understand v. 32? Throughout Mark, wonder is the reaction to interventions of God as the rule of God breaks in to human affairs to save. It was noted, for example, in the paradigmatic miracle, 1.21-28, that wonder is used twice as that which strikes the people in response to the authority present in Jesus' teaching, the same authority which subdues (גער, ἐπιτιμᾶν) the forces of evil. The response is καὶ ἐθαμβήθησαν ἅπαντες. Later, Jesus calms a storm, and the response is καὶ ἐφοβήθησαν φόβον μέγαν (4.41). The reaction of a woman experiencing the salvation of God is φοβηθεῖσα καὶ τρέμουσα. Reactions of wonder are responses to the saving words and acts of God, both to those who receive them (5.33-34) and to those who later reject them (6.2). I suggest that by his redactional portrait depicting the journey of Jesus to Jerusalem as striking those with him with the same wonder as previously, the evangelist is informing the readers and hearers that the same intervention of God to save, which was present at other places in the gospel, is also present now as Jesus moves toward the passion. The rule of God is again breaking in to save, even in the passion. The result is that reactions of wonder strike those traveling with Jesus. Further, the expression καὶ ἦν προάγων ὁ Ἰησοῦς is critical in Mark for presenting Jesus as the leader of the disciples in context of the passion and resurrection (14.28; 16.7). Although the passion may seem to be the abandonment of Jesus by God and humans, in fact the audience are being told that God is present and ruling even as Jesus moves to the cross. There are ways other than the motif of wonder which indicate the intervention of God in the passion and resurrection, but her it is crucial to note that by the reactions of wonder on the way to Jerusalem, the narrative is relating that God is indeed present even as Jesus moves toward the passion. While I agree with Otto that 10.32 renders with force the immediate impression of the numinous that issues from the man Jesus,[64] I would want to emphasize here that wonder is experienced as the result of the intervention and presence of God in a situation which may seem to be abandonment by God.

It should also be noted at this point that the reactions of wonder in 10.32 do not paralyze those present from following Jesus.[65] Although their understanding

64. Otto, *Holy*, p. 158.
65. This is well expressed by M.J. Selvidge, 'And Those Who Followed Feared (Mk. 10.32)', *CBQ* 45 (1983), p. 400.

is very imperfect, those present are still 'following Jesus on the way', with wonder. This will become important to remember when we come to 16.8.

The bare historical event of the crucifixion looks for all intents and purposes as the abandonment of Jesus by God. The evangelist, however, places the event in a different light by the insertion of the motif of wonder in the predictions of 9.32 and 10.32. That which may seem to be the abandonment of Jesus by God actually involves the presence of God to save as Jesus moves to the cross. The reactions of wonder show that God is involved and active.[66] The ways in which we saw reactions of wonder in Greco-Roman and early Jewish literature show that wonder was the reaction at the intervention of God or gods, and indicates that the gospel readers and hearers would in fact have recognized it as such, even if it comes in unexpected places and in unusual ways.

Mark 11.18

The motif of wonder occurs next following Jesus' temple act in 11.18: καὶ ἤκουσαν οἱ ἀρχιερεῖς καὶ οἱ γραμματεῖς, καὶ ἐζήτουν πῶς αὐτὸν ἀπολέσωσιν. ἐφοβοῦντο γὰρ αὐτόν, πᾶς γὰρ ὁ ὄχλος ἐξεπλήσσετο ἐπὶ τῇ διδαχῇ αὐτοῦ. There is a general acceptance of the historicity of Jesus' act in the temple, especially on a smaller scale.[67] The location of the incident in the Markan account draws attention now, especially within the context of ch. 11.

---

66. In an illuminating paper read at the 1988 annual meeting of the Society of Biblical Literature in Chicago on 19 November, 1988, Robert Gundry called Mark an 'apology for the cross'. He said that the basic problem in Mark is how to fit the theology of glory together with the theology of suffering. While he did not deal in any detail with the motif of wonder, he suggested that Mark in fact glorifies the passion, for example by presenting Jesus' flesh as strong on the cross (he cries out with a 'loud voice'); there is acceptance of the title, 'King of the Jews'; the guilt of Barabbas is a foil for the innocence of Jesus; the bandits alongside Jesus also paint his innocence in strong relief; the confession of the centurion shows that Christ's identity as the 'Son of God' continues; and by the fact that Jesus' predictions (passion and resurrection) all come true. Gundry said that Mark is placing the cross in a position of glory. My suggestion is amiable to his, seeing the movement to the cross and events surrounding the passion and resurrection as colored redactionally with wonder in order to show that in those events, God was in fact breaking-in to rule and save, with the same reactions resulting which occurred when he intervened to save earlier in the gospel. Gundry's views have now been detailed in his commentary, *Mark: A Commentary on His Apology for the Cross* (Grand Rapids: Eerdmans, 1993).

67. E.P. Sanders, *Jesus and Judaism* (Philadelphia: Fortress Press, 1985), pp. 301-308; C.K. Barrett, 'The House of Prayer and the Den of Thieves', in *Kümmel*, p. 13; B.F. Meyer,

6. *Mark II*

Chapter 11 beings with the 'triumphal entry' in vv. 1-11. There is a clear messianic understanding in the entry on the πῶλος δεδεμένος (Gen. 49.11) and especially in the cry, Εὐλογημένη ἡ ἐρχομένη βασιλεία τοῦ πατρὸς ἡμῶν Δαυίδ.[68] In fact, the sequence in Mark 11 may come from a traditional pattern.[69] The temple incident itself is framed by the cursing of the fig tree in 11.12-13 and 20-25, and this arrangement shows that what is intended in the incident is not 'cleansing' but destruction.[70] In the Markan context, the coming of the messiah and kingdom means condemnation for the temple.

I would especially want to emphasize that there is a clear relation in Mark between the temple incident and the breaking-in of the kingdom. It has been suggested that the temple act epitomized in action the message of the reign of God and was calculated to bring the imminence of God's reign abruptly and forcibly to all (note the context of 11.10).[71] Without the authority of the Sanhedrin or Roman procurator, such an act as this, which was an interference in the sovereign economic affairs of the temple, must have been taken as a direct claim to kingship.[72] The action suggests comparison with these Old Testament passages: Zech. 14.21 (a chapter which emphasizes the eschatological order within which God's kingship is activated, especially vv. 5, 9 and 16-21);[73] Isa. 56.7; Jer. 7.11 and Mal. 3.1-3.

The Aims of Jesus (London: SCM Press, 1979), p. 170, ('solidly probable'); V. Epstein, 'The Historicity of the Gospel Account of the Cleansing of the Temple', *ZNW* 55 (1964), p. 58.

68. H.-W. Kuhn, 'Das Reittier Jesu in der Einzugsgeschichte des Markusevangelium', *ZNW* 50 (1959), p. 87.

69. D. Catchpole, 'The Triumphal Entry', in *Jesus and the Politics of His Day* (ed. E. Bammel and C.F.D. Moule; Cambridge: Cambridge University Press, 1984), p. 321, says that ch. 11 contains some major recurrent features in a number of Jewish stories. First, victory is achieved and status recognized for a central person; second, a formal and ceremonial entry; third, either greetings or acclamations, or both, together with invocations of God; fourth, entry to the city climaxed by entry to the temple; fifth, cultic activity, either positive (offering of sacrifice) or negative (expulsion of objectionable persons and cleansing away of uncleanness). He sees this pattern in Josephus's *Ant.* 2.325-29; 13.304-306; 16.12-15; 22.342-45; *War* 1.73-74; *2 Macc.* 4.21-22; *1 Macc.* 4.19-25; 5.45-54; 10.86; 13.43-48, 49-51.

70. W.R. Telford, *The Barren Temple and the Withered Tree* (JSNTSup, 1; Sheffield: JSOT Press, 1980), pp. 238-39; Sanders, *Jesus*, p. 70; Barrett, 'House', p. 14; Kelber, *Kingdom*, p. 102.

71. Meyer, *Aims*, p. 197.

72. N.Q. Hamilton, 'Temple Cleansing and Temple Bank', *JBL* 83 (1964), pp. 370-71.

73. Catchpole, 'Entry', p. 333.

There is a special relation within Mark between 11.15-19 and the paradigmatic pericope of 1.21-28. In both cases, Jesus has entered the city, and goes to the place of worship (the synagogue in 1.21-28, the temple here). He casts out those who defile the temple as he exorcized the unclean spirit in the synagogue in 1.25-26. In both cases, Jesus teaches and the crowd marvels (1.22 and 11.18 both have similar language). Jesus' teaching was initially contrasted with that of the scribes in 1.22 and in 1.18 the scribes and other leaders confront him. It may be that just as the rule of God breaking-in gave Jesus authority to exorcize the demon in 1.21-28, so here the authority (see 11.18, 29, 33) for this act comes also from the rule of God. It is especially notable that amazement in both cases comes in a different way than might be expected. Neither the exorcism nor the temple act provokes amazement, but in both cases the teaching does, and though the content is not given in 1.22, the reader is drawn back to the summary of Jesus' message in 1.14-15. Here, we are drawn to 11.17's καὶ ἐδίδασκεν... The assumption is that divine authority was again inherent in the teaching.

There is one other point which must be raised in relation to the temple act. J. Neusner has emphasized that the casting out of the buyers and sellers was an act directly aimed at the temple cultus and the daily sacrifice which was an atonement for sin for the community.[74] The Mishnaic evidence (*m. Sheq* 1.3 and *Tos. Sheq.* 1.6) indicates that the money-changers changed the diverse coinage into the shequel required for the temple tax, which provided the public daily whole offerings for the year, and Jesus' act would have called into question the belief that the daily whole offering brought about expiation for sin.[75] There is in view, then, another expiation which points to Mk 10.45 and 14.24.

In 11.18 ἐφοβοῦντο γὰρ αὐτόν reminds of 6.20 ὁ δὲ Ἡρῴδης ἐφοβεῖτο τὸν Ἰωάννην. This γὰρ clause is followed by another (similar to the γὰρ ... γὰρ of 9.6), πᾶς γὰρ ὁ ὄχλος ἐξεπλήσσετο ἐπὶ τῇ διδαχῇ αὐτοῦ. This is almost identical to 1.22 (καὶ ἐξεπλήσσοντο ἐπὶ τῇ διδαχῇ αὐτοῦ), with the only change being that the subject is now definite (πᾶς γὰρ ὁ ὄχλος). The only other place in Mark where ὁ ὄχλος is the subject of amazement is 9.15. The key to understanding the verse seems to be in the use of γὰρ...γὰρ.

The first statement, that the scribes and chief priests 'were afraid of Jesus', is

---

74. J. Neusner, 'Money Changers in the Temple: The Mishnah's Explanation', *NTS* 35 (1989), pp. 387-90, and 'The Absoluteness of Christianity and the Uniqueness of Judaism: Why Salvation is Not of the Jews', *Int* 43 (1989), especially pp. 22-26.

75. Neusner, 'Money', p. 289.

related by the first γάρ to the previous statement (καὶ ἤκουσαν οἱ ἀρχιερεῖς καὶ οἱ γραμματεῖς, καὶ ἐζήτουν πῶς αὐτὸν ἀπολέσωσιν). The illative sense of would not be very meaningful here, since (numinous) fear of Jesus would not seem a reason to kill him. On the other hand, could the notion that the people were struck with wonder at Jesus' teaching provide a reason for wanting to destroy him, that is, envy (15.10)? However, in the context of the pericope, the reason for wanting to destroy Jesus would seem to go back to v. 17, namely the accusation of having made the temple a robbers' cave. The καὶ...καὶ connective in v. 18a, the usual Markan style of stringing sentences together, would serve as co-ordinating the accusation and the attempt to destroy Jesus. Amazement at Jesus' teaching would not very well fit as a *reason* for wanting to destroy him, since amazement at his teaching (1.22 and similar) did not provoke this desire previously. Nor would amazement at Jesus' teaching by the people be an *explanation* of why there was a desire to kill him. The accusation in v. 17 provides all the explanation necessary.[76] We are back, then, to asking the meaning of the γὰρ...γὰρ in v. 18.

I noted in the previous chapter that there are occasions in Mark related to amazement when γάρ has a function other than that of providing a specific explanation (see n. 172 in the previous chapter, and on 9.6b). It seems that there is such a case here. Sometimes γάρ can serve the purpose of a parenthesis.[77] Verse 18b would indeed make better sense as a parenthetical statement than as an explanation or a reason for v. 18a. It interrupts the flow of thought to provide a redactional comment (as we shall see) about the reaction of both the leaders and the people to Jesus. Verse 19 picks up the flow of thought of v. 18a again without any problem. The leaders were afraid of Jesus, a comment which underscores his exalted nature and appearance.[78] The people were struck with wonder at his teaching, just as at the beginning (1.22). It may well be that Mark is providing a redactional comment on why Jesus was able to stop traffic in the temple without opposition, rather than a reason why the leaders wanted to destroy Jesus. Just as the holiness of John made Herod afraid, so the authority of Jesus made the leaders afraid. In the same way that those in the synagogue at Galilee were struck with wonder at Jesus' authoritative teaching (with the authority manifesting itself in the exorcism), so those in the temple in Jerusalem

---

76. Roloff, *Kerygma*, p. 92, notes that v. 18b is not congruent with v. 18a, since v. 18a goes directly back to the temple incident, but v. 18b is a general statement.
77. Robertson, *Grammar*, pp. 433-35.
78. Gnilka, *Evangelium*, II, p. 130.

are also awe-struck at the (authoritative) teaching (manifesting itself in Jesus' taking authority over the temple). Although Jesus does no miracles in Jerusalem as in Galilee and in Gentile territories, the same authority is at work with him, to bring God's rule to the very temple itself.

As stated earlier, v. 18b is with little question redactional.[79] One can note γάρ...γάρ, ὄχλος, διδαχή and ἐκπλήσσομαι, which are all Markan indications,[80] along with the fact that the narrative makes sense without it. Also the shaping is similar to 1.22.

I suggest, then, that v. 18b is a redactional insertion which was not intended as an explanation of why the leaders sought to destroy Jesus, but rather a general comment about the authority of Jesus in the temple act. I have noted how authority becomes the question in 11.28, and since the authority of Jesus' teaching led to amazement in 1.22, 27, it is likely that the authority leads to the fear of Jesus in 11.18b. One wonders why Jesus was not stopped at the temple, or why the temple guard or Roman soldiers were not summoned. Discussions of the historicity of the event scale it down to a smaller size to explain how the act occurred without an immediate arrest. The insertion of v. 18b may be an answer to the question of why Jesus was not immediately seized, namely, due to the fear and amazement which the supernatural authority (as 'the Lord coming to his temple') evoked. Mark may also be telling the reader or hearer that the same authority which sprang from the rule of God in Galilee and Gentile territories now operates in Jerusalem, as the rule of God is brought to the temple which has been usurped by robbers from its rightful Lord. Though Jesus will be rejected and killed, a process even now under way (v. 18a), the authority remains the same, as is shown by the fact that the reactions remain the same. The rule of God is still breaking-in with Jesus, even as the passion draws nearer and opposition increases.

---

79. Pryke, *Redactional Style*, p. 168; G.W. Buchanan, 'Mark 11.15-19: Brigands in the Temple', *HUCA* 30 (1959), p. 176; Roloff, *Kerygma*, p. 92; E. Trocmé, 'L'expulsion des merchands du Temple', *NTS* 15 (1968), p. 7; Taylor, *Gospel*, p. 461; Mann, *Mark*, p. 450; Nineham, *Gospel*, p. 298; Gnilka, *Evangelium*, II, p. 127; Lohmeyer, *Evangelium*, p. 237; Klostermann, *Markusevangelium*, p. 117; Schmithals, *Evangelium*, II, p. 482; W. Schenke, *Der Passionsbericht nach Markus* (Forschung zur Bibel 4; Gütersloh: Mohn, 1974), p. 158; Bultmann, *History*, p. 36; Catchpole, 'Entry', p. 331.

80. Stein, 'Methodology', pp. 184, 197; Pryke, *Redactional Style*, p. 168.

Mark 11.32

I must note in passing 11.32: ἀλλὰ εἴπωμεν Ἐξ ἀνθρώπων; ἐφοβοῦντο τὸν ὄχλος, ἅπαντες γὰρ εἶχον τὸν Ἰωάννην ὄντως ὅτι προφήτης ἦν. There is not a reaction of wonder here, but rather a remark expressing the fear of the Jewish leaders in view of the crowd (12.12 also). There is a good possibility that this verse is intended to be in tension with 11.18, namely that the leaders not only had a fear of Jesus, but also of the crowd. It may be that Prov. 29.25 is in the background here.

The question of the pericope 11.27-33 revolves around Jesus' authority (vv. 28-29, 33), which has been seen as central in 1.22, 27 and 2.10. The narrative has indicated that the authority comes because Jesus is the anointed Son of God and proclaimer of the kingdom. The authority question inquires, Ἐν ποίᾳ ἐξουσίᾳ ταῦτα ποιῇς. The plural of ταῦτα in connection with ἐξουσία probably refers, in the context of the gospel, to more than the temple act, to all of the activities of Jesus which have been related, and in particular to his exercise of authority as the proclaimer of the kingdom.[81] Jesus' response indicates that his authority was from the same place as John's, namely from heaven.

The note ἐφοβοῦντο τὸν ὄχλος, ἅπαντες γὰρ εἶχον τὸν Ἰωάννην ὄντως ὅτι προφήτης ἦν is most likely redactional. There is a clear and sudden break between it and the preceding Ἐξ ἀνθρώπων, a transition from the first person plural to the third person plural, and the expected apodosis following v. 32a is never given.[82] Along with the redactional 11.18b, then, the evangelist is relating the double-mindedness of the Jewish leaders, and a further reason why Jesus was not immediately seized. At this point popular approval was still with Jesus and John as messengers from heaven.

---

81. G.S. Shae, 'The Question of the Authority of Jesus', *NovT* 16 (1974), P. 26; V.N. Makrides, 'Considerations on Mark 11.27-33 par', Deltion Biblikon Meleton 14 (1985), pp. 47-48; Schweizer, *Good News*, p. 237.

82. Shae, 'Question', p. 8. Also viewing it as redactional are Nineham, *Gospel*, p. 308 and Lohmeyer, *Evangelium*, p. 242.

Mark 12.11, 12

I would note next the conclusion to the parable in 12.1-9 which is found in vv. 10-11:

οὐδὲ τὴν γραφὴν ταύτην ἀνέγνωτε,
λίθον ὃν ἀπεδοκίμασαν οἱ οἰκοδομοῦντες
οὗτος ἐγενήθη εἰς κεφαλὴν γωνίας
παρὰ κυρίου ἐγένετο αὕτη
καὶ ἔστιν θαυμαστὴ ἐν ὀφθαλμοῖς ἡμῶν.

The parable of the rejected son or wicked tenants in vv. 1-9 is related to the context of the entire gospel in that the owner or lord of the vineyard (v. 9) has sent his 'beloved son' to gain some fruit after the rejection of the servants on the same question. Although the question of whether this is a parable or an allegorical invention of the early church is outside the scope of the issue at hand,[83] as is the question of the original form of the parable,[84] I would especially underscore that 'beloved son' in v. 6 in the context of the gospel must allude to 1.11 and 9.7. It could also be said again that the mystery of the kingdom is illustrated in the parable, namely how God can be 'Lord of the vineyard', but people could reject the messengers and the beloved son sent to them.

By all accounts the parable is related to Isa. 5.1-7. The elements of the planting, the fencing and the digging of the winepress and the building of the tower all derive from Isa. 5.2 LXX.[85] Recent studies on that passage have shown that it was understood as being of the genre 'judicial parable', and that at some point

---

83. See J. Jeremias, *The Parables of Jesus* (New York: Charles Scribner's Sons, 1972), pp. 71-76; M. Hengel, 'Das Gleichnis von den Weingärtnern Mk. 12.1-12 in Lichte der Zenonpapyri und der rabbinischen Glichnisse', *ZNW* 59 (1968), p. 30; C.H. Dodd, *The Parables of the Kingdom* (Glasgow: Collins, 1983), pp. 93-97; A.M. Hunter, *Interpreting the Parables* (London: SCM Press, 1984), pp. 116-18; against the theory of A. Jülicher, *Die Glichnisreden Jesu* (Tübingen: Mohr, 1910) that the parable is an allegorical invention of the early church.

84. Since the parable is also in *Thomas* 65, it has been suggested that the form there is more original: J.D. Crossan, 'The Parable of the Wicked Husbandmen', *JBL* 90 (1971), p. 461; for the contrary view see K.R. Snodgrass, 'The Parable of the Wicked Husbandmen: Is the Gospel of Thomas Version the Original?', *NTS* 21 (1974), pp. 142-44; and B. Dehandschutter, 'La parabole des vignerons homocides (Mc. 12.1-12) et l'Evangile selon Thomas' in (ed.) M. Sabbe, *L'Evangile*, especially pp. 208-18.

85. Crossan, 'Parable', p. 452.

subsequent to the Babylonian exile and during the emergence of the Targumic tradition, it came to be understood as a prediction of the destruction of the temple (*Targum Isa.* 5.2, 5; *1 En.* 89.56; 66b-67).[86] In both Isaiah 5 and Mark 12 the function is a critique of unwarranted assumptions of unconditional security in the convenant by Israel.[87] Ellis suggests that Mk 12-1-11 reflects a midrashic pattern current in synagogue addresses where the speaker reproduces part of the scripture lesson for the day (Isa. 5.1-7), illuminates it with a parable, and underscores his words by a further biblical passage (Ps.118.22-23), a proem midrash.[88] On the other hand, Black has suggested that the parable is a midrash on Ps. 118.22-23 based on a word-play on בן-אבן in the tradition of 1 Q. Hod 6.26, 1 QS 8.7-10. Since the parable is a pesher of the testimonia, it is not a parable of the wicked husbandmen, but of the rejected stone-son.[89] The suggestions of Ellis and Black have in common the element that the quotation of Ps. 118.22-23 is seen as an integral part of the parable, and that is where the language which draws our attention occurs.

Ps. 118.22 was probably originally related to an enthronement festival in which an anointed king-priest took his place as Yahweh's regent. As he mounts the steps of the throne, a new and and highly decorated coping stone is added to the cornice which the builders have failed to complete until now.[90] As stated earlier, the metaphor is related to the parable through a play on אבן and בן.[91] The picture given is of a stone unsuitable for its position, which specialists in masonry would not normally have placed in this prominent position: εἰς κεφαλὴν γωνίας.[92] The reference is to the most prominent position in the building (*T. Sol.* 22.7-23.8), or perhaps to the pinnacle of the temple.[93]

The citation of Ps. 118.23 in Mk 11.11 is striking. Luke does not include it, and Matthew makes it less important than the following statement (Mt. 21.43)

---

86. C.A. Evans, 'On the Vineyard Parables of Isaiah 5 and Mark 12', *BZ* 28 (1984), pp. 82-83.

87. Evans, 'Vineyard', p. 86.

88. E.E. Ellis, 'New Directions in Form Criticism', in *Jesus Christus in Historie und Theologie: Neutestamentliche Festschrift für Hans Conzelmann zum 60. Geburtstag* (ed. G. Strecker; Tübingen: Mohr, 1975), pp. 312-14.

89. M Black, 'The Christological Use of the Old Testament in the New Testament', *NTS* 18 (1971/2), p. 13.

90. B. Lindars, *New Testament Apologetic* (London: SCM Press, 1961), pp. 169-70.

91. Pesch, *Markusevangelium*, II, p. 222; Black, 'Christological', p. 12.

92. J.D.M. Derrett, 'Allegory and the Wicked Vinedresser', *JTS* 25 (1974), p. 181.

93. F.F. Bruce, 'The Corner Stone', *ExpTim* 84 (1973), p. 232.

that the kingdom will be taken away and given to others. Mark, on the other hand, makes it the center of the passage. The language strikes us due to the similarity to the wonder-terms in the gospel: καὶ ἔστιν θαυμαστὴ ἐν ὀφθαλμοῖς ἡμῶν. It is a direct quotation from the Septuagint, translating the Hebrew phrase היא נפלאת בעינינו. The niphal of פלא has the meaning of 'extraordinary, wonderful or marvelous' (2 Sam. 1.26; Ps. 119.18; 139.14). This latter part of the passage is all the more striking because it did not need to be included, since the psalm would have been so well known that the quotation of v. 22 would have implied the remainder.[94] In light of this, the Greek θαυμαστή strikingly reminds us of other places in Mark where θαυμάζω is used (5.20; 6.6a; 15.5, 44), and indeed the motif of wonder throughout the gospel. Is there a relationship?

The following pericope, which will be examined in due course, ends with this redactional note, καὶ ἐξεθαύμαζον ἐπ' αὐτῷ. It is not necessary to the pericope, nor do any of the other controversy stories in ch. 11 contain such a conclusion. the intensity of the preposition ἐκ added to θαυμάζω, the fact that it is added onto the very next pericope, and that v. 11 has a central place in the passage, all direct to the likelihood of an intentional shaping, directing his readers and hearers to relate the reactions of people marveling at Jesus throughout the gospel to the marvelous thing which God has done in making the rejected stone (son) the head of the corner. After all, what is Mark relating in the gospel except the things from the Lord which have come about in Jesus (miracles, forgiveness, exorcism, salvation, rejection, death, resurrection)? Also, in light of the way in which wonder carries throughout the early part of the gospel into the passion and resurrection (15.5, 44; 16.5, 6, 8), the quotation makes good sense. Both the rejection and the exaltation are marvelous (and involve the rule of God), and when people are made to marvel in the gospel, it would seem a clear indication that they are marveling at the wondrous act of the Lord. Although the wonder language utilizes various verbs, adjectives and nouns as we have seen, this should not deter us, since surely Mark must not be required to use the same word in a pedantic way, but must be allowed the freedom of using many synonyms. I would say, then, that an unusually striking ending in v. 11, in light of another striking ending in the very next pericope, and the way wonder is used throughout the gospel can serve for understanding the individual reactions of wonder as part of the wonderful thing which the Lord has accomplished making the rejected stone (son) the head of the corner.

Mark 12.12 follows with this remark: Καὶ ἐζήτουν ἐπ' αὐτὸν κρατῆσαι, καὶ

---

94. Derrett, 'Allegory', p. 186.

ἐφοβήθησαν τὸν ὄχλον, ἔγνωσαν γὰρ ὅτι πρὸς αὐτοὺς τὴν παραβολὴν εἶπεν. καὶ ἀφέντες αὐτὸν ἀπῆλθον. This verse is most likely redactional.[95] There is ἐζήτεν, κρατεῖν, ὄχλον, φοβεῖσθαι and γὰρ explanatory.[96] As with 11.32, the crowd again serves as a buffer between the intentions of the leaders and Jesus. This is not a reaction of wonder as such, but again shows the double-mindedness of the leaders who fear Jesus (11.18), marvel at him (12.17) and yet want to kill him, but are hindered from doing so now because they also fear the crowd.

Mark 12.17

The next place where the motif of wonder occurs is in the verse mentioned above, 12.17: ὁ δὲ Ἰησοῦς εἶπεν αὐτοῖς, Τὰ Καίσαρος ἀπόδοτε Καίσαρι καὶ τὰ τοῦ θεοῦ τῷ θεῷ. καὶ ἐξεθαύμαζον ἐπ' αὐτῷ. The pericope is on the question of the Pharisees and Herodians about the payment of the tribute to Caesar. The question revolves around the concept of kingship, as we shall see, and is thus related to the breaking-in of the kingdom of God. There is also the redactional title Διδάσκαλε[97] given to Jesus is v. 14, which connects to the picture of the 'new teaching with authority', in 1.22, 27. Just as in 1.21-28, the powerful authority of the teaching of Jesus will amaze the hearers. I have also noted previously the way v. 17 may emphasize the amazing work of God in v. 11 (Ps. 118.23).

The intensive noun ἐκθαυμάζω, 'to be greatly astonished', occurs only here in the New Testament. It is rare in the Septuagint, only occurring in Sir. 27.23a (ἀπέναντι τῶν ὀφθαλμῶν σου γλυκανεῖ τὸ στόμα αὐτοῦ, καὶ ἐπὶ τῶν λόγων σου ἐκθαυμάσει, describing the hypocrite as 'honey-tongued before your eyes, he is lost in wonder at your words); Sir. 43.18 (κάλλος λευκότητος αὐτῆς ἐκθαυμάσει ὀφθαλμός, καὶ ἐπὶ τοῦ ὑετοῦ αὐτῆς ἐκστήσεται καρδιά, speaking about snow, 'the eye is greatly astonished at the beauty of its whiteness and the heart is besides itself at its raining down'); and *4 Macc.* 17.17 (ἐξεθαύμασαν αὐτῶν τὴν ὑπομονήν, of the young martyrs). The parallelism of Sir. 43.18 is especially striking for our look at Mark's wonder language. The verb

---

95. Pryke, *Redactional Style*, p. 168; Schweizer, *Good News*, p. 239; Gnilka, *Evangelium*, II, p. 142; Nineham, *Gospel*, p. 314; Klostermann, *Markusevangelium*, p. 123; Hengel, 'Gleichnis', p. 1.
96. Pryke, *Redactional Style*, p. 162.
97. E. Schweizer, 'Anmerkung', in *Cullmann*, pp. 37-39; Stein, 'Methodology', p. 197.

ἐξίστημι (2.12; 3.21; 5.42) is compared to ἐκθαυμάζω, which indicates that ἐξίστημι ('beside themselves') should be seen as stronger than ἐκθαυμάζω, and that ἐκθαυμάζω has the strong sense of 'beside themselves with astonishment', or 'utterly astonished'. The verb ἐκθαυμάζω also occurs in *Ep. Arist.* 312 (λίαν ἐξεθαύμασε τὴν τοῦ νομοθέτου διάνοιαν: the king, Ptolemy II Philadelphus is said to be beside himself with astonishment at the genius of the lawgiver), and Dionysius of Halicarnassus, *De Thuc.* 34 (ὅσοι μὲν οὖν ἐκτεθαυμάκασιν, 'those who admired him immoderately', compare Philo, *De Somn.* 2.70). It can be seen that ἐκθαυμάζω describes an amazement that is thought excessive at some points, and describes in general 'being lost in amazement'. The reaction in 12.17 at first glance also seems almost overly dramatic.

It would be beyond the issue at hand to go into detail about the background of the pericope 12.13-17,[98] but it should be noted that doubt has risen of late about the reality of an organized Zealot movement prior to the period shortly before the war of 66-70 CE.[99] These doubts seem to be gaining a consensus among scholars.[100] However, due to the current state of the discussion, the use of an organized Zealot party as a foil (refusing to pay taxes to Caesar, though individual pious Jews may have refused) for the background to this passage may need to be held in abeyance.

The traditional interpretation of the answer of Jesus preceding the reaction of amazement in v. 17 understands the statement as legitimating the payment of taxes as ordained under God. Some things can be given to Caesar, and other things can be given to God, and there is no necessary conflict between the two.

---

98. See the fine discussion by F.F. Bruce in 'Render to Caesar', in (ed.) Bammel and Moule, *Jesus*, pp. 251-54. The sensitivity surrounding the coin can be seen by the fact that in the revolts of 66-70 CE and 132-35 CE the Jews minted their own coins.

99. See R.A. Horsley with J.S. Hanson, *Bandits, Prophets and Messiahs: Popular Movements at the Time of Jesus* (Minneapolis: Winston Press, 1985), pp. xiii-xv, 190-243; R.A. Horsley, 'The Zealots: Their Origin, Relationships and Importance in the Jewish Revolt', *NovT* 27 (1986), pp. 159-92; M. Borg, *Conflict, Holiness and Politics in the Teaching of Jesus* (Lewiston, NY: Mellon, 1984), pp. 34-36; and M. Borg, 'The Currency of the Term Zealot', *JTS* 22 (1971), pp. 504-12.

100. M. Hengel, *The Zealots: Investigations into the Jewish Freedom Movement in the Period from Herod I until 70 AD* (Edinburgh: T. & T. Clark, 1989), a revision of his 1961 original in German (Leiden: Brill), argues the opposite view to Horsley and Borg, cited above, and must still be the starting point for discussion of the issue. Horsley and Borg note that Josephus does not use the term 'Zealot' prior to the war, and the 'Zealots' need not be identified with the 'fourth philosophy'.

Goppelt, for example, says that the statement is a call to 'eschatological existence', and that the faith that honors the God of Israel as the God of all history recognizes that God has placed the region of Judea under the dominion of the Roman emperor, and what a ruler has due to him is to be paid to him. Jesus is summoning people to both total devotion to God and compensation to Caesar.[101] Derrett believes that Jesus, relying on Qoh. 8.2, was teaching what oriental teachers had taught for millenia, namely that a ruler must pass decrees and orders to which obedience is due, provided God is not disobeyed.[102] Bruce has written that Jesus' answer implies that Caesar is entitled to demand tribute, and to pay him tribute is simply to give him back what is his.[103] These similar views have been somewhat traditional since the reformation, and make the answer of Jesus in v. 17 essentially equivalent to 'yes'. Perhaps the fact that Jesus did not simply answer 'yes' should warn us against seeing his answer as straightforwardly affirmative.[104] We might also ask what was so amazing about an answer which essentially agreed to the legitimacy of payment. It would also seem a mistake to interpret the answer of Jesus here in light of Rom. 13.1-7.

One must take the answer of Jesus in v. 17, which leads to the strong amazement, in the context of Jesus' teaching in the rest of Mark. His teaching in Mark is for 'those who have ears to hear' (4.9), while 'those outside' will receive all things in parables, since they are unable to understand (4.12). Further, Jesus' teaching must be placed within the context of the breaking-in of the rule of God. Also, Jesus places an absolute contrast in Mark between τὰ τοῦ θεοῦ and τὰ τῶν ἀνθρώπων (8.33). Though the answer of Jesus in v. 17 may seem ambiguous, it will not be for those who know that the rule of God is breaking-in, who have ears to hear and who think the things of God. On the other hand, those outside who think human things will not understand, but only hear a confusing or unclear parable.

The questioners are clearly 'those outside', and are recognized as such by Jesus (vv. 13,17). The questioners ask if it is right to 'give' (δοῦναι) the tribute

---

101. L. Goppelt, 'Die Freiheit zur Kaisersteuer zu Mk. 12.17 und Rom. 13.1-7', in *Christologie und Ethik: Aufsätze zum Neuen Testament* (Göttingen: Vandenhoeck & Ruprecht, 1968), pp. 208, 210, 214-15; and L. Goppelt, 'The Freedom to Pay the Imperial Tax, Mk. 12.17', *SE* II (1964), pp. 183, 185-87.

102. J.D.M. Derrett, *Law in the New Testament* (London: Darton, Longman & Todd, 1970), pp. 313-37.

103. Bruce, 'Render', pp. 258-59.

104. K. Wengst, *Pax Romana and the Peace of Jesus Christ* (Philadelphia: Fortress Press, 1987), p. 59.

to Caesar, but the answer is worded with ἀπόδοτε in v. 17. The difference between δίδωμι and ἀποδίδωμι is slight, but should not be overlooked. The question phrased with 'give' is answered with 'give back'.[105] The answer, in contrast with the question, is phrased in the gospel in the terms by which people recognize the rightful claims of others, as a debtor 'gives back' what he or she owes. Jesus is emphasizing and extrapolating on the understanding of tribute in Roman Imperial culture: duty is owed to an emperor because of his lordship.[106] The phrases τὰ Καίσαρος and τὰ τοῦ θεοῦ remind one distinctly of 8.33, where τὰ τῶν ἀνθρωπῶν and τὰ τοῦ θεοῦ are not subordinate, but diametrically opposed. The request of Jesus to bring the coin to him implies that he did not have one,[107] and the question regarding ἡ εἰκών must be seen in light of the Old Testament teaching that human creation is in the image and likeness of God (Gen. 1.26). Although the coin has Caesar's image, humans have God's image. If one asks the question, 'What is God's?' in light of v. 17 ('Give to God the things which are God's'), the answer from the Old Testament is clear and definite: 'The earth is the Lord's and all it contains, the world and those who dwell in it' (Ps. 24.1). The answer from Jesus' teaching is also clear: 'God has become king, the rule of God is breaking-in'. If everything belongs to God, if God has become king, what is left for Caesar? Can Caesar be king also?

Although Jesus has not unambiguously answered the question of the 'hypocrites', the answer is clear for those who 'have ears to hear'. I agree here with Horsley, who says:

> There is simply no evidence anywhere else in the gospel tradition which would lead us to believe that Jesus would compromise the Lordship of God with regard to Caesar any more than he would with regard to the high-priestly aristocracy, Satan, or Mammon. The key in the saying 'render to Caesar what is Caesar's and to God what is God's' must lie in what is Caesar's and what is God's. Jesus would appear consistent with later rabbinic teaching in this regard, only more adamant about it—that everything is God's (Avot 3.8). Hence, the implication seems obvious in the saying: there is not much left to be rendered to Caesar.[108]

---

105. See BAGD, p. 90; Lk. 4.20; 7.42; 12.59; Mt. 5.26; 18.25.

106. R.A. Horsley, *Jesus and the Spiral of Violence* (San Francisco: Harper & Row, 1987), p. 309. Bruce, 'Render', p. 258, agrees that ἀποδίδωμι implies that the rightful owner has something returned to him, something that he is entitled to demand.

107. Bruce, 'Render', p. 259, recognizes that there may have been the implication in Jesus' answer that such a coin as was produced for his inspection was fit only for Gentiles to handle.

108. Horsley, *Spiral*, p. 313.

Such an interpretation may run contrary to the usual understanding, and seem quite radical for Jesus' followers (whatever the hermeneutical problems might be for our day, which is not our question, and should not be an objection in interpretation), but in the context of Mark the answer makes sense. This is especially true in light of the notion that God has become king and there is an absolute antithesis between 'the things of God' and 'human things'. This view makes better sense than interpretations which basically answer the question of paying the tax with 'yes'. If the objection is raised that when 'render to God' is to be understood as nullifying the superficial meaning of the words preceding them ('render to Caesar'), then this thought would have been expressed so cryptically that it might easily have been missed,[109] I would reply that the answer is clear 'for those who have ears to hear'. The rest receive the answer in a hidden *maschal*. Perhaps the objection might be raised that this answer would place the disciples of Jesus in great danger of persecution for non-payment. We must also remember that Jesus said that those who would follow him must deny themselves and be prepared to die (8,34-35). It may well be that as a carpenter who had left his craft (6.3), as fishermen who had left their nets (1.16-20), and as a publican who had left his post (6.3), Jesus and the disciples would not have had an income anyway, and so would not have been taxed (except perhaps at toll booths). Taxation was escaped, at the price of a very uncertain existence.[110] Again, our purpose is not to answer hermeneutic questions for our day, or to interpret Mk 12.17 in light of Rom. 13.1-7.

I would understand the reaction in v. 17b as redactional.[111] The fact that the ending is not necessary to the story, and the unusual ἐκθαυμάζω, indicate an insertion. The focus of the insertion is clear in light of this discussion. The question and answer center on who is king. Jesus replies with the authority given by God. Just as the 'new teaching with authority' amazed in 1.22, 27, so here the authority is also evident. In reality, Jesus' answer is a pronouncement about the kingdom, and comes with the authority of the kingdom. The listeners, though hypocrites and enemies, are beside themselves with astonishment.

---

109. Bruce, 'Render', p. 259.
110. Wengst, *Pax*, p. 59. Tolls due at toll booths are another issue.
111. Also Pryke, *Redactional Style*, p. 167; and Nineham, *Gospel*, p. 314. Pesch, *Markusevangelium*, II, p. 228, sees this pericope as part of his pre-Markan passion story, but says that the evidence is weighty that this was appended to the story.

Mark 14.33

The next place where the motif of wonder occurs is in the unusual and puzzling verse 14.33: καὶ παραλαμβάνει τὸν Πέτρον καὶ τὸν Ἰάκωβον καὶ τὸν Ἰωάννην μετ' αὐτοῦ, καὶ ἤρξατο ἐκθαμβεῖσθαι καὶ ἀδημονεῖν. The pericope 14.32-42 is about the prayer in Gethsemane, and it is related to the rest of the gospel in several ways. There is the initial separation of Peter, James and John in v. 33a, which reminds us of 5.37 and 9.2. In each prior separation, there had been a miraculous and mysterious intervention of God, and the separation prepares us for another here.[112] The term, παραδίδωμι, so important in Mark (1.14; 3.19; 9.31; 10.33; 13.9, 11, 12; 14.10, 11, 18, 21, 42, 44; 15.1, 10, 15 and others) occurs in vv. 41 and 42. When John was 'delivered over' in 1.14, Jesus began to preach, and now Jesus is 'delivered over'. It has been suggested that there is an eschatological significance to the arrival of 'the hour' in v. 41, especially with the coming near (ἤγγικεν, 1.15) of ὁ παραδιδούς (1.14, τὸ παραδοθῆναι) in v. 42. In Mark, ἤγγικεν is an 'eschatologically loaded term' which recalls the programmatic summary of the message of Jesus in 1.14-15 in such a way as to relate the 'coming near' of the passion to the 'coming near' of the kingdom.[113] There is also a sense in which the prayer, 'not my will, but yours', in v. 36, can be said to summarize the entire message of the kingdom of God in Mark.[114] Since God has become king, God's will must be done. Also the call to prayer directed toward the disciples and exemplified by Jesus in the pericope is a call to theo-centricity and a summons to radical trusting faith in

---

112. A. Kenny, 'The Transfiguration and the Agony in the Garden', *CBQ* 19 (1957), pp. 444-52, notes the following illuminating parallels between the transfiguration and the Gethsemane scene: there is the separation of the three 'Abba, Father' echoes, 'This is my beloved son'; Peter is in the foreground of both incidents; οὐ γὰρ ᾔδει τί ἀποκριθῇ in 9.6 corresponds to καὶ οὐκ ᾔδεισαν τί ἀποκριθῶσιν in 14.40; and in the transfiguration the father testifies of his love for the son, while in Gethsemane the son accepts the father's will.

113. W. Kelber, 'The Hour of the Son of Man and the Temptation of the Disciples (Mk. 14.32-42)', in (ed.) W. Kelber, *Passion*, 1976, p. 45. Kelber notes that the eschatological perspective is also suggested by the emergence of the designation 'king' in the passion narrative (15.2, 9, 12, 18, 26, 32). There is a sense in which the cross confirms the coming of the kingdom and legitimates Jesus as king, for the 'hour' of the crucifixion is also the 'hour' of coronation (p. 46).

114. T. Söding, 'Gebet und Gebetsmahnung Jesu in Getsemani: Eine redaktionskritische Auslegung von Mk. 14.23-42', *BZ* 31 (1987), p. 93.

the light of the call to belief and repentance (1.15).[115] In sum, the Gethsemane pericope is about Jesus submitting to the rule and will of the father, and this then becomes a summons for the community to also 'watch and pray'.

There have been questions regarding the unity of vv. 32-42. K.G. Kuhn has suggested that two sources are joined together, and others have followed him.[116] Tensions in the account include Jesus separating from the disciples to pray, but in v. 33 taking the three with him; the prayer of Jesus is reported twice (v. 35 in indirect speech, and v. 36 in direct speech); and the return of Jesus to the disciples is reported in vv. 37-38 and again in v. 41. Also, it is strange to some that Peter alone is asked to watch in v. 37b, but all sleep in v. 37a. Others argue for the unity of the passage.[117] Kelber is more radical in arguing for Mark as the creator of the story 'to a high degree'.[118] Others argue that the story rests on primitive tradition.[119] Still others see differing layers in the pericope,[120] or a primitive

---

115. Söding, 'Gebet', p. 93. Söding also notes that the Gethsemane prayer in 14.35-36, 39, is related to the kingdom proclamation in that it shows the proclamation of the kingdom to service, which has as its consequence that Jesus is delivered over into the hands of sinners (see p. 80).

116. K.-G. Kuhn, 'Jesus in Gethsemane', *EvT* 12 (1952/53), pp. 260-85, especially pp. 266-67. Kuhn sees one source as a christological statement of the hour of the son of man (vv. 32, 35, 40, 41) and the other source as parenetic, with Jesus as the master example of how to stand in temptation (vv. 33-34, 36-38). Kuhn sees v. 42 as redactional, also πάλιν of v. 40, and καὶ ἔρχεται τὸ τρίτον of v. 41. Also seeing two sources joined is R. Barbour, 'Gethsemane in the Tradition of the Passion', *NTS* 16 (1969/70), especially pp. 232-33; T. Lescow, 'Jesus in Gethsemane', *EvT* 26 (1966), pp. 141-59; and Schweizer, *Good News*, pp. 309-10.

117. E. Lohse, *Die Geschichte des Leidens und Sterbens Jesu Christi* (Gütersloh: Mohn, 1964) p. 65. Lohmeyer, *Evangelium*, p. 313, describes v. 32-42 as a literary unity. Also Pesch, *Markusevangelium*, II, p. 385, sees vv. 32-42 as following his pre-Markan passion story, and does not believe the evangelist has broken into the story.

118. W. Kelber, 'Mark 14.32-42: Gethsemane', *ZNW* 63 (1972), especially p. 176.

119. Taylor, *Gospel*, p. 551; Mann, *Mark*, pp. 588-89; Cranfield, *Gospel*, p. 430.

120. W. Schenk, *Markus*, p. 206, sees a historical present layer in 32, 33a, 34a, b, 36, 37a, 37b, 40b, 40c, 41a and 42; an apocalyptic tradition in 33b, 35b, c, 38, 41b, c; and Markan redaction in 33b, 34a, 35a, b, 36a, 37a, b, 38a, part of 39, 40a, 41a, b (partly). E. Linnemann, *Studien zur Passionsgeschichte* (FRLANT 102; Göttingen: Vandenhoeck & Ruprecht, 1970), p. 32, sees the original composition as 32, 35, 37a, 39a, 40a, b, 40c, 41a, 41b; a second draft of vv. 33, 34a, 36; and a third draft of vv. 32-37a, 38-40a, b, 41a, 40c, 41b; and the evangelist then added 37b, 41c, 42, and moved 40c to its present place. D. Dormeyer, *Die Passion Jesu als Verhaltensmodell: Literarische und theologische Analyse der Traditions und Redaktionsgeschichte der Markuspassion* (Münster: Aschendorff, 1974), p. 133, sees

tradition which has been greatly expanded.[121] Perhaps the wide variety of divisions of the pericope show that source-critical analysis is not an exact science.[122] For the purposes at hand, I would note that the two key themes in the pericope, the prayer of Jesus and the admonition to prayer directed to the disciples, are introduced in the opening verse, v. 32.[123] I will focus on v. 33, and the unusual language there.

It has been said that there is nothing comparable to the distress of v. 33 in other Jewish or Christian martyrdoms.[124] Taylor calls the verse, 'one of the most important statements in Mark'.[125] Certainly the language is unique, and may have been scandalous to Matthew and Luke. The expression καὶ ἤρξατο ἐκθαμβεῖσθαι καὶ ἀδημονεῖν is striking. This is the second of four occurrences of the intensive ἐκθαμβεῖσθαι in Mark (also 9.15; 16.5, 6). Previously noted was the parallelism of Sir. 30.9: τιθήνησον τέκνον, καὶ ἐκθαμβεῖσθαι σε, σύμπαιξον αὐτῷ, καὶ λυπήσει σε. Sirach uses ἐκθαμβεῖσθαι and λυπεῖσθαι as parallel, and Mk 14.34 uses περίλυπος in Jesus' explanation of the experience of v. 33. Both Mark and Sirach connect an element of grief with ἐκθαμβεῖσθαι, while Mt. 27.37 links ἀδημονεῖν with λυπεῖσθαι. The preposition ἐκ may add a shade of terror to the awe of θαμβεῖσθαι (note 16.5, 6, also ἔκθαμβος in 1 Kgdms 4.13 Sym.), and this may be evident in both Sir. 30.9 and Mk 14.33. We have here, then, a terrified awe along with a deep anxiety (ἀδημονεῖν; Phil. 2.26; Aq. Job 18.20).

There have been numerous proposals for understanding the language of v. 33b. The three main options would include v. 33b as indicating horror of the terrible fate ahead of Jesus;[126] an encounter with the mystery and power of

---

v. 32a as traditional; 32b, 35a, 36, 37a and 41b as a secondary redaction, and vv. 33, 34, 35b, 37b, 38, 39, 40, 41a, c, and 42 as from a final redactor. The secondary redaction has the *Gattung* of an epic prayer-struggle, while the final redactor makes Jesus a type of the model prayer. Also with three layers is T. Boman, 'Der Gebetskampf Jesu', *NTS* 10 (1963/64), pp. 261-73.

    121. W. Mohn, 'Gethsemane (Mk. 14.32-42)', *ZNW* 64 (1973), p. 202, sees a *Vorlage* in v. 32 (Gethsemane, καθίσατε ὧδε ἕως προσεύξωμαι); vv. 35, 37a, 41b. While the *Vorlage* had an apocalyptic origin, it was expanded to warn against an interpretation of the historical Jesus apart from the cross and the resurrection (p. 205).

    122. I agree here with Schmithals, *Evangelium*, II, p. 634.
    123. Söding, 'Gebet', p.77.
    124. Schweizer, *Good News*, p. 311.
    125. Taylor, *Gospel*, p. 552.
    126. Cranfield, *Gospel*, p. 340; Lane, *Mark*, p. 516; A. Feuillet, *L'agonie de*

evil;[127] or a shuddering awe at an encounter with the holy.[128] I would suggest that the best option is the last of the three, namely that Jesus is having an encounter with God, and is dramatically confronted with the divine will.

I note first of all that where θαμβέομαι or ἐκθαμβέσθαι are used in Mark, it is when people are confronted with supernatural intervention (1.27; 16.5, 6), or a revelation of the divine will (10.24, 32). Jesus has separated from the disciples to pray (v. 32), and there is indication elsewhere in Mark that in prayer Jesus seeks the will of God (1.35-39). The confrontation with evil comes later, with the arrival of the betrayer in v. 43. The reaction, ἀδημονεῖν, can serve as an agony in understanding and following the will of God (Ezek. 3.15 Sym.). Both shuddering awe and agony are experienced in the Bible by those encountering God and the divine will (Isa. 6.5; Jer. 20.7 פתה [God has 'overcome' Jeremiah]; 20.9; Hab. 3.16; Dan. 10.8), and in light of v. 34, the portrait of the 'righteous sufferer' is appropriate to this passage.[129] In light of the examples of the prophets Isaiah, Jeremiah and Habbakuk experiencing awe and agony in confrontation with God and God's will for their mission, it seems legitimate to join the two concepts in v. 33b. Jesus encounters God and the divine will regarding the passion is reconfirmed (these cannot be separated). The response is deep, shuddering awe and agony.

Verse 33b is most likely redactional.[130] The construction ἄρχομαι with the infinitive is identifiable as a Markan feature,[131] and the unusual ἐκθαμβέσθαι is also Markan.[132] There are also Markan evidences in v. 33a, namely the separation and naming of the three.

The purpose of v. 33b is to show Jesus confronted with the presence of God and the agony of the revelation of the divine will. Just as others in the gospel

Gethsémani: Enquête exégétique et théologique suivie d'un étude du 'Mystere de Jésus' de Pascal (Paris: Gabalda, 1977), pp. 79-80.

127. Barbour, 'Gethsemane', p. 236; Kelber, 'Gethsemane', p. 177.

128. Pesch, *Markusevangelium*, II, p. 389; Söding, 'Gebet', p. 85; and Rawlinson, *Mark*, p. 211, who says it is a shuddering awe, as of one conscious of being in the presence of a supernatural mystery which excites terror.

129. J. Héring , 'Zwei exegetische Probleme in der Perikope von Jesus in Gethsemane', in (eds.) Ellis and Grässer, *Cullmann*, p. 67; L. Schenke, *Studien zur Passionsgeschichte des Markus: Tradition und Redaktion in Markus 14.1-42*, (FB 4; Würzburg: Echter Verlag), p. 549.

130. Pryke, *Redactional Style*, p. 122; Kelber, 'Passion', p. 174; Mohn, 'Gethsemane', p. 202; Dormeyer, *Passion*, p. 125; Feuillet, *Agonie*, pp. 79-80; Söding, 'Gebet', p. 80.

131. Peabody, *Composer*, p. 54.

132. Pryke, *Redactional Style*, p. 172.

have reacted with awe when God has broken-in powerfully, so now here Jesus has the same reaction. This serves to put the coming passion in the light of the rule and acts of God, rather than to present Jesus as abandoned by God. God has directed Jesus to this fate, and the same terrifying awe which the miracles of Jesus caused observers is now experienced by Jesus himself. The result is to show that God is present in both the early acts and the passion in the same way. Also, just as the journey to Jerusalem brought awe to those with Jesus (10.32), so now Jesus experiences shuddering awe to a greater degree. The presence and power of God are being revealed even as Jesus is betrayed into the hands of sinners, for this too is the will of the father who rules.

Mark 15.5

The next place where the motif of wonder occurs is in 15.5: ὁ δὲ Ἰησοῦς οὐκέτι οὐδὲν ἀπεκρίθη, ὥστε θαυμάζειν τὸν Πιλᾶτον. The pericope 15.1-5 presents Jesus before Pilate, and as part of the passion, there is an important relationship between ch. 15 and the theme of the rule of God in the gospel. It has been suggested by Rhoads and Michie that the narrator wants the reader to see God's ruling king in the dying Jesus. Irony is used by Mark to present this. The crucifixion is portrayed with many elements of mockery, which the reader sees as ironically true. Jesus is six times called king (15.2, 9, 12, 18, 26, 32). There is one person on his right and one on the left (see 10.37). He was dressed in purple earlier and wore a crown of thorns. 'The mockery is ironic testimony to the true kingship of Jesus as he hangs in agony; God's rule is triumphant in Jesus' death'.[133] Jesus as the Son of God in the gospel is the regent of the kingdom and the death is ironically the coronation.

It must also be noted here that with Pilate's amazement (and 15.44), the circle is complete. Previously Jesus amazed the Jewish people (1.22, 27), the scribes and other leaders (2.12; 12.17), the disciples (6.50-51) and Gentiles (5.15, 20; 7.37). Now a Gentile ruler is amazed. This is surely a shaping of the gospel to present Jesus as amazing to all, Jew and Gentile, leader and people.

Tensions have been noted in 15.1-5, including the element that Pilate knows the accusation in v. 2, but further accusations come in v. 3; Jesus is silent in v. 5, but has spoken in v. 2; and the accusations differ in vv. 2 and 3.[134] Verse 2

---

133. Rhoads and Michie, *Story*, p. 115; and see Chronis, 'Veil', pp. 103-107; and Kelber, *Passion*, pp. 45-46.
134. Schmithals, *Evangelium*, II, pp. 670-71; Grundmann, *Evangelium*, p. 306; Nineham, *Gospel*, pp. 415-16.

may be redactional, to bring forth the kingship idea.[135] The accusations of v. 3 may simply be further claims related to the principal charge of v. 2.

The construction ὥστε θαυμάζειν τὸν Πιλᾶτον reminds of ὥστε ἐξίστασθαι πάντας of 2.12 (ὥστε with amazement). The double negative οὐκέτι οὐδὲν reminds of other double negatives in Mark (1.44: μηδενὶ μηδὲν εἴπῃς; 16.8: καὶ οὐδενὶ οὐδὲν εἶπαν). In each case these relate to the tension between speech and silence. The similarity between ὥστε θαυμάζειν τὸν Πιλᾶτον and Isa. 52.15 (οὕτως θαυμάσονται ἔθνη πολλὰ ἐπ᾽ αὐτῷ) has been recognised.[136] This raises the question of the relation of the portrait of the servant of Isaiah and the 'righteous sufferer' to the Markan portrait of Jesus' passion.

It is probably better to see a general portrait of the 'righteous sufferer', as is evidenced through the traditions from Ps. 38.13-16; 39.10; Wis. 2-5; 4 Macc. 7, as shaping the Markan passion, than a specific appropriation of Isa. 52.13-53.12.[137] There may be a tradition of Isa. 52.15 behind Wis. 5.2 (the servant of Isaiah generated the portrait in Wisdom), but it is probably better to relate Mk 15.5 to Markan amazement in the first instance.

In light of the way reactions of wonder have functioned in Mark, it is hard to see 15.5 as indicating a mere surprise or admiration for Jesus. Especially in light of 5.20, and the supernatural silence in front of the accusers in v. 5a, it is better to see this as awe before the uncanny.[138] Just as the witness to the Gentiles

---

135. Gnilka, *Evangelium*, II, p. 296.
136. Pesch, *Markusevangelium*, II, p. 454, says there is perhaps an allusion intended, as does Cranfield, *Gospel*, p. 449, and Maurer, 'Knecht', pp. 1-38.
137. J. Donahue, 'Temple', p. 66, notes many parallels between Wisdom and the Markan passion: the enemies lie in wait for the righteous man (2.12); his ways are strange (2.15); he boasts that God is his father (2.16); he is tested with insults and torture (2.19); he is condemned to a shameful death (12.20); but will stand with great confidence before his accusers (5.1-2); the accusers will be shaken with fear and amazed (5.2); at the righteous man's death he will be numbered among the sons of God (5.5). Donahue also sees parallels to David (p. 76): like David, Jesus makes a sorrowful ascent to the Mount of Olives (Mk. 14.26, 33; 2 Sam. 15.30); is accompanied by companions in his hour of trial (Mk. 14.33; 2. Sam. 15.19-24); one of these proclaims his enduring fidelity to his master (Mk. 14.29; 2 Sam. 15.19-21); one of David's friends wants to strike with a sword when David is attacked (Mk. 14.42; 2 Sam. 15.31). Donahue's parallels show how polyvalent the portrait in Mark is, and warns against over-dependence on only Isaiah 53. See Kee, 'Function', p. 171; Dormeyer, *Passion*, p. 177; Maurer, 'Knecht', p. 10; L. Schenke, *Der gekreuzigte Christus: Versuch einer literarkritischen und traditionsgeschichtlichen Bestimmung der vormarkinischen Passionsgeschichte* (SBS 69; Stuttgart: Katholisches Bibelwerk, 1974), p. 65; and especially Nickelsburg, 'Genre', pp. 153-84.

of Jesus' deed in 5.20 amazed them, so the silence of Jesus now amazes the Gentile procurator. The tradition in Jn 19.8 may pick up another element of the effect Jesus had on Pilate. Wonder at the supernatural interventions of God took place throughout Mark, and here the supernatural silence of Jesus in the face of accusers is also an act of God manifesting a divine presence. Even in the non-defense of Jesus, God is present to save. The irony of a powerful Roman procurator in awe before a Jewish peasant on the way to death shows the message of the entire gospel of Mark: God has acted and broken-in to rule and save in a very unusual way, and the greatness of that divine power is most keenly manifested in the powerlessness of suffering.

Although the construction, ὥστε with the infinitive, is a Markan construction,[139] it is probably better to see 15.5 as traditional.[140] Perhaps it was rewritten by Mark, and Jn 19.8 may indicate an independent tradition about the fear of Pilate before Jesus was in circulation.

The reaction of amazement of Pilate indicates to the readers that God is present even in the silence of Jesus which leads to the cross. In other words, even in the sentencing of Jesus there is the reign of God. The Roman authority has not overruled God! The reaction of Pilate is not the only way the gospel indicates this in the passion story. The fulfillment of scripture (vv. 24, 34), the fulfillment of the predictions of Jesus (8.31; 9.30-32; 10.32-34), the sudden darkness (v. 33), the tearing of the temple curtain (v. 38), the extraordinarily quick death, and the confession of the centurion all testify to the crucifixion being part of the plan and will of God.[141] The special contribution of a reaction of wonder is that the passion is related to other events in the gospel where the rule of god has broken-in to save. The passion is put in the same light, as a divine intervention to save.

Another element of the breaking-in of the rule of God must also be mentioned here in relation to the passion. I have noted earlier that Mark emphasizes

---

138. Gnilka, *Evangelium*, II, p. 300; Grundmann, *Evangelium*, p. 307; Schniewind, *Evangelium*, p. 195; H. Schlier, *Die Markuspassion* (Einsiedeln: Johannes Verlag, 1974), p. 64; Pohl, *Evangelium*, p. 546; G. Bertram, *Die Leidensgeschichte Jesu und der Christkult* (FRLANT 21; Göttingen: Vandenhoeck & Ruprecht, 1922), p. 63; and Bertram, 'θαῦμα', p. 38.

139. Peabody, *Composer*, p. 45.

140. Schenk, *Markus*, p. 246; Dormeyer, *Passion*, p. 177; Schmithals, *Evangelium*, II, pp. 670-71; Gnilka, *Evangelium*, II, pp. 296-97; Schenke, *Gekreuzigte*, pp. 55-58; Pesch, *Markusevangelium*, II, p. 454 (part of Pesch's pre-Markan passion story).

141. A helpful article on this is H.M. Jackson, 'The Death of Jesus in Mark and the Miracle from the Cross', *NTS* 33 (1987), pp. 16-37.

'the mystery of the kingdom of God', namely how God's power can rule and yet humans can remain in bondage to sin and Satan. The passion brings forth this thought above all, as God acts in the midst of the rejection of Jesus. 15.1-5 shows this mystery very clearly. Evil still exists and seems to win the day, but in the silence of Jesus and the ironic truthfulness of the accusation of kingship, God is in fact acting to save. In the supernatural silence of Jesus, who is submitting to the will of the father, God is present. Wonder results at this unusual, and even unrecognized, revelation of the holy.

Mark 15.44

The motif ofwonder occurs again with Pilate in 15.44: ὁ δὲ Πιλᾶτος ἐθαύμασεν εἰ ἤδη τέθνηκεν, καὶ προσκαλεσάμενος τὸν κεντυρίωνα ἐπηρώτησεν αὐτὸν εἰ πάλαι ἀπέθανεν.[142] The pericope 15.42-27 is on the burial of Jesus. The person who takes responsibility for the body of Jesus is Joseph of Arimathea, who is one of Mark's heroic 'little people'. The narrative relates in v. 43 that he was waiting for the kingdom of God. He takes a risk of coming under suspicion of treason and collaboration by asking for the body of Jesus.[143] While the pericope may serve as a transition to the resurrection of 16.1-8, it also secures the fact that Jesus has truly died.

It has been suggested that two traditions have been joined in the pericope, namely one concerning Pilate and the other centering on the women.[144] Some see v. 44 as continuing a pre-Markan passion story.[145] Others have thought vv. 44-45 are a later addition to the gospel,[146] with possible apologetic purposes affirming the reality of the death of Jesus. The purpose of v. 44 may rather be to indicate God's action in yet another way in the death of Jesus.

---

142. There is a textual difficulty with εἰ πάλαι, which is attested in ℵ, A, C, K, L, X^vid, Π, Ψ, f¹, f¹³ and many miniscules, but εἰ ἤδη is also attested by B, D, W, Θ, 1009 and some versions, but the latter is probably a repetition from εἰ ἤδη τέθνηκεν earlier in the verse. Admittedly, however, the use of πάλαι is odd here.

143. R.E. Brown 'The Burial of Jesus (Mk. 15.42-47)', *CBQ* 50 (1988), p. 241, who notes that Joseph is called a βουλευτής, which Brown takes to mean a member of the Sanhedrin (in Josephus's *War* 2.17.1, the term is used of belonging to the Sanhedrin).

144. Lohmeyer, *Evangelium*, pp. 351-52; Grundmann, *Evangelium*, pp. 317-18.

145. Pesch, *Markusevangelium*, II, p. 509; Schenke, *Gekreuzigte*, p. 102, vv. 42-47 as a unit.

146. Bultmann, *History*, p. 274; Dormeyer, *Passion*, pp. 217, 220; Weiss, *Älteste*, p. 340; and Gnilka, *Evangelium*, II, p. 331, says vv. 44-45 are a later ingredient which may not have been read by Matthew or Luke.

Since early in church history, the quick death of Jesus (crucifixion most often took days) has been seen as a marvel.[147] Since Mark is likely presenting the quick death as miraculous (15.37), the reaction of Pilate in v. 44, ὁ δὲ Πιλᾶτος ἐθαύμασεν εἰ ἤδη τέθνηκεν, is not surprise, but wonder. Gnilka calls it a numinous reaction, as at 15.5.[148] There is evidence of God's acting even in the death of Jesus, in that it occurs unusually fast, and this brings amazement once more to Pilate.

The construction, ἐθαύμασεν εἰ, is not as common as ὅτι following might be, but still occurs on occasion. 1 Jn 3.13 is the only other New Testament use of this construction (Philo, *Mech.* 77.41; *Migr. Abr.* 26; Josephus, *Apion* 1.68; Polybius 3.33.17; Pap. *Hib.* 159; 3 Cor. 3.2; Dg. 10.4; MPol. 16.1).[149] The idea in 15.44 is that Pilate is amazed that Jesus had already died. There is something unusual and uncanny about a man who refuses self-defense and whose death by crucifixion turns out to be so sudden.

Verse 44 need not be redactional. It fits the flow of the story since the request of Joseph expects an answer from Pilate,[150] and θαυμάζω is not an unusual or favorite Markan term. Other than v. 47, the pericope is simply the account of the burial, with a minimum of Markan characteristics and theological elaboration which may rest on old tradition.[151] If the quick death was seen as a marvel, amazement is the expected result.

The use of tradition by an evangelist is sometimes overlooked as not as important as redaction. However, what is used may sometimes be as important as what is added for the entire theology of a work. There is in 15.44 another place in which divine intervention in the death of Jesus is portrayed. Amazement is the logical result. Within the contours of the gospel, the motif of wonder has placed the death in the very same light as the earthly works of Jesus. In the former, God has broken-in to rule and save just as clearly as in the latter. This unusual event strikes even the hardened Roman procurator.

---

147. Klostermann, *Markusevangelium*, p. 169, quotes Origen: *miraculum einim erat quoniam post tres horas receptus est, qui forte biduum victurus erat in cruce*. See Lohmeyer, *Evangelium*, p. 350; Schenke, *Gekreuzigte*, pp. 80-81.

148. Gnilka, *Evangelium*, II, p. 333; Also, J. Schreiber, 'Die Bestattung Jesu', *ZNW* 72 (1981), p. 148; Bertram, 'θαῦμα', p. 39.

149. BAGD, p. 352.

150. R. Pesch, 'Der Schluss der vormarkinischen Passionsgeschichte und das Markusevangelium: Mk. 15.42-16.8', in (ed.) Sabbe, *Evangile*, p. 376.

151. Mann, *Mark*, p. 656; Schweizer, *Good News*, p. 361; Brown, 'Burial', pp. 240-43.

One should note also here that the gospel is showing that just because a character is struck with wonder at the uncanny or unusual, this does not necessitate that belief will follow. Rather, the emphasis is that all, believers and unbelievers, Jews and Gentiles, disciples and enemies, of necessity marvel. Whether or not one accepts it, God has acted, and the amazement of even staunch enemies testifies to this. In light of the Roman persecution of the Christians under Nero, it would have been a tremendous affirmation to the Christian community at Rome to recount how even the ranking Roman official in Judea stood in awe of Jesus on two occasions. There is a power at which even Rome is astounded. Even in death, Jesus the Son of God is beyond the ability of the Roman officials to grasp. As Mark has so ironically and yet truthfully presented, Jesus is God's appointed regent. Paradoxically, in his powerlessness such power was released that even Rome's representative, the one holding earthly power, would tremble. The power of earth means little compared with the power of heaven.

Mark 16.5, 6, 8.

Perhaps the most puzzling of all the places where the motif of wonder occurs in Mark is in 16.5-6, 8: καὶ εἰσελθοῦσαι εἰς τὸ μνημεῖον εἶδον νεανίσκον καθήμενον ἐν τοῖς δεξιοῖς περιβεβλημένον στολὴν λευκήν, καὶ ἐξεθαμβήθησαν. ὁ δὲ λέγει αὐταῖς, Μὴ ἐκθαμβεῖσθε. Ἰησοῦν ζητεῖτε τὸν Ναζαρηνὸν τὸν ἐσταυρωμένον. ἠγέρθη, οὐκ ἔστιν ὧδε. ἴδε ὁ τόπος ὅπου ἔθηκαν αὐτόν...καὶ ἐξελθοῦσαι ἔφυγον ἀπὸ τοῦ μνημείου, εἶχεν γὰρ αὐτὰς τρόμος καὶ ἔκστασις. καὶ οὐδενὶ οὐδὲν εἶπαν, ἐφοβοῦντο γὰρ. The problems surrounding the ending of Mark are vexing, and the secondary literature is enormous, so although I must deal with some of the textual problems, I will attempt to focus most of our attention on the place of the motif of wonder.

It has been stated recently that at present, scholarly opinion may be moving more closely to a consensus on the Markan ending, with a majority of interpreters, approaching the text from a variety of theological perspectives, now appearing to favor 16.8 as the intended end of the gospel.[152] There are six textual possibilities on the ending: first, the text ends at 16.8 (ℵ, B, 304, syr^s, cop^{sa}, ^{ms}, arm^{mss}, geo^{1,a} and this was known by Clement, Origen, Eusebius, Jerome, Ammonius, Victor of Antioch and Euthymius); second, 16.1-8 with the so-called shorter ending (only k); third, 16.1-8 with vv. 9-20, with a sign showing doubt of the originality of vv. 9-20 (f^1, 22, 138, 205, 1110, 1210, 1221, 1582 and

---

152. Black, *Disciples*, p. 35.

others); fourth, 16.1-8 with vv. 9-20 in a consecutive text (A, C, D, K, X, Δ, Θ, Π, f[13], 28, 33, 274[txt], 565, 700, 892, 1009, 1010, 1071, 1079, 1195, 1230, 1242, 1253, 1344, 1365, 1546, 1646, 2148, 2174 and versions); fifth, 16.1-8 with vv. 9-14 and free logion and vv. 15b-20 (W, Hieronymus); sixth, 16.1-6 with a shorter ending and vv. 9-20 (L, Ψ, 099, 0112, 274[mg], 579, I[1602], syr[h mg], cop[sa mss bo mss] and eth[mss]).[153] The best probability textually, however, for both internal and external reasons, leaves us with an ending at 16.8.[154]

The problem with an ending at 16.8 is that ἐφοβοῦντο γὰρ seems very unusual for an ending, and the fact that differing endings were added in the early church shows that it was judged inadequate, perhaps even by the other evangelists. It is supposed by some that the text was either never finished, or the conclusion was either lost or destroyed by some accident, or the conclusion was deliberately suppressed.[155] The supposition that the ending was lost or destroyed has led to some attempts at reconstruction of the original ending.[156] One would have to say, however, that if the ending was lost or destroyed, it would have had to have been at such an early date that not only was it never recopied, but also

---

153. See Gnilka, *Evangelium*, II, pp. 350-51; Pesch, *Evangelium*, I, pp. 40-47.

154. B.M. Metzger, *The Text of the New Testament: Its Transmission, Corruption and Resoration* (New York: Oxford University Press, 1982), pp. 226-29; K. Aland, 'Der Schluss der Markusevangeliums' in *L'Evangile selon Marc*, pp. 435-70; K. Aland, 'Bemerkung zum Schluss des Markusevangeliums' in *Neotestamentica et Semitica: Studies in Honour of Matthew Black*, (eds. E.E. Ellis and M. Wilcox; Edinburgh: T. & T. Clark, 1969), pp. 157-80; K. Aland, 'Der wiedergefundene Markusschluss? Eine methodologische Bemerkung zur text kritischen Arbeit', *ZTK* 67 (1970), pp. 3-13. The last article is written against the perspective of E. Linnemann, 'Der wiedergefundene Markusschluss', *ZTK* 66 (1969), pp. 255-87, attempting to salvage 16.15-20. W.R. Farmer, *The Last Twelve Verses of Mark* (SNTSMS, 25; Cambridge: Cambridge University Press, 1974), has argued for the authenticity of vv. 9-20, as has H. Lubsczyk, 'Kurios Jesus: Beobachtungen und Gedanken zum Schluss des Markusevangeliums' in *Die Kirche des Anfangs: Festschrift für Heinz Schürmann zum 65. Geburtstag* (ed. R. Schackenburg, J. Ernst and J. Wanke; Leipzig: St. Benno, 1977), pp. 133-74. In spite of these and other attempts, it is generally recognized that 16.1-8 is the best ending textually.

155. These options are given in Cranfield, *Gospel*, p. 470.

156. For example, Linnemann, 'Markusschluss'; G.W. Trompf, 'The First Resurrection Appearance and the Ending of Mark's Gospel', *NTS* 18 (1972), pp. 308-330; W. Schmithals, 'Die Markusschluss, die Verklärungsgeschichte und die Aussendung der Zwolf', *ZTK* 69 (1972), pp. 379-411; H.R. Balz, 'Furcht vor Gott?', *EvT* 29 (1969), especially p. 633; C.F.D. Moule, 'St. Mark 16:8 Once More', *NTS* 2 (1955), pp. 58-59.

no one was sufficiently familiar with the ending to restore it from memory.[157] If the gospel was never finished, why was it canonized? The objection of Cranfield is that a gospel needs resurrection appearances, and Mark must surely have had some at one point.[158] This assumes that the outline of a gospel follows the kerygma of 1 Cor. 15.3-7 (for example). One must note that the apostolic proclamation did not always include appearances (note Acts 2.24; 13.33-34), and one must not judge Mark by the later Matthew or Luke. It is also possible that oral presentation of resurrection appearances in the church could have supplemented the gospel (or made it unnecessary for Mark to include them). The linguistic possibility of a book ending with ἐφοβοῦντο γὰρ has been shown repeatedly.[159] It is outside the scope of this investigation to give a case for Mark ending intentionally with 16.8, but I can approve the comment of Burkill, 'The primary duty of the exegete is to elucidate the gospel as it stands, not as he [sic] thinks it ought to be...'.[160] As it stands, Mark ends with 16.8, and the exegete must first seek to understand it as such without recourse to reconstructed endings.

The reaction to the 'young man' in 16.5 uses the intensive verb ἐξεθαμβήθησαν again (9.15; 14.33). The response is Μὴ ἐκθαμβεῖσθε, which occurs nowhere else. The common response of comfort after an angelophany or epiphany is μὴ φοβοῦ or μὴ φοβεῖσθε (6.50; Lk. 1.12, 29; Acts 27.24; Rev. 1.17) no matter what the verb is which describes the startled reaction. For example, in 6.50 the startled reaction is ἐταράχθησαν, but the word of comfort is μὴ φοβεῖσθε, not μὴ ταρασσου. The word of comfort, μὴ ἐκθαμβεῖσθε, obviously picking up the verb from the reaction, is unusual and draws attention to the rare Markan word.

Mark 16.7 has the command to the women to tell the disciples 'and Peter', Ππροάγει ὑμας εἰς τὴν Γαλιλαίαν. The verb προάγω follows the move to the

---

157. M.S. Enslin, 'ἐφοβοῦντο γὰρ, Mk. 16.8', *JBL* 46 (1927), p. 68.
158. C.E.B. Cranfield, 'St. Mark 16.1-8', *SJT* 5 (1952), p. 406.
159. P.W.v.d. Horst, 'Can a book end with *GAR*? A Note on Mk. 16.8', *JTS* 23 (1972), pp. 1212-24; L.J.D. Richardson, 'St. Mark 16.8', *JTS* 49 (1948), pp. 144-45; R. Lightfoot, *The Gospel Message of St. Mark* (Oxford: Clarendon Press, 1950), pp. 85-86 and *Locality and Doctrine in the Gospels* (London: Hodder & Stoughton, 1938), pp. 11-15; C.H. Kraeling, 'A Philological Note on Mark 16.8', *JBL* 44 (1925), p. 357; R.R. Ottley, 'ἐφοβοῦντο γὰρ: Mark 16.8', *JTS* 27 (1926), p. 408; Enslin, 'ἐφοβοῦντο γὰρ', p. 63.
160. T.A. Burkill, *Mysterious Revelation: An Examination of the Philosophy of St. Mark's Gospel* (Ithaca, NY: Cornell University Press, 1963), p. 5.

passion in 10.32, and here is a fulfillment of the promise of 14.28. Though some have seen this as a summons to a parousia in Galilee,[161] one should especially note the tense change from 14.28 (προάξω) to 16.7 (προάγει), because the indication is that what was in the future before the resurrection (a meeting with the disciples in Galilee) is now a present reality after the resurrection. Jesus is going before them to Galilee. If the reference was to the parousia, that event would still have been future and Stein has argued no tense shift would be needed.[162] Galilee, the place where the ministry first began, will now be the place of the appearance.

After the announcement, the response of the women is to flee: καὶ ἐξελθοῦσαι ἔφυγον ἀπὸ μνημείου. Flight is a common response to confrontation with the supernatural (*1 En.* 106.4; Dan. 10.7; Mk 5.14). Kee suggests here an allusion to Dan. 10.7: θ ἀλλ᾽ ἢ ἔκστασις μεγάλη ἐπέπεσεν ἐπ᾽ αὐτούς, καὶ ἔφυγον ἐν φόβῳ,[163] and the similarities are striking: ἔκστασις, φόβος, and ἔφυγον. I shall return to these similarities later. Flight has negative connotations in Mk 5.14 and 14.50, 52, but is commanded in 13.14. It may be an element of the message and angelophany here rather than having a negative connotation as such. Could they be expected to stroll casually away?

A double γάρ clause follows, as in 9.6 and 11.18 (each with wonder also).[164] The first is εἶχεν γὰρ αὐτὰς τρόμος καὶ ἔκστασις. I would attribute the meaning 'to take hold of' to εἶχεν.[165] In 5.33 the woman with the flow of blood had the reaction φοβηθεῖσα καὶ τρέμουσα, very similar to here, and there her reaction is in faith (v. 34) and is commended by Jesus. The raising of Jairus's daughter by Jesus in 5.42 brought the reaction καὶ ἐξέστησαν ἐκστάσει μεγάλῃ. Thus the reactions τρόμος, ἔκστασις and φόβος are consistent with reactions to divine interventions early in the gospel, especially experiences of confrontations with divine power and resurrections, which are commended and co-exist with faith. One must note the response to the coming of God's rule in Zech. 14.13: καὶ ἔσται ἐν τῇ ἡμέρᾳ ἐκείνῃ ἔκστασις κυρίου ἐπ᾽ αὐτοὺς μεγάλη..., and the language of Wis. 5.2 and the vindication of the righteous sufferer:

---

161. Notably Lohmeyer, *Evangelium*, pp. 357ff; and Marxsen, *Mark*, p. 90.
162. R.H. Stein, 'A Short Note on Mark 14.28 and 16.7', *NTS* 20 (1972/74), p. 449.
163. Kee, *Community*, pp. 46, 68.
164. F.-J. Niemann, 'Die Erzählung vom leeren Grab bei Markus', *ZKT* 101(1979), p. 194, notes a parallelism in the two parts of v. 8, with καὶ and an action followed by γὰρ and an explanation repeated twice.
165. Taylor, *Gospel*, p. 609.

...ἰδόντες ταραχθήσονται φόβῳ δεινῷ καὶ ἐκστήσονται ἐπὶ τῷ παραδόξῳ τῆς σωτηρίας. The common elements here again are striking: ταράσσω or τρόμος, ἔκστασις or ἐξίστημι and φόβος.

The next clause, καὶ οὐδενὶ οὐδὲν εἶπαν, has brought much vexation to interpreters. At this point, let us only compare the double negatives related to speech in 1.44: Ὅρα μηδενὶ μηδὲν εἴπῃς (with the sense of speaking to no one at all except the appropriate party, the priest) and 15.5: ὁ Ἰησοῦς οὐκέτι οὐδὲν ἀπεκρίθη (the silence at divine constraint). However, not even in 15.5 is Jesus' silence absolute (compare v. 2). We note also that there are other occasions in the Bible where silence, for a time, results from a divine encounter (1 Sam. 3.15; Dan. 7.28; Ezek. 3.26-27; 2 Cor. 12.4). I would also point to Isa. 6.5, where the encounter with God left Isaiah lamenting the uncleanness of his lips. In Mk 9.6, the reaction at the transfiguration was noted: ἔκφοβοι γὰρ ἐγένοντο, and it was related to the answer of Peter in v. 5. It must be remembered, however, that the reaction of v. 6b is in the plural, ἐγένοντο. Terror befell all three. The response of Peter was mindless speech, but the response of James and John, often overlooked, was silence! They said nothing. Again, an encounter with God terrified them and two became silent (but spoke in due time, v. 11).

The final clause, ἐφοβοῦντο γάρ, must be related to other reactions of fear in Mark (4.41; 5.15; 9.6, 32; 10.32; 11.18). It has been the response at divine interventions. In the double γάρ clauses at 9.6 and 11.18, there was the understanding that to take both as explanatory was awkward, and it was noted in 6.51 that Mark uses γάρ at times as a general statement regarding wonder in a passage, not a specific explanation of the last thing said. Here, however, the first γάρ could be understood as explanatory, the reason they fled from the tomb. The second γάρ then gives an explanation for the clause καὶ οὐδενὶ οὐδὲν εἶπαν. The reaction τρόμος καὶ ἔκστασις can explain the flight of the women. It is not necessary to stereotype the three γάρ...γάρ clauses in Mark, but better to let them fit each context.

It is best to attempt to understand 16.8 in light of the gospel context, and the gospel use of wonder. Although Petersen suggests two alternatives, namely to interpret 16.8 in light of everything before it, or everything before 16.8 in light of it,[166] it would seem that both must be held tension in interpreting 16.8. In terms of 16.8, it has been noted that the verse follows narrative techniques which have been used elsewhere in Mark. 16.8 is a final short sentence which contains an inside view and a narrative comment. Inside views conclude stories at 6.51-52; 9.32 and 12.17. Short sentences conclude stories in 6.6; 11.14; 12.12, 17, 34, 37; 14.11 and 31. A narrative commentary ends a story in 6.52

and 14.1-2. Mark 6.52 is both an inside view an a final short sentence. All three of these techniques for ending a pericope are combined in 16.8.[167]

J. Lee Magness has related 16.1-8 to Markan miracle stories in some detail.[168] He sees five key patterns in them. First, fear, a reaction motivated by a situation which is unknown, uncontrollable or unsolvable; second, a recognition or confrontation with Jesus, the personification of divine power; third, the factum, the thing done which is the miracle itself; fourth, a new level of fear which may be expressed as amazement, fear or astonishment based on knowledge or sight, as well as fear of one who can control the uncontrollable; fifth, proclamation as either a rehearsal of the miracle, a confession of faith in Jesus or a statement of joy. Magness sees this pattern in 1.21-28, 32-34 (partially), 40-45 (partially); 2.1-12; 4.35-41; 5.1-20, 21-43; 6.45-51 and 7.31-37.[169] Mark 16.1-8 follows this pattern, according to Magness, in a 'muted, allusive way'. The stumbling block is the fifth of the list, the proclamation. Magness notes that commands to silence and silences in Mark are not necessarily absolute in intention or result, even when the language of the command sounds absolute (note 1.25 where the whole scene is in public; 1.40-45 where the silence is not total; 5.43 where the deed would be obviously known), and the reference to silence may apply only to certain periods of time, until the target groups are reached (1.43; 5.19). Also, the silence may refer to a specific audience.[170]

Magness notes further that there are two levels on which proclamation and non-proclamation may operate (indiscriminate proclamation is discouraged by Jesus, but discriminate proclamation is frequently commanded). Silence is not necessarily a result of ignorance, but is a function of knowledge (the recipient knows what has happened). Fear, astonishment and amazement are appropriate responses to the display or report of the display of divine power, and these responses and proclamation are not mutually exclusive in 2.1-12; 4.35-41; 5.33; 7.31-37 (as has been seen). Also, Magness notes that in Markan miracle stories the closing proclamation is often reported but rarely quoted (1,45; 5.20; 7.36).[171]

---

166. N.R. Petersen, 'When is the End not the End? Literary Reflections on the Ending of Mark's Narrative', *Int* 34 (1980), p. 159.

167. T.E. Boomershine and G.L. Bartholemew, 'The Narrative Technique of Mark 16.8', *JBL* 100 (1981), especially pp. 214-19.

168. Magness, *Sense*, pp. 93-102.

169. Magness, *Sense*, pp. 93-98.

170. Magness, *Sense*, pp. 98-99.

171. Magness, *Sense*, p. 99.

Magness relates 16.18 to these observations by saying that the silence of the women is not necessarily absolute. It may be silence about the circumstances of their experience rather than the fact that they have learned about the resurrection, or their silence may not be permanent (they 'said nothing to anyone' refers to passing soldiers changing their guard or merchants opening their stalls, but the disciples were told when the women reached them). The implication is that they kept silence before inappropriate audiences until the message could be told to the appropriate audience (see 1.44). It has been learned from Markan miracle stories that silence is a function of knowledge and understanding of Jesus' person and power on the basis of observation. Fear and amazement are not helpless reactions, but rather the result of a confrontation with divine power, and in 5.33 the reactions precede the woman telling Jesus the 'whole truth'. Thus, the reaction does not rule out later proclamation.[172]

I have related the helpful observations of Magness in great detail because they join three crucial factors in an understanding of 16.1-8: the silence of the women; the reactions of wonder; and the indication of a display of divine power. Let me discuss these in that order.

First, what about the silence of 16.8? This statement may be taken as either absolutely factual (the women in fact said nothing to anyone at any time),[173] or as provisional (the women spoke in due time to the disciples, but no one else),[174] or as an address or summons to the reader (will the reader be silent like the women, or proclaim the message?).[175] Although there are combinations of these choices possible (of the second and third choices, for example), I believe the second choice best places 16.8 in the context of Mark. When one compares καὶ

172. Magness, *Sense*, pp. 100-101.
173. This is the view of Weeden, *Traditions*, pp. 45-50, 110-17 (Mark has a 'vendetta against the disciples'); J.D. Crossan, 'Empty Tomb and Absent Lord (Mk. 16.1-8)', in (ed.) Kelber, *Passion*, pp. 135-52; J.D. Crossan, 'A Form for Absence: The Markan Creation of Gospel', *Semeia* 12 (1978), pp. 41-53; and H. Waetjen, 'The Ending of Mark and the Gospel's Shift in Eschatology', *ASTI* 4 (1965), especially p. 127.
174. Moule, 'Mark', pp. 58-59; Lane, *Gospel*, p. 590; Pesch, 'Schluss', p. 393; Pesch, *Markusevangelium*, II, p. 536; Magness, *Sense*, pp. 100-101; Cranfield, 'Mark 16', p. 297; D. Catchpole, 'The Fearful Silence of the Women at the Tomb', *JThSAf* 18 (1977), p. 6; Malbon, 'Fallible', p. 45.
175. Petersen, 'When?', p. 162; Gnilka, *Evangelium*, II, p. 345; Rhoads and Michie, *Story*, pp. 61-62; T. Boomershine, 'Mark 16.8 and the Apostolic Commission', *JBL* 100 (1981), p. 237; A. Lindemann, 'Die Osterbotschaft des Markus: Zur Theologischen Interpretation von Mark 16.1-8', *NTS* 26 (1980), p. 316.

οὐδενὶ οὐδὲν εἶπαν with 1.44, "Ορα μηδενὶ μηδὲν εἴπῃς and 15.5 ὁ δὲ Ἰησοῦς οὐκέτι οὐδὲν ἀπεκρίθη, which are both plainly provisional, it is best to see 16.8 not as absolute (they never told the disciples), but provisional in the sense that they told no one else, or told no one until they told the disciples. After all, the reader or hearer assumes that the women told the disciples about the resurrection, because someone told the narrator who now tells the reader or hearer.[176]

Second, what about the wonder of 16.8 (and 16.5-6)? I would suggest that too much attention has been paid to the silence and too little attention to the awe.[177] The silence is a function of the wonder, subordinate to it, and not the main feature of the narrative.[178] As was suggested by Magness, I would agree that wonder elsewhere in Mark can help one understand 16.8. One can especially compare 6.45-52, where there is an initial fear at the sight of the 'phantom', which is comforted, and then a greater awe follows. Also, in 4.35-41 there is an initial cowardice (the question Τί δειλοί ἐστε) at the storm which is rebuked, but then a greater awe follows (4.41). Similarly, 5.35-43 also follows this pattern. Jairus fears (implicit, but present in light of v. 36) when the news comes that his daughter has died. This fear is comforted (v. 36). After Jesus raises the daughter, a greater wonder follows (v. 42). 16.1-8 follows the same pattern. There is a reaction at the 'young man' (vv. 5-6) which is soon comforted. After the message of the resurrection, a greater and more lasting wonder follows. The sight of the 'young man' causes astonishment, but this is not what the women should be astonished about. When they are told that God has intervened and raised Jesus from the dead and that Jesus will appear in Galilee, they are struck with a greater wonder. This is more lasting, and fully appropriate.

Thirdly, interventions of God throughout Mark have caused amazement, and this is the case here also (the passive ἠγέρθη). Flight and silence occur throughout the Bible as responses to divine encounters, as was noted previously. Here the women are struck with an exceeding wonder (three words are used) because they have seen an act of God which is greater and indeed sums up all the other acts in the gospel. The tomb is empty, Jesus has been raised! God has

176. Malbon, 'Fallible', p. 45
177. F.W. Synge, 'Mark 16.1-8', *ThSAf* (1985), p. 72, says that it is likely that the possibility never occurred to Mark that any reader of his narrative would pay more attention to the frightened women than to the vision which took their tongues away.
178. N.B. Stonehouse, *The Witness of Matthew and Mark to Christ* (Philadelphia: Presbyterian Guardian, 1944), p. 105.

established the divine rule over death and vindicated Jesus.

I suggest that the reactions in 16.5-6 are traditional, part of angelophanies, but likely rewritten with the Markan ἐκθαμβέομαι. 16.8, however, has redactional characteristics: two γάρ explanatory clauses, the double negative οὐδενὶ οὐδὲν, φοβεῖσθαι and ἔκστασις, and I would for those reasons take it as redactional.[179]

Throughout Mark, the various acts of God have been related to the breaking-in of the rule of God and divine triumph over evil. The indication in Dan. 12.2 is that the resurrection signals the end times, and in light of the similarities in Mk 16.8 to Dan. 10.7 (introducing the vision of the latter days), it is likely that Mk 16.1-8 also signifies the new age has come.[180] The theme of Mk 1.14-15 is thus complete. God has begun to rule (death has been overruled) and again amazement is the result. The conclusion of Mark can be seen as fitting with the rest of the gospel.

It should also be stated that we have seen that at times amazement is followed by faith, and at times it leads to stumbling and rejection of Jesus. How is it understood in 16.8? When one leaves aside the questionable assumption that the women never told to anyone the message from the angel, one is then free to see the amazement of 16.8 as not necessarily negative or positive, but simply a function of the marvelous act of God. This intervention is more important than the silence. Mark has shown that God has begun to rule in the ministry of Jesus, even in the weakness and seeming abandonment in the crucifixion. The conclusive confirmation is that indeed God has vindicated Jesus, overruled death, and restored the creation. Death is not the end. The victory and rule of God is supreme, even though the mystery of the kingdom indicates that there is yet evil and resistance. There can be no doubt that God has begun to rule.

---

179. 16.8b is taken as redactional by Weeden, *Traditions*, pp. 48-50; Pryke, *Redactional Style*, p. 176; Catchpole, 'Silence', p. 6; Gnilka, *Evangelium*, II, p. 338; L. Schenke, *Auferstehungsverkündigung und leeres Grab: Eine traditionsgeschichtliche Untersuchung von Mk. 16.1-8* (SBS, 33; Stuttgart: Katholisches Bibelwerk, 1969), p. 47; H. Paulsen, 'Mk. 16.1-8', *NovT* 22 (1980), pp. 174-75. Dormeyer, *Passion*, p. 226, sees 16.8b as a gloss. It is not likely that the entire pericope 16.1-8 is a Markan creation; see Crossan, 'Empty', p. 135. A summary of various positions on tradition and redaction in 16.1-8 through 1980 is given in F. Neirynck, 'Mark 16.1-8: Tradition et rédaction', *ETL* 56 (1980), pp. 56-88. Verse 8a is sometimes seen as tradition, but the γάρ explanatory argues for redaction, as does the verb εἶχεν. See Turner, 'Usage', *JTS* 28 (1927), p. 357.

180. Waetjen, 'Ending', p. 119; Grundmann, *Evangelium*, p. 324.

Summary

I will save a full conclusion which will draw our various chapters together until the following chapter, but seek here to integrate the two chapters on Mark with previous results. I have surveyed the places in Mark where the motif of wonder occurs and noted that often it is related to the authority which Jesus exercises because of the rule of God over Satan, illness, nature, sin and death in order to act for salvation. The teaching of Jesus comes with this same authority, especially on pronouncements regarding the kingdom. The passion and resurrection of Jesus has been placed in this same light. Even in the powerlessness and weakness of the cross, the rule of God was breaking-in to save. This was confirmed in the dramatic and definitive act of God, the triumph over death in the resurrection.

The motif is mostly redactional (1.21, 28; 2.12; 3.21; 5.15, 20, 33, 42; 6.2, 51; 7.37; 9.6, 15, 32; 10.24, 26, 32; 11.18; 14.33; 16.8) and fitted into pericopae in which it is an unusual intrusion. In a way consistent with the Old Testament and early Jewish expectation of amazement at the end times, the breaking-in of the rule of God in Mark evokes these reactions, although definite quotations of prophesies are not used. In a way consistent with wonder in Greco-Roman sources, the intervention of God evokes the wonder. In a way consistent with amazement in other early Christian canonical and apocryphal literature, either faith or unbelief may follow.

An unusual twist is that even Jesus experiences this reaction in 14.33, and in related language is thought mad in 3.21. God is intervening *with* Jesus as well as *by* Jesus. The presence of God is even experienced by Jesus himself, as he submits to the will and rule of the father.

There is a remarkable consistency in the emphasis of pericopae in which wonder is introduced. Although I have followed a verse-by-verse approach, I have also sought to pay careful attention to the context and content of these pericopae, in order to see how wonder may be functioning around a common theme in the gospel. The theme of the breaking-in of the rule of God, as the central idea of the gospel (1.14-15) provided us a point of integration, and showed up with a remarkable consistency in places where wonder occurs. God has acted, broken-in with divine rule to save, and amazement results. That intervention and rule is diversified and evident in healing, exorcism, authoritative teaching, kingdom pronouncement, forgiveness, restoration to community, storm-calming, transfiguration, passion predictions, passion and resurrection.

6. *Mark II*

Just as the rule of God is manifested in a variety of ways, so amazement occurs in a variety of ways in the gospel. Both kingdom and amazement break human expectations as the uncanny is dramatically experienced in Mark. The transcendent is met as humanity encounters the possibility of the impossible in salvation.

The climax of the gospel is 16.1-8. The motif of wonder there underscores the event in a way which may make an appearance perhaps unnecessary. In a definitive and final way, God has overruled death and vindicated Jesus. The intensity of wonder there goes beyond any other expression in Mark. This is no accident. Initial fear is comforted and gives way to greater wonder. God has broken-in and dramatic amazement results, which should not be overshadowed by the (temporary) silence of the women. The earthly has met the heavenly, and one is left with an impression of the numinous surrounding the entire gospel of Mark.

Chapter 7

CONCLUSION

This study began with a discussion of the need for a study on wonder in Mark, and sought some clarification on the meaning of wonder as a 'motif' following the work of W. Freedman. An attempt was made to determine how the interests of the evangelist might be ascertained, and a comparison on the use of wonder in Mark and the other synoptic gospels rounded out the first chapter. After examining the way in which Matthew and Luke edit Mark, it was noted that Mark uses wonder with an intensity, frequency and mystery that surpasses the other synoptics. The Markan use of wonder is continually softened by Matthew and Luke.

Rarely has wonder in the ancient world been studied. Reactions of wonder in Greco-Roman, early Jewish and early Christian literature provided an interpretative framework and showed the diversity of uses in the literary world of Mark (Chapters 2–4). To approach Mark without this research base would be problematic, limiting the context in which the gospel is set. Research in these areas has shown that wonder is not common in miracle stories or so-called 'divine man' literature, and is infrequently directed at the subject in the biographical literature (Chapter 2), and thus did not likely enter Mark based on sources with these models. Neither is wonder often used to draw attention to esteemed teachers of antiquity. The 'fear and pity' evoked by ancient drama, related to wonder in Mark to Stock and Standaert is something quite different than Mark's wonder. It is also unlikely that wonder entered Mark as a rhetorical convention. The evidence indicates that wonder in Greco-Roman literature is predominantly used in reference to signs, portents, dreams or divine interventions in general.

The use of wonder in early Jewish literature is an area which is also necessary to examine to set Mark in context. In a survey of this material, it was seen that wonder is a common response to God and God's acts, but there was also an important eschatological expectation that, in the last days, God would 'amaze' Israel (Chapter 3). This expectation is in both canonical texts such as Hos. 3.5

7. Conclusion

and non-canonical texts such as *1 En.* 1.4-5. Also, it was observed that this was at times related to messianic expectation. It was also seen that there was a defense of the idea that God was revealed to Israel in the use of wonder in such propagandistic texts as *2 Maccabees, Joseph and Asenath*, and the *Letter of Aristeas*. These results enabled us to approach wonder in Mark in a new way, and with new questions.

In early Christian texts it was seen that reactions of wonder can have either a positive or a negative connotation, and can be followed by either faith or deception, even within the same text (such as the book of Acts). In fact, in *Gospel of Thomas* 2, wonder is the first step towards enlightenment. In 2 Thess. 1.10 believers will marvel at the return of Jesus. This insight would urge caution when some attempt to see wonder in Mark as entirely deficient, indicating a lack of faith and understanding. Wonder in early Christian literature in general represented the entrance into a realm beyond the natural, and served an important function. As the excursus on the numinous and religious experience at the end of Chapter 4 showed, the experience of the mortal with the immortal, the uncanny and the numinous is depicted by wonder. Wonder is often a *necessary* experience.

Exegesis of Mark in Chapters 5-6 indicated nuances of wonder in Mark. The study sought to understand wonder in the light of the central proclamation of the kingdom in 1.14-15. The linkage between wonder and belief in 5.33, and the report of those following 'on the way' with wonder in 10.32, indicates the untenability of the view that wonder in Mark is exclusively negative (indicated above). Rather it is the necessary experience when the mortal meets the uncanny.

Further, the detailed examination of the verses in Mark, because of the focus on wonder and the previous information produced, enabled many pericopae to be seen in a fresh way. We saw the clear programmatic importance of the pericope 1.21-28, and the two reactions of wonder there. An essential relation of the reactions in 1.22 and 27 to the breaking-in of the kingdom in the authority of Jesus' teaching was seen. Wonder was not a mere response to an exorcism, and in 2.12 it is the response to healing *and* forgiveness. Jesus' experience was indicated in 3.21. Mark 4.41 and 6.50-51 were determined to be wonder not at the exorcism, but at the restoration of the individual into community. Mark 7.37 indicates a clear understanding of what is taking place in Jesus' ministry (a restoration of the creation by God's kingly power) by a redactional reaction and scriptural acclamation by Gentiles. The wonder at the transfiguration was seen as less negative than had been previously thought. The puzzling verses of 9.15 and 10.32 were seen as redactional presentations relating wonder directly to the upcoming passion. Hellenistic magic sources need not be behind 10.32. Mark 10.24 and 26 were seen as the response to pronouncements on the kingdom by Jesus which contained kingdom authority. The reason for the wonder in 11.18 added insight into the temple incident. Mark 14.33 was noted to be Jesus' experience with the will and rule of God. Also, the conclusion of 16.8 was able to be seen in a fresh way by focusing on the wonder, and the (probably temporary) silence as a function of the wonder. A pattern of conclusion was present in other pericopae in the gospel (such as 4.35-41, 6.50-51) was seen to be followed in 16.8, where fear is present, is comforted and then a greater awe follows. Facile schematization of wonder in Mark becomes untenable due to these nuances. Reactions of wonder come from friend, enemy, Jew, Gentile, people, leaders, those 'on the way' and those opposed, as co-existent with faith and understanding, and as co-existent with murderous opposition. Wonder in Mark appears to be a multivalent motif which resists paradigms and simplified categories. If anything, the reaction is necessary and essential as God breaks in to rule and save with power.

My thesis, in light of the evidence presented, is as follows. In a way consistent with the manner in which wonder is used in Greco-Roman and early Jewish literature, wonder in Mark is a response to the divine intervention of the breaking-in of the kingdom or rule of God in power to save and restore the creation. Wonder is a response to Jesus' authoritative words on the kingdom, the vanquishing of Satan in exorcisms, the submission of creation to the creator, and the healing and restoring of individuals into community. The passion and resurrection, through wonder, can then also be seen in the light of the breaking-in of the rule of God to save. The final chapter of the gospel leaves one with a sense of dramatic awe. This is because in the kingly one, Jesus of Nazareth, God has intervened in creation. Even a situation which might seem to be void of the presence of God, the passion of Jesus, can be seen as marked by the manifest presence of God by intensive and repeated reactions of wonder in Mark 10–16.

In a way similar to *2 Maccabees*, *Joseph and Asenath*, and the *Letter of Aristeas*, wonder in Mark attests that God has indeed been revealed in the ministry of Jesus of Nazareth in saving activity. The textually inscribed situation in life of Mark may call for this use of wonder. Those who have undergone persecution (note 10.20; 13.9-13) can see in Mark a vindication that God had broken-in to rule in the ministry of Jesus of Nazareth. The proof of divine activity was that reactions of wonder and awe occurred, even as Jesus seemed abandoned by all. Those who may have felt abandoned by God in their perse-

7. Conclusion

cutions could be encouraged in the fact that God continues to rule in situations of powerlessness. Perhaps more attention needs to be paid in the future to the apologetic thrust of Mark in light of this. Combined with ecclesiastical concerns, Mark appears to be a kind of 'pastoral apologetic'.

There is an inevitable interest in the christology of the gospel of Mark, and our study has some relevance for this question. If one can recognize that christology must go beyond titles for Jesus, and that Mark is 'narrative christology', the evidence from this study indicates that a primary portrait of Jesus in Mark is as the spirit-anointed agent of the kingdom. In other words, the kingdom is the framework for the christology of Mark as well as for the wonder. As the 'son of God' (1.1, 11; 3.11; 9.7; 14.61; 15.39), even Jesus responds with wonder at times. 3.21 indicates Jesus' experience of the eschatological spirit, and in 14.33 Jesus encounters the rule and will of God. Thus, for Mark, even Jesus is under the will and rule of God. Instead of the 'christology of awe' of Trocmé, it may be best to speak of a 'divine rule of awe'.

Some have seen wonder in Mark as a distinct element of the numinous. The evidence indicates that this is likely true, but this needs to be carried further. A reason wonder may be either positive or negative in Mark has been clarified by the history-of-religions research examined in the excursus following Chapter 4 and integrated into our exegesis of the gospel. When one experiences the realm of the uncanny or the Wholly Other, there is an overwhelming sense of stupefaction and 'creature-consciousness'. The creature is submerged and overwhelmed by that which is beyond him or her. A sense of 'energy' or 'urgency' overpowers the individual. With this experience there is a sense of both fascination and terror. One may flee, or one may worship. Neither response is necessarily negative (see 16.8). This is evident in Mark where the breaking-in of the kingdom confronts people with ineffable energy. This is a crisis experience, as the research indicates. Some follow Jesus as a result, but others will be 'scandalized' and stumble, manifesting the attraction *and* avoidance of the *mysterium tremendum*. Two further elements of the *mysterium tremendum* relate to wonder in Mark, which I have just alluded to. First, the sense of creature-feeling would be natural in light of a confrontation with the rule of the creator restoring creation as the kingdom of God irrupts into the world (see Chapter 5 on 7.37). Secondly, the sense of uncanny energy would also be expected with the rule of God coming near with miracles and exorcisms.

This understanding of wonder seems to fit with Bruce Chilton's understanding of the breaking-in of the kingdom as 'God coming in strength'.[1] If the kingdom is the self-revelation of God, as Chilton asserts, this explains the reactions of wonder in Mark as the crisis experiences of people with the various manifestations of the self-revelation of God in strength. A Markan focus, however, provides more of an eschatological element ('the time is fulfilled'; 'we have never seen anything like this') than Chilton's targumic orientation allows.

Mark's use of wonder in the second half of the gospel is especially aided by an understanding of it as a response to the kingdom in light of Chilton's concept of the kingdom as the self-revelation of God. In Mark 9.15, 32; 10.32; 14.33, 15.5, 44; wonder shows the passion as being depicted as also the human encounter with the overwhelming energy of the rule of God. This, in turn, may shed some light on why the gospel could have ended at 16.8. In view of the way in which the passion has been shown to be the self-revelation of the rule of God, there is a sense in which a resurrection appearance is not necessary to further verify that the saving work of God has taken place. The reaction of 16.8 of itself can serve for verification, and apologetic for the message of the 'young man' that Jesus has been raised. God has overruled death, and that rule is evident in the wonder.

The all-encompassing nature of the rule of God is indicated in the responses of wonder by opponents of Jesus, but the summons to believe and obey then must be carried out by those who would be disciples. Faith in Mark means the voluntary assumption of social powerlessness, even as those in the miracle stories demonstrate.[2] This consequently may entail suffering and death (13.12-13) for the followers of Jesus as also for their Lord, but just as the presence and rule of God was active in the sufferings of the Lord, so the followers can also know that God is with them in their hour of trial, and even this is not out of the will of God. After all, even Rome's authority was struck with awe at their Lord (15.5, 44).

Mark also encourages his readers that the rule and presence of God is also active in their proclamation. Mark 5.20, again in a Gentile setting, is a special aid in demonstrating this. Also, 16.8 is the response to the message of the

1. B. Chilton, 'Regnum Dei Deus Est', in *Targumic Approaches to the Gospels* (Lanham, MD: University Press of America, 1986), pp. 99-107, 'Gottesherrschaft als Gotteserfahrung: Erkenntnisse der Targumforschung für den neutestamentlischen Begriff "Königsherrschaft Gottes"', in the same book, pp. 85-97, and *God in Strength: Jesus' Announcement of the Kingdom* (SUNT, 1; Göttingen: Vandenhoeck & Ruprecht, 1979).

2. C.D. Marshall, *Faith as a Theme in Mark's Narrative* (SNTSMS, 64; Cambridge: Cambridge University Press, 1989), p. 175.

resurrection, not a resurrection appearance. It was not only in the earthly ministry of Jesus that the rule of God was present, but also in the present proclamation of Jesus' followers. Also, in the restoration of the disenfranchised to community, which is a continuing ministry of the believers, the rule of God is yet active (5.15 and 5.33, the latter in a Gentile setting). Thus the breaking-in of the rule of God to save extends beyond the historical Jesus to the community receiving the gospel.

Are the reactions of wonder intended to evoke a similar response in the readers and hearers? This is proposed by Dahl[3] and Donahue[4] among others. The question is complicated because it is the experience of the numinous which excites awe, and the numinous is not something that can be humanly effected. In other words, the uncanny is not subject to human manipulation.[5] Wonder and awe result from encounters with the uncanny. I would hesitate to state that Mark intended to evoke these feelings among the readers and hearers, because that would be saying that the gospel was intended to be a vehicle for the numinous. Religious studies research indicates that the numinous is not subject to human control. It would rather be best to say that Mark wants to present a record of the way in which the numinous excited wonder and awe in the breaking-in of the kingdom of God in the person and work of Jesus of Nazareth. If, however, the reactions of wonder indicate the power of the revelation of God in Jesus to unsettle and challenge human existence,[6] certainly the gospel story as narrated by Mark would continue to unsettle and challenge human existence, as it has to this day.

As a narrative, Mark was probably the first such way of relating the ministry, death and resurrection of Jesus. The evangelist heightens in the story the degree to which those involved were meeting awesome power beyond human categories and understanding. The possibility of the impossible, the unknown and the uncontrollable is met. As such, the gospel of Mark has a powerful drama and impact. The audience learns about the ineffable, but not in a didactic way for the ineffable is not taught but experienced. A narrative about the uncanny is

---

3. N.A. Dahl, 'The Purpose of Mark's Gospel', in *Jesus in the Memory of the Early Church* (Minneapolis: Augsburg, 1976), p. 55.

4. J. Donahue, *The Gospel in Parable* (Philadelphia: Fortress Press, 1988), p. 196.

5. I am aware of the practices of some mystics and charismatics here, but see these practices as something different than reactions of wonder indicated in the history-of-religions research and exegesis of Mark.

6. Donahue, *Gospel*, p. 197.

experienced, striking humans with awesome terror. In a real sense we are reading about God in all transcendence and mystery, not in a reasoned lecture or analytical tome, but in a story. The basic element of human religious experience, understood by the Jews as Yahweh and related in the Old Testament in the thunder at Sinai and the visions of Isaiah and Ezekiel, has again been revealed. Humanity is again reminded that it is not supreme, but dependent. It trembles in awe before that which is simply 'Other'. The incredible thing is that the 'Other' has come to save and heal and help in compassion and kindness. Mark's story is is indeed a story of the numinous and the uncanny, but it is also a story of 'good news'. The good news is that the 'Wholly Other', God, Yahweh, has come to rule and save through Jesus the Messiah. Humankind still trembles with wonder before the 'Other', but we are assured that God is good and for us and with us in our human predicament. Thus Mark has written what can be truly characterized as 'the good news of Jesus the Messiah, the Son of God'.

BIBLIOGRAPHY

Achtemeier, P.J., 'An Exposition of Mk. 9.30-37', *Int* 30 (1976), pp. 178-82.
—'"He Taught Them Many Things": Reflections on Markan Christology', *CBQ* 42 (1980), pp. 465-81.
—'Jesus and the Disciples as Miracle Workers in the Apocryphal New Testament', in *Aspects of Religious Propaganda in Judaism and Early Christianity* (ed. E.S. Fiorenza; Notre Dame: University of Notre Dame Press, 1976), pp. 149-86.
—'Miracles and the Historical Jesus: A Study of Mark 9.14-29', *CBQ* 37 (1975), pp. 471-91.
—'The Origin and Function of the Pre-Markan Miracle Catanae', *JBL* 91 (1972), pp. 198-221.
—'Person and Deed: Jesus and the Storm-Tossed Sea', *Int* 16 (1962), pp. 169-76.
Aland, K., 'Bemerkungen zum Schluss des Markusevangeliums', in *Neotestamentica et Semitica: Studies in Honour of Matthew Black* (ed. E.E. Ellis and M. Wilcox; Edinburgh: T. & T. Clark, 1969), pp. 157-80.
—'Der Schluss des Markusevangeliums', in *L'Evangile selon Marc: Tradition et rédaction* (BETL 34; Leuven: Leuven University Press, 1974) pp. 435-70.
—'Der wiedergefundene Markusschluss? Eine methodische Bemerkung zur text-kritischen Arbeit', *ZTK* 67 (1970), pp. 3-13.
Alexander, J.A., *The Gospel According to Mark* (Grand Rapids: Baker, repr. 1980 [1858]).
Allen, W.C., '"Fear" in St. Mark', *JTS* 48 (1946), pp. 201-203.
—'St. Mark 16.8: They Were Afraid. Why?', *JTS* 47 (1946), pp. 46-49.
Ambrozic, A.M., 'New Teaching with Power (Mark 1.27)', in *Word and Spirit: Essays in Honor of David M. Stanley on his 60th Birthday* (ed. J. Plevnik; Willowdale, Ontario: Regis College, 1975), pp. 113-49.
—*The Hidden Kingdom: A Redaction-Critical Study of the References to the Kingdom of God in Mark's Gospel* (CBQMS, 2; Washington: The Catholic Bible Society of America, 1972).
Anderson, G., *Philostratus: Biography and Belles Lettres in the Third Century AD* (London: Croon Helm, 1986).
Annen, F., *Heil für die Heiden: Zur Bedeutung und Geschichte der Tradition von besessenen Gerasener (Mk 5.1-20 par.)* (Frankfurter Theologischer Studien, 20; Frankfurt am Main: Josef Knecht, 1976).
Attridge, H., 'Jewish Historiography', in *Early Judaism and its Modern Interpreters* (ed. G.W.E. Nickelsburg and R. Kraft; Philadelphia: Fortress Press; Atlanta: Scholars Press, 1986), pp. 311-43.
Aune, D., *The New Testament in its Literary Environment* (Philadelphia: Westminster Press, 1987).
Aune, D., ed., *Studies in New Testament and Early Christian Literature: Essays in Honor of Allen Wikgren* (NovTSup, 33; Leiden: Brill, 1972).
Balz, H.R., 'Furcht vor Gott?', *EvT* 29 (1969), pp. 626-44.
Bammel, E., and C.F.D. Moule, *Jesus and the Politics of His Day* (Cambridge: Cambridge University Press, 1984).

Barbour, R.H., 'Gethsemane in the Tradition of the Passion', *NTS* 16 (1969/70), pp. 231-51.
Barrett, C.K., *The Gospel According to St. John* (London: SPCK, 1978).
—'The House of Prayer and the Den of Thieves', in *Jesus und Paulus: Festschrift für Werner Georg Kümmel zum 70. Geburtstag* (ed. E.E. Ellis and E. Grässer; Göttingen: Vandenhoeck & Ruprecht, 1975), pp. 13-20.
Barthes, R., *et al.*, eds., *Structural Analysis and Biblical Exegesis: Interpretational Essays* (Pittsburgh: Pickwick Press, 1974)
Bartsch, H.W., 'Der Schluss der Markus-Evangeliums: Ein überlieferungsgeschichtliches Problem', *TZ* 27 (1971), pp. 241-54.
Bassler, J., Review of *Jesus the Teacher* by V.K. Robbins, *JBL* 106 (1987), pp. 339-41.
Bauckham, R., 'The Worship of Jesus in Apocalyptic Christianity', *NTS* 27 (1980/81), pp. 322-41.
Beasley-Murray, G., *Jesus and the Kingdom of God* (Grand Rapids: Eerdmans; Exeter: Paternoster Press, 1986).
—*John* (WBC; Waco, TX: Word Books, 1987).
Becker, J., *Das Evangelium des Johannes* (OTKNT; 2 vols.; Würzburg: Mohn, 1979).
—'Wunder und Christologie', *NTS* 16 (1969/70), pp. 130-48.
Beckwith, I.T., *The Apocalypse of John* (repr.; Grand Rapids: Baker; 1967 [1919]).
Berger, K., 'Zum Problem der Messianität Jesu', *ZTK* 71 (1974), pp. 1-30.
Bertram, G., 'θάμβος, θαμβέω, ἔκθαμβος, ἐκθαμβέομαι', in *TDNT*, III, pp. 4-7.
—'θαῦμα, θαυμάζω, θαυμάσιος, θαυμαστός', in *TDNT*, III, pp. 27-42.
—*Leidensgeschichte Jesu und der Christkult* (FRLANT, 21; Göttingen: Vandenhoeck & Ruprecht, 1922).
Best, E., *Disciples and Discipleship: Studies in the Gospel According to Mark* (Edinburgh: T. & T. Clark, 1986).
—*Following Jesus: Discipleship in the Gospel of Mark* (JSNTSup, 4; Sheffield: JSOT Press, 1981).
—*Mark: The Gospel as Story* (Edinburgh: T. & T. Clark, 1983).
—'The Purpose of Mark', *Proceedings of the Irish Biblical Association* 6 (1982), pp. 19-35.
—*The Temptation and The Passion: The Markan Soteriology* (SNTSMS, 2; Cambridge: Cambridge University Press, 1965.
Betz, H.D., 'The Early Christian Miracle Stories: Some Observations on the Form-Critical Problem', *Semeia* 11 (1978), pp. 69-81.
—*Galatians: A Commentary on Paul's Letter to the Churches in Galatia* (Hermeneia Commentaries; Philadelphia: Fortress Press, 1979).
—'Jesus as Divine Man', in *Jesus and the Historian* (ed. F.T. Trotter; Philadelphia: Westminster Press, 1968).
—'The Literary Composition and Function of Paul's Letter to the Galatians', *NTS* 21 (1975), pp. 353-79.
—'The Problem of Rhetoric and Theology According to the Apostle Paul', in *L'Apôtre Paul* (ed. A. Vanhoye; Leuven: Peteers–Leuven University, 1986), pp. 16-48.
—Review of *New Testament Interpretation through Rhetorical Criticism* by G. Kennedy, *JTS* 37 (1986), pp. 166-67.
Betz, H.D., ed., *Christology and a Modern Pilgrimage: A Discussion with Norman Perrin* (Claremont, CA: The New Testament Colloquium, 1971).
—*The Greek Magical Papyrus in Translation* (Chicago: University of Chicago Press, 1986).

Bibliography

Betz, O., 'The Concept of the So-Called "Divine Man" in Mark's Christology', in *Studies in New Testament and Early Christian Literature: Essays in Honor of Allen Wikgren* (ed. D. Aune; NovTSup, 33; Leiden: Brill, 1972), pp. 229-40.

—'Das Problem des Wunders bei Flavius Josephus im Vergleich zum Wunderproblem bei den Rabbinen und im Johannesevangelium', in *Josephus-Studies: Untersuchungen zu Josephus, dem antiken Judentum und dem Neuen Testament. Otto Michael zum 70. Geburtstag gewidmet* (ed. O. Betz, K. Haacker and M. Hengel; Göttingen: Vandenhoek & Ruprecht, 1974), pp. 23-24.

Bianchi, H., et al., eds., *Gnosis: Festschrift für Hans Jonas* (Göttingen: Vandenhoeck & Ruprecht, 1978),

Bible and Culture Collective, The, *The Postmodern Bible* (New Haven: Yale University Press, 1995).

Bieler, L., ΘΕΙΟΣ ANHP: *Das Bild des göttlichen Menschen in Spätantike und Frühchristentum* (2 vols.; Vienna: Oscar Hofels, 1935).

Bilezikian, G.G., *The Liberated Gospel: A Comparison of the Gospel of Mark and Greek Tragedy* (Grand Rapids: Baker, 1977).

Bird, C.H., 'Some γάρ clauses in St. Mark's Gospel', *JTS* 4 (1953), pp. 171-87.

Black, C.C., *The Disciples according to Mark: Markan Redation in Current Debate* (JSNTSup, 27; Sheffield: JSOT Press, 1989).

—'The Quest of Mark the Redactor: Why It Has Been Pursued, and What Has It Taught Us?', *JSNT* 33 (1988), pp. 19-39.

Black, D.A., 'The Text of Mark 6.20', *NTS* 34 (1988), pp. 141-45.

Black, M., 'The Christological Use of the Old Testament in the New Testament', *NTS* 18 (1971/72), pp. 1-14.

Blackburn, B., *A Critique of the Theios Aner Concept as an Interpretative Background of the Miracle Traditions Used by Mark* (Unpublished PhD Thesis: University of Aberdeen, 1986).

—'Miracle Working θεῖοι ἄνδρες in Hellenism (and Hellenistic Judaism)', in *Gospel Perspectives* (ed. D. Wenham and C. Blomberg; Sheffield: JSOT Press, 1986), VI, pp. 185-218.

Bligh, J., 'The Gerasene Demoniac and the Resurrection of Christ', *CBQ* 31 (1969), pp. 383-90.

Bonner, C., 'Note on Mark 6:20', *HTR* 37 (1944), pp. 41-44.

—'Traces of Thaumaturgic Technique in the Miracles', *HTR* 20 (1927), pp. 171-181.

Boomershine, T.E., 'Mark 16.8 and the Apostolic Commission', *JBL* 100 (1981), pp. 225-39.

Boomershine, T.E., and G.L. Bartholomew, 'The Narrative Technique of Mark 16.8', *JBL* 100 (1981), pp. 213-23.

Booth, W., *The Rhetoric of Fiction* (Chicago: University of Chicago Press, 1961).

Borg, Marcus, *Conflict, Holiness and Politics in the Teachings of Jesus* (Lewiston, NY: Edwin Mellen, 1984).

—'The Currency of the Term Zealot', *JTS* 22 (1971), pp. 504-12.

—*Jesus: A New Vision* (San Francisco: Harper & Row, 1987).

Borgen, P., 'Philo of Alexandria', in *Jewish Writings of the Second Temple Period* (CRINT, 2; ed. M. Stone; Philadephia: Fortress Press; Assen: Van Gorcum, 1984), pp. 233-82.

Bornkamm, G., 'Pneuma alalon: Einer Studie zum Markusevangelium', in *Gesammelte Aufsätze, Geschicte und Glaube* (Munich: Chr. Kaiser Verlag, 1971), IV, pp. 21-36.

Bovon, F. et al., *Les Actes Apocryphes des Apôtres: Christianism et monde païen* (Geneva: Laber, 1981).

Boman, T., 'Der Gebetskampf Jesu', *NTS* 10 (1963/64), pp. 261-73.

Branscomb, B.H., *The Gospel of Mark* (London: Hodder & Stoughton, 1948).

Broadhead, E.K., *Teaching with Authority: Miracles and Christology in the Gospel of Mark* (JSNTSup, 74; Sheffield: JSOT Press, 1992).
Brown, R.E., 'The Burial of Jesus (Mark 15.42-47)', *CBQ* 50 (1988), pp. 233-45.
—*The Gospel According to John* (2 vols.; AB; Garden City, NY: Doubleday, 1966).
—'The Gospel of Peter and Canonical Gospel Priority', *NTS* 33 (1987), pp. 321-43.
—'Jesus and Elisha', *Perspective* 12 (1971), pp. 85-104.
—'The Relation of the "Secret Gospel of Mark" to the Fourth Gospel', *CBQ* 36 (1974), pp. 466-85.
Bruce, F.F., *The Acts of the Apostles* (London: Tyndale Press, 1952).
—'The Corner Stone', *ExpTim* 84 (1973), pp. 231-35.
—'Render to Caesar', in *Jesus and the Politics of His Day* (ed. E. Bammel and C.F.D. Moule; Cambridge: Cambridge University Press, 1984), pp. 249-63.
Bryan, C., *A Preface to Mark: Notes on the Gospel in its Literary and Cultural Settings* (Cambridge: Cambridge University Press, 1993).
Buchanan, G.W., 'Mark 11.15-19: Brigands in the Temple', *HUCA* 30 (1959), pp. 169-77.
Bultmann, R., *The Gospel of John: A Commentary* (Oxford: Basil Blackwell, 1971).
—*History of the Synoptic Tradition* (Oxford: Basil Blackwell, 1968).
—*Theology of the New Testament* (2 vols.; London: SCM Press, 1983).
Burch, E.W., 'Tragic Action in the Second Gospel: A Study in the Narrative of Mark', *JR* 11 (1931), pp. 346-58.
Burkill, T.A., *Mysterious Revelation: An Examination of the Philosophy of St. Mark's Gospel* (Ithaca, NY: Cornell University Press, 1963).
Burridge, R.A., *What are the Gospels?* (SNTSMS, 70; Cambridge: Cambridge University Press, 1992).
Burrus, V., 'Chastity as Autonomy: Women in the Stories of the Apocryphal Acts', *Semeia* 38 (1986), pp. 101-17.
Busemann, R., *Die Jüngergemeinde nach Markus 10* (Bonn: Peter Hanstein, 1983).
Calvin, J., *The Gospel According to St. John* (2 vols.; Edinburgh: Oliver & Boyd, 1959, 1961).
Cameron, R., ed., *The Other Gospels: Non-Canonical Gospel Texts* (Philadelphia: Westminster Press, 1982).
Catchpole, D., 'The Fearful Silence of the Women at the Tomb', *JThSAf* 18 (1977), pp. 3-10.
—'The Triumphal Entry', in *Jesus and the Politics of His Day* (ed. E. Bammel and C.F.D. Moule; Cambridge: Cambridge University Press, 1984), pp. 319-34.
Cave, C.H., 'The Obedience of the Unclean Spirits', *NTS* 11 (1964), pp. 93-97.
Charles, R.H., ed., *The Apocryphya and Pseudepigrapha of the Old Testament* (2 vols.; Oxford: Oxford University Press, 1913).
—*A Critical and Exegetical Commentary on the Revelation of St. John* (ICC; 2 vols.; Edinburgh: T. & T. Clark, 1920).
Charlesworth, J.H., ed., *The Old Testament Pseudepigrapha* (2 vols.; Garden City, NY: Doubleday, 1983, 1985).
—*The Pseudepigrapha and the New Testament* (SNTSMS, 54; Cambridge: Cambridge University Press, 1985).
Chatman, S., *Story and Discourse: Narrative Structure in Fiction and Film* (Ithaca, NY: Cornell University Press, 1980).
Chilton, B.D., 'Exorcism and History: Mark 1.21-28', in *Gospel Perspectives* 6 (ed. D. Wenham and C. Blomberg; Sheffield: JSOT Press, 1986), pp. 253-71.
—*A Galilean Rabbi and His Bible* (Wilmington, DE: Michael Glazier, 1984).

—*God in Strength: Jesus' Announcement of the Kingdom* (SUNT, 1; Göttingen: Vandenhoeck & Ruprecht, 1979).
—'Gottesherrschaft als Gotteserfahrung: Erkenntnisse der Targumforschung für den neutestamentlichen Begriff "Königsherrschaft Gottes"', in *Targumic Approaches to the Gospels* (Lanham, MD: University Press of America, 1986), pp. 85-97.
—'Regnum Dei Deus Est', in *Targumic Approaches to the Gospels*, pp. 99-107.
Chronis, H.L., 'The Torn Veil: Cultus and Christology in Mark 15.37-39', *JBL* 101 (1982) pp. 97-114.
Clarke, M.L., *Rhetoric at Rome* (London: Cohen and West, 1953).
Cohen, S.J.D., *Josephus in Galilee and Rome: His Vita and Development as a Historian* (Leiden: Brill, 1979).
Collins, A.Y., *Crisis and Cartharsis: The Power of the Apocalypse* (Philadelphia: Westminster Press, 1986).
—'Narrative, History and Gospel: A General Response', *Semeia* 43 (1988), pp. 145-53.
—'The Political Perspective of the Revelation to John', *JBL* 96 (1977), pp. 241-56.
Collins, J.J., *Between Athens and Jerusalem* (New York: Crossroad, 1983).
— Pseudonymity, Historical Reviews and the Genre of the Revelation of John', *CBQ* 34 (1977), pp. 329-43.
—'The Sibylline Oracles', in Stone (ed.), *Jewish Writings of the Second Temple Period*, pp. 357-82.
—'Testaments', in Stone (ed.), *Jewish Writings of the Second Temple Period*, pp. 325-56.
Conzelmann, H., *The Acts of the Apostles* (Hermeneia Commentaries; Philadelphia: Fortress Press, 1987).
Corley, B.C., ed., *Colloquy on New Testament Studies* (Macon, GA: Mercer University Press, 1983)
Corrington, G.P., *The Divine-Man: His Origin and Function in Hellenistic Popular Religion* (American University Studies Series; Theology and Religion, 8.17; New York: Peter Lang, 1986)
Cox, P., *Biography in Late Antiquity: A Quest for the Holy Man* (Berkley, CA: University of California Press, 1983).
Craghan, F.J., 'The Gerasene Demoniac', *CBQ* 30 (1968), pp. 522-36.
Cranfield, C.E.B., *The Gospel According to St. Mark* (CGTC; Cambridge: Cambridge University Press, 1979).
—'St. Mark 9.14-29', *SJT* 3 (1950), pp. 57-67.
—'St. Mark 16.1-8', *SJT* 5 (1952), pp. 282-98, 398-414.
Crossan, J.D., 'Aphorism in Discourse and Narrative', *Semeia* 43 (1988), pp. 121-36.
—'Empty Tomb and Absent Lord (Mark 16.1-8)', in *The Passion in Mark: Studies on Mark 14-16* (ed. W. Kelber; Philadelphia: Fortress Press, 1976), pp. 135-52.
—'A Form for Absence: The Markan Creation of Gospel', *Semeia* 12 (1978), pp. 41-53.
—*Four Other Gospels: Shadows on the Contours of Canon* (New York: Winston Press, 1985).
—'Mark and the Relatives of Jesus', *NovT* 15 (1973), pp. 81-113.
—'The Parable of the Wicked Husbandmen', *JBL* 90 (1971), pp. 451-65.
Culpepper, R.A., *Anatomy of the Fourth Gospel* (Philadelphia: Fortress Press, 1983).
—'Mark 11.15-19', *Int* 34 (1980), pp. 176-81.
Dahl, N.A., 'The Purpose of Mark's Gospel', in *Jesus in the Memory of the Early Church* (Minneapolois: Augsburg, 1976), pp. 52-65.
Daube, D., *The New Testament and Rabbinic Judaism* (London: Athlone Press, 1956).
Dauer, A., *Die Passionsgeschichte im Johannesevangelium: Eine traditionsgeschichtliche und theologische Untersuchung zu Joh. 18.1-19.30* (Munich: Kösel, 1972).

Dautzenberg, G., 'Die Zeit des Evangeliums. Mk. 1.1-15 und die Komposition des Markusevangeliums', *BZ* 21 (1977), pp. 219-234, 22 (1978), pp. 76-91.
Davids, P.H., *The Epistle of James* (NIGTC; Grand Rapids: Eerdmans, 1982).
Davies, S.L., *The Gospel of Thomas and Christian Wisdom* (New York: Seabury Press, 1983).
—*The Revolt of the Widows: The Social World of the Apocryphal Acts* (Carbondale, IL; Southern Illinois University Press, 1980).
Dehandschutter, B. 'La parabole des vignerons homocides (Mc 12.1-12) et l'évangile selon Thomas', in *L'Evangile selon Marc*, pp. 203-19.
Delling, G., 'Josephus und das Wunderbare', *NovT* 2 (1958), pp. 291-309.
Derrett, J.D.M., 'Allegory and the Wicked Vinedressers', *JTS* 25 (1974), pp. 426-32.
—'Contributions to the Study of the Gerasene Demoniac', *JSNT* 3 (1979), pp. 2-17.
—*Law in the New Testament* (London: Darton, Longman & Todd, 1970).
—*The Making of Mark* (2 vols.; Shipston-on-Stour: P. Drinkwater, 1985).
—'Mark's Technique: The Haemorrhaging Woman and Jairus' Daughter', *Bib* 63 (1982), pp. 474-505.
—'The Stone that the Builders Rejected', *SE* 4 (1968), pp. 180-86.
Dewey, J., 'The Literary Structure of the Controversy Stories of Mk. 2.1-3.6', *JBL* 92 (1973), pp. 394-401.
Dibelius, M., *From Tradition to Gospel* (London: Ivor, Nicholson & Watson, 1934).
Dimant, D., 'Qumran Sectarian Literature', in Stone, (ed.), *Jewish Writings in the Second Temple Period*, pp. 483-550.
Dobschütz, E.v., 'Der Roman in der altchristlichen Literature', *Deutsche Rundschau* 111 (1902), pp. 87-106.
Dodd, C.H., 'The Appearances of the Risen Christ: An Essay in Form-Criticism of the Gospels', in *Studies in the Gospels: Essays in Memory of Robert H. Lightfoot* (ed. D.E. Nineham; Oxford: Basil Blackwell, 1955), pp. 9-35.
—*Historical Tradition in the Fourth Gospel* (Cambridge: Cambridge University Press, 1963).
—*The Parables of the Kingdom* (Glasgow: Collins, 1983).
Dodds, E.R., *Pagans and Christians in an Age of Anxiety* (Cambridge: Cambridge University Press, 1965).
Donahue, J., *The Gospel in Parable, Metaphor, Narrative and Theology in the Synoptic Gospels* (Philadelphia: Fortress Press, 1988).
—'Jesus as the Parable of God in the Gospel of Mark', *Int* 32 (1978), pp. 369-88.
—'A Neglected Factor in the Theology of Mark', *JBL* 101 (1982), pp. 563-94.
—'Temple, Trial and Royal Christology (Mark 14.53-65)', in Kelber (ed.), *The Passion in Mark*, pp. 61-79.
Doran, R., *Temple Propaganda: The Purpose and Character of 2 Maccabees* (CBQMS, 12; Washington: Catholic Biblical Association, 1981).
Dormeyer, D., 'Die Kompositions Metaphor "Evangelium Jesu Christi, des Sohnes Gottes" Mk. 1.1. Ihre theologische und literarische Aufgabe in der Jesus-Biographie des Markus', *NTS* 33 (1987), pp. 452-68
—*Die Passion Jesu als Verhaltensmodell: Literarische und theologische Analyse der Traditions–und Redaktionsgeschichte der Markuspassion* (Münster: Aschendorff, 1974).
Doughty, D.J., 'The Authority of the Son of Man (Mk. 2.1-3.6)', *ZNW* 74 (1983), pp. 161-81.
Drury, J., 'Mark', in *The Literary Guide to the Bible* (ed. R. Alter and F. Kermode, Cambridge, MA: Harvard University Press, 1987), pp. 402-217.

Duke, P., *Irony in the Fourth Gospel* (Atlanta, GA; John Knox Press, (1985).
Dunn, J.D.G., *Jesus and the Spirit: A Study of the Religious and Charismatic Experiences of Jesus and the First Christians as Reflected in the New Testament* (London: SCM Press, 1975).
Dupont-Summer, A., ed., *The Essene Writings from Qumran* (trans. G. Vermes; Gloucester, MA: Peter Smith, 1973).
Ebeling, G., E. Jüngel and G. Schunak, eds., *Festschrift für Ernst Fuchs* (Tübingen: Mohr [Siebeck], 1973)
Edelstein, E.J., and L. Edelstein, eds., *Asclepius: A Collection and Interpretation of the Testimonies* (2 vols.; Baltimore: Johns Hopkins Press, 1945).
Egger, W., *Nachfolge als Weg zum Leben: Chancen neuer exegetischen Methoden dargelegt an Mk. 10.17-31* (Klosterneuberg: Österreichisches Katholisches Bibelwerk, 1979).
Ellis, E.E., 'New Directions in Form Criticism', in *Jesus Christus in Historie und Theologie: Neutestamentliche Festschrift für Hans Conzelmann zum 60. Geburtstag* (ed. G. Strecker; Tübingen: Mohr, 1975), pp. 299-315.
Ellis, E.E., and E. Grässer, eds., *Jesus und Paulus: Festschrift für Werner Georg Kümmel zum 70. Geburtstag* (Göttingen: Vandenhoeck & Ruprecht, 1975).
Ellis, E.E., and M. Wilcox, eds., *Neotestamentica et Semitica: Studies in Honour of Matthew Black*, (Edinburgh: T. & T. Clark, 1969), pp. 157-80.
Enslin, M., ' ἐφοβοῦντο γάρ, Mk. 16.8', *JBL* 46 (1927), pp. 62-68.
Epstein, V., 'The Historicity of the Gospel Account of the Cleansing of the Temple', *ZNW* 55 (1964), pp. 42-58.
Evans, C.A., 'On the Vineyard Parables of Isaiah 5 and Mark 12', *BZ* 28 (1984), pp. 82-86.
Farmer, W.R., *The Last Twelve Verses of Mark* (SNTSMS, 25; Cambridge: Cambridge University Press, 1974).
Farrer, A., *A Study in St. Mark* (London: Dacre Press, 1951).
Feuillet, A., *L'agonie de Gethsémani: Enquête exégétique et théologique suivie d'un étude du "Mystére de Jésus" de Pascal* (Paris: Gabalda, 1977).
Fiebig, P., *Die jüdisches Wundergeschichten* (Tübingen: Mohr, 1911).
Fiorenza, E.S., ed., *Aspects of Religious Propaganda in Judaism and Early Christianity* (Notre Dame: University of Notre Dame Press, 1976)
Fitzmyer, J., *The Gospel According to Luke 1-9* (AB; Garden City, NY; Doubleday, 1984).
—'The Oxyrhynchus *logoi* of Jesus and the Coptic Gospel According to Thomas', in *Essays on the Semitic Background of the New Testament* (London: Geoffrey Chapman, 1971), pp. 355-433.
Fleddermann, H., 'And He Wanted to Pass by Them (Mk. 6.48a)', *CBQ* 45 (1983), pp. 389-95.
Ford, J.M., 'Money Bags in the Temple, *Bib* 57 (1976), pp. 249-53.
— *Revelation: A New Translation with Introduction and Commentary* (AB; Garden City, NY: Doubleday, 1975).
Fortna, R.T., *The Gospel of Signs* (SNTSMS, 11; Cambridge: Cambridge University Press, 1970).
—*The Fourth Gospel and its Predecessor: From Narrative Source to Present Gospel* (Philadelphia: Fortress Press, 1970).
Fowler, R., *Loaves and Fishes* (SBLDS, 54; Chico, CA: Scholars Press, 1981).
France, R.T., 'Mark and the Teaching of Jesus', in *Gospel Perspectives*, I, pp. 101-36.
Freedman, W., 'The Literary Motif: A Definition and Evaluation', *Novel* 4 (1971), pp. 123-31.
Freyne, S., 'The Charismatic', in *Ideal Figures in Ancient Judaism* (ed. G.W.E. Nickelsburg and J.J. Collins; Chico, CA: Scholars Press, 1980), pp. 233-58.
—'The Disciples in Mark and the *Maskilim* in Daniel: A Comparison', *JSNT* 16 (1982).

Friedrich, J., W. Pohlmann and P. Stuhlmacher, eds., *Rechtfertigung: Festschrift für Ernst Käsemann zum 70. Geburtstag* (Göttingen: Vandenhoeck & Ruprecht, 1976).
Frye, N., *The Great Code: The Bible and Literature* (New York: Harcourt Brace Jovanovich, 1981).
Frye, R.M., 'A Literary Perspective for the Criticism of the Gospels', in *Jesus and Man's Hope* (ed. D. Miller and D. Y. Hadadian; Pittsburgh: Pittsburgh Theological Seminary, 1971), II, pp. 193-221.
Fuller, R., 'Classics and the Gospels: The Seminar', in *The Relationships Among the Gospels: An Interdisciplinary Dialogue* (San Antonio, TX: Trinity University Press, 1978).
Gallagher, E.V., *Divine Man or Magician: Celsus and Origen on Jesus* (SBLDS, 64; Chico, CA: Scholars Press, 1982).
Gaston, L., *No Stone on Another* (NovTSup, 23; Leiden: Brill, 1970).
Georgi, D., *The Opponents of Paul in Second Corinthians* (Edinburgh: T. & T. Clark, 1987).
Gerber, W., 'Die Metamorphose Jesu: Mark 9.2f., par.', *TZ* 23 (1967), pp. 385-95.
Giblin, C.H., '"The Things of God" in the Question Concerning Tribute to Caesar, *CBQ* 33 (1971), pp. 510-27.
Guelich, R., ed., *Unity and Diversity in New Testament Theology: Essays in Honor of George E. Ladd* (Grand Rapids: Eerdmans, 1978)
Gnilka, J., 'Das Elend vor dem Menschensohn', in *Jesus und der Menschensohn: Für Anton Vögtle* (ed. R. Pesch and R. Schnackenburg; Freiburg: Herder, 1975), pp. 196-209.
—*Das Evangelium nach Markus* (EKKNT; 2 vols.; Zürich: Benzinger Verlag, 1978, 1979).
—'Das Martyrium Johannes des Taufers (Mk. 6.17-29)', in *Orientierung an Jesus: Für Josef Schmid* (ed. P. Hoffman; Freiburg: Herder, 1973), pp. 78-92.
— *Johannesevangelium* (Die neue Echter-Bibel; Würzburg: Echter Verlag, 1983).
Goldstein, J.A., *2 Maccabees: A New Translation with Introduction and Commentary* (AB; Garden City, NY: Doubleday, 1984).
Goodenough, E.R., *An Introduction to Philo Judaeus* (London: Basil Blackwell, 1962).
Goodspeed, E.J., *A History of Early Christian Literature* (Chicago: University of Chicago Press, 1966; repr. with revisions by R.M. Grant [1942]).
Goppelt, L., 'The Freedom to Pay the Imperial Tax, Mk. 12.17', *SE* II (1964), pp. 183-94.
—'Die Freiheit zur Kaiserteuer zu Mk. 12.17 und Rom. 13.1-7', in *Christologie und Ethik: Aufsätze zum Neuen Testament* (Göttingen: Vandenhoeck & Ruprecht, 1968), pp. 208-19.
—*Theology of the New Testament* (trans. J.A. Alsup; 2 vols.; Grand Rapids: Eerdmans, 1981), I.
Grant, R.M., 'The Coming of the Kingdom', *JBL* 67 (1948), pp. 297-303.
Grässer, E., 'Jesus in Nazareth (Mark 6.1-6a): Notes on the Redaction and Theology of St. Mark', *NTS* 16 (1969), pp. 1-23.
Greeley, A.M., *Ecstacy: A Way of Knowing* (Englewood Cliffs, NJ: Prentice-Hall, 1974).
Grenfell, H., and R. Hunt, eds., *The Oxyrhynchus Papyri* (60 vols.; London: Oxford University Press, 1904), IV.
Grunmann, W., *Das Evangelium nach Markus* (THKNT; Leipzig: Deichart, 1968).
Guillemette, P., 'Un Enseignment noveau, plein d'autorité', *NovT* 22 (1980), pp. 232-47.
Gundry, R., *Mark: A Commentary on His Apology for the Cross* (Grand Rapids: Eerdmans, 1993).
—'Mark: An Apology for the Cross', unpublished paper.
Hadas, M., and M. Smith, *Heroes and Gods: Spiritual Biographies in Antiquity* (Freeport, NY: Books for Libraries Press, 1970).
Haenchen, E., *The Acts of the Apostles* (Oxford: Basil Blackwell, 1971).
—*A Commentary on the Gospel of John* (2 vols., Philadelphia: Westminster Press, 1984).

Hall, R.G., 'The "Christian Interpolation" in the *Apocalypse of Abraham*', *JBL* 107 (1988), pp. 107-10.
Halliday, W.R., *Greek Divination* (London: Macmillan, 1913).
Hamilton, N.Q., 'Temple Cleansing and Temple Bank', *JBL* 83 (1964), pp. 365-72.
Harnisch, W., 'Die Berufung des Reichen: Zur Analyse von Markus 10.17-27', in *Festschrift für Ernst Fuchs* (ed. G. Ebeling, E. Jüngel and G. Schunack; Tübingen: Mohr [Siebeck], 1973), pp. 161-76.
Harrington, D.J., 'The Jewishness of Jesus: Facing Some Problems', *CBQ* 49 (1987), pp. 1-13.
—'Palestinian Adaptations of Biblical Narratives and Prophesies', in (ed.), Nicklesburg and Kraft, *Early Judaism and its Modern Interpreters*, pp. 239-58.
Hartmann, G., *Der Aufbau des Markusevangeliums* (Neutestamentliche Abhandlungen, 17, 2-3; Münster: Aschendorff, 1936).
—'Mk. 3.20f', *BZ* 11 (1913), pp. 249-79.
Heil, J.P., *Jesus Walking on the Sea: Meaning and Gospel Functions of Matthew 14.22-23, Mark 6.45-52 and John 6.15b-21* (AnBib, 87; Rome: Biblical Institute Press, 1981).
Hengel, M., *Between Jesus and Paul* (London: SCM Press, 1983).
—*Earliest Christianity* (London: SCM Press, 1986).
—'Das Gleichnis v. den Weingärtnern Mc. 12.1-12 in Lichte der Zenonpapyri und der rabbinischen Gleichnisse', *ZNW* 59 (1968), pp. 1-39.
—*The Son of God* (London: SCM Press, 1976).
—*Studies in the Gospel of Mark* (London: SCM Press, 1985).
—*The Zealots: Investigations into the Jewish Freedom Movement in the Period from Herod I until 70 AD* (Edinburgh: T. & T. Clark, 1989 [1961]).
Hennecke, E., and W. Schneemelcher, eds., *The New Testament Apocryphya* (2 vols.; Philadelphia: Westminster Press, 1963, 1965).
Héring, J., 'Zwei exegetische Probleme in der Perikope v. Jesus in Gethsemane', in *Neotestamentica et Patristica: Eine Freundesgabe Herrn Professor Dr Oscar Cullmann zu seinem 60. Geburtstag überreicht* (ed. E.E. Ellis and E. Grässer; NovTSup, 6; Leiden: Brill, 1962), pp. 64-69.
Hiers, R.H., 'Purification of the Temple: Preparation for the Kingdom of God', *JBL* 90 (1971), pp. 82-90.
Hingston, J.,'John 18.5, 6', *ExpTim* 32 (1920/21), p. 232.
Hobbs, E.C., 'Norman Perrin on Methodology in the Interpretation of Mark: A Critique of 'The Christology of Mark" and "Toward An Interpretation of the Gospel of Mark"', in *Christology and a Modern Pilgrimage: A Discussion with Norman Perrin* (ed. H.D. Betz; Claremont, CA: New Testament Colloquium, 1971), pp. 79-91.
Hoehner, H., *Herod Antipas* (SNTSMS, 17; Cambridge: Cambridge University Press, 1972).
Hoffman, P,. ed., *Orientierung an Jesus: Für Josef Schmid* (Freiburg: Herder, 1973).
Holladay, C., *Theios Aner in Hellenistic Judaism: A Critique of the Use of this Category in New Testament Christology* (SBLDS, 40; Chico, CA: Scholars Press, 1977).
Horsley, R.A., *Jesus and the Spiral of Violence* (San Francisco: Harper & Row, 1987).
—'The Zealots, Their Origin, Relationships, and Importance in the Jewish Revolt', *NovT* 27 (1986), pp. 159-192.
Horsley, R.A., with J.S. Hanson, *Bandits, Prophets and Messiahs: Popular Movements at the Time of Jesus* (Minneapolis: Winston Press, 1985).
Horst, P.W. v.d., 'Can a Book End with *gar*?: A Note on Mk. 16.1-8', *JTS* 23 (1972), pp. 121-24.

Hort, F.J.A., *The Epistle of St. James* (London: Macmillan, 1909).
Hunter, A.M., *Interpreting the Parables* (London: SCM Press, 1984).
Iersel, B.M.F. v., and A.J.M. Linmans, 'The Storm on the Lake, Mk 4.35-41 and Mt. 8.18-27 in the Light of Form-Criticism, "Redaktionsgeschichte" and Structural Analysis', in *Miscellanea Neotestamentica* (ed. T. Baarda, A.F.J. Klijn and W.C. v. Unnik (NovTSup, 48; Leiden: Brill, 1978), pp. 17-48.
Jackson, H.M., 'The Death of Jesus in Mark and the Miracle from the Cross', *NTS* 33 (19870, pp. 16-37.
James, W., *Varieties of Religious Experience* (New York: Random House, 1902).
Jeremias, J., *The Parables of Jesus* (New York: Charles Scribner's Sons, 1972).
—*Unknown Sayings of Jesus* (London: SPCK, 1957).
Jeremias, J., and W. Zimmerli, *The Servant of God* (SBT, 20; London: SCM Press, 1957).
Johnson, L.T., *The Writings of the New Testament: An Interpretation* (London: SCM Press, 1986).
Johnson, S., 'Greek and Jewish Heroes: Fourth Maccabees and the Gospel of Mark', in *Early Christian Literature and the Classical Intellectual Tradition: In Honor of Robert M. Grant* (ed. W.R. Schoedel and R.L. Wilken; Paris: Editions Beauchesne, 1979), pp. 157-75.
Jülicher, A., *Die Gleichnisreden Jesu, 1-2* (Tübingen: Mohr, 1910).
Junod, E., 'Les Vies de philosophes et les actes apocryphes des apôtres, poursuivent-ils un dessein similaire?', in F. Bovon *et al.* (eds.), *Les actes apocryphes des apôtres*, pp. 209-19.
Kaestli, J.-D., 'Les principles orientations de la recherche sur les actes apocryphes des apôtres', in F. Bovon *et al.* (eds.), *Les actes apocryphes des apôtres*, pp. 49-67.
Keck, L., 'Mark 3.7-12 and Mark's Christology', *JBL* 84 (1965), pp. 341-58.
Kee, H.C., 'Aretalogy and Gospel', *JBL* 92 (1973), pp. 402-22.
—*Community of the New Age* (London: SCM Press, 1977).
—'The Function of Scriptural Quotations and Allusions in Mark 11-16', in *Jesus und Paulus: Festschrift für Werner Georg Kümmel zum 70. Geburtstag* (ed. E.E. Ellis and E. Grässer; Göttingen: Vandenhoeck & Ruprecht, 1975), pp. 165-88.
—*Miracle in the Early Christian World* (New Haven: Yale University Press, 1983).
—'The Terminology of Mark's Exorcism Stories', *NTS* 14 (1967/68), pp. 232-46.
—'The Transfiguration in Mark: Epiphany or Apocalyptic Vision?', in *Understanding the Sacred Text: Essays in Honor of Morton S. Enslin on the Hebrew Bible and Christian Beginnings* (ed. J. Reumann; Valley Forge, PA; Judson Press, 1972), pp. 135-52.
Kelber, W., 'The Hour of the Son of Man and the Temptation of the Disciples (Mk. 14.32-42)', in *The Passion in Mark: Studies on Mark 14–16* (ed. W. Kelber; Philadelphia: Fortress Press, 1976), pp. 41-60.
—*The Kingdom in Mark: A New Place and A New Time* (Philadelphia: Fortress Press, 1974).
—'Mark 14.32-42: Gethsemane', *ZNW* 63 (1972), pp. 166-87.
—*The Oral and Written Gospel* (Philadelphia: Fortress Press, 1983).
Kennedy, G., *The Art of Persuasion in Greece* (London: Routledge & Kegan Paul, 1963).
—*The Art of Rhetoric in the Roman World 300 BC–AD 300* (Princeton: Princeton University Press, 1972).
—*New Testament Interpretation through Rhetorical Criticism* (Chapel Hill, NC; University of North Carolina Press, 1984).
Kenny, A., 'The Transfiguration and the Agony in the Garden', *CBQ* 19 (1957), pp. 444-52.
Kermode, F., *The Genesis of Secrecy: On the Interpretation of Narrative* (Cambridge, MA; Harvard University Press, 1979).

—*The Sense of An Ending* (London: Oxford University Press, 1976).
Kertlege, K., 'Die Epiphanie Jesu im Evangeliums (Markus)', in *Gestalt und Anspruch des Neuen Testaments* (ed. J. Schreiner; Würzburg: Echter Verlag, 1969), pp. 153-172, repr. in W. Telford, ed., *The Interpretation of Mark* (Philadelphia: Fortress Press, London: SPCK, 1985), pp. 78-94.
—*Die Wunder Jesu im Markusevangelium* (Munich: Kösel, 1970).
Kiilunen, J., *Die Vollmacht im Widerstreit: Untersuchungen zum Werdegang v. Mk. 2.1-3.6* (Helsinki: Suomalainen Tiedeakatemia, 1985).
Kingsbury, J.D., *The Christology of Mark's Gospel* (Philadelphia: Fortress Press, 1983).
—*Conflict in Mark* (Philadelphia: Fortress Press, 1989).
—'The "Divine Man" as the Key to Mark's Christology—The End of an Era?', *Int* 35 (1981), pp. 243-57.
Kline, M., 'The Old Testament Origins of the Gospel Genre', *WTJ* 38 (1975), pp. 1-27.
Klostermann, E., *Das Markusevangelium* (HNT; Tübingen: Mohr, 1971).
Knox, W., *The Sources of the Synoptic Gospels* (2 vols.; Cambridge: Cambridge University Press, 1953), I.
Koch, D.-A., *Die Bedeutung der Wundererzählungen für die Christologie des Markusevangeliums* (Berlin: de Gruyter, 1968).
Koester, H., 'Apocryphal and Canonical Gospels', *HTR* 73 (1980), pp. 105-30.
—'Gnomai Diaphoroi: The Origin and Nature of Diversification in theHistory of Early Christianity', *HTR* 58 (1965), pp. 279-318.
—'The Historical Jesus: Some Comments and Thoughts on Norman Perrin's *Rediscovering the Teaching of Jesus*', in H.D. Betz (ed.), *Christology and a Modern Pilgrimage*, pp. 123-36.
—'History and Development of Mark's Gospel (from Mark to Secret Mark and "Canonical" Mark)', in *Colloquy on New Testament Studies* (ed. B. Corley; Macon, GA: Mercer University Press, 1983), pp. 35-57.
—*Introduction to the New Testament. I. History, Literature and Culture of the Hellenistic Age. II. History and Literature of Early Christianity* (Philadelphia: Fortress Press; Berlin: de Gruyter, 1982).
—'One Jesus and Four Primitive Gospels', in H. Koester and J. Robinson (eds.), *Trajectories through Early Christianity* (Philadelphia: Fortress Press, 1971).
Kraeling, C.H., 'A Philological Note on Mark 16.8', *JBL* 44 (1925), pp. 357-58.
Kuhn, H.-W., *Ältere Sammlungen im Markusevangelium* (Göttingen: Vandenhoeck & Ruprecht, 1971).
—'Das Reittier Jesu in Einzugsgeschichte des Markusevangelium', *ZNW* 50 (1959), pp. 82-91.
Kuhn, K.-G., 'Jesus in Gethsemane', *EvT* 12 (1952/53), pp. 260-85.
Kümmel, W.G., *Introduction to the New Testament* (London: SCM Press, 1984).
Kysar, R., *The Fourth Evangelist and His Gospel* (Minneapolis: Augsburg, 1975).
Lane, W.L., *The Gospel of Mark* (NICNT; Grand Rapids: Eerdmans 1979).
—'Theios Aner Christology and the Gospel of Mark', in *New Dimensions in New Testament Study* (ed. R. Longenecker and M.C. Tenney; Grand Rapids: Zondervan, 1974), pp. 144-61.
Lang, F.G., 'Kompositionsanalyse des Markusevangeliums', *ZTK* 74 (1977), pp. 1-24.
—'Sola Gratia im Markusevangelium: Die Soteriologie des Markus nach 9.14-29 und 10.117-31', in *Rechtfertigung: Festschrift für Ernst Käsemann zum 70. Geburtstag* (ed. J. Friedrich, W. Pohlmann and P. Stuhlmacher; Göttingen: Vandenhoeck & Ruprecht, 1976), pp. 321-37.
Lapide, P., 'A Jewish Exegesis of the Walking on the Water', *Concilium* 138 (1980), pp. 37-40.

Laws, S., *A Commentary on the Epistle of James* (BNTC; London: A. & C. Black, 1980).
Layton, B., ed., *The Gnostic Scriptures: A New Translation with Annotations and Introductions* (Garden City, NY; Doubleday, 1987).
Leenhardt, F.J., 'An Exegetical Essay: Mark 5.1-20', in *Structural Analysis and Biblical Exegesis: Interpretational Essays* (ed. R. Barthes *et al.*; Pittsburgh: Pickwick Press, 1974).
Lee-Pollard, D.A., 'Powerlessness as Power: A Key Emphasis in the Gospel of Mark', *SJT* 40 (1987), pp. 173-88.
Leeuw, G. v.d., *Religion in Essence and Manifestation* (2 vols.; New York: Harper & Row, 1963).
Légasse, S., *L'appel du riche (Mc 10.17-31 et paralléles): Contribution à l'étude des fondements scripturaires de l'état religieux* (Paris: Beauchesne, 1966).
—'Jésus, a-t-il annoncé la conversion finale d'Israël? (à propos de Mark 10.23-37)', *NTS* 10 (1964), pp. 480-87.
Lenski, R.C.H., *The Interpretation of St. Mark's Gospel* (Minneapolis: Augsburg, 1964).
Lescow, T., 'Jesus in Gethsemane', *EvT* 26 (1966), pp. 141-59.
Lewis, I.M., *Ecstatic Religion: An Anthropological Study of Spirit Possession and Shamanism* (Harmondsworth: Penguin Books, 1975).
Lightfoot, R., *The Gospel Message of St. Mark* (Oxford: Clarendon Press, 1950).
—*Locality and Doctrine in the Gospels* (London: Hodder & Stoughton, 1938).
Lindars, B., *Behind the Fourth Gospel* (London: SPCK, 1971).
—'Elijah, Elisha and the Gospel Miracles', in *Miracles: Cambridge Studies in Their Philosophy and History* (ed. C.F.D. Moule; London, Mowbray, 1965), pp. 63-79.
—*The Gospel of John* (NCB; London: Oliphants, 1972).
—*New Testament Apologetic* (London: SCM Press, 1961).
Lindars, B., and S.S. Smalley, eds., *Christ and the Spirit in the New Testament: Studies in Honour of C.F.D. Moule* (Cambridge: Cambridge University Press, 1973)
Lindemann, A., 'Die Osterbotschaft des Markus: Zur theologischen Interpretation v. Mark 16.1-8', *NTS* 26 (1986), pp. 298-317.
Linnemann, E., *Studien zur Passionsgeschichte* (FRLANT, 102; Göttingen: Vandenhoeck & Ruprecht, 1970).
—'Der (wiedergebundene) Markusschluss', *ZTK* 66 (1969), pp. 255-87.
Lohmeyer, E., *Das Evangelium des Markus* (MeyerK; Göttingen: Vandenhoeck & Ruprecht, 1963).
—'Und Jesu ging vorüber', *NedTTs* 23 (1934), pp. 206-24.
—*Die Offenbarung des Johannes* (HNT; Tübingen, Mohr, 1971).
Lohse, E., *Die Offenbarung des Johannes* (NTD; Göttingen: Vandenhoeck & Ruprecht, 1971).
—*Die Geschichte des Leidens und Sterbens Jesu Christi* (Gütersloh: Mohn, 1964)
Longenecker, R., and M.C. Tenney, eds., *New Dimensions in New Testament Study* (Grand Rapids: Zondervan, 1974)
Lubsczyk, H., 'Kurios Jesus: Beobachtungen und Gedanken zum Schluss des Markusevangeliums', in *Die Kirche des Anfangs: Festschrift für Heinz Schürmann zum 65. Geburtstag* (ed. R. Schnackenburg, J. Ernst and J. Wanke; Leipzig: St. Benno, 1977), pp. 133-74.
Lührmann, D., *Das Markusevangelium* (HNT; Tübingen: Mohr, 1987).
Luz, U., 'The Secrecy Motif and the Markan Christology', in *The Messianic Secret* (ed. C. Tuckett; Philadelphia: Fortress Press; London: SPCK, 1983), pp. 75-96.
MacDonald, D.R., *The Legend and the Apostle: The Battle for Paul in Story and Canon* (Philadelphia: Westminster Press, 1983).
Mack, B.L., 'The Kingdom Sayings in Mark', *Foundations and Facets Forum* 3 (1987), pp. 3-47.

MacKay, B.S., 'Plutarch and the Miraculous', in C.F.D. Moule (ed.), *Miracles: Cambridge Studies in Their Philosophy and History*, pp. 93-111.
MacRae, G., 'Miracles in the *Antiquities* of Josephus', in C.F.D. Moule (ed.), *Miracles: Cambridge Studies in Their Philosophy and History*, pp. 127-47.
Magness, J.L., *Sense and Absence: Structure and Suspension in the Ending of Mark's Gospel* (SBLDS; Chico, CA: Scholars Press, 1986).
Maier, J., *The Temple Scroll: An Introduction, Translation and Commentary* (Sheffield: JSOT Press, 1985).
Maisch, I., *Die Heilung des Gelähmten: Eine exegetisch traditions-geschichtliche Untersuchung zu Mk. 2.1-12* (SB, 52; Stuttgart: Katholisches Bibelwerk, 1971).
Makrides, V.N., 'Considerations on Mark 11.27-33 par.', *Deltion Biblikon Meleton* 14 (1985), pp. 43-55.
Malbon, E.S., 'Disciples, Crowds, Whoever: Markan Characters and Readers', *NovT* 28 (1986), pp. 104-30.
—'Fallible Followers: Women and Men in the Gospel of Mark', *Semeia* 28 (1983), pp. 29-48.
—'The Jesus of Mark and the Sea of Galilee', *JBL* 103 (1984), pp. 363-77.
—*Narrative Space and Mythic Meaning in Mark* (San Francisco: Harper & Row, 1986).
Mann, C.S., *Mark: A New Translation with Introduction and Commentary* (AB; Garden City, NY: Doubleday, 1986).
Marcus, J., *The Mystery of the Kingdom of God* (SBLDS, 90; Chico, CA: Scholars Press, 1986).
—*The Way of the Lord: Christological Exegesis of the Old Testament in the Gospel of Mark* (Lousiville, KY: Westminster–John Knox, 1992).
Marshall, C.D., *Faith as a Theme in Mark's Narrative* (SNTSMS, 64; Cambridge: Cambridge University Press, 1989).
Marshall, I.H., *Commentary on Luke* (NIGTC; Exeter: Paternoster Press, 1978).
—'Son of God or Servant of Yahweh? A Reconsideration of Mark 1.11', *NTS* 15 (1968–69), pp. 326-33.
Martitz, W. v., 'υἱός', *TDNT*, VIII.
Martyn, J.L., *History and Theology in the Fourth Gospel* (New York: Harper & Row, 1968).
Marxsen, W., *Mark the Evangelist: Studies in the Redaction of the Gospel* (trans. J. Boyce *et. al.*; Nashville: Abingdon Press, 1969).
Maslow, A.H., *Religions, Values and Peak-Experiences* (New York: Viking Press, 1973).
Masson, C., *Les deux épîtres de Saint Paul aux thessaloniens* (CNT; Neuchâtel: Delachaux & Niestlé, 1957)
Matera, F., *The Kingship of Jesus: Composition and Theology in Mark 15* (SBLDS, 66; Chico, CA: Scholars Press, 1981).
Maurer, C., 'Knecht Gottes und Sohn Gottes im Passionsbericht des Markusevangeliums', *ZTK* 50 (1953), pp. 1-38.
Mayer, B., 'Überlieferungs- und redaktionsgeschichtliche Überlegungen zu Mk. 6.1-6a', *BZ* 22 (1978), pp. 187-98.
McCasland, S.V., 'Portents in Josephus and in the Gospels', *JBL* 51 (1932), pp. 323-35.
McCurley, F.R., Jr, '"And After Six Days" (Mark 9.2): A Semitic Literary Device', *JBL* 93 (1974), pp. 67-81.
McKinnis, R., 'An Analysis of Mark 10.32-34', *NovT* 18 (1976), pp. 81-100.
Mead, R.T., 'The Healing of the Paralytic—A Unit?', *JBL* 80 (1961), pp. 348-54.

Meechem, H.G., ed., *The Letter of Aristeas: Greek Text* (Manchester: Manchester University Press, 1935).
Mein, P., 'A Note on John 18.6', *ExpTim* 65 (1953–54), pp. 286-87.
Metzger, B.M., *The Text of the New Testament: Its Transmission, Corruption and Restoration* (Oxford: Oxford University Press, 1982).
—*A Textual Commentary on the Greek New Testament* (London: United Bible Societies, 1971).
Meye, R.P., *Jesus and the Twelve: Discipleship and Revelation in Mark's Gospel* (Grand Rapids: Eerdmans, 1968).
—'Psalm 107 as Horizon for Interpreting the Miracle Stories of Mark 4.35 to 8.26', in *Unity and Diversity in New Testament Theology: Essays in Honor of George E. Ladd* (ed. R. Guelich; Grand Rapids: Eerdmans, 1978), pp. 1-13.
Meyer, B.F., *The Aims of Jesus* (London: SCM Press, 1979).
Meyer, E., *Ursprung und Anfange des Christentums* (Berlin: J.G. Colta'sche Buchhandlung Nachfolger, 1921), I.
Miller, D.C., and D.Y. Hadadian, eds., *Jesus and Man's Hope* (Pittsburgh: Pittsburgh Theological Seminary, 1971)
Miller, D., and P. Miller, *The Gospel of Mark as Midrash on Earlier Jewish and Christian Literature* (Lewiston, NY: Edwin Mellen, 1990).
Minear, P., 'The Needle's Eye', *JBL* 61 (1942), pp. 157-69.
Mohn, W., 'Gethsemane (Mk. 14.32-42)', *ZNW* 64 (1973), pp. 194-208.
Momigliano, A., *The Development of Greek Biography* (Cambridge, MA: Harvard University Press, 1972).
—'The Second Book of Maccabees', *Classical Philology* 70 (1975), pp. 81-88.
Moore, S., *Literary Criticism and the Gospels* (New Haven: Yale University Press, 1989).
—*Mark and Luke in Post-structuralist Perspectives: Jesus Begins to Write* (New Haven: Yale University Press, 1992).
Moore, S., and J.C. Anderson, eds., *Mark and Method* (Minneapolis: Augsburg, 1992).
Morgenthaler, R., *Statische Synopse* (Zürich: W. Gotthelf, 1971).
Morris, L., *The Gospel According to St. John* (NICNT; Grand Rapids: Eerdmans, 1972).
Moule, C.F.D., *An Idiom Book of New Testament Greek* (Cambridge: Cambridge University Press, 1982).
—'St. Mark 16.1-8 Once More', *NTS* 2 (1955/56), pp. 58-59.
Moule, C.F.D., ed., *Miracles: Cambridge Studies in their Philosophy and History* (London: Mowbray, 1965).
Mounce, R., *The Book of Revelation* (London: Marshall, Morgan & Scott, 1977).
Müller, H.P., 'Die Verklärung Jesu: Eine motivgeschichtliche Studie', *ZNW* 51 (1960), pp. 55-64.
Müller, U.B., 'Die christologische Absicht des Markusevangelium und die Verklärungsgeschichte', *ZNW* 64 (1973), pp. 159-93.
Murphy-O'Connor, J., 'The Judean Desert', in G.W.E. Nickelsburg and R. Kraft (eds.), *Early Judaism and Its Modern Interpreters*, pp. 119-56.
Müssner, F., 'Gottesherrschaft und Sendung Jesu nach Mk. 1.14f. zugleich ein Beitrag über die innere Struktur des Markusevangeliums', in *Praesentia Salutis: Gesammelte Studien zu Fragen und Themen des Neuen Testaments* (Düsseldorf: Patmos Verlag, 1967), pp. 81-98.
Neirynck, F., *Duality in Mark: Contributions to the Study of the Markan Redaction* (Leuven: Leuven University Press, 1972).
—'Mark 16.1-8: Tradition et rédaction', *ETL* 56 (1980), pp. 56-88.

—'The Redactional Text of Mark', *ETL* 57 (1981), pp. 144-62.
Neirynck, F., et al., *Jean et les synoptiques: Examen critique de l'exégèse de M.E. Boismard* (BETL, 49; Leuven: Leuven University Press, 1979).
Neusner, J., 'The Absoluteness of Christianity and the Uniqueness of Judaism: Why Salvation is Not of the Jews', *Int* 43 (1989), pp. 18-31.
—'Money Changers in the Temple: The Mishnah's Explanation', *NTS* 35 (1989), pp. 287-90.
Newell, J.E., and R.R. Newell, 'The Parable of the Wicked Husbandman', *NovT* 14 (1972), pp. 226-37.
Nickelsburg, G.W.E., 'The Genre and Function of the Markan Passion Narrative', *HTR* 73 (1980), pp. 153-84.
—*Jewish Literature Between the Bible and the Mishnah* (Philadelphia: Fortress Press, 1981).
—'Introduction: The Modern Study of Early Judaism', in *Early Judaism and its Modern Interpreters* (ed. G. Nickelsburg and R. Kraft; Philadelphia: Fortress Press; Atlanta, CA: Scholars Press, 1986), p. 3.
Nickelsburg, G.W.E., and J.J. Collins, eds., *Ideal Figures in Ancient Judaism* (Chico, CA: Scholars Press, 1980)
Nickelsburg, G.W.E., and R. Kraft, eds., *Early Judaism and Its Modern Interpreters* (Philadelphia: Fortress Press; Atlanta, CA: Scholars Press, 1986).
Nicol, W., *The Semeia in the Fourth Gospel* (NovTSup, 32; Leiden: Brill, 1972).
Niditch, S., 'The Visionary', in *Ideal Figures in Ancient Judaism* (ed. G.W.E. Nickelsburg and J.J. Collins; Chico, CA: Scholars Press, 1980), pp. 153-79.
Niemann, F-J., 'Die Erzählung vom leeren Grab bei Markus', *ZKT* 101 (1979), pp. 188-99.
Nineham, D.E., *The Gospel of St. Mark* (Pelican Gospel Commentaries; Harmondsworth: Penguin Books, 1986).
Nineham, D.E., ed., *Studies in the Gospels: Essays in Memory of Robert H. Lightfoot* (Oxford: Basil Blackwell, 1955).
Nock, A.D., 'Religious Attitudes of the Ancient Greeks', in *Essays on Religion and the Ancient World* (2 vols.; Oxford: Clarendon Press, 1972).
Nützel, J.M., *Die Verklärungserzählung im Markusevangelium* (Würzburg: Echter Verlag, 1973).
O'Neill, J.C., *The Theology of Acts in Its Historical Setting* (London: SPCK, 1970).
Ottley, R.R., 'ἐφοβοῦντο γάρ, Mk.16.8', *JTS* 27 (1926), pp. 407-409.
Otto, R., *The Idea of the Holy* (ET; London: Oxford University Press, 1923 [1917]).
Pagels, E., with H. Koester, 'Report on the Dialogue of the Savior', in *Nag Hammadi and Gnosis* (ed. R.McL. Wilson; Leiden: Brill, 1978), pp. 66-72.
Paulsen, H., 'Mk. 16.1-8', *NovT* 22 (1980), pp. 138-75.
Peabody, D.B., *Mark as Composer* (New Gospel Studies, 1; Macon, GA: Mercer University Press, 1987).
Perrin, N., 'The Christology of Mark: A Study of Methodology', in *The Interpretation of Mark* (ed. W. Telford; Philadelphia: Fortress Press; London: SPCK, 1985), pp. 95-108.
—'The Interpretation of Mark', *Int* 30 (1976), pp. 115-24.
—*A Modern Pilgrimage in Christology* (Claremont, CA: The New Testament Colloquium, 1971).
—*The New Testament, An Introduction: Proclamation and Parenesis, Myth and History* (New York: Harcourt Brace Jovanovich, 1974).
—*What is Redaction Criticism?* (Guides to Biblical Scholarship; Philadelphia: Fortress Press, 1976).
Pervo, R., *Profit with Delight: The Literary Genre of the Acts of the Apostles* (Philadelphia: Fortress Press, 1987).

Pesch, R., *Der Besessene von Gerasa: Entstehung und Überlieferung einer Wundergeschichte* (SBS, 56; Stuttgart: Katholisches Bibelwerk, 1972).
—*Die Apostelgeschichte* (EKKNT; 2 vols.; Zürich: Benzinger Verlag, 1986).
—*Das Markusevangelium* (HTKNT; 2 vols.; Freiburg: Herder, 1976, 1977).
—'Der Schluss der vormarkinischen Passionsgeschichte und des Markusevangeliums, Mk. 15.42-16.8', in *L'Evangile selon Marc: Tradition et rédaction*, pp. 365-409.
Pesch, R., and R. Schnackenburg, eds., *Jesus und der Menschensohn: Für Anton Vögtle* (Freiburg: Herder, 1975)
Petersen, N.R., *Literary Criticism for New Testament Critics* (Guides to Biblical Scholarship; Philadelphia: Fortress Press, 1978).
—'Point of View in Mark's Narrative', *Semeia* 12 (1978), pp. 97-121.
—'When is the End not the End? Literary Reflections on the Ending of Mark's Narrative', *Int* 34 (1980), pp. 151-66.
Peterson, E., ΕΙΣ ΘΕΟΣ: *Epigraphische, formgeschichtliche und religionsgeschichtliche Untersuchungen* (FRLANT, 41; Göttingen: Vandenhoeck & Ruprecht, 1926).
Petzke, G., 'Die historische Frage nach den Wundertaten Jesu: Dargestellt am Beispiel des Exorzismus Mk. 9.14-29 par.', *NTS* 22 (1976), pp. 180-204.
Pfister, F., 'Ekstase', in *Reallexikon für Antike und Christentum* (17 vols.; Stuttgart: Anton Hiersemann, 1959), IV, pp. 944-87.
—'Epiphanie', in *Paulys Real-Encyclopädie des classischen Altertums-Wissenschaft* (Stuttgart: J.B. Metzlersche Verlasbuch-handlung, 1924), Suppl. IV, pp. 227-323.
Plevnik, J., ed., *Word and Spirit: Essays in Honor of David M. Stanley on his 60th Birthday*, (Willowdale, Ontario: Regis College, 1975)
Pohl, A., *Das Evangelium des Markus* (Wuppertaler Studien Bible, Ergänzungsband; Wuppertal: R. Brochaus, 1986).
Porter, C.A., 'John 9.38-39a: A Liturgical Addition to the Text', *NTS* 13 (1966/67), pp. 387-94
Presendanz, K., ed., *Papyri Graecae Magicae: Die griechischen Zauberpapyri* (2 vols.; Leipzig: B.G. Teubner, 1928).
Prigent, P., *L'Apocalypse de Saint Jean* (CNT; Paris: Delachaux & Niestlé, 1981).
Pryke, E.J., *Redactional Style in the Markan Gospel: A Study of Syntax and Vocabulary as Guides to Redaction in Mark* (SNTSMS, 33; Cambridge: Cambridge University Press, 1978).
Quesnell, Q., 'The Mar Saba Clementine: A Question of Evidence', *CBQ* 37 (1975), pp. 48-67.
—*The Mind of Mark: Interpretation and Method through the Exegisis of Mark 6.52* (AnBib, 38; Rome: Biblical Institute Press, 1969).
Quispel, G., '"The Gospel of Thomas" and "The Gospel of the Hebrews"', *NTS* 12 (1965–66), pp. 371-82.
Rau, G., 'Das Markusevangelium: Komposition und Intention der ersten Darstellung christichler Mission', in *Aufstieg und Niedergang der römischen Welt* (Berlin: de Gruyter, 1985), II.25.3, pp. 2036-57.
Rawlinson, A.E.J., *St. Mark* (Westminster Commentaries; London: Methuen, 1925).
Reed, D.S., *Epochs of Greek and Roman Biography* (New York: Biblio & Tanner, 1967).
Reese, J.M., 'Plan and Structure in the Book of Wisdom', *CBQ* 27 (1965), pp. 391-99.
Reitzenstein, R., *Hellenistiche Wundererzählungen* (Leipzig: Teubner, 1906).
—*Die hellenistischen Mysterienreligionen* (Leipzig: Teubner, 1910).
Reploh, K.-G., *Markus-Lehrer der Gemeinde* (SBM, 9; Stuttgart: Katholisches Bibelwerk, 1969).

Reumann, J., ed., *Understanding the Sacred Text. Essays in Honor of Morton S. Enslin on the Hebrew Bible and Christian Beginnings* (Valley Forge, PA; Judson Press, 1972).
Rhoads, D., 'Narrative Criticism and the Gospel of Mark', *JAAR* 50 (1982), pp. 411-34.
Rhoads, D., and D. Michie, *Mark as Story* (Philadelphia: Fortress Press, 1982).
Richardson, L.J.D., 'St. Mark 16.8', *JTS* 49 (1948), pp. 144-45.
Riedl, J., *Das Heilswerk Jesu nach Johannes* (Freiburg: Herder, 1973).
Riesenfeld, H., *Jésus transfiguré: L'Arrière du récit évangélique de la transfiguration de notre-Seigneur* (Copenhagen: Ejnar Munksgaard, 1947).
Rigaux, B., *Saint Paul: Les épîtres aux thessaloniens* (Paris: Gabalda, 1956).
Ritt, H., 'Der Seewandel Jesu (Mk. 6.45-52 par.): Literarische und theologische Aspekte', *BZ* 23 (1979), pp. 71-84.
Roberts, W.R., *Greek Rhetoric and Literary Criticism* (London: George G. Harrup, 1928).
Robbins, V.K., *Jesus the Teacher* (Philadelphia: Fortress Press, 1984).
Robertson, A.T., *A Grammar of the Greek New Testament in the Light of Historical Research* (Nashville: Broadmann Press, 1934).
Robinson, J., 'Gnosticism and the New Testament', in *Gnosis: Festschrift für Hans Jonas* (ed. H. Bianchi *et al.*; Göttingen: Vandenhoeck & Ruprecht, 1978), pp. 125-43.
—'Logoi Sophoi: On the Gattung of Q', in J. Robinson and H. Koester, *Trajectories through Early Christianity* (Philadelphia: Fortress Press, 1971), pp. 114-57, 158-204.
—'On the Gattung of Mark (and John)', in *Jesus and Man's Hope* (ed. D.C. Miller and D.Y. Hadidian; Pittsburgh, PA: Pittsburgh Theological Seminary, 1970), pp. 99-129.
—*The Problem of History in Mark* (London: SCM Press, 1971).
Roloff, J., *Das Kerygma und der irdische Jesus: Historische Motive in den Jesus-Erzählungen der Evangelien* (Göttingen: Vandenhoeck & Ruprecht, 1973).
Roth, C., 'The Cleansing of the Temple and Zechariah 14.21', *NovT* 4 (1960), pp. 174-181.
Roth, W., *Hebrew Gospel: Cracking the Code of Mark* (Bloomington, IN: Meyer-Stone, 1988).
Rowland, C., *The Open Heaven: a Study of Apocalyptic in Judaism and Early Christianity* (London: SPCK, 1982).
Sabbe, M., ed., *L'Evangile selon Marc* (BETL, 34; Gembloux: Duculot; Leuven: Leuven University Press, 1974).
Saldarini, H., 'Rabbinic Judaism', in *Early Judaism and Its Modern Interpreters*, pp. 437-77.
Salin, H., 'Die Perikope v. gerasenischen Besessen und der Plan des Markusevangeliums', *ST* 18 (1964), pp. 159-72.
Sanders, E.P., *Jesus and Judaism* (Philadelphia: Fortress Press, 1985).
—*The Tendencies of the Synoptic Tradition* (SNTSMS, 9; Cambridge: Cambridge University Press, 1969).
Sandmel, S., *The First Christian Century in Judaism and Christianity: Certainties and Uncertainties* (New York: Oxford University Press, 1969).
—'Palestinian and Hellenistic Judaism: The Question of the Comfortable Theory', *HUCA* 50 (1979), pp. 137-48.
—'Parallelomania', *JBL* 81 (1962), pp. 1-13.
—*Philo of Alexandria: An Introduction* (Oxford: Oxford University Press, 1979).
Schenk, W., *Der Passionsbericht nach Markus* (Gütersloh: Gerd Mohn, 1974).
—'Tradition und Redaktion in der epileptiker Perikope Mk. 9.14-29', *ZNW* 63 (1972), pp. 76-94.
Schenke, L., *Auferstehungsverkündigung und leeres Grab: Eine traditionsgeschichtliche Untersuchung von Mk. 16.1-8* (SBS, 33; Stuttgart: Katholisches Bibelwerk, 1969).

—*Der gekreuzigte Christus: Versuch einer literarkritischen und traditionsgeschichtlichen Bestimmung der vormarkinischen Passionsgeschichte* (SBS, 69; Stuttgart: Katholisches Bibelwerk, 1974).
—*Studien zur Passionsgeschichte des Markus: Tradition und Redaktion in Markus 14.1-42* (FB, 4; Würzburg: Echter Verlag, 1971).
—*Die Wundererzählungen des Markusevangelium* (Stuttgart: Katholisches Biblewerk, 1974).
Schille, G., *Die Apostelgeschichte des Lukas* (THNT; Berlin: Evangelische Verlagsanstalt, 1984).
—'Die Seesturmerzählung Markus 4.35-41 als Beispiel neutestamentlicher Aktualisierung', *ZNW* 56 (1965), pp. 30-40.
Schlatter, A., *Der Evangelist Johannes* (Stuttgart: Calwer Verlag, 1948).
Schlier, H., *Die Markuspassion* (Einsiedeln: Johannes Verlag, 1974).
Schmid, J., *The Gospel According to Mark* (Regensburg New Testament; Staten Island, NY: The Mercier Press, 1968).
Schmithals, W., *Das Evangelium nach Markus* (2 vols.; Ökumenischer Taschenbuch Kommentar zum Neuen Testament; Würzburg: Gerd Mohn; Gütersloh: Gütersloher & Echter Verlag, 1979).
—Schulz, S., 'Marcus und das Alte Testament', *ZTK* 58 (1961), pp. 184-97.
—'Mark's Significance for the Theology of Early Christianity', in *The Interpretation of Mark*, pp. 158-66.
—*Die Stunde der Botschaft* (Hamburg: Furche; Zürich: Zwingli, 1970).
Schweizer, E., 'Anmerkung zur Theologie des Markus', in *Neotestamentica et Patristica: Eine Freundesgabe Herrn Professor Dr Oscar Cullmann zu seinem 60. Geburtstag überreicht* (NovTSup, 6, Leiden: Brill, 1962), pp. 35-46.
—*The Good News According to Mark* (London: SPCK, 1987).
—'Mark's Contribution to the Quest of the Historical Jesus', *NTS* 10 (1963–64), pp. 421-32.
—'Neuere Markus-Forschung in USA', *EvT* 33 (1973), pp. 533-37.
Selvidge, M.J., 'Mark 5.25-34 and Leviticus 15.19-20: A Reaction to Restrictive Purity Regulations', *JBL* 103 (1984), pp. 619-23.
—'And Those Who Followed Feared (Mark 10.32)', *CBQ* 45 (1983), pp. 396-400.
Shae, G.S., 'The Question of the Authority of Jesus', *NovT* 16 (1974), pp. 1-29.
Shuler, P.L., *A Genre for the Gospels: The Biographical Character of Matthew* (Philadelphia: Fortress Press, 1982).
Simonsen, H., 'Zur Frage der grundlegenden Problematik in form- und redaktionsgeschichtlicher Evangelienforschung', *ST* 26 (1972), pp. 1-23.
Smith, D.M., 'John and the Synoptics: Some Dimensions of the Problem', in *Johannine Christianity: Essays on Its Setting, Sources and Theology* (Columbia, SC: University of South Carolina Press, 1984), pp. 145-72.
Smith, M., *Clement of Alexandria and A Secret Gospel of Mark* (Cambridge, MA: Harvard University Press, 1973).
—'The Origin and History of the Transfiguration Story', *USQR* 36 (1980), pp. 39-44.
—'Prolegomena to a Discussion of Aretalogies, Divine Men, the Gospels and Jesus', *JBL* 90 (1971), pp. 174-99.
—*The Secret Gospel: The Discovery and Interpretation of the Secret Gospel of Mark* (New York: Harper & Row, 1973).
Snodgrass, K.R., 'The Parable of the Wicked Husbandman: Is the Gospel of Thomas Version the Original?', *NTS* 21 (1974), pp. 142-44.

Snoy, T., 'Marc 6.48, "... et il voulait les dés passer"': Proposition pour la solution d'un enigme', in Sabbe (ed.), *L'Evangile selon Marc*, pp. 347-63.
Soards, M.L., 'The Question of a Pre-Markan Passion Narrative', *Bible bhashyam* 11 (1985), pp. 144-69.
Söder, R., *Die apokryphen Apostelgeschichten und die romanhafte Literatur der Antike* (repr.; Stuttgart: W. Kohlhammer, repr. 1969, [1932]).
Söding, T., 'Gebet und Gebetsmahnung Jesu in Getsemani: Eine redaktionskritische Auslegung v. Mk. 14.32-42', *BZ* 31 (1987), pp. 76-100.
Solages, M. de, *Jean et les synoptiques* (Leiden: Brill, 1979).
Stacy, R.W., *Fear in the Gospel of Mark* (Doctoral thesis; Southern Baptist Theological Seminary, 1979).
Standaert, B.H., *L'Evangile selon Marc: Composition et genre littéraire* (Nijmegen: Stichting Studentpress, 1978).
Starobinski, J., 'An Essay in Literary Analysis: Mark 5.1-20', *EcumRev* 23 (1971), pp. 377-97.
Steichele, H.-J., *Der leidende Sohn Gottes: Eine Untersuchung einiger alttestamentlicher Motive in der Christologie des Markusevangeliums* (Münchener Universitäts Schriften; Munich: Friedrich Pustet Revensburg, 1980).
Stein, R.H., 'Is the Transfiguration (Mark 9.2-8) a Misplaced Resurrection Account?', *JBL* 95 (1976), pp. 79-96.
—'The Proper Methodology for Ascertaining a Markan Redaction History', *NovT* 13 (1971), pp. 181-98.
—'The *redaktionsgeschichtliche* Investigation of a Markan Seam (Mk. 1.21ff)', *ZNW* 61 (1970), pp. 70-94.
—'A Short Note on Mark 14.28 and 16.7', *NTS* 20 (1973/74), pp. 445-52.
—'What is *Redaktionsgeschichte*?', *JBL* 88 (1969), pp. 45-56.
Steinmueller, J.E., 'Jesus and the οἱ παρ' αὐτοῦ', *CBQ* 4 (1942), pp. 355-59.
Sternberg, M., *The Poetics of Biblical Narrative* (Bloomington, IN: Indiana University Press, 1985).
Stock, A., *Call to Discipleship: A Literary Study of Mark's Gospel* (Wilmington, DE: Michael Glazier, 1982).
—*The Method and Message of Mark* (Wilmington, DE: Michael Glazier, 1989).
Stone, M.E., 'Apocalyptic Literature', in *Jewish Writings of the Second Temple Period* (ed. M.E. Stone, CRINT; Philadelphia: Fortress Press; Assen: Van Gorcum, 1984), pp. 383-442.
—'Judaism at the Time of Christ', in AASOR Newsletter 1 (1974), pp. 1-6.
Stonehouse, N.B., *The Witness of Matthew and Mark to Christ* (Philadelphia: The Presbyterian Guardian, 1944).
Strecker, G., 'The Passion and Resurrection Predictions in Mark's Gospel (Mark 8.31, 9.31, 10.32-34)', *Int* 22 (1968), pp. 421-42.
Strecker, G., ed., *Jesus Christus in Historie und Theologie: Neutestamentliche Festschrift für Hans Conzelmann zum 60. Geburtstag* (Tübingen: Mohr, 1975).
Stroker, W.D., 'Extra-canonical Parables and the Historical Jesus', *Semeia* 44 (1988), pp. 95-120.
Stronstad, R., *The Charismatic Theology of St. Luke* (Peabody, MA: Hendrickson, 1984).
Suhl, A., *Die Funktion der alttestamentlichen Zitaten und Anspielungen im Markusevangelium* (Gütersloh: Gerd Mohn, 1965).
Sweet, J.P.M., 'The Theory of Miracles in the Wisdom of Solomon', in *Miracles: Cambridge Studies in Their Philosophy and History*, pp. 113-26.
Swete, H.B., *Commentary on Mark* (repr.; Grand Rapids: Kregel Publications, 1977 [1913]).

—'The New Oxyrhynchus Sayings', *ExpTim* 15 (1903–1904), pp. 488-95.
Synge, F.W., 'Mark 16.1-8', *JThSAf* 11 (1975), pp. 71-73.
Tagawa, K., *Miracles et Evangile* (Paris: Presses Universitaires de France, 1966).
Talbert, C., *What is a Gospel? The Genre of the Canonical Gospels* (Philadelphia: Fortress Press, 1977).
Tannehill, R.C., 'The Disciples in Mark: The Function of a Narrative Role', *JR* 57 (1977), pp. 386-405; repr. in W. Telford, ed., *The Interpretation of Mark* (Philadelphia: Fortress Press; London: SPCK, 1985), pp. 134-57.
—'The Gospel of Mark as Narrative Christology', *Semeia* 16 (1979), pp. 57-95.
—*The Narrative Unity of Luke–Acts* (Philadelphia: Fortress Press, 1986), I.
Taylor, V., *The Formation of the Gospel Tradition* (London: Macmillan, 1949).
— *The Gospel According to St. Mark* (London: Macmillan, 1952).
Teeple, H., *The Literary Origins of the Gospel of John* (Evanston, IL: Religion and Ethics Institute, 1974).
Telford, W., *The Barren Temple and the Withered Tree* (JSNTSup, 1; Sheffield: JSOT Press, 1980).
Telford, W., ed., *The Interpretation of Mark* (Philadelphia: Fortress Press; London: SPCK, 1985).
Theissen, G., *The Miracle Stories of the Early Christian Tradition* (Edinburgh: T. & T. Clark, 1983).
Thrall, M.E., 'Elijah and Moses in Mark's Account of the Transfiguration', *NTS* 16 (1970), pp. 305-17.
Tiede, D.L., *The Charismatic Figure as Miracle Worker* (SBLDS; Chico, CA: Scholars Press, 1973).
Tillesse, M.d., *Le Secret messianique dans l'Evangile de Marc* (Paris: Cerf, 1968), pp. 116-17.
Tov, E., 'Jewish Greek Scriptures', in *Early Judaism and Its Modern Interpreters*, pp. 223-37.
Trocmé, E., 'L'Expulsion des marchands du temple', *NTS* 15 (1968), pp. 1-22.
—'Is there a Markan Christology?', in *Christ and the Spirit in the New Testament: Studies in Honour of C.F.D. Moule* (ed. B. Lindars and S.S. Smalley; Cambridge: Cambridge University Press, 1973), pp. 3-13.
Trompf, G.W., 'The First Resurrection Appearances and the Ending of Mark's Gospel', *NTS* 18 (1972), pp. 308-30.
Trotter, F.T., ed., *Jesus and the Historian* (Philadelphia: Westminster Press, 1968).
Tuckett, C., ed., *The Messianic Secret* (Philadelphia: Fortress Press, London: SCM Press, 1983).
Turner, C.H., 'Markan Usage: Notes, Critical and Exegetical, on the Second Gospel', *JTS* 25 (1923–24), pp. 378-86; 26 (1924–25), pp. 12-20; 145-56, 225-40, 337-46; 27 (1925–26), pp. 58-62; 28 (1926–27), pp. 9-30, 349-62; 29 (1927–28), pp. 275-89, 346-61.
Tyson, J., 'The Blindness of the Disciples in Mark', in *The Messianic Secret*, pp. 35-43.
Vanhoye, A., ed., *L'Apôtre Paul* (Leuven: Peeters–Leuven University Press, 1986).
Vermes, G., *Jesus the Jew* (London: Collins, 1973).
—*Post-Biblical Jewish Studies* (Leiden: Brill, 1975).
Via, D.O., *The Ethics of Mark's Gospel: In the Middle of Time* (Philadelphia: Fortress Press, 1985).
—*Kerygma and Comedy in the New Testament* (Philadelphia: Fortress Press, 1975).
Vielhauer, P., *Geschichte der urchristlichen Literatur* (Berlin: de Gruyter, 1975).
Vischer, E., *Die Offenbarung Johannes, eine jüdische Apokalypse in christlicher Überarbeitung* (Texte und Untersuchungen zur Geschichte der altchristlichen Literatur, 2.3; Leipzig: Hinrichs, 1886).
Votaw, C.W., *The Gospels and Contemporary Biographies in the Greco-Roman World* (repr.; Philadelphia: Fortress Press, 1970 [1915]).
Wach, J., *Types of Religious Experience: Christian and Non-Christian* (Chicago: University of Chicago Press, 1972).

Waetjen, H., 'The Ending of Mark and the Gospel's Shift in Eschatology', *ASTI* 4 (1965), pp. 114-31.
Walter, N., 'Zur Analyse v. Mc. 10.17-31', *ZNW* 53 (1962), pp. 200-18.
Wansbrough, H., 'Mark 3.21: Was Jesus Out of His Mind?', *NTS* 18 (1972), pp. 233-23.
Ward, R.A., *Commentary on 1 and 2 Thessalonians* (Waco, TX: Word Books, 1975), pp. 148-49.
Wardman, A., *Plutarch's Lives* (London: Paul Elek, 1974).
Watson, F., 'The Social Function of Mark's Secrecy Theme', *JSNT* 24 (1985), pp. 49-69.
Weeden, T.J., 'The Heresy that Necessitated Mark's Gospel', *ZNW* 59 (1968), pp. 145-58.
—*Mark: Traditions in Conflict* (Philadelphia: Fortress Press, 1971).
Weiss, J., *Das älteste Evangelium* (Göttingen: Vandenhoeck & Ruprecht, 1903).
Wengst, K., *Pax Romana and the Peace of Jesus Christ* (Philadelphia: Fortress Press, 1987).
Wenham, D., 'The Meaning of Mk. 3.21', *NTS* 21 (1975), pp. 295-300.
Westermann, A., ed., *Paradoxographoi* (London: Brunsvigae, 1839).
Wikenhauser, A., *Die Offenbarung des Johannes* (RNT; Regensburg: Pustet, 1959).
Williams, J.G., *Gospel Against Parable: Mark's Language of Mystery* (Sheffield: JSOT Press, 1985).
Wilson, R.McL., '"Thomas" and the Growth of the Gospels', *HTR* 53 (1960), pp. 231-50.
—'"Thomas" and the Synoptic Gospels', *ExpTim* 72 (1960–61), pp. 36-39.
Windisch, H., 'Kleine Beiträge zur evangelischen Überlieferung. I. Zum Gastmahl des Antipas', *ZNW* 18 (1917–18), pp. 73-81.
Winston, D., *The Wisdom of Solomon: A New Translation with Introduction and Commentary* (AB; Garden City, NY: Doubleday, 1981).
Wohlenberg, G., *Das Evangelium des Markus* (KNT; Leipzig: A. Deichert, 1910).
Wrede, W., *The Messianic Secret* (Cambridge, MA: James Clarks, rev. edn, 1971 [1901])
Wuellner, W.H., 'Greek Rhetoric and Pauline Argumentation', in *Early Christian Literature and the Classical Intellectual Tradition: In Honor of Robert M. Grant* (ed. W.R. Schoedel and R.L. Wilken; Paris: Editions Beauchesne, 1979), pp. 177-88.
—*The Meaning of 'Fishers of Men'* (Philadelphia: Westminster Press, 1967).
—'Paul's Rhetoric of Argumentation in Romans', *CBQ* 38 (1976), pp. 330-51.
—'Where is Rhetorical Criticism Taking Us?', *CBQ* 49 (1987), pp. 448-63.
Ziesler, J.A., 'The Transfiguration Story and the Markan Soteriology', *ExpTim* 81 (1970), pp. 263-68.
Zimmerli, W, 'Die Frage des Reichen nach dem ewigen Leben (Mc. 10:17-31 par.)', *EvT* 19 (1959), pp. 90-97.

INDEXES

INDEX OF REFERENCES

OLD TESTAMENT

Genesis		33.22	129	Judges	
1.26	174	34.6	129	2.28	118
1.31	136	34.29-35	147	9.4	95
2.21	56	34.29	139	13.7	80
15.2	51	34.30	70, 139	13.20	51
15.12	56, 57	34.35	139	16.25	141
17.3	51				
22	64	*Leviticus*		*Ruth*	
27.33	56, 119	9.24	51, 53, 56, 131	2.8	117
27.34	109			3.9	117
28.17	51, 70	12.7	117	4.13	178
32.31	80	15.19-20	118		
41.8	51	15.21	117	*1 Samuel*	
42.28	131	15.25	117	1.6	109
49.11	163	20.18	117	3.15	189
Exodus		*Numbers*		*2 Samuel*	
3.6	51, 70	14.5	51	1.26	170
3.14	129	16.4	51	12.13	99
10.19	67	16.22	51	15.19-24	181
14.21	129	16.45	51		
14.24	129	20.6	51	*1 Kings*	
15.14-16	52, 67			1.12	109
15.16	81	*Deuteronomy*		4.13	95
18.9	53, 55, 67, 131	9.19	142	6.9	53
		28.26	141	13.7	95
19.18	53, 56, 67, 131	28.28-29	56	16.4	95
		33.2	129	16.14	95
20.29	53			18.39	11
24.12	139	*Joshua*		19.11	129
24.16	139	3.4	129	21.1	95
25.9	139	5.1	55	23.26	95
33.19	129	5.14	51	28.5	95
33.20	80				

Index of References

2 Kings		77.20	129	35.6	100
6	61, 62, 64	80.16	94	40.9	72
6.20-27	102	88.14	129	42.9	93
9.20	104	89.9	109, 111	43.1-4	129
15.1-5	102	93.3-4	109	43.10-11	129
15.31	181	107	112	43.16	129
		107.10-16	113	43.18-19	93
3 Kings		107.28-29	109, 111	43.25	102
10.5	61	115.2	95	44.8	95
18.39	51, 53	117.13	54	44.22	99, 102
		118.22-23	169	52.13–53.12	55, 181
2 Chronicles		118.22	169, 170	52.13-20	54
6.13	51	118.23	169, 171	52.15	50, 54, 67, 181
7.3	51	119.18	170		
7.14	102	121.1	135	56.7	163
20.18	51	123.1	135	65.1-5	113
		139.14	170	65.1	113
Job				65.3-4	113
4.14	51	Proverbs		65.17	93
7.14	51	1.28	86		
9.8	129	8.15	86	Jeremiah	
18.20	178	8.17	86	7.11	163
38.16	129	15.27	109	20.7	179
42.11	53	31.21	106	20.9	179
				31.8	100
Psalms		Qohelet			
2	55	7.16	95	Lamentations	
2.7	55	8.2	173	1.8	109
2.11	54				
5.6	94	Song of Songs		Ezekiel	
14.5	109	2	117	1.28	51, 80
15.1	152	4.15	117	3.15	179
19.22	102	5.1	117	3.26-27	189
24.1	174			9.8	51
27.2	75	Isaiah		11.13	51
35.4	75	1.10	152	18	152
38.13-16	181	2	85	30.9	95
38.17	102	2.10	81		
39.10	181	5	169	Daniel	
46.6	129	5.1-7	168, 169	2.46	51
47.6	51	5.2	168	4.16	95
52.6	109	6.5	51, 80, 179, 189	4.19	51, 142
54.5	81			5.6	79
55.10	75	8.12	131	5.9	51
57.18-19	102	17.3	94	5.19	118
68.6	113	19.21	81	7.15	51, 54, 79
68.31	94	35.5-6	102, 135, 136	7.28	51, 79, 142, 189
76.7	94				

8.17	51	Zechariah		14.11	54
8.18	80	3.2	94	17.3	51, 55
8.27	51, 79	9–14	53	17.6	141
10	140	14.5	163	17.9	141
10.7-9	80	14.9	163	17.19	141
10.7-8	79	14.13	53, 64, 138	19.15	54
10.7	51, 141, 188, 193	14.16-21	163		
		14.21	163	Sirach	
10.8	179, 188			4.11	86
10.12	80, 131	Malachi		6.18	86
10.15-19	80	3.1-3	163	9.1-9	72
10.19	131			30.9	148, 178
12.2	193	2 Esdras		39.16	136
12.3	139	2.43	51	43.18	171
		3–14	54	47.17	55, 95
Hosea		10.30	79		
2.19-20	117	13.30	54	Susanna	
3.5	53, 64, 67, 100, 138, 196			33	106
		Tobit			
		12.16	51	1 Maccabees	
10.8	81			4.19-25	163
		Judith		5.45-54	163
Amos		11.16	55	6.8	95
5.4-7	152	11.20	95	9.44	106
5.16-17	130			10.8	109
		Wisdom of Solomon		10.86	163
Jonah		2–5	181	13.2	141
1.16	53, 109	2.20	54	13.43-48	163
		3.7	54	13.49-51	163
Micah		3.9	54		
6.8	152	3.13	54	2 Maccabees	
7.15-17	138	3.18	54	1.22	51
7.15	53, 64, 111	4.7	86	3	52
7.17	53, 64, 112	4.15	54	3.24	51
		5.1-23	54	4.21-22	163
Habakkuk		5.2-23	54	6.18-31	126
1.5	76, 78	5.2	53, 131, 181, 188	7.12	95
2.4	117			8.35-39	52
3.3	129	8.13	86	10.10–15.36	52
3.15	129	8.16	86	12.22	51
3.16	179	11.19	141	15.23	52
		13.4	95		
Zephaniah					
3.17-29	117				

NEW TESTAMENT

Matthew		2.22	21	5.26	174
2.3	21	4.18	132	7.28	20, 94

Index of References

7.38	136	1.1-15	19, 121,		73, 92-94,
8.10	21		122, 124		96, 97, 99,
8.18-27	110	1.1-13	39		113, 115,
8.25	108	1.1	19, 95, 98,		117, 122,
8.27	20-22		110, 137,		136, 146,
9.1-7	102		153, 199		147, 149,
9.8	20, 21	1.2-3	93, 125		151, 152,
9.33	20, 21	1.4-5	99		154, 156,
11.29-30	86	1.9-11	93, 98, 110,		164-67,
12.23	20, 21, 107,		137		171, 175,
	115	1.10	106, 108		180, 197
12.28	108	1.11	55, 138,	1.23-24	96
12.33	100		146, 153,	1.23	95, 112
13.24	85		168, 199	1.24	83, 108,
13.54	21, 100, 136	1.12-28	108		112, 127
14.5	21, 125-27	1.13	108	1.25	94, 96, 108,
14.26	20, 21	1.14-15	18, 19, 25,		112, 145,
14.30	21		92, 93, 98,		190
14.34	178		108, 124,	1.26	95-97
15.29-31	134		137, 139,	1.27-28	97
15.31	20, 21, 100,		145, 151,	1.27	13, 20, 21,
	135		164, 176,		23, 92-99,
16.6	80		193, 194,		102, 103,
17.6	21		197		108, 110,
17.23	22	1.14–8.26	39		113, 115,
18.25	174	1.14–3.6	39		117, 121-
19.25	21, 136	1.14	19, 93, 99,		23, 136,
21.5	20		176		143, 145,
21.15	21	1.15	99, 108,		147, 148,
21.20	20, 21		109, 121,		152-54,
21.26	21		176, 177		156, 159,
21.42	21	1.16-20	92, 146, 175		166, 167,
21.43	169	1.16-17	132		171, 175,
21.46	21	1.17	151		179, 180,
22.21	21	1.20-25	163		197
22.22	21	1.20	160	1.28	96, 194
22.23	136	1.21-28	39, 92-94,	1.29	164
22.33	20, 21, 94		99, 109,	1.31	135
27.14	21, 100		112, 115,	1.32-34	190
27.51-54	89		121, 145,	1.32	160
27.54	20, 21		151, 152,	1.33	13, 164
28.4	21		161, 164,	1.35-39	179
28.5	131		171, 190,	1.40-45	190
28.8	21, 89		197	1.43	190
		1.21-22	97, 123	1.44	135, 181,
Mark		1.21	94-96, 145,		189, 191,
1	145		194		192
		1.22	13, 20, 21,	1.45	136, 190

2–4	25		194, 197,	5.1-2	113, 181
2.1-12	99, 190		199	5.2	112, 181
2.2	100	3.22-30	116	5.6-7	113
2.3-5	101	3.22	105	5.7	112
2.3	100	3.23-30	106	5.8	112, 113
2.4	100	3.23	108	5.9	113
2.5-10	100-102	3.26	108	5.10	127
2.5	99, 101, 121	3.29	108	5.13	113
2.6-10	101	3.31	107	5.14-15	114
2.6	100, 101	4–6	27	5.14	113, 114,
2.7	99, 101, 110	4	87		188
2.9	100, 102	4.1-34	109	5.15	20, 21, 110,
2.10	99-101, 167	4.1-20	121, 122		112-14, 148-
2.11-12	101, 103	4.1-2	107		51, 159, 180,
2.11	100, 102	4.1	94		189, 194,
2.12	20, 21, 23,	4.2	94		201
	46, 56, 95,	4.9	173	5.16-17	114
	99-105,	4.10-12	109, 121,	5.16	114
	115, 119,		122, 124	5.17	115
	122, 131,	4.10	106	5.18-20	113-15
	133, 135,	4.12	173	5.19	190
	136, 143,	4.13	127	5.20	20, 21, 23,
	148, 149,	4.17	122		95, 112,
	153, 172,	4.29	108		113, 115,
	180, 181,	4.35–5.43	110, 121,		122, 123,
	194, 197		124		135, 137,
2.13	94	4.35-41	109, 110,		149, 170,
2.15	132, 181		112, 129,		180-82,
2.16	181		133, 134,		190, 194,
2.19	181		190, 192,		200
3.4	143		198	5.21-43	116, 120,
3.6	39, 40	4.35-36	110		190
3.7–8.26	39	4.37	110	5.21-24	116
3.7-30	105	4.38	94, 108, 110	5.21	117
3.7-12	27	4.39	110, 145	5.22	117
3.8-9	107	4.40	121, 129	5.23	116, 117,
3.11-12	105	4.41	20-23, 95,		135, 143
3.11	199		108-11,	5.24-34	116
3.12	127		113, 119,	5.24	117
3.13-19	106		121, 125,	5.25-34	118
3.15	105		143, 150,	5.25	116, 117
3.19	176		152, 159,	5.26	106, 116,
3.20	105		161, 189,		117
3.21-22	105		192, 197	5.27	83, 117
3.21	20, 21, 23,	5	22	5.28	116, 143
	57, 100,	5.1-20	112, 113,	5.29	117, 118
	104-108,		115, 136,	5.33-34	123, 156,
	123, 172,		190		161

Index of References

5.33	20, 21, 23, 24, 89, 110, 113, 116, 119, 127, 137, 149-51, 159, 160, 188, 190, 191, 194, 197, 201	6.6	20, 21, 23, 94, 115, 120, 121, 123, 124, 170, 189	6.53	110
				6.56	143
				7.7	94
				7.24-30	110, 135
				7.24	160
		6.14-29	116, 124	7.27	143
		6.14	127	7.28	21
		6.17-29	125	7.31-37	134, 135, 190
		6.17	125		
		6.19	125	7.31-36	136, 137
5.34	116, 121, 143, 188	6.20-28	128	7.32-37	110
		6.20	20, 23, 113, 124-28, 150, 159, 164	7.32	135
5.35-43	192			7.33	135
5.35	94, 117			7.34	135
5.36	110, 113, 116, 121, 131, 150, 159, 192	6.29	125	7.35	135
		6.30	94, 124	7.36	135, 136, 190
		6.32-51	130		
		6.34-44	110	7.37	13, 20, 21, 23, 46, 95, 100, 122, 131, 134-37, 143, 152, 153, 156, 180, 194, 197, 199
5.37	176	6.34	94		
5.40	135	6.45–8.26	134		
5.41	117, 121, 135	6.45-52	112, 128, 129, 192		
5.42	20, 21, 23, 24, 56, 100, 116, 117, 119, 120, 131-33, 136, 156, 172, 188, 192, 194	6.45-51	110, 190		
		6.45-47	130		
		6.47	130		
		6.48-50	130		
		6.48	129, 130	8	22
		6.49-50	130	8.1-10	110, 135
		6.49	70	8.11	106
		6.50-52	128	8.22-26	110, 135, 137, 147
5.43	117, 120, 127, 135, 190	6.50-51	180, 197, 198	8.22	135
				8.23-25	135
		6.50	20, 21, 23, 72, 95, 113, 130, 131, 148, 150, 159, 187	8.23	135
6	22			8.24	135
6.1-6	121, 122, 124			8.26	135
				8.27–16.8	139
6.2-3	123			8.27–10.53	39
6.2	20, 21, 23, 73, 94, 95, 120-23, 136, 138, 152-54, 161, 194	6.51-52	189	8.27–10.52	40, 150-52, 157
		6.51	20, 21, 23, 70, 100, 130-34, 136, 152, 156, 189, 194	8.27–10.45	138, 146
				8.27-91	138
				8.27-33	138
				8.27-30	135
6.3	122, 123, 175	6.52	15, 129, 130, 132, 133, 153, 189, 190	8.29	149
				8.31–9.1	138, 149
6.4	123			8.31-33	127, 135, 150
6.5	135, 156				
6.6-13	124				

8.31	94, 150, 182	9.23	146	10.24	20, 21, 23, 95, 148, 151-56, 159, 179, 194, 198
8.33	173, 174	9.24	146		
8.34-37	40	9.25	145, 146, 148		
8.34-35	175				
8.35-38	43	9.26	127, 146		
9	140	9.27	135	10.25	151, 152, 155
9.1	139	9.28-29	146		
9.2-13	138	9.29	153	10.26-27	152
9.2-9	51, 149	9.30-37	150	10.26	20, 21, 23, 95, 122, 131, 136, 151-53, 155, 156, 194, 198
9.2-8	140	9.30-35	138		
9.2	139, 140, 176	9.30-32	182		
		9.30	149		
9.3-6	140	9.31	94, 150, 176		
9.5	141, 189	9.32	20, 22, 113, 127, 149-51, 157, 159, 162, 189, 194, 200	10.27	152, 153, 156
9.6	20, 23, 24, 125, 127, 138, 140-42, 164, 165, 188, 189, 194			10.28-31	152
				10.28-30	152
				10.28	152-55, 159
				10.29-30	152
		9.38	94	10.31	159
9.7	140, 146, 149, 153, 168, 199	9.43	152	10.32-34	138, 150, 157, 158, 160, 182
		9.45	152		
		9.47	152		
9.8	140	9.49-29	145		
9.9-13	149	10–16	198	10.32	18, 20, 21, 23, 95, 113, 125, 127, 148, 150, 152, 157-62, 179, 180, 188, 189, 194, 197, 198, 200
9.9	135, 140	10	152, 159		
9.10-13	149	10.1	94, 138		
9.10	153	10.2-12	152		
9.11	189	10.2-9	152		
9.14-29	112, 145	10.11	152		
9.14	146, 148	10.13-16	152, 156		
9.15	18, 20, 21, 23, 95, 113, 115, 145, 147, 149, 158, 159, 164, 178, 187, 194, 197, 200	10.14	152		
		10.17-31	145, 151, 152		
		10.17-27	152	10.33	157, 176
		10.17-22	152	10.34	158
		10.17	94, 151	10.35-45	152
		10.20	94, 151, 198	10.35-40	152
		10.21	152, 153, 160	10.35	94
9.17-18	146			10.37	180
9.17	94, 145, 146, 148	10.23-27	152	10.39	40
		10.23-26	152	10.42-45	43
9.18	145, 146	10.23-24	152	10.42	152
9.19	145, 146	10.23	151, 152, 154-56	10.43-45	152
9.20-27	146			10.45	132, 164
9.20	146	10.24-27	152	10.46-52	138
9.22	146	10.24-25	152, 155, 156	10.49	131
9.23-24	145, 157			10.52	160

11.1–15.39	40	12.13	173	14.32-37	177	
11.1–13.7	39	12.14	94, 171	14.32	177-79	
11	162, 163	12.17	20, 21, 23,	14.33	18, 20, 21,	
11.1-23	138		24, 103,		23, 57, 123,	
11.1-11	163		171-75,		147, 148,	
11.8	159		180, 189		150, 159,	
11.9	159	12.19	94		176-79,	
11.10	163	12.20	181		187, 194,	
11.11	169, 170	12.31	106		198-200	
11.12-13	163	12.32	94	14.34	148, 177-79	
11.13	132	12.34	138, 150,	14.35-36	177	
11.14	189		189	14.35	177, 178	
11.15-19	116, 164,	12.35-17	138	14.36-38	177	
	166	12.35	94	14.36	40, 176-78	
11.17	94, 164, 165	12.37	126, 127,	14.37-38	177	
11.18	20, 23, 94,		189	14.37	177, 178	
	95, 113,	12.38	94	14.38-40	177	
	115, 122,	12.41-44	138	14.38	178	
	125, 126,	13	22	14.39	177, 178	
	136, 141,	13.1	94	14.40	176, 177	
	150, 152,	13.5-7	43	14.41	176-78	
	162, 164-	13.6	129	14.42	176-78, 181	
	67, 171,	13.9-13	198	14.43	106, 179	
	188, 189,	13.9	125, 176	14.44	125, 176	
	194, 198	13.11-12	138	14.46	125	
11.19	159, 165	13.11	125, 176	14.49	40, 94, 125	
11.27-33	138, 167	13.12-13	200	14.50	125, 188	
11.28-29	167	13.12	125, 176	14.52	188	
11.28	166	13.14	188	14.61	199	
11.31	153	13.33-34	177	14.62	129	
11.32	20, 23, 113,	13.54	21	15	157, 180	
	159, 167,	14.1–16.8	138	15.1-5	180, 183	
	171	14.1–15.39	39	15.1	125, 176	
11.33	167	14.1	125	15.2	157, 176,	
12	169	14.3-9	116		180, 181,	
12.1-12	138, 168	14.4	153		189	
12.1-11	169	14.10	176	15.3	180, 181	
12.1-9	168	14.11	176, 189	15.5	23, 50, 100,	
12.2	106	14.13	188		103, 115,	
12.7	153	14.18	176		123, 150,	
12.10-11	168	14.21	176		159, 170,	
12.11	23, 106,	14.24	164		180-82,	
	168, 171	14.26	181		184, 189,	
12.12	20, 113,	14.28	159, 161,		192, 200	
	125, 159,		188	15.9	157, 176,	
	167, 168,	14.31	189		180	
	170, 189	14.32-42	148, 176,	15.10	165, 176	
12.13-17	138, 172		177			

Reference	Pages	Reference	Pages	Reference	Pages	Reference	Pages
15.12	157, 176, 180				126, 133, 138, 141, 150, 159, 160, 162, 170, 185-87, 189, 191-94, 198-201	8.25	23, 77
15.15	176					8.35	23
15.18	157, 176, 180					8.37	23, 77
15.23	127					8.39	115
15.24	182					8.47	23, 24, 118
15.26	157, 176, 180					8.56	23, 24, 77
						9.34	23, 24
15.32	157, 176, 180	16.9-20	185, 186			9.43	23, 136
		16.9			159	9.45	23
15.33	182	16.15-20			186	10.26	123
15.34	182	16.18			191	11.14-15	107
15.37	184	16.20			115	11.14	23, 115
15.38	182	16.22			185	11.38	23
15.39	199	19.25			21	12–19	22
15.42-47	183	20.15			156	12.59	174
15.44-45	183	22.33			21	13.13	23
15.44	20, 23, 50, 115, 123, 150, 159, 170, 180, 183, 184, 200					17.15	23
		Luke				18.13	135
		1				18.43	23
		1.12			22	20.19	23
					23, 77, 81, 187	20.26	23, 24
					131	21.25	81
		1.13				22.2	23
		1.21			23	24.5	23, 141
15.47	184	1.29			23, 187	24.12	23, 123
16.1-8	18, 43, 134, 183, 185, 186, 190-92, 195	1.30			131	24.22	23, 77
		1.63			23	24.37	23, 141
		1.65-66			77	24.41	23
		1.65			23, 77		
16.5-8	39	2			22	*John*	
16.5-6	147, 185, 192, 193	2.9			23	2.11	71
		2.18			23, 77	3.6	71, 76
16.5	20, 21, 23, 148, 150, 159, 170, 178, 179, 185, 187	2.33			23	3.7	82
		2.47			23, 77, 88, 100	3.10	74
						4.27	71, 76
		2.48			23	5	71, 73
		4.20			174	5.18	72
16.6-8	115	4.22			23, 73, 77, 123	5.19	72
16.6	21, 23, 131, 150, 159, 170, 178, 179, 185					5.20	72
		4.32			23, 94	5.28	71-73, 76, 82
		4.36			23, 77, 97		
		5.9			23	5.31-47	73
16.7	159, 161, 187, 188	5.26			23	6.19	70-72, 76
		6.8			81	7.12	73
16.8	18, 20, 21, 23, 40, 56, 57, 113, 119, 120,	7.9			23, 123	7.13	72
		7.16			23, 46	7.14	73
		7.42			174	7.15-24	73
		8.24			108	7.15	73

7.20	73	7.32	76	*2 Thessalonians*	
7.21	71, 73	8.9-11	82, 89	1.7-8	83
7.25	73	8.9	76-78	1.10	83, 197
7.49	73	8.11	76-78		
9.2	102	8.13	76, 78	*2 Timothy*	
9.6	135	8.32-33	55	1.17	110
9.12-13	128	9.7	76		
9.22	72	9.21	76, 77, 100	*Hebrews*	
9.30	73	10.4	76, 141, 142	12.21	141, 142
9.38	74, 80	10.10	56		
10.18	75	10.45	76, 77	*James*	
10.20	105	11.5	56	2.19	83
12.15	72	12.16	76, 77	5.15	102
13.22	127	13.12	76, 89, 94		
17.1	135	13.33-34	187	*1 Peter*	
18.6	71, 74, 75	13.33	55	3.14	131
19.8	71, 75, 126, 182	13.41	76, 78		
		16.29	76-78, 89	*1 John*	
19.38	72	19.17	76, 77, 81	3.13	71, 76, 82, 184
20.19-20	72	22.17	56		
20.19	72	24.25	76, 78, 81, 126, 141	*Revelation*	
		26.14	76	1.17	80, 187
Acts		27.24	187	4.10	80, 81
2.5	77			5.8	80
2.6	77	*Romans*		6.15-17	81
2.7-11	77	7.2	132	7.11	81
2.7	76-78, 100, 129	13.1-7	173, 175	11.11	81
				11.13	81, 141
2.12-13	77			13.3	81, 82, 89
2.12	76, 77	*1 Corinthians*		13.4	82
2.14	77	2.3	118	14.7	81
2.24	187	14.23	105	16.6	81
2.43	76-78, 89	15.3-7	187	16.9	81
3.10	56, 76, 77			16.13	81
3.11	76, 77	*2 Corinthians*		17.6	82
3.12	76, 78, 123	5.13	105	17.7	82, 123
4.13	76, 77	7.15	118	17.8	82, 89
4.25-26	55	12.4	189	19.10	80
5.5	76-78, 81, 89	*Ephesians*		21.8	110
5.11	76-78, 81, 89	6.5	118	22.8-9	80
7.31	76, 123	*Philippians*			
		2.12	118		
		14.33	178		

PSEUDEPIGRAPHA

Apoc. Abr.		22.4	64	3 Maccabees	
10.2	64	39.8	64	2.23	53
17.1-3	64	69.16	64		
		71.18	64	4 Maccabees	
2 Baruch				1.11	30
50.10	139	3 Enoch		4.10	31, 118, 141
70.2	64	15.48	139	5.1–6.30	126
				6.13	30, 126
1 Enoch		Ep. Arist.		7	181
1.4-5	64, 197	96-99	65	7.13	30
1.5	80	312	172	8.4	31, 95
1.45	67			8.5	31
14.9	79	4 Ezra		9.26	30, 126
14.13-15	79	7.97	139	17.16	30, 95
14.14	80	13.30	65	17.17	30, 126, 171
14.24	63, 79			18.3	30
45.4	93	Jos. Asen.			
52.6	74	9.1	65	T. Job	
60.3-4	63, 67, 79	14.3	65	39.13	105
72.1	93	14.10	65		
89.56	169	28.1	66	T. Mos.	
89.66-67	169			10.4	64
106.4	188	Jubilees			
		18.10	63	T. Sol.	
2 Enoch				22.7-23.8	169
2.7	80				

OTHER ANCIENT REFERENCES

Qumran		2.13	63	Targum Micah	
1QH				7.14	93
4.26	78	Manual of Discipline			
6.26	169	11.3	62	Mishnah	
		11.9	62	Aboth.	
1QM		11.21	63	3.10-11	66
14.9-15	94, 109				
		War Scroll		Ber.	
1QS		8.9	63	5.5	66
8.7-10	169				
		Targums		Sheq.	
Genesis Apocryphon		Targ. Isa.		1.3	164
20.9	63	5.2	169		
		5.5	169		
Hymn Scroll		52.15	55	Sot.	
1.21	63			9.15	66

Index of References

Ta'an		On the Life of Moses		1.255	60
3.8	66	1.190	135	2.82	61
		1.14.78	31	2.83	61
Talmuds		1.14.81	31	2.206	61
b. Ber.		1.16.91	31	2.210–4.331	29
34b	66	1.32.177	31	2.267	31
		1.32.180	31	2.270	31
b. Bk.		1.36.200	31	2.274	31
50a	66	1.38.213	31	2.280	30, 31
		1.6.27	29	2.325-29	163
b. Ta'an		2.14.70	29	2.339	60
23a	66	2.48.264	31	3.38	31
24b	66			3.82	31
25a	66	On Migration of Abraham		4.66	31
		26	184	4.111	31
y. Ber.		34	58	8.48	113
9d	66			9.58	61
		On Providence		9.60	61
Tosefta		2.10	58	10.114	105
Ber.				11.268	61
3.20	66	On Rewards and		12.101	61
		Punishments		12.110	61
Sheq.		164	58	12.90	61
1.6	164			13.304-306	163
		On Special Laws		14.22-24	66
Midrashim		1.186	58	15.141	61
Genesis Rabbah				15.388	61
13.7	66	On Virtues		15.414	61
		217	58	15.416	61
Rabbinic				16.12-15	163
Pirqe Aboth		Question and Answers		18.168-70	61
1.5	72	on Exodus		18.268	62
		24	58	18.286	60
Philo		3.117	58	18.309	62
Account of Creation				18.5.2	125, 126
2.17	58	Questions and Answers		22.342-45	163
2.7	58	on Genesis		27.12	64
		3.9	56, 57		
Decalogue				Apion	
46	58	Who is Heir?		1.19	29, 30
		249-51	56	1.27	29, 30
On Dreams		23	58	1.68	184
1	58	249-52	105	2.221	61
2.70	172	257-60	105	3.16	29
				3.40	29, 30
On Joseph		Josephus		4.3	29
8	58	Antiquities		4.20.25	30
80	58	1.10.5	106	4.21	29

4.31	29, 30	Dio Chrysostom		*On Marvelous Things*	
4.44	29, 30	29 [46] 1	94	*Heard*	
6.3	29, 30			1.24	44
7.22	29	*Gospel of Peter*		1.34	44
7.32	29	6.21	88	3.3	44
7.36	29, 30	13.57	89	4.28	45
8.8	29, 30			7.38	44
8.9	29, 30	*Gospel of Thomas*		8.37-38	44
8.30	29	2	69, 84, 86,	8.65	45
8.31	29		197	9.120	45
9.20	30	24	86	9.65	45
		27	86		
War		29	86	*On the Sublime*	
1.73-74	163	38	86	35.5	43
1.328	60	49	86		
2.553	60	50	86	*Physiog.*	
2.61	60	51	86	812b.29	141
3.188	61	76	86		
3.237	60	80	86	*Poet.*	
5.472	60	86	86	6.2	40
6.180	60	90	86	9.1452.22-3	40
6.288-309	60	92	86	14.1453.3-6	40
7.63-74	82	94	86		
		107	86	*Rhetoric*	
Christian Authors				2.8.1-2	40
Acts of John		*Infancy Stories of Thomas*		3.14.7	43
61	88	2.5	88		
		6.1	88	Cicero	
Acts of Peter		13.2	88	*De div.*	
5.12	88	17.7	88	1.26.55	102
		19.2	88		
Acts of Pilate				*De Inv.*	
8.1	89	*Latin Infancy Gospel*		1.3.98	43
		71	89		
Barnabas		*Protevangelium of James*		*De Or.*	
7.10	94	11.18	89	2.77.311	43
16.10	94				
		Classical Authors		Dionysius of Halicarnassus	
Clement		Aristides		*De Thuc.*	
Strom.		*Hymns to Serapis*		34	172
2.9.45	85	33	130		
5.1.96	85			*Demos*	
6.96.1	127	Aristotle		4.22	95
		Hist. An.		4	38
The Gospel of		622.12	105	5.3	35
Bartholemew				22	38
4.9	89	*Nic. Eth.*			
		7.71149b35	105	*Lysias*	
				3	95

Index of References

Dio Cassius		31	135	Polybius	
66.8	135	31.16	113	3.33.17	184
		12	30		
Diodorus Siculus				Porphyry	
4.43	30	*Abdic.*		*Vit. Pyth.*	
		5	30	25.21	29
Euripedes				28.12	29
Bacc.		Philostratus			
291-310	105	*Vit. Ap.*		Suetonius	
449	30	3.38	112	*Ves.*	
850	105	4.10	112	7	135
		4.20	112		
Eusebius		4.43	112	Tacitus	
Praep. Ev.		4.45	135	*Hist.*	
1.2	127			4.81.1-3	135
9.27.24-26	75	Plato			
		Phaedra		Xenophon	
Herodotus		251a	84	*Cyr.*	
4.79	105			1.4.27	94
		Plutarch		4.2.15	35
Homer		*Brut.*		4.10	46
Iliad		20.9	95		
8.77	46			Papyri	
		Ca. Ma.		Oxyrhynchus Papyri	
Hymns		31.3	95	1.53.18	148
33.12	130			654.7	84
		Cor.			
Livy		24.3	102	*PGM*	
2.36	102			13.527	95
		Fab.		13.945	135
Lucian		6.8	141	4.161	47
Philop.				4.245	30
9	135	*Lys.*		4.775	47
12	135	25.2	36	4.791	47

INDEX OF AUTHORS

Achtemeier, P.J. 93, 110, 111, 117, 146, 150
Aland, K. 186
Alexander, J.A. 127, 132, 136
Allen, W.C. 118
Alter, R. 16
Ambrozic, A.M. 18, 93, 96, 98
Anderson, J.C. 14
Annan, F. 114, 115
Attridge, H. 52
Aune, D. 32

Balz, H.R. 186
Bammel, E. 163, 172
Barbour, R. 177, 179
Barrett, C.K. 69, 75, 162, 163
Barthes, R. 17
Bartholemew, G.L. 190
Bauckham, R. 79, 80
Bauer, W. 94
Beasley-Murray, G. 73
Becker, J. 71, 73
Berger, K. 28
Bertram, G. 12, 24, 71, 182, 184
Best, E. 15, 94, 97, 103, 107, 108, 123, 124, 138, 141, 142, 146, 150-55, 157, 160
Betz, H.D. 27, 28, 41, 47, 50, 102
Betz, O. 59, 60
Bianchi, H. 87
Bieler, L. 27, 28
Bilezikian, G.G. 39, 40
Bird, C.H. 132
Black, C.C. 15, 16, 185
Black, D.A. 125
Black, M. 169
Blackburn, B. 28, 30

Blass, F. 106, 109, 160
Bligh, J. 113, 114
Blomberg, C. 96
Boman, T. 178
Bonner, C. 126, 127, 136
Boomershine, T.E. 190, 191
Booth, W. 17
Borg, M. 108, 172
Borgen, P. 56, 57
Bornkamm, G. 146-48
Bovon, F. 88
Boyce, J. 14
Branscomb, B.H. 122, 123, 147
Broadhead, E.K. 12, 13
Brown, R.E. 49, 71, 72, 74, 75, 183, 184
Bruce, F.F. 78, 169, 172-75
Bryan, C. 43, 103
Buchanan, G.W. 166
Bultmann, R. 13, 27, 30, 70, 72, 73, 75, 100, 123, 129, 130, 139, 142, 146, 148, 152, 166, 183
Burch, E.W. 39
Burkill, T.A. 13, 187
Burns, V. 88
Burridge, R.A. 26, 32, 33
Busemann, R. 152-55, 160

Calvin, J. 72
Cameron, R. 68, 89
Catchpole, D. 163, 166, 191, 193
Cave, C.H. 114
Charles, R.H. 81
Charlesworth, J.H. 49, 63
Chatman, S. 17
Chilton, B.D. 55, 66, 96, 98, 200
Chronis, H.L. 50, 180

Index of Authors

Clarke, M.L. 42
Cohen, S.J.D. 59
Collins, A.Y. 19, 79
Collins, J.J. 59, 66, 79, 80
Conzelmann, H. 77, 78
Corley, B.C. 68, 158
Corrington, G.P. 27
Cowley, A.E. 109
Cox, P. 34
Craghan, F.J. 113, 114
Cranfield, C.E.B. 98, 101, 106, 118, 125, 139, 145-47, 151, 159, 160, 178, 181, 186, 187, 191
Crossan, J.D. 15, 68, 86, 87, 97, 107, 122, 123, 168, 191, 193
Culpepper, R.A. 71

Dahl, N.A. 201
Daube, D. 101
Dauer, A. 74
Dautzenberg, G. 19
Davids, P.H. 83
Davies, S.L. 69, 84, 86, 88
Debrunner, A. 106, 109, 160
Dehandschutter, B. 168
Delling, G. 59, 60
Derrett, J.D.M. 50, 113, 117, 169, 170, 173
Derrida, J. 17
Dewey, J. 101
Dibelius, M. 13
Dimant, D. 62
Dobschütz, E. von 88
Dodd, C.H. 75, 139, 168
Dodds, E.R. 46
Donahue, J. 54, 181, 201
Doran, R. 52
Dormeyer, D. 19, 177, 179, 181, 183, 193
Doughty, D.J. 100, 102
Drury, J. 16
Duke, P.D. 74
Dunn, J.D.G. 108

Ebeling, E. 152
Edelstein, E.J. 26
Edelstein, L. 26
Egger, W. 154, 155

Ellis, E.E. 169, 186
Enslin, M.S. 187
Epstein, V. 163
Ernst, J. 186
Evans, C.A. 169

Farmer, W.R. 186
Feuillet, A. 178, 179
Fitzmyer, J.A. 85, 87
Fleddermann, H. 129, 130
Ford, J.M. 79, 81, 82
Fortna, R.T. 71
Fowler, R. 16
Freedman, W. 17, 18, 25, 196
Freyne, S. 50, 51, 66
Friedrich, J. 145
Frye, R.M. 16
Fuller, R.H. 26

Gallagher, E.V. 27
Gerber, W. 139
Gnilka, J. 12, 72, 92, 93, 96, 97, 99, 100, 102, 108, 114, 115, 120, 123-26, 128, 130, 134, 135, 137, 140, 141, 148, 150, 151, 154, 155, 160, 165, 166, 171, 181-84, 186, 191, 193
Goldstein, J.A. 52
Goodenough, E.R. 56, 57
Goppelt, L. 99, 173
Grant, R.M. 53
Grässer, E. 121-24
Greeley, A.M. 90, 91
Grenfell, H. 84
Grundmann, W. 93, 100, 114, 127, 130, 137, 152, 182, 183, 193
Guelich, R. 50
Guillemette, P. 96
Gundry, R. 162

Haacker, K. 59
Hadas, M. 27, 28
Haenchen, E. 70, 75, 78
Hall, R.G. 64
Hamilton, N.Q. 163
Hanson, J.S. 172
Harnisch, W. 152, 154, 155
Harrington, D.J. 48, 59

Hartman, G. 49
Hartmann, G. 104
Heil, J.P. 132
Hengel, M. 59, 168, 171, 172
Héring, J. 179
Hingston, J. 74
Hobbs, E.C. 50
Hoehner, H. 126
Holladay, C. 28
Horsley, R.A. 172, 174
Horst, P.W. van der 187
Hort, F.J.A. 84
Hunt, R. 84
Hunter, A.M. 168

Iersel, B.M.F. van 110

Jackson, H.M. 182
James, W. 90, 91
Jeremias, J. 50, 85, 168
Johnson, L.T. 11
Johnson, S.E. 29
Jülicher, A. 168
Jürgen, E. 152

Kautzsch, E. 109
Keck, L. 27
Kee, H.C. 26, 28, 49, 50, 94, 109, 140, 141, 181, 188
Kelber, W. 13, 19, 111, 124, 142, 163, 176, 177, 179, 180
Kellogg, R. 17
Kennedy, G. 26, 41, 42
Kenny, A. 176
Kermode, F. 16, 17
Kertelge, K. 96, 99-104, 110, 111, 114, 115, 117, 120, 124, 129, 131, 132, 136, 146
Kiilunen, J. 103
Kingsbury, J.D. 13, 16, 27, 28, 157
Kline, M. 50
Klostermann, E. 93, 96, 102, 118, 122, 126, 128, 132, 140, 147, 159, 166, 171, 184
Knox, W. 122, 123
Koch, D.-A. 100, 102, 112-14, 128, 130, 132, 146-48
Kock, D.-A. 96

Koester, H. 27, 49, 68, 69, 87, 158, 159
Kraeling, C.H. 187
Kraft, R. 50, 52
Kuhn, H.-W. 27, 100, 152, 154, 155, 163, 177
Kümmel, W.G. 70
Kysar, R. 72

Lane, W.L. 28, 100, 122, 131, 132, 137, 139, 157, 160, 178, 191
Lang, F.G. 39, 40, 145
Lapide, P. 134
Layton, B. 84
Lee-Pollard, D.A. 158
Leenhardt, F.J. 114
Leeuw, G. van der 90, 91
Légasse, S. 153, 154
Lenski, R.C.H. 118, 126
Lescow, T. 177
Lightfoot, R. 187
Lindars, B. 12, 49, 169
Lindemann, A. 191
Linmans, A.J.M. 110
Linnemann, E. 177, 186
Lohmeyer, E. 12, 80-82, 98, 100, 118, 122, 127, 130, 131, 133, 166, 183, 188
Lohse, E. 80, 177
Longenecker, R. 28
Lubsczyk, H. 186
Lührmann, D. 97, 109, 151

MacDonald, D.R. 88
MacKay, B.S. 36
MacRae, G. 59, 60
Mack, B.L. 19
Magness, J.L. 133, 190, 191
Maisch, I. 101, 102
Makrides, V.N. 167
Malbon, E.S. 109, 119, 120, 160, 191, 192
Mann, C.S. 92, 111, 118, 127, 140, 151, 160, 166, 184
Marcus, J. 50, 122
Marshall, C.D. 200
Marshall, I.H. 55
Martitz, W. von 27
Martyn, J.L. 73

Marxsen, W. 14, 15, 188
Maslow, A.H. 90, 91
Masson, C. 83
Matera, F. 157
Maurer, C. 50, 55, 181
Mayer, B. 123, 124
McCasland, S.V. 59, 60
McCurley, F.R. 140, 141
McKinnis, R. 158, 160
Mead, R.T. 101, 103
Mein, P. 74
Metzger, B.M. 116, 128, 186
Meye, R. 50
Meye, R.P. 15, 112, 113, 160
Meyer, B.F. 162, 163
Michie, D. 16, 19, 24, 119, 124, 125, 180, 191
Miller, D. 16
Miller, D.C. 70
Minear, P. 152
Mohn, W. 178, 179
Momigliano, A. 33, 34, 52, 65
Moore, S. 14, 16, 17
Morgenthaler, R. 20
Morris, L. 74
Moule, C.F.D. 36, 49, 148, 163, 172, 186, 191
Mounce, R. 80
Müller, U.B. 140
Müssner, F. 19

Neirynck, F. 15, 16, 70, 119, 193
Neusner, J. 164
Nickelsburg, G.W.E. 48, 50, 52, 54, 66, 80
Nicol, W. 70, 71
Niditch, S. 80
Niemann, F.-J. 188
Nineham, D.E. 114, 115, 129, 132, 137, 166, 171, 175
Nock, A.D. 35
Nützel, J.M. 141, 142

O'Neill, J.C. 76
Ottley, R.R. 187
Otto, R. 80, 90, 91, 161

Pagels, E. 86

Paulsen, H. 193
Peabody, D. 15, 16, 179, 182
Peabody, D.B. 103
Perrin, N. 14, 16, 50
Pesch, R. 12, 19, 24, 77, 78, 95, 96, 100, 102, 109, 110, 113, 117, 124, 126, 128, 130, 132, 138, 147, 152, 154, 155, 169, 175, 179, 181, 183, 184, 191
Petersen, N.R. 14, 16, 104, 189-91
Peterson, E. 45, 46
Petzke, G. 148
Pfister, F. 46, 60
Plevnik, J. 93
Pohl, A. 103, 105, 111, 119, 127, 182
Pohlmann, W. 145
Porter, C.A. 74
Preisendanz, K. 47
Prigent, P. 80, 82
Pryke, E.J. 15, 16, 96, 103, 107, 113-15, 119, 123, 128, 131, 133, 137, 141, 148, 151, 154, 155, 160, 166, 171, 175, 179, 193

Quesnell, Q. 15
Quispel, G. 87

Rau, G. 19, 119, 139
Rawlinson, A.E.J. 110, 154, 179
Reed, D.S. 34
Reese, J.M. 54
Reitzenstein, R. 27
Reploh, K.-G. 153, 155
Rhoads, D. 16, 19, 24, 119, 124, 125, 180, 191
Richardson, L.J.D. 187
Riedl, J. 72
Riesenfeld, H. 140
Rigaux, B. 83
Ritt, H. 129, 134
Robbins, V.K. 37, 94
Roberts, W.R. 42
Robertson, A.T. 132, 165
Robinson, J.M. 70, 87
Roloff, J. 146, 165, 166
Roth, W. 50, 104
Rowland, C. 80

Sabbe, M. 168, 184
Salin, H. 113
Sanders, E.P. 22, 162
Sandmel, S. 26, 48, 49, 56
Schenk, W. 148, 177, 182
Schenke, L. 96, 110, 114, 115, 119, 123, 132, 134-36, 147, 166, 179, 181, 183, 184, 193
Schille, G. 78, 110
Schlatter, A. 72
Schlier, H. 182
Schmid, J. 120, 140
Schmithals, W. 114, 128, 129, 131-33, 136, 137, 146, 147, 151, 159, 160, 166, 178, 180, 182, 186
Schnackenburg, R. 71-73, 75, 100, 186
Schneider, G. 77, 78
Schniewind, J. 146, 155, 182
Schoedel, W.R. 29
Scholes, R. 17
Schreiber, J. 15, 184
Schroeder, H.-H. 104
Schulz, S. 27
Schunak, G. 152
Schweizer, E. 19, 28, 50, 94, 97, 98, 100, 108, 115, 116, 119, 128, 134, 137, 139, 140, 146, 154, 159, 160, 167, 171, 177, 178, 184
Selvidge, M.J. 118, 161
Shae, G.S. 167
Shuler, P.L. 32-34
Shultz, S. 50
Simonsen, H. 101
Smalley, S.S. 12
Smith, D.M. 70
Smith, M. 27-29, 140, 158, 159
Snodgrass, K.R. 168
Snoy, T. 130
Soards, M.L. 138
Söder, R. 88
Söding, T. 176-79
Solages, M. de. 70
Stacy, R. 13, 24
Standaert, B.H. 39, 196
Starobinski, J. 114
Stein, R.H. 15, 16, 96, 97, 140, 141, 160, 166, 171, 188

Steinmueller, J.E. 104
Sternberg, M. 16
Stock, A. 196
Stone, M.E. 48, 56, 62
Stonehouse, N.B. 192
Strecker, G. 169
Stroker, W.D. 69
Stuhlmacher, P. 145
Suhl, A. 50
Sweet, J.P.M. 54
Swete, H.B. 85, 113, 123, 131
Synge, F.W. 192

Tagawa, K. 12, 21, 23, 24, 93, 97, 132, 133, 147-49, 154, 155, 160
Talbert, C. 32, 33
Tannehill, R.C. 16, 24
Taylor, V. 55, 100, 106, 112, 118, 120, 127, 136, 137, 139, 147, 148, 150, 157, 159, 166, 177, 178, 188
Teeple, H. 71
Telford, W.R. 163
Tenney, M.C. 28
Theissen, G. 11, 13, 26, 28, 30, 45, 118, 130, 136, 146
Thrall, M.E. 140-42
Tillesse, M. de 100, 103, 112, 119, 147, 148
Tov, E. 50
Trocmé, E. 12, 166
Turner, C.H. 15, 114, 131, 153, 160, 193
Tyson, J. 111, 132

Vermes, G. 66, 102
Via, D.O. 19, 39, 153, 155
Vielhauer, P. 69, 87, 88
Vischer, E. 79
Votaw, C.W. 29, 32, 33, 37

Wach, J. 90, 91
Waetjen, H. 191, 193
Walter, N. 152, 154, 155
Wanke, J. 186
Wansbrough, H. 104, 106, 107
Ward, R.A. 83
Wardman, A. 35
Watson, F. 124

Index of Authors

Weeden, T.J. 13, 15, 27, 28, 132, 141, 142, 191, 193
Weiss, J. 33, 160, 183
Wengst, K. 173, 175
Wenham, D. 96, 104, 107
Wikenhauser, A. 80-82
Wilcox, M. 186
Wilken, R.L. 29
Williams, J.G. 50, 55

Wilson, R.McL. 87
Windisch, H. 126
Winston, D. 54
Wohlenburg, G. 159
Wrede, W. 13, 124, 160
Wuellner, W.H. 41, 93

Zeisler, J.A. 139
Zimmerli, W. 50, 152

JOURNAL FOR THE STUDY OF THE NEW TESTAMENT
SUPPLEMENT SERIES

1 W.R. Telford, *The Barren Temple and the Withered Tree: A Redaction-Critical Analysis of the Cursing of the Fig-Tree Pericope in Mark's Gospel and its Relation to the Cleansing of the Temple Tradition*
2 E.A. Livingstone (ed.), *Studia Biblica 1978, II: Papers on the Gospels (Sixth International Congress on Biblical Studies, Oxford, 1978)*
3 E.A. Livingstone (ed.), *Studia Biblica 1978, III: Papers on Paul and Other New Testament Authors (Sixth International Congress on Biblical Studies, Oxford, 1978)*
4 E. Best, *Following Jesus: Discipleship in the Gospel of Mark*
5 M. Barth, *The People of God*
6 J.S. Pobee, *Persecution and Martyrdom in the Theology of Paul*
7 C.M. Tuckett (ed.), *Synoptic Studies: The Ampleforth Conferences of 1982 and 1983*
8 T.L. Donaldson, *Jesus on the Mountain: A Study in Matthean Theology*
9 S. Farris, *The Hymns of Luke's Infancy Narratives: Their Origin, Meaning and Significance*
10 R. Badenas, *Christ the End of the Law: Romans 10.4 in Pauline Perspective*
11 C.J. Hemer, *The Letters to the Seven Churches of Asia in their Local Setting*
12 D.L. Bock, *Proclamation from Prophecy and Pattern: Lucan Old Testament Christology*
13 R.P. Booth, *Jesus and the Laws of Purity: Tradition History and Legal History in Mark 7*
14 M.L. Soards, *The Passion According to Luke: The Special Material of Luke 22*
15 T.E. Schmidt, *Hostility to Wealth in the Synoptic Gospels*
16 S.H. Brooks, *Matthew's Community: The Evidence of his Special Sayings Material*
17 A.T. Hanson, *The Paradox of the Cross in the Thought of St Paul*
18 C. Deutsch, *Hidden Wisdom and the Easy Yoke: Wisdom, Torah and Discipleship in Matthew 11.25-30*
19 L.J. Kreitzer, *Jesus and God in Paul's Eschatology*
20 M.D. Goulder, *Luke: A New Paradigm*
21 M.C. Parsons, *The Departure of Jesus in Luke–Acts: The Ascension Narratives in Context*
22 M.C. de Boer, *The Defeat of Death: Apocalyptic Eschatology in 1 Corinthians 15 and Romans 5*
23 M. Prior, *Paul the Letter-Writer and the Second Letter to Timothy*
24 J. Marcus & M.L. Soards (eds.), *Apocalyptic and the New Testament: Essays in Honor of J. Louis Martyn*
25 D.E. Orton, *The Understanding Scribe: Matthew and the Apocalyptic Ideal*
26 T.J. Geddert, *Watchwords: Mark 13 in Markan Eschatology*

27 C.C. Black, *The Disciples according to Mark: Markan Redaction in Current Debate*
28 D. Seeley, *The Noble Death: Graeco-Roman Martyrology and Paul's Concept of Salvation*
29 G.W. Hansen, *Abraham in Galatians: Epistolary and Rhetorical Contexts*
30 F.W. Hughes, *Early Christian Rhetoric and 2 Thessalonians*
31 D.R. Bauer, *The Structure of Matthew's Gospel: A Study in Literary Design*
32 K. Quast, *Peter and the Beloved Disciple: Figures for a Community in Crisis*
33 M.A. Beavis, *Mark's Audience: The Literary and Social Setting of Mark 4.11-12*
34 P.H. Towner, *The Goal of our Instruction: The Structure of Theology and Ethics in the Pastoral Epistles*
35 A.P. Winton, *The Proverbs of Jesus: Issues of History and Rhetoric*
36 S.E. Fowl, *The Story of Christ in the Ethics of Paul: An Analysis of the Function of the Hymnic Material in the Pauline Corpus*
37 A.J.M. Wedderburn (ed.), *Paul and Jesus: Collected Essays*
38 D.J. Weaver, *Matthew's Missionary Discourse: A Literary Critical Analysis*
39 G.N. Davies, *Faith and Obedience in Romans: A Study in Romans 1–4*
40 J.L. Sumney, *Identifying Paul's Opponents: The Question of Method in 2 Corinthians*
41 M.E. Mills, *Human Agents of Cosmic Power: in Hellenistic Judaism and the Synoptic Tradition*
42 D.B. Howell, *Matthew's Inclusive Story: A Study in the Narrative Rhetoric of the First Gospel*
43 H. Räisänen, *Jesus, Paul and Torah: Collected Essays* (trans. D.E. Orton)
44 S. Lehne, *The New Covenant in Hebrews*
45 N. Elliott, *The Rhetoric of Romans: Argumentative Constraint and Strategy and Paul's Dialogue with Judaism*
46 J.O. York, *The Last Shall Be First: The Rhetoric of Reversal in Luke*
47 P.J. Hartin, *James and the Q Sayings of Jesus*
48 W. Horbury (ed.), *Templum Amicitiae: Essays on the Second Temple Presented to Ernst Bammel*
49 J.M. Scholer, *Proleptic Priests: Priesthood in the Epistle to the Hebrews*
50 D.F. Watson (ed.), *Persuasive Artistry: Studies in New Testament Rhetoric in Honor of George A. Kennedy*
51 J.A. Crafton, *The Agency of the Apostle: A Dramatistic Analysis of Paul's Responses to Conflict in 2 Corinthians*
52 L.L. Belleville, *Reflections of Glory: Paul's Polemical Use of the Moses–Doxa Tradition in 2 Corinthians 3.1-18*
53 T.J. Sappington, *Revelation and Redemption at Colossae*
54 R.P. Menzies, *The Development of Early Christian Pneumatology, with Special Reference to Luke–Acts*
55 L.A. Jervis, *The Purpose of Romans: A Comparative Letter Structure Investigation*
56 D. Burkett, *The Son of the Man in the Gospel of John*

57   B.W. Longenecker, *Eschatology and the Covenant: A Comparison of 4 Ezra and Romans 1–11*
58   D.A. Neale, *None but the Sinners: Religious Categories in the Gospel of Luke*
59   M. Thompson, *Clothed with Christ: The Example and Teaching of Jesus in Romans 12.1–15.13*
60   S.E. Porter (ed.), *The Language of the New Testament: Classic Essays*
61   J.C. Thomas, *Footwashing in John 13 and the Johannine Community*
62   R.L. Webb, *John the Baptizer and Prophet: A Socio-Historical Study*
63   J.S. McLaren, *Power and Politics in Palestine: The Jews and the Governing of their Land, 100 BC–AD 70*
64   H. Wansbrough (ed.), *Jesus and the Oral Gospel Tradition*
65   D.A. Campbell, *The Rhetoric of Righteousness in Romans 3.21-26*
66   N. Taylor, *Paul, Antioch and Jerusalem: A Study in Relationships and Authority in Earliest Christianity*
67   F.S. Spencer, *The Portrait of Philip in Acts: A Study of Roles and Relations*
68   M. Knowles, *Jeremiah in Matthew's Gospel: The Rejected-Prophet Motif in Matthaean Redaction*
69   M. Davies, *Rhetoric and Reference in the Fourth Gospel*
70   J.W. Mealy, *After the Thousand Years: Resurrection and Judgment in Revelation 20*
71   M. Scott, *Sophia and the Johannine Jesus*
72   S.M. Sheeley, *Narrative Asides in Luke–Acts*
73   M.E. Isaacs, *Sacred Space: An Approach to the Theology of the Epistle to the Hebrews*
74   E.K. Broadhead, *Teaching with Authority: Miracles and Christology in the Gospel of Mark*
75   J. Kin-Man Chow, *Patronage and Power: A Study of Social Networks in Corinth*
76   R.W. Wall & E.E. Lemcio, *The New Testament as Canon: A Reader in Canonical Criticism*
77   R. Garrison, *Redemptive Almsgiving in Early Christianity*
78   L.G. Bloomquist, *The Function of Suffering in Philippians*
79   B. Charette, *The Theme of Recompense in Matthew's Gospel*
80   S.E. Porter & D.A. Carson (eds.), *Biblical Greek Language and Linguistics: Open Questions in Current Research*
81   In-Gyu Hong, *The Law in Galatians*
82   B.W. Henaut, *Oral Tradition and the Gospels: The Problem of Mark 4*
83   C.A. Evans & J.A. Sanders (eds.), *Paul and the Scriptures of Israel*
84   M.C. de Boer (ed.), *From Jesus to John: Essays on Jesus and New Testament Christology in Honour of Marinus de Jonge*
85   W.J. Webb, *Returning Home: New Covenant and Second Exodus as the Context for 2 Corinthians 6.14–7.1*
86   B.H. McLean (ed.), *Origins of Method: Towards a New Understanding of Judaism and Christianity—Essays in Honour of John C. Hurd*

87 M.J. Wilkins & T. Paige (eds.), *Worship, Theology and Ministry in the Early Church: Essays in Honour of Ralph P. Martin*
88 M. Coleridge, *The Birth of the Lukan Narrative: Narrative as Christology in Luke 1–2*
89 C.A. Evans, *Word and Glory: On the Exegetical and Theological Background of John's Prologue*
90 S.E. Porter & T.H. Olbricht (eds.), *Rhetoric and the New Testament: Essays from the 1992 Heidelberg Conference*
91 J.C. Anderson, *Matthew's Narrative Web: Over, and Over, and Over Again*
92 E. Franklin, *Luke: Interpreter of Paul, Critic of Matthew*
93 J. Fekkes, *Isaiah and Prophetic Traditions in the Book of Revelation: Visionary Antecedents and their Development*
94 C.A. Kimball, *Jesus' Exposition of the Old Testament in Luke's Gospel*
95 D.A. Lee, *The Symbolic Narratives of the Fourth Gospel: The Interplay of Form and Meaning*
96 R.E. DeMaris, *The Colossian Controversy: Wisdom in Dispute at Colossae*
97 E.K. Broadhead, *Prophet, Son, Messiah: Narrative Form and Function in Mark 14–16*
98 C.J. Schlueter, *Filling up the Measure: Polemical Hyperbole in 1 Thessalonians 2.14-16*
99 N. Richardson, *Paul's Language about God*
100 T.E. Schmidt & M. Silva (eds.), *To Tell the Mystery: Essays on New Testament Eschatology in Honor of Robert H. Gundry*
101 J.A.D. Weima, *Neglected Endings: The Significance of the Pauline Letter Closings*
102 J.F. Williams, *Other Followers of Jesus: Minor Characters as Major Figures in Mark's Gospel*
103 W. Carter, *Households and Discipleship: A Study of Matthew 19–20*
104 C.A. Evans & W.R. Stegner (eds.), *The Gospels and the Scriptures of Israel*
105 W.P. Stephens (ed.), *The Bible, the Reformation and the Church: Essays in Honour of James Atkinson*
106 J.A. Weatherly, *Jewish Responsibility for the Death of Jesus in Luke–Acts*
107 E. Harris, *Prologue and Gospel: The Theology of the Fourth Evangelist*
108 L.A. Jervis & P. Richardson (eds.), *Gospel in Paul: Studies on Corinthians, Galatians and Romans for R.N. Longenecker*
109 E.S. Malbon & E.V. McKnight (eds.), *The New Literary Criticism and the New Testament*
110 M.L. Strauss, *The Davidic Messiah in Luke–Acts: The Promise and its Fulfillment in Lukan Christology*
111 I.H. Thomson, *Chiasmus in the Pauline Letters*
112 J.B. Gibson, *The Temptations of Jesus in Early Christianity*
113 S.E. Porter & D.A. Carson (eds.), *Discourse Analysis and Other Topics in Biblical Greek*
114 L. Thurén, *Argument and Theology in 1 Peter: The Origins of Christian Paraenesis*

115 S. Moyise, *The Old Testament in the Book of Revelation*
116 C.M. Tuckett (ed.), *Luke's Literary Achievement: Collected Essays*
117 K.G.C. Newport, *The Sources and Sitz im Leben of Matthew 23*
118 T.W. Martin, *By Philosophy and Empty Deceit: Colossians as Response to a Cynic Critique*
119 D. Ravens, *Luke and the Restoration of Israel*
120 S.E. Porter & D. Tombs (eds.), *Approaches to New Testament Study*
121 T.C. Penner, *The Epistle of James and Eschatology: Re-reading an Ancient Christian Letter*
122 A.D.A. Moses, *Matthew's Transfiguration Story in Jewish-Christian Controversy*
123 D.L. Matson, *Household Conversion Narratives in Acts: Pattern and Interpretation*
124 D.M. Ball, *'I Am' in John's Gospel: Literary Function, Background and Theological Implications*
125 R.G. Maccini, *Her Testimony is True: Women as Witnesses According to John*
126 B.H. Mclean, *The Cursed Christ: Mediterranean Expulsion Rituals and Pauline Soteriology*
127 R.B. Matlock, *Unveiling the Apocalyptic Paul: Paul's Interpreters and the Rhetoric of Criticism*

GENERAL THEOLOGICAL SEMINARY
NEW YORK